COMMON GROUND

READING AND WRITING ABOUT AMERICA'S CULTURES

LAURIE G. KIRSZNER
Philadelphia College of Pharmacy and Science

STEPHEN R. MANDELL
Drexel University

ST. MARTIN'S PRESS, NEW YORK

Senior Editor: *Karen Allanson*
Development Editor: *Mark Gallaher*
Managing Editor: *Patricia Mansfield-Phelan*
Project Editor: *Amy Horowitz*
Production Supervisor: *Alan Fischer*
Art Director: *Sheree Goodman*
Text Design: *Jeannette Jacobs Design*
Photo Research: *Elnora Bode*
Cover Art: *Bill Jacklin, "Promenade, Fifth Avenue," 1986*

8 7 6 5 4
f e d c b a

For information, write:
St. Martin's Press, Inc.
175 Fifth Avenue
New York, NY 10010

ISBN: 0–312–07586–3

*Acknowledgments and copyrights can be found on pages 478–480 and
constitute an extension of the copyright page.*

PREFACE

Our years of teaching have demonstrated to us that students learn to write by writing, and that they write best when they are engaged by their subject matter. To some extent most students are already interested in the issues discussed in *Common Ground*. They live in a nation composed of many ethnic and racial groups, and they have almost certainly come into contact with cultures other than their own. They may even have witnessed—or experienced—some form of discrimination. As a result of their experiences, they may have had occasion to question their values or to challenge the values of others, and they may have struggled to understand and be understood. (Such struggles, in fact, seem to be the price we pay for living in a multicultural society.) The goal of *Common Ground* is to take students' unfocused reactions to their experiences and to turn them into subjects for critical discussion and writing.

It is our hope that by reading and writing about their lives and the lives of others, students will be able to see not just the differences that exist between themselves and others, but also the common ground shared by all groups: the hope for a better life, the desire for an education, and the need for self-respect. Certainly there were times during the writing of this book when we worried that no such common ground existed. We feared that nothing could transcend the mutual suspicion and distrust that emerged in Los Angeles and throughout the nation in 1992 after the acquittal of the police officers charged with beating motorist Rodney King. Still, we wanted to assert our belief in shared goals and values, and we wanted to affirm our conviction that a dialogue could and should continue. Perhaps it is the last vestige of our 1960s idealism, but we feel strongly that voices such as those in this book still can make a difference. We also believe that part of our mission as teachers is to help our students transcend the bigotry and misunderstanding they see around them and learn to live in a culturally diverse society. For this reason—and despite some evidence to the contrary—we decided to keep this book's working title, *Common Ground*, which expresses our hopes for our students and for our country.

Common Ground puts cultural diversity in the United States at the center of the composition classroom. Some of the essays in this book will reinforce the preconceptions that students have, but others will challenge these ideas, forcing students to reexamine and possibly to redefine their values. As they read, engage in discussion, and respond in writing, we expect that students will develop questions, interpret ideas, and evaluate arguments—in short, that they will begin to think critically about what they hear and what they read. The result, we hope, will be that students acquire the confidence and the judgment necessary for more sophisticated critical reading and writing.

 Features

A thematically and rhetorically unified organization *Common Ground* begins with the assumption that reading and writing are intimately connected. Few composition readers that focus on cultural diversity offer much in the way of writing instruction; our goal in this text has been to provide as much support for student writers as possible. To do so, we begin by giving *Common Ground* a unique dual organization, with each chapter focusing on both a particular theme and a specific rhetorical purpose:

Culture and Personal History: Recounting Experiences

Culture and Environment: Describing One's World

Culture and Custom: Explaining Processes

Perceptions of Culture: Discovering through Examples

Society and Culture: Exploring Causal Connections

Across Cultures: Comparing and Contrasting

Categorizing Cultures: Classifying and Dividing

Culture and Identity: Defining Terms

Culture and Diversity: Taking a Stand

The introduction to each of these chapters discusses how the particular rhetorical purpose can illuminate an aspect of American culture and offers **detailed guidance for writing** with that purpose in mind. Each introduction ends with a **review checklist**.

An introductory chapter that contains a case study showing the connections between the reading and writing processes in one student's work Chapter 1 begins with a brief historical overview of the American experience, introduces some of the problems and challenges of living in a multicultural society, and provides an exercise to engage students and stimulate discussion. The chapter then introduces the reading and writing processes, following a student as he reads and analyzes the provocative essay "The 'Black Table' Is Still There" by Lawrence Otis Graham, which addresses the issue of segregated tables in a school cafeteria. We reproduce the student's **marginal annotations** on the essay, his **notebook entries** in response to his reading, and some of the ideas that came out in class discussion. The student's writing process includes an **initial draft** of an essay on the same topic, a discussion of **revision and editing strategies,** and a **final draft** of the essay, "High School U.S.A."

Examples of student writing in every chapter In addition to the student case study in Chapter 1, each subsequent chapter includes two further examples of student writing: **a student paragraph** that introduces a particular cultural perspective and orients readers to the rhetorical purpose of the chapter and **a complete student essay** that reflects the chapter's theme and purpose. The **nineteen student writers** represented in the book range from white Anglo-Saxon Protestant to Filipino American to Palestinian American to Vietnamese American to African American.

A diverse collection of readings by some of the country's most dynamic and provocative writers One of the great pleasures of putting together this book has been the discovery of so many new and exciting voices, representing a variety of styles, viewpoints, and purposes. Like the student essays, the professional essays present **a rich mixture of multicultural perspectives** in terms of class, geographic origin, and sexual orientation as well as race and ethnicity. We wanted *Common Ground,* like the United States, to represent many voices.

Unusually complete headnotes We have tried in every case to go beyond standard headnote information and provide in addition **direct commentary by the writers about their lives, their writing, and their cultural identities.** Many of the quotations—collected through our correspondence with the writers—address issues related to the composition of the essay at hand. Thus students can get a better sense of each writer's voice and purpose.

Apparatus that encourages critical thinking and classroom collaboration In addition to its thought-provoking essays, *Common Ground* contains a wealth of material designed to stimulate critical thinking, discussion, collaborative work, and writing. Each professional essay is followed by four kinds of apparatus. "Opening the Dialogue" questions encourage students to respond to the writer's ideas. "Keeping a Notebook" questions ask students to explore in their writing journals an issue raised in a reading selection. "Working Together" exercises present innovative collaborative activities that encourage students to exchange ideas and thus examine the wider cultural implications of ideas introduced in an essay. Finally, "Writing an Essay" asks students to make connections between the reading selection and their own experiences. Each chapter ends with additional writing assignments that encourage students to explore ideas that run through the chapter.

Detailed Instructor's Manual In addition to suggestions for teaching individual essays, the Instructor's Manual includes ideas for classroom activities to get students thinking about cultural identity; advice for helping students annotate and think critically about what they read; and an alternative thematic table of contents that offers suggestions for making connections among essays throughout the text for additional discussion and writing.

Acknowledgments

Support for *Common Ground* has come from many sources. Karen Allanson at St. Martin's and Mark Gallaher, our development editor, helped us define the project and worked closely with us to shape it into the book it became. Their imagination, generosity, and professionalism have been much appreciated. In addition, we thank Amy Horowitz at St. Martin's for her careful project management; Paul Ciccarelli and Alex DiGiovanni for their indispensable work on the headnotes; and our friend Ben Obo for performing tasks large and small.

We are also grateful to the following colleagues, who provided much useful commentary on the various drafts of the book: Patricia Bates, Louisiana State University—Shreveport; Kitty Chen Dean, Nassau

Community College; Patricia Durfy, Broome Community College; Kathy Evertz, University of Wyoming; Joyce Flamm, Eastern Arizona College; Joan Gilson, University of Missouri—Kansas City; Elton Higgs, University of Michigan—Dearborn; Jacquelyn Jackson, Middle Tennessee State University; Jake Jakaitis, Indiana State University; Arden Jensen, Gulf Coast Community College; Richard Nordquist, Armstrong State College; Shirley Rose, San Diego State University; Barbara Sloan, Santa Fe Community College; Victor Villanueva, Northern Arizona University; and Maria Elena Yepes, East Los Angeles College.

We are especially grateful to the students who shared their written work with us. Despite their busy schedules and the pressures of school and part-time jobs, they wrote, revised, and edited conscientiously, communicating their thoughts about their own and others' cultures with honesty and sincerity.

Our families are another source of support. As they have so many times before, Mark, Adam, and Rebecca Kirszner and Demi, David, and Sarah Mandell tolerated the constant phone calls, clutter, and commotion that are part of a book-in-progress and survived to tell the tale. And so, once again, did we.

Laurie Kirszner
Stephen Mandell

CONTENTS

4   Culture and Custom: Explaining Processes   154

7 Across Cultures:
Comparing and Contrasting   **275**

ALTERNATE TABLE OF CONTENTS: CULTURAL GROUPS

FEMALE CULTURE

MALE CULTURE

Chapter 1

Reading and Writing about America's Cultures

Jacob Lawrence: Bumbershoot (1976)

American culture at the end of the twentieth century is the product of the interaction—often unequal, sometimes volatile—among many cultures: ethnic, racial, generational, regional, economic, sexual, educational, professional. Despite the check-off designations that appear on census forms and scholarship applications, we all define ourselves in terms of a variety of cultures: middle class, college-educated, Latina; midwestern, blue-collar, African-American male; unmarried, white, urban, working mother. The labels may vary according to the winds of political and social change; in any event, the search for self-identity within our broadly diverse society is ongoing. So too is the search to understand other cultures and to make sense of American culture as a whole—to see how all these diverse, often competing interests contribute to the shifting fabric of American life.

Among various racial and ethnic groups, significant differences exist in historical experiences, educational and economic opportunity, and values and social goals. The result of these differences, more often than not, has been conflict. This struggle—as troubling as it may be at times—is characteristic of life in the United States. Whether it is Puerto Ricans wanting bilingual education, African Americans calling for affirmative action, women demanding equal pay for equal work, Native Americans asking for an end to negative stereotypes, gay men and lesbians lobbying for more representation in local government, or people with disabilities working to change building codes, the various ethnic, racial, cultural, and special interest groups that make up the United States are engaged in a constant process of definition, redefinition, and negotiation. As various individuals and groups question the roles they play in society, they also challenge the status quo.

The essays collected in *Common Ground: Reading and Writing about America's Cultures* highlight the experiences of writers (and readers) of diverse cultural backgrounds and thus reveal the extent to which each of us is engaged in interpreting and reinterpreting American culture in light of its diversity. As you read these essays, keep in mind that in a multicultural society each group has an effect on every other group. This fact is reason enough for each of us to pay close attention to what others have to say.

Defining the American Experience

At one time the image of the melting pot defined the way diverse groups were supposed to achieve a national identity. First introduced in 1908 by the English writer Israel Zangwill, the term reflects the unique nature of the United States, all of whose residents, except for Native Americans, are immigrants. It also suggests that the different races that make up America will eventually lose or abandon their distinctive languages, customs, and cultures and assume a new homogenous American character:

> There [in America] lies the great Melting Pot—listen! Can't you hear the roaring and the bubbling? There gapes her mouth—the harbor where a thousand mammoth feeders come from the ends of the world to pour in their human freight. Ah, what a stirring and a seething! Celt and Latin, Slav and Teuton, Greek and Syrian,— black and yellow. . . . (*The Melting Pot,* Act I)

Much of the force of the idea of the melting pot came from the faith that as a new country with seemingly endless resources, America could absorb all the immigrants who came to its shores. Initially, this course of action seemed both possible and desirable, and for this reason very few restrictions were placed on immigration. The first great wave of nineteenth-century immigration—bringing mostly Irish, Germans, and English—began around 1815 and lasted until the 1840s. The second major wave—bringing primarily Germans, Scandinavians, and English— began in the 1860s, after the Civil War, and lasted until the 1880s. A third wave—bringing eastern European Jews as well as Russians, Poles, Ukrainians, Lithuanians, Italians, Greeks, and others—began in the 1880s and lasted until World War I, when strict immigration quotas brought it to an end.

Over the years, some people began to question how accurately the melting pot described the American experience. They saw that even as various groups came voluntarily to America in search of greater opportunity, some were more easily assimilated—and more welcome—than others. In 1965, over half of the immigrants to the United States still came from Europe. Today, however, most immigrants come from Mexico, the

Philippines, Jamaica, El Salvador, Haiti, Vietnam, Korea, India, China, and other developing countries. Some people find the new face of the American population (more and more diverse in terms of race, religion, and national origin) disturbing, prompting them to question how—and sometimes whether—some groups can ever adapt to life in the United States. In addition, studies have shown that many groups do not really "melt"; rather, they maintain their racial or ethnic identities from generation to generation. Whether by choice or as a result of discrimination, they hold on to a core of traditional values—especially where religion and language are concerned.

Also challenging the concept of the melting pot was the emerging awareness that some groups had been (and continued to be) specifically excluded from the American mainstream. African Americans, who were brought to America against their will, were first enslaved and then held back by Jim Crow laws, which legalized segregation between blacks and whites. Chinese, who came to the United States before most eastern European and Mediterranean immigrants did, were expelled from several western states and specifically barred from citizenship by the Chinese Exclusion Act of 1882. Hispanic Americans, whose families had been living in the American West and Southwest one hundred years before the Pilgrims landed at Plymouth Rock, were driven off their land and forcibly expatriated. Native Americans, who occupied the land before Europeans came, were conquered and consigned to reservations. (Native-American children were forced to attend "Indian schools" where white teachers attempted to strip them of their traditional values.) Other native cultures— such as those in Alaska, Hawaii, Puerto Rico, and American Samoa— were absorbed against their wills when their lands were ceded to the United States.

Still other factors called the concept of the melting pot into question. The post–World War II years saw the evolution of an enormous "baby boom," which by the 1950s had developed into a culture of youth and by the 1960s into a culture of adolescence. In addition, lifestyle changes and developing social and political movements modeled on the civil rights movement of the 1950s and 1960s led senior citizens, feminists, people with disabilities, environmentalists, welfare recipients, gays and lesbians, and other special interest groups to develop cultures based on common values and common social and political agendas. Thus, not only ethnic and racial groups, but also other emerging communities have come to enrich (and, in fact, define) the American experience.

Because the melting pot image is so problematic, many social critics now use other images to describe America. Some prefer to compare America to a salad bowl—in which all items retain their individual textures and flavors. Others, less optimistic about the ideal of equality, see it as a stew, in which various components are mixed together but one—the meat—predominates (as white, middle class, northern European males so often do). Some see America as a mosaic, emphasizing both the individual parts and the whole picture they form, while others stress conflict, characterizing America as a seething caldron. At this time, when the idea of difference is so much at the forefront, it should not be surprising that there is little agreement on a metaphor for the American experience. Whatever image is used, however, it is clear that people are questioning what America is and what it is becoming. Are we, as some suggest, moving toward cultural compromises that will allow us to live—despite our differences—as a single nation? Or are we, as others suggest, moving toward two nations: one mostly white, middle class, and affluent, and another composed mainly of people of color, mostly alienated, poor, and marginalized?

The difficulty of answering these questions is illustrated by the variety of perspectives represented in *Common Ground*. Despite their differences, however, the writers whose essays appear in this book are united to some extent by their common concern with defining their individual cultures in relation to the reality of American life. Therefore, underlying the essays in *Common Ground* is a sense of the ambivalence involved in being a member of one or more minority cultures in America. On the one hand, many write of seeking to fit in and adapt to the dominant culture of the United States, just as, traditionally, many immigrants try to dress, speak, and act like the "real" Americans they see around them. On the other hand, these same writers are obviously trying to preserve those parts of their unique cultures that define their identity. This is especially true for later generations, who often zealously try to recover the past that their parents or grandparents left behind. In many cases, then, these writers present a record of conflict, of their ongoing struggle to find answers about themselves, their families, and their cultures—and about the roles all three play in American society.

EXERCISE: OPENING THE DIALOGUE

1. To what racial or ethnic groups does each of your parents belong?

2. If you were outside the United States and someone asked you your nationality, how would you answer?

3. What do you say when someone in this country asks your nationality? How do your parents answer?

4. Is it possible for someone with three Irish grandparents and one Italian grandparent to consider him or herself Italian American? What about someone who is three-quarters African American and one-quarter Italian American?

5. How do you think each of these five Americans would describe himself or herself?

   • A black Catholic whose parents emigrated from Haiti
   • A Jew whose grandparents came from Poland
   • A Protestant whose ancestry is German
   • A naturalized U.S. citizen raised as a Buddhist in Korea
   • A Muslim of Indian ancestry who emigrated to the U.S. from South Africa

   How do you explain any inconsistencies or discrepancies?

6. Did you ever wish you were a member of a race, religion, or ethnic group other than your own? Why?

7. In addition to your ethnic or racial heritage, what other factors do you take into account when you define your culture? What labels do you think others use to define you?

 Exploring Cultural Identity

Whether explicitly or implicitly, any examination of America's cultures poses a fundamental question: What does it mean to be American? Because the population is constantly assimilating alternative experiences and values, the characteristics that make a person an American are difficult, if not impossible, to identify. Do Americans, for example, have a common set of religious, political, or social assumptions? Does being an

American mean striving for material wealth or attaining a certain level of education? Do Americans look or act a certain way, share certain goals, or even speak a common language? Does being an American mean be-lieving in a set of abstract principles, such as those embodied in the Bill of Rights, that guarantee equality of opportunity and individual free-doms?

When writers focus on their experiences as Americans, on the ways in which cultural influences shape their sense of themselves as Americans individually and collectively, they may examine broad issues such as *relo-cation, assimilation, aspiration, conflict,* and *compromise.* Thus some writers may discuss relocating from one country to another or from one part of the United States to another, either voluntarily or involuntarily, focusing on their own journeys or on those undertaken by their ancestors. Essays about relocation tend to look backward, often with a sense of loss, at the journey and what motivated it.

Writers may also focus on facing the realities, both positive and negative, of assimilating into the new world or a new community. They may examine opportunity and commonality as well as isolation, discrim-ination, religious differences, language difficulties, and cultural misunder-standings. Writers may also talk about their aspirations and their ability to adapt to or come to terms with the concepts of progress and success. In focusing on these aspirations, writers often deal with realizing—or failing to realize—their dreams and desires. In many cases, these dreams focus on educational, economic, and social advancement.

Many writers choose to focus on the conflicts inherent in American life—conflicts that shaped their ideas about themselves and about their cultures. Essays about conflict often involve issues of questioning, rebel-ling, and testing limits; frequently such essays examine generational con-flicts—in particular, deciding whether to be more (or less) "American" than other generations—or chronicle a struggle for acceptance and iden-tity. Finally, some writers discuss their efforts to balance individual, cul-tural, and assimilationist instincts, both internally and externally. These writers may focus on a search for compromise and consensus as they seek to define what it means to be an American. In doing so, writers may ex-amine (or reexamine) the meaning and value of their cultural heritage and consider whether (and to what extent) they should participate in the wider American society.

✦ Reading Critically

As you read the essays in this book, both those written by professional writers and those written by students, you should have two goals: to discover what the writers think and to discover what you think. In a sense, all the reading you do in college has this dual purpose, and so does much of your writing. After all, education involves a constant testing of ideas, a continuous process of evaluating new perspectives and reconsidering, refining, and rejecting old ones. By reading, you learn about others and about your world. By responding critically to reading—in discussion and in writing—you learn about yourself.

As you read, and prepare to write, essays about America's cultures, you may want to ask yourself some of the following questions:

- What political, social, economic, and religious ideas have shaped the writer's viewpoint?
- In what ways has the writer's race, gender, social or economic class, or ethnicity affected his or her ideas?
- What is your emotional reaction to the writer's ideas? Why do you think you react as you do? How do you think other readers might react? Why?
- How are the writer's experiences like and unlike yours?
- What in your own reading, education, observations, or experiences suggests parallels with the essay or gives you a wider perspective?
- What do various writers have in common? What problems do they share? How are their solutions different?
- What specific points does the writer make? Do you agree or disagree with these points?
- What conclusions does the writer draw? Do you draw similar conclusions?

Your responses to these questions will help you become an active participant in the reading process. This dialogue between you and the text will go a long way toward helping you become a thoughtful and perceptive reader.

Writing as a Process

As you prepare to compose your own essays, you should be aware of some basic principles about writing. Even before they begin to write, writers often engage in specific activities designed to help them discover what they have to say about a topic. Next, they identify the points they want to discuss and arrange them in the order in which they intend to discuss them. Then, consulting their notes, they write several drafts of their essay. Finally, they revise and edit their work so that it is ready for an audience. The techniques writers use to get from initial idea to finished paper are collectively called the **writing process.**

Of course, the process we have just described does not accurately represent the way many writers actually compose. The writing process is seldom this orderly, and it almost never goes from stage to stage sequentially. More often, several activities occur at once, and an activity that you first engage in at the beginning of the process may be repeated several times throughout the process. For example, as you draft an essay you may discover an order for your ideas. As you revise, you may rethink the points you wish to make about your topic. Thus the writing process is a creative and dynamic activity.

CONSIDERING AUDIENCE

Before you begin to write, you should consider who will be reading your essay. Usually, your readers will be your fellow students and your instructor. Because these readers may not be familiar with your culture, they may not share your values or opinions. In order to accommodate your diverse audience, then, you must take care to provide the background readers will need to understand your ideas and to define terms and explain traditions with which they might be unfamiliar. Moreover, when you write about other cultures, you should make a special effort to be sensitive to the feelings of the individuals who define themselves as members of that culture. Be careful not to inadvertently employ cultural stereotypes, which will be offensive to members of the group you are discussing—and, in fact, to all fair-minded readers. Be particularly careful to use only those terms to refer to members of a group that they would use to describe themselves—*disabled*, not *handicapped* or *crippled*, for example.

CONSIDERING PURPOSE

You should also consider your purpose before you begin to write. Sometimes you might set out to explore your reactions to members of a particular group or to communicate your mixed feelings about a culture or its values. At other times, your purpose might be to explain a practice associated with a group. Finally, your goal might be to persuade others to consider your ideas or to adopt a course of action. Whatever the case, your purpose for writing determines what kind of information you include and how you present it.

DISCOVERING IDEAS

Before you begin to write, you should approach any reading selection you will write about as a critical reader. Prepare to read carefully and to question both what you read and what you already think.

MAKING ANNOTATIONS   Annotating what you read can be a great help to you as you prepare for writing. When you **annotate** an essay, you underline key passages and write comments and questions on the page as you read. Not only will the reactions you record help you clarify your ideas, but they will also provide you with subject matter for your writing.

Thomas J. Togno, a student in a composition class, was assigned to read the essay "The 'Black Table' Is Still There," by Lawrence Otis Graham, in preparation for class discussion. Tom's instructor told students that afterward they would be writing an essay which, like Graham's, discussed a personal encounter with racism. Graham's essay, along with Tom's annotations, is reproduced here. Notice how Tom highlights material selectively and uses familiar symbols and brief comments to identify important points and to indicate ideas that he might want to explore later.

LAWRENCE OTIS GRAHAM
The 'Black Table' Is Still There

During a recent visit to my old junior high school in   1
Westchester County, I came upon something that I never ex-

pected to see again, something that was a source of fear and dread for three hours each school morning of my early adolescence: the all-black lunch table in the cafeteria of my predominantly white suburban junior high school.

As I look back on 27 years of often being the first and   2 only black person integrating such activities and institutions as the college newspaper, the high school tennis team, summer music camps, our all-white suburban neighborhood, my eating club at Princeton or my private social club at Harvard Law School, the one scenario that puzzled me the most then and now is the all-black lunch table.

Why was it there? Why did the black kids separate   3 themselves? What did the table say about the integration that was supposedly going on in home rooms and gym classes? What did it say about the black kids? The white kids? What did it say about me when I refused to sit there, day after day, for three years?

Each afternoon, at 12:03 P.M., after the fourth period   4 ended, I found myself among 600 12-, 13- and 14-year-olds who marched into the brightly lit cafeteria and dashed for a seat at one of the 27 blue formica lunch tables.

<u>No matter who I walked in with—usually a white</u>   5 <u>friend</u>—no matter what mood I was in, there was one thing that was certain: I would not sit at the black table.

I would never consider sitting at the black table.   6
What was wrong with me? What was I afraid of?   7

I would like to think that my decision was a heroic   8 one, made in order to express my solidarity with the theories of integration that my community was espousing. But I was just 12 at the time, and there was nothing heroic in my actions.

I avoided the black table for a very simple reason: I was   9 afraid that by sitting at the black table I'd lose all my white friends. I thought that by sitting there I'd be making a racist, anti-white statement.

Is that what the all-black table means? Is it a rejection   10 of white people? I no longer think so.

At the time, I was angry that there was a black lunch   11

[Handwritten margin annotations:]
Because they have interests in common?
because they feel more comfortable?
Why didn't he sit with them?

are most of his friends white?

Maybe he's afraid of being black.

table. I believed that the black kids were the reason why other kids didn't mix more. I was ready to believe that their self-segregation was the cause of white bigotry.

Ironically, I even believed this after my best friend (who was white) told me I probably shouldn't come to his bar mitzvah because I'd be the only black and people would feel uncomfortable. I even believed this after my Saturday afternoon visit, at age 10, to a private country club pool prompted incensed white parents to pull their kids from the pool in terror.

In the face of this blatantly racist (anti-black) behavior, I still somehow managed to blame only the black kids for being the barrier to integration in my school and my little world. What was I thinking?

I realize now how wrong I was. During the same time, there were at least two tables of athletes, an Italian table, a Jewish girls' table, a Jewish boys' table (where I usually sat), a table of kids who were into heavy metal music and smoking pot, a table of middle class Irish kids. Weren't these tables just as segregationist as the black table? At the time, no one thought so. At the time, no one even acknowledged the segregated nature of these other tables.

Maybe it's the color difference that makes all-black tables or all-black groups attract the scrutiny and wrath of so many people. It scares and angers people; it exasperates. It did those things to me, and I'm black.

As an integrating black person, I know that my decision *not* to join the black lunch table attracted its own kind of scrutiny and wrath from my classmates. At the same time that I heard angry words like "Oreo" and "white boy" being hurled at me from the black table, I was also dodging impatient questions from white classmates: "Why do all those black kids sit together?" or "Why don't you ever sit with the other blacks?"

The black lunch table, like those other segregated tables, is a comment on the superficial inroads that integration has made in society. Perhaps I should be happy that even this

is a long way from where we started. Yet, I can't get over the
fact that the 27th table in my junior high school cafeteria is
still known as the "black table"—14 years after my adolescence.

KEEPING A NOTEBOOK　Like annotating, keeping a **notebook,**—a
journal in which you record ideas you may be able to use in your writing—is another useful strategy. In your notebook you can *brainstorm*—jot
down ideas, questions, and connections as they occur to you, without
paying attention to the style or form of your responses. These notes can
be responses to your reading, observations, memories, discussions, or a
record of your instructor's comments or questions. You can also use your
notebook as a place to engage in a dialogue with a writer—or with yourself—debating the merits of various positions or questioning lines of reasoning. Finally, your notebook is an ideal place in which to try out different versions of sentences and paragraphs you plan to use in your writing.

　　The following entries are from Thomas Togno's writer's notebook.
You can see how he uses his entries to develop ideas reflected in his annotations of Lawrence Otis Graham's essay.

9/21
Westville[1] H. S.--"minority" cafeteria and white cafeteria. (But now whites are the minority.) Graham sees
separate tables as a problem--We have separate <u>rooms</u>.
Would this be a problem if kids didn't fight? Is it
necessarily a bad thing? (Would I want my children to
go to Westville High? Would a black parent want this?)
Graham grew up in an upper-middle-class suburb, and
now he's a lawyer, so the segregation he describes
didn't exactly hurt him. Maybe he's just feeling
guilty because he sees what an Oreo he was.

9/23
In our college cafeteria, there are tables for jocks,
commuters, Deadheads, frats, geeks--and some for

[1]Because this essay discusses actual incidents, the names of the town and the high school
have been changed.

blacks, Asians, Hispanics, etc. So what? This so-
called segregation isn't such a bad thing. Everyone
chooses where to sit; they're not forced, and everyone
seems happy. I like to sit with people like me, and so
do blacks and other groups. No problem.

9/28
In class we talked about the idea of a melting pot, and
Westville sure isn't it. The professor even said Westville still has some KKK activity. Now that I think of
it, it isn't surprising. So maybe the high school cafeteria just reflects what people in the town want. Is
this OK? Maybe not. But even if it's not OK, what can
anyone do about it? I remember an article we read about
gangs in LA fighting over turf. That's what's going on
at Westville.

WORKING TOGETHER One final strategy for generating and testing ideas is **working together**—exchanging ideas with others and trying
out your ideas on an audience to find out how others respond.

When Thomas Togno discussed his ideas with other students in his
composition class, he discovered that many of them did not see the separate tables in their college cafeteria as either desirable or natural. Although many agreed that such separation was the result of free choice,
others believed these seating patterns were actually determined by social
pressures both from within individual groups and from society as a whole.
Some students thought their college cafeteria reflected their community's
values. (One student even pointed out that the tendency to sit with individuals of the same background was reflected in classroom seating patterns as well.)

In addition to comparing his reaction to separate tables in the college cafeteria to those of his classmates, Tom discussed with them his
reactions to Graham's essay. The biggest surprise came when he talked
about his own high school and discovered how shocked the other students were when they heard that it had segregated facilities. The existence of two separate cafeterias was something that Tom had always
taken for granted. Now his classmates' strong reactions led him to appreciate the seriousness of the situation and to consider for the first time the
dangers of his own complacency.

ARRANGING IDEAS

Once you have collected the ideas you want to examine in an essay, you should select the major points you want to discuss. Then, you should gather supporting details and decide what material should be added, deleted, or modified. Finally, you should decide on the order in which to present your main points. Sometimes an outline is helpful; more often, however, reviewing notes and jotting down your main points works just as well.

After reviewing his annotations and notebook entries and thinking about the points his classmates made, Tom jotted down the following points he thought he could discuss in his essay:

- Atmosphere at Westville High School
- Separate cafeterias
- Graham's essay
- Violent incidents at high school
- Effects of experiences

USING PATTERNS OF ORGANIZATION   As you think about a subject, your mind arranges ideas in a variety of familiar ways. For example, you can react to a subject by narrating (telling what happened), by describing places and things, by explaining a process, by presenting a series of examples, by analyzing causes and effects, by classifying and dividing, by comparing and contrasting, by defining, or by trying to persuade an audience. Each of these ways of thinking about a subject corresponds to a way of arranging material in an essay. Moreover, you can use these options not only for shaping your essay but also for discovering new ways of looking at your subject. Notice how the following familiar patterns can help shape your thinking and writing about cultural experiences:

You can narrate an event from your personal, family, or community history.
- Tell about a difficulty you encountered in understanding your cultural heritage.
- Trace the changing ethnic makeup of your town's population.

You can describe an environment that has significance to a particular culture.
- Describe an ethnic neighborhood in a large city.
- Describe a community's cultural center (a building, a monument, a meeting place).

You can explain the process of performing a custom.
- Tell how to make or do something unique to a particular cultural group.
- Describe a ritual or tradition that embodies a special set of values.

You can use examples to show how a culture is perceived.
- Illustrate how people of a given age group, profession, or region are perceived by outsiders.
- Examine how a group—union members, the elderly, evangelical Christians, single parents, the wealthy—is presented in the media.

You can explore the causes that shape cultural identity or examine the effects of diverse cultures on the larger society.
- Examine the major influences on your ethnic group's attitudes toward race or gender.
- Consider the effects of a confrontation between people of different cultures.

You can compare and contrast cultures.
- Explore the ways in which your values are similar to or different from those of others.
- Compare the perspectives of urban and rural communities on a given environmental issue.

You can classify and divide people, experiences, or cultures.
- Classify a group of individuals according to their attitudes about education, economic success, or politics.
- Divide a cultural group into subgroups on the basis of their respective degrees of assimilation.

You can define a culture or a cultural identity.
- Is there a culture of poverty?
- How might one of the following groups define its culture: White

Anglo-Saxon Protestants, Vietnam veterans, people with AIDS, suburban homeowners, college students, the visually impaired?

You can persuade readers to accept ideas about culture and diversity.

- Persuade readers that Native Americans are (or are not) entitled to reparations from the government of the United States.
- Persuade readers that the 1991 Americans with Disabilities Act goes too far (or not far enough).

In subsequent chapters, you will find these options for exploring ideas discussed in detail, along with suggestions about how each can be used as a pattern for organizing an essay. Keep in mind, though, that two or more of these strategies may often be used together within a single essay, depending on an essay's subject and purpose. In any case, a pattern is not imposed on a piece of writing; it emerges from the way in which the writer interprets his or her experience.

As you think about how to approach your subject—the pattern and strategies you will use to develop and organize your ideas—you should also begin to consider a tentative **thesis**, a statement that summarizes the main point of your essay and gives your writing its focus. Sometimes, particularly in essays that are predominantly narrative or descriptive, the thesis will be implied. Generally, however, you will want to state your thesis directly, often in your opening paragraph. Your thesis can then serve as a guide to help you decide what to include from among the notes you have already made about your subject.

As he read over his notes and considered the main points he wanted to discuss in his essay, Thomas Togno realized his best strategy would be to use a series of provocative, even shocking, examples to support the tentative thesis that Westville High School's cafeteria reflects the community's racial strife.

DRAFTING

Writing and revising an essay requires careful planning and thoughtful reflection. Ideally, a fully thought out essay emerges over several drafts and changes significantly as it takes shape. As Thomas Togno drafted his essay and continued to discuss his ideas with other students, he began to realize that the pattern of segregation he had accepted was a sign of a serious problem—not just inside his school but outside it as well. As a result, he began to modify his ideas and eventually took a strong stand against the racism he witnessed at his high school.

The following first draft enabled Tom to shape his ideas about his experiences and to connect them to the ideas expressed in Lawrence Otis Graham's "The 'Black Table' Is Still There."

Thomas J. Togno
Assimilate vs. Segregate (*draft*)

Are Americans united? This is a question that I often ask myself. Coming from a culturally diverse city, I have been exposed to a multitude of unique backgrounds. The segregated nature of my city became apparent to me when I entered high school and learned that Westville High's cafeteria reflected the community's racial strife.

The social atmosphere of my high school showed me that the   2
United States is not a melting pot. Entering high school was the beginning of my exposure to many different races. Coming from a Catholic school that was predominantly white, I was ignorant of the fact that different races selectively chose segregation. The change of schools also introduced me to a very uneven balance of whites to blacks and Hispanics. It now seemed that whites were the minority, and that blacks and Hispanics were the majority. This was a very uncomfortable situation which I, like all new white students, had to adjust to.

The first high school experience that led me to believe that some-   3
thing was wrong occurred at lunch time. I knew that there were two cafeterias that were used by students for three fifty-minute lunch periods each day. They were both normal cafeterias decorated with green tiles and stained furniture. The problem was not with the appearance or the furnishings, but rather with the people who occupied each cafeteria.

What I learned was that although the cafeterias were called "east" and "west" cafeterias, they were actually "black" and "white" cafeterias. Naturally, I ate in the white cafeteria, but I didn't understand the system. Why did students want to separate themselves into racial groups? This was a question I could never answer.

As Lawrence Otis Graham says, "the black lunch table, like those   4 other segregated tables, is a comment on the superficial inroads that integration has made in society." These "superficial inroads" that were introduced into society have not joined the separated cultures of blacks and whites in my high school, but instead have literally deprived them of one another.

Violence also contributed to the racial atmosphere of my high   5 school. Throughout my four years of high school, I witnessed many fights between blacks and whites over school territory. One example of this occurred when a white student mistakenly came into the black cafeteria. A small riot occurred during which whites and blacks not only fought with their hands but also with weapons. Incidents like this one were not formed overnight. After all, the two "separate but equal" cafeterias had been there for years.

Before I ever entered the Westville school system, vicious fights   6 took place between blacks and whites. The violence I witnessed in high school was also seen by my older brother, who is now twenty-seven. The event that intensified the racial tension that exists happened when my older brother was in his junior year of high school. The fight had been started by a few students who apparently placed a black doll on a cross. They then set the doll on fire, and flaunted it around the black cafeteria. The incident sparked a large and violent confrontation between blacks and whites. The riots forced many students, both black and white, to stay home and forced others to be escorted to classes. The riot that occurred almost ten years ago still affects students today. Police, who were called in during the riots, are still stationed at the end of each hallway of the school.

The violence that occurred at my high school, initiated by a few   7
ignorant people, has left scars that go beyond superficial wounds. The resulting racial tension will not be easily forgotten. Bad feelings have been passed on to the younger generation. Because the conflicts between the different racial groups continue to be fed by anger, the trouble that has occurred can only be heightened by more, increasingly violent, incidents. As in the Westville school system, the gaps among the many unique races in the United States also seem to be too wide to be bridged at this time.

Revising

When you **revise**, you look at your draft and determine how effectively it communicates your ideas. As you reread your work, you attempt to see your draft as your readers do, making sure that the content and structure of your essay help you achieve your purpose. Asking the following general questions will help you revise the first draft of your essay:

- Do you have a clear sense of your audience and your purpose?
- Do you clearly state your thesis?
- Are the points you discuss relevant to your thesis?
- Do these points adequately develop your thesis?
- Have you supplied enough material—examples and statistics—to support your points?
- Is the organizational pattern of the essay suited to your purpose?
- Does your organization help you present your ideas effectively?
- Do your paragraphs and sentences clearly flow into one another?
- Do you have an effective introduction and conclusion?

As Thomas Togno revised, he asked himself each of these questions. In addition, he discussed his draft with other students. As a result, he made several decisions. First, he decided that he should sharpen his thesis to make his point more explicitly. Next, he deleted the references in his fourth paragraph to "The 'Black Table' Is Still There" after a classmate reminded him that the assignment asks students to discuss a situation *like* the one Graham describes, not to make a specific connection. Many of the students agreed this paragraph should be deleted, saying that they thought the reference to Graham's essay was distracting. Another student suggested that Tom emphasize the fact that his thinking has changed since he attended Westville High. Tom decided to make this point in his conclusion as he discussed the wider implications of his experience. Finally, he substituted a new title that stressed the universality of the prejudice he had witnessed in high school.

EDITING

Unlike revision, which is concerned with large-scale changes, **editing** focuses on smaller concerns such as punctuation, mechanics, and manuscript form. When you edit, you concentrate on the surface features of your draft. Editing is the final thing you do before you submit a paper. It is your last chance to make sure that you have attended to the many smaller elements in your paper, correcting errors that could, if uncorrected, distract readers and undercut your credibility. As you edit, you should ask yourself the following questions:

- Is your writing free of sentence fragments, run-on sentences, and other sentence-level errors?
- Is your spelling correct?
- Is your punctuation correct?
- Have you capitalized, hyphenated, and abbreviated according to accepted usage?
- Have you followed the manuscript format prescribed by your instructor?

As Thomas Togno edited his essay, he made his sentences more concise and corrected problems with grammar, spelling, and punctuation. Here is the revised and edited draft of his essay.

STUDENT VOICE: THOMAS J. TOGNO

High School U.S.A.

Coming from a culturally diverse city, I have been exposed to   1
people from a number of different backgrounds. As I grew up, the
cultural variety I saw led me to believe that my hometown, Westville, New Jersey, was a true melting pot. But the ethnic divisions of
my city became apparent to me when I entered high school. My
experiences there forced me to realize that Westville—and possibly the United States—has a long way to go before it can be considered a true melting pot.

My first real social contacts with people of other races occurred   2
when I got to high school. Coming from a Catholic school that
was predominantly white, I did not know that different races would
often choose to be segregated. High school also introduced me to
a situation where whites were the minority, and blacks and Hispanics were the majority. This was a very uncomfortable situation to
which I, like all new white students, had to adjust.

My first day in the cafeteria convinced me that something was   3
wrong. I knew there were two cafeterias that were used by students
for three fifty-minute lunch periods each day. They were similar in
all respects—decorated with green tiles and stained furniture. The
problem was not with the appearance or the furnishings, but rather
with the people who occupied each cafeteria. Although the cafeterias were designated "east" and "west," they were actually "black"
and "white." Each day as I took my tray to the "white" cafeteria
while black and Hispanic students took theirs to the "black" cafeteria, I had a weird feeling in my stomach. I asked myself why we

wanted to separate ourselves from each other. Unfortunately, I never was able to answer this question.

Violence seemed to be an almost daily part of my high school. 4 Whether because of the separation of the races or because of long-standing anger between them, fights between blacks and whites regularly occurred over territory. One fight took place when a white student walked into the "black" cafeteria. A small riot occurred in which whites and blacks fought viciously not only with their hands, but also with weapons.

I now realize that the attitudes that fueled these fights were not 5 formed overnight. After all, the two "separate but equal" cafeterias had existed for years. According to my older brother, who is now twenty-seven, the racial tension had always been present. He told me about one example that to him typified the racial climate he encountered at Westville High School. A few white teens apparently put a black doll on a cross, set the doll on fire, and flaunted it in the black cafeteria. The incident sparked a large, very violent confrontation between black and white students. The riots that occurred forced many students to stay home and others to be escorted by guards to certain classes. Even today, ten years after the event, police are still stationed in every hallway.

The violence that I saw at my high school has left scars. Each 6 generation of students that comes into the school seems to be infected by the prejudice and intolerance that exists there. Because the conflicts between the different races continue, the cycle goes on. Meanwhile, the two cafeterias, the symbol of all that is wrong with my school, are still present. In my mind the racial tension that exists in the Westville school system mirrors the racial situation throughout the rest of the United States. Instead of coming together and talking, we seem to be segregating ourselves into two distinct "cafeterias." If we do not want our children to eat in separate cafeterias, we need to do something now—while there is still time.

The purpose of *Common Ground* is not just to introduce you to a variety of perspectives on ethnic and cultural diversity, but also to encourage you to explore your own identity, find various ways to describe your version of the American experience, and discover the similarities and differences between yourself and others. Both the student and professional writers whose work is collected in this book explore a variety of issues related to the American experience. Their essays are here to get you thinking about your own experiences and about how you might respond in discussion or writing when you examine the ideas in this book. Like these writers, you will be considering your own culture, your family's relationship to other cultures, and the characteristics that define (or should define) a multicultural society.

The student and professional writers represented in this book approach the issue of cultural identity in America in a number of ways. Each chapter presents a set of essays illustrating a particular rhetorical approach to a cultural theme. The essays in Chapter 2 use **narrative** to focus on how we identify ourselves and our culture through the stories we tell about our personal past. The essays in Chapter 3 **describe** cultural environments—the homes, neighborhoods, and landscapes that shape, and are shaped by, the people who live there. Chapter 4 examines **process,** looking at customs within particular cultures, the rituals and processes that set cultures apart and provide points of identification for individuals within them. The writers in Chapter 5 seek to characterize their cultures through **examples,** identifying images that they themselves, or outsiders, use to describe them; those in Chapter 6 examine how culture shapes a sense of personal identity, exploring **causal connections** between what a person is and the forces that shaped him or her.

In Chapter 7 the writers **compare and contrast** cultures, focusing in particular on parallels and differences among ethnic groups, social classes, and generations. Essays in Chapter 8 **classify and divide**, thereby identifying categories within cultures, the ways in which types and stereotypes both illuminate and obscure the reality of particular cultures. Chapter 9 finds writers attempting to **define** a cultural heritage for themselves as individuals, and the writers in Chapter 10 try to **persuade** readers to accept a particular position concerning the cultural diversity of American life.

As you read the essays in this book, look for connections among different writers' experiences and for similarities and differences between their lives and your own. Think of these connections as starting points for your own process of reading and writing and as the first steps in the process of discovering ideas and communicating them to others.

CHAPTER 2

CULTURE AND
PERSONAL HISTORY
RECOUNTING
EXPERIENCES

My father was the second oldest of seven children born and raised on a farm in South Korea. The farm had no electricity and no indoor plumbing, and everything was done by manual labor and hard work. My father, the first-born male, was the only one to receive a proper education. After he graduated from college he married my mother, and a year later my brother was born. Two and a half years later I was born, and then my family moved out of the country and into the city of Seoul. Because of the intense competition for jobs, my college-educated father had to settle for a position as a manager of a tire plant. After two years of being miserable in this job, he decided that this was not what he wanted to do for the rest of his life. Soon after my third birthday, my parents decided that their future was limited in South Korea and that they wanted to start somewhere new where there was more freedom of choice and more opportunities.

Judy Kim, student

Culture and Personal History

Narrative—recounting events to tell a story—is a useful pattern of organization for a variety of academic assignments. For example, you can use narrative to relate historical events, present a case study, review the background of a court decision, or summarize the plot of a novel. Because narrative tells a story, it is also an appropriate choice for writing about culture and personal history. A narrative can, for example, trace the history of a family—or of an ethnic group, a town, or a neighborhood. It can chronicle a journey—either a physical journey, from one region or country to another, or an emotional or spiritual journey, from one state of mind to another. Narrative can follow a person's educational development or measure progress toward personal or professional goals. Writers also use narrative to relate anecdotes about memorable people or events or to recount experiences that served as turning points or offered moral lessons.

In this chapter, writers with very different backgrounds and experiences use narrative as they explore their cultural heritages and consider what it means to be part of American society. More specifically, these writers remember key encounters and confrontations, trace (and try to come to terms with) the evolution of their family histories, recall both triumphant and painful memories, and tell about their efforts to assimilate into a larger American culture. As they do so, they recount experiences that are familiar to many Americans: They struggle to achieve success; they face setbacks caused by physical disabilities and racial bias; and they are challenged by confrontations with people different from themselves.

Recounting experiences in a narrative essay can help you to understand your own cultural and personal history and explore its significance. Narrative also provides a structure within which you can chronicle the lives and times of family members or examine your involvement with people who have had an important influence on your life or shaped your values or beliefs.

In the essay that follows, a student gives an account of his mother's early years, learning as he does so about his heritage.

STUDENT VOICE: JEAN-LIONEL REMISE

My Mother's Life

In the countryside of Haiti, where my mother was born, life   1
could be very difficult for a child with no parents. Haiti is a country
of strong traditions, and the institution of family is highly esteemed. An orphaned child was therefore denied the privileges and
respect that other children had. The fact that both of my mother's
parents were dead by the time she was twelve influenced her life
tremendously.

The early years of my mother's childhood were not much differ-   2
ent from mine or any other child's. She remembers being in the
Girl Scouts and playing games on the Rue Saint Honoré in

Mirebalais, where she grew up. One of her favorite games was Oselet. Oselet is very similar to the American game of Jacks, except that the jacks used are made not of aluminum but of the ankle bone of a cow. My mother recalls many other games, such as Tirée Conte (Folklores) and La Ronde (Ring around the Rosy), which were very special to her as a child.

Amid all of the sunshine in my mother's childhood there were   3
dark clouds, and there was rain. My mother's father died when she was only three months old. Her single mother tried her best to provide a solid home for her children, but the male presence was very important in a Haitian family, and there were certain things that a girl without a father could not do. For example, my mother did not go to many parties. It was understood in Haiti that a young girl did not go to "balls" or any other social gatherings without a male figure. My mother also never dared to have boyfriends. Many of the young men who were interested in her knew that she did not have a father; therefore, they believed they could treat her in any manner they pleased, knowing there was no father to intervene.

In retrospect, these were minor inconveniences. The true de-   4
spair in my mother's life did not come until after her mother's death. Things were still normal at first: she and her sister lived with their grandmother and attended school. After a short time, however, her grandmother's health failed, and soon she too died, leaving my mother and her sister alone. Most of her maternal relatives were dead, and she did not know her paternal relatives well. Although several of her surviving relatives wanted to take the girls in, none could afford to. Some relatives and neighbors were willing to

take in one but not both of the girls, but the girls resisted this because their mother's dying wish had been to keep them together always. As a result, they had trouble finding shelter.

For the next few years, my mother and her sister migrated from   5
the home of one family to the next. They were given shelter, but no food or clothing. Sometimes they would be lucky: there would be leftovers, and the mistress of the house would let them eat. My mother refers to this time as the "nothing stage." She remembers going barefoot and having only one dress. I asked her once if her peers were cruel to her. She said, "Never. If you respect yourself, others will respect you as well. I may have had only one dress, but I was always clean and well-kept."

One term, my mother found herself with none of the supplies   6
she needed to attend school. Haiti's school system was a combination of our public and parochial systems: While there was no tuition, students and their families were responsible for buying uniforms and books. Because Mirebalais was such a small town, her professor knew my mother's situation. "It is a shame," he said, "that a good kid like you has a desire to learn but cannot afford to." Because the professor admired her determination, he bought all of the necessary books and supplies for her that term.

My mother's life was never without hardship or struggle, but   7
with faith in God and the love of a few individuals—particularly her sister—she made it. It is her faith and determination that have gotten her this far. And it is these same qualities, which she has instilled in all of her children, that have made us what we are today.

My mother has set a tremendous example for me. I often com-   8 plain about how tough it is to be black and how many obstacles there are in my path. Then I remember my mother's struggle just to stay alive, and I am thankful. I am thankful for my home; I am thankful for my education; and, most important, I am thankful for the sacrifices that my mother has made for me.

Recounting Experiences

A **narrative** recounts a series of events in order to tell a story. Thus it can trace progress, summarize experiences, chart milestones, or record moments of insight. Often, a narrative essay has a thesis—that is, it tells a story in order to make a point.

USING CHRONOLOGICAL SEQUENCE

When you write narrative essays, you *present key events in an orderly, logical sequence,* generally beginning with the first event that occurred and moving toward the most recent. This order helps your readers follow your story and understand the chronological relationships among the events. Sometimes, however, you may use a *flashback,* a glimpse back in time, to present one or more events that occurred prior to the main action of the narrative. Professional writers frequently use this technique in an essay's introduction, when an incident in the recent past triggers memories of an earlier experience. In "A Giant Step" (p. 36), for example, Henry Louis Gates, Jr., begins his narrative in the relatively recent past (" 'What's this?' the hospital janitor said to me as he stumbled over my right shoe.") and then moves back in time ("We had been together since 1975, those shoes and I.") and then still further back ("It all started 26 years ago . . . ") to explain the significance of the orthopedic shoes that so dominated his life.

USING DIALOGUE AND DESCRIPTION

Whenever possible, *use dialogue and physical description* to evoke the character of the storyteller (yourself), to enrich your characterizations of the people you discuss, and to make events more memorable and vivid to your readers. (For detailed information about using physical description, see Chapter 3, "Culture and Environment: Describing One's World.")

In "The Struggle to Be an All-American Girl" (p. 42), for example, Elizabeth Wong quotes her brother's critical comments to their mother in order to illustrate his frustration with her limited command of English: " 'It's not "What it is," Mom,' he'd say in exasperation. 'It's "What *is* it, what *is* it, what *is* it!" ' " Similarly, Audre Lorde's (p. 46) careful characterization of her family's proud physical appearance—"a proper caravan, mother bright and father brown, the three of us girls step-standards in-between"; "Corded and crisp and pinafored"—underscores the injustice of the white waitress's embarrassed refusal to serve them.

USING VERB TENSES

You should also *use verb tenses carefully* to help readers understand the relationship in time between one event and another. Be sure verb tenses are consistent and accurate, with no unwarranted shifts from one tense to another.

A narrative generally uses past tense to look back at events that have already occurred and explore their significance. In "Foul Shots" (p. 52), for instance, Rogelio R. Gomez uses past tense verbs in the body of his essay as he recounts events that happened to him over twenty years ago: "But my teammates and I *smiled* sardonically at one another, and our sneakers *squeaked* as we nervously *rubbed* them against the waxed hardwood floors of our gym." In similar fashion, Mary Clearman Blew uses past tense in " The Unwanted Child" (p. 71) to recount events in her mother's life: "My mother *was* an unwanted child. The fourth daughter of a homesteading family racked by drought and debt, she *was* only a year old when the sister nearest her in age *died* of a cancerous tumor." When the focus of Blew's narrative is on her own life, however, she uses present tense to recapture past events: "December 1958. I *lie* on my back on an examination table in a Missoula clinic. . . . " This technique gives a sense of immediacy to her own story and keeps her experiences distinct from those of her mother.

A narrative may also use present tense to express the writer's current feelings about past events. Thus Gomez uses present tense verbs in the introduction of his essay: "Now and then I *can* still *see* their faces, snickering and laughing, their eyes mocking me. And it *bothers* me that I should remember." In his conclusion too he uses present tense to comment on past events: "Two decades later, the memory of their gloating *lives* on in me."

USING TRANSITIONS

In addition to selecting verb tenses carefully, be sure to *include transitions* to clarify the sequence of events, indicate shifts from one time period to another, and show how much time passes between events.

KEY TRANSITIONS: NARRATIVE

First	Later	On April 12
Then	Meanwhile	In 1940
Next	When	Finally
After that	Twenty years ago	Now
Afterwards	Six years earlier	Today
Soon	Ten years later	At the present time
Earlier	After six months	Recently

Effective transitions can also help make your narrative flow smoothly. In "A Giant Step" (p. 36), for instance, Gates's use of transitions that serve as time markers ("It all started . . . "; "A few weeks later . . . "; "I limped through the next decade . . . "; "In the meantime . . . "; " This year, my 40th, . . . "; " Twenty-four hours later, . . . "; " The next day . . . ") enables readers to follow easily a story that stretches over twenty-five years. In "My Mother's Life" (p. 28) Jean-Lionel Remise also uses transitions to indicate the sequence of events, with words and phrases such as "at first," "For the next two years," "Sometimes," and "one term."

VARYING SENTENCE LENGTHS AND OPENINGS

Finally, when you write and revise narratives, you should try to *vary sentence lengths and openings* to avoid monotony. When you are recounting a family history, for instance, rather than writing a series of short sentences and beginning each sentence with the subject—producing a narrative that reads like a shopping list—connect and combine sentences smoothly, making causal and sequential relationships clear:

MONOTONOUS

Her grandmother's health failed. Soon she too died. Her death left my mother and her sister alone. Most of her maternal relatives were dead. She did not know her paternal relatives well. Several of her surviving relatives wanted to take the girls in. None could afford to, though. Some relatives and neighbors were willing to take in one but not both of the girls. The girls resisted this. Their mother's dying wish had been to keep them together. They had trouble finding shelter.

REVISED

After a short time, however, her grandmother's health failed, and soon she too died, leaving my mother and her sister alone. Most of her maternal relatives were dead, and she did not know her paternal relatives well. Although several of her surviving relatives wanted to take the girls in, none could afford to. Some relatives and neighbors were willing to take in one but not both of the girls, but the girls resisted this because their mother's dying wish had been to keep them together always. As a result, they had trouble finding shelter.

Although repetition of stylistic patterns may be tedious, intentional repetition of sentence openings may be an effective stylistic strategy, one that adds clarity and emphasis to your ideas. Audre Lorde uses this technique effectively when she lists the items her mother packed for their trip: *"There were* violently yellow iced cakes. . . ."; *"There was* a spice bun. . . ."; *"There were* sweet pickles. . . ."; "And, for neatness, *there were* piles of napkins. . . ." (p. 47). In this instance, the parallel sentence openings work well, partly because Lorde is careful to vary the length of her sentences.

REVIEW CHECKLIST: RECOUNTING EXPERIENCES

✓ Present key events in chronological sequence, unless you are using a flashback.

✓ Use dialogue and physical description to make narratives more vivid.

✓ Choose verb tenses carefully, avoiding unwarranted tense shifts.

✓ Include appropriate transitions to clarify the sequence of events.

✓ Vary sentence lengths and openings to avoid monotony.

HENRY LOUIS GATES, JR.

A Giant Step

Henry Louis Gates, Jr. (b. 1950), grew up in a poor Appalachian mountain community on the border between West Virginia and Maryland. After high school he earned degrees from Yale and Cambridge, served as London correspondent for *Time* magazine, and worked in corporate public relations before beginning a distinguished career as a professor and literary critic. He is currently on the faculty at Harvard University.

A strong advocate of multicultural studies, Gates traces his own achievements to his early reading of *The Fire Next Time*, by the African-American writer and social critic James Baldwin: "A wonderful thing happens when you encounter images of your cultural self in a book at an early age. . . . I felt like Baldwin was naming me in a way that I didn't even know I needed to be named. It changed my life. That's where I first got the idea that I might want to be a scholar, to serve my people through print. How could anybody deny—right, left, or center—the importance of that experience in shaping a young intellect?"

First published as a magazine article in 1989, "A Giant Step" traces Gates's long struggle to overcome a childhood injury. As you read, notice how Gates manages time in narrating his experiences, covering more than twenty-five years by compressing some incidents while expanding others in detail.

"**W**HAT'S THIS?" the hospital janitor said to me as he stumbled   1
over my right shoe.

"My shoes," I said.   2

"That's not a shoe, brother," he replied, holding it to the light.   3
"That's a brick."

It *did* look like a brick, sort of.   4

"Well, we can throw these in the trash now," he said.   5

"I guess so."   6

We had been together since 1975, those shoes and I. They were   7
orthopedic shoes built around molds of my feet, and they had a 2¼-inch
lift. I had mixed feelings about them. On the one hand, they had given
me a more or less even gait for the first time in 10 years. On the other
hand, they had marked me as a "handicapped person," complete with
cane and special license plates. I went through a pair a year, but it was
always the same shoe, black, wide, weighing about four pounds.

It all started 26 years ago in Piedmont, W.Va., a backwoods town   8
of 2,000 people. While playing a game of touch football at a Methodist
summer camp, I incurred a hairline fracture. Thing is, I didn't know it yet.
I was 14 and had finally lost the chubbiness of my youth. I was just learning tennis and beginning to date, and who knew where that might lead?

Not too far. A few weeks later, I was returning to school from lunch   9
when, out of the blue, the ball-and-socket joint of my hip sheared apart.
It was instant agony, and from that time on nothing in my life would be
quite the same.

I propped myself against the brick wall of the schoolhouse, where   10
the school delinquent found me. He was black as slate, twice my size,
mean as the day was long and beat up kids just because he could. But the
look on my face told him something was seriously wrong, and—bless
him—he stayed by my side for the two hours it took to get me into a taxi.

"It's a torn ligament in your knee," the surgeon said. (One of the   11
signs of what I had—a "slipped epithysis"—is intense knee pain, I later
learned.) So he scheduled me for a walking cast.

I was wheeled into surgery and placed on the operating table. As   12
the doctor wrapped my leg with wet plaster strips, he asked about my
schoolwork.

"Boy," he said, "I understand you want to be a doctor."   13

I said, "Yessir." Where I came from, you always said "sir" to white   14
people, unless you were trying to make a statement.

Had I taken a lot of science courses?   15

"Yessir. I enjoy science."   16

"Are you good at it?"   17

"Yessir, I believe so."   18

"Tell me, who was the father of sterilization?"   19

"Oh, that's easy, Joseph Lister."   20
Then he asked who discovered penicillin.   21
Alexander Fleming.   22
And what about DNA?   23
Watson and Crick.   24
The interview went on like this, and I thought my answers might   25
get me a pat on the head. Actually, they just confirmed the diagnosis he'd
come to.

He stood me on my feet and insisted that I walk. When I tried, the   26
joint ripped apart and I fell on the floor. It hurt like nothing I'd ever
known.

The doctor shook his head. "Pauline," he said to my mother, his   27
voice kindly but amused, "there's not a thing wrong with that child. The
problem's psychosomatic. Your son's an overachiever."

Back then, the term didn't mean what it usually means today. In   28
Appalachia, in 1964, "overachiever" designated a sort of pathology: the
overstraining of your natural capacity. A colored kid who thought he
could be a doctor—just for instance—was headed for a breakdown.

What made the pain abate was my mother's reaction. I'd never, ever   29
heard her talk back to a white person before. And doctors, well, their
words were scripture.

Not this time. Pauline Gates stared at him for a moment. "Get his   30
clothes, pack his bags—we're going to the University Medical Center,"
which was 60 miles away.

Not great news: the one thing I knew was that they only moved   31
you to the University Medical Center when you were going to die. I had
three operations that year. I gave my tennis racket to the delinquent,
which he probably used to club little kids with. So I wasn't going to make
it to Wimbledon. But at least I wasn't going to die, though sometimes I
wanted to. Following the last operation, which fitted me for a metal ball,
I was confined to bed, flat on my back, immobilized by a complex system
of weights and pulleys. It was six weeks of bondage—and bedpans. I
spent my time reading James Baldwin, learning to play chess and quarreling daily with my mother, who had rented a small room—which we
could ill afford—in a motel just down the hill from the hospital.

I think we both came to realize that our quarreling was a sort of   32
ritual. We'd argue about everything—what time of day it was—but the
arguments kept me from thinking about that traction system.

I limped through the next decade—through Yale and Cam-   33
bridge . . . as far away from Piedmont as I could get. But I couldn't escape
the pain, which increased as the joint calcified and began to fuse over the
next 15 years. My leg grew shorter, as the muscles atrophied and the ball
of the ball-and-socket joint migrated into my pelvis. Aspirin, then
Motrin, heating pads and massages, became my traveling companions.

Most frustrating was passing store windows full of fine shoes. I used   34
to dream about walking into one of those stores and buying a pair of
shoes. "Give me two pairs, one black, one cordovan," I'd say. "Wrap 'em
up." No six-week wait as with the orthotics in which I was confined.
These would be real shoes. Not bricks.

In the meantime, hip-joint technology progressed dramatically.   35
But no surgeon wanted to operate on me until I was significantly older, or
until the pain was so great that surgery was unavoidable. After all, a new
hip would last only for 15 years, and I'd already lost too much bone. It
wasn't a procedure they were sure they'd be able to repeat.

This year, my 40th, the doctors decided the time had come.   36

I increased my life insurance and made the plunge.   37

The nights before my operations are the longest nights of my   38
life—but never long enough. Jerking awake, grabbing for my watch, I
experience a delicious sense of relief as I discover that only a minute or
two have passed. You never want 6 A.M. to come.

And then the door swings open. "Good morning, Mr. Gates," the   39
nurse says. "It's time."

The last thing I remember, just vaguely, was wondering where am-   40
nesiac minutes go in one's consciousness, wondering if I experienced the
pain and sounds, then forgot them, or if these were somehow blocked
out, dividing the self on the operating table from the conscious self in the
recovery room. I didn't like that idea very much. I was about to protest
when I blinked.

"It's over, Mr. Gates," says a voice. But how could it be over? I had   41
merely blinked. "You talked to us several times," the surgeon had told me,
and that was the scariest part of all.

Twenty-four hours later, they get me out of bed and help me into   42
a "walker." As they stand me on my feet, my wife bursts into tears. "Your
foot is touching the ground!" I am afraid to look but it is true: the surgeon
has lengthened my leg with that gleaming titanium and chrome-cobalt
alloy ball-and-socket-joint.

"You'll need new shoes," the surgeon says. "Get a pair of Dock-   43
Sides; they have a secure grip. You'll need a ¾-inch lift in the heel, which
can be as discreet as you want."

I can't help thinking about those window displays of shoes, those   44
elegant shoes that, suddenly, I will be able to wear. Dock-Sides and
sneakers, boots and loafers, sandals and brogues. I feel, at last, a furtive
sympathy for Imelda Marcos, the queen of soles.

The next day, I walk over to the trash can, and take a long look at   45
the brick. I don't want to seem ungracious or unappreciative. We have
walked long miles together. I feel disloyal, as if I am abandoning an old
friend. I take a second look.

Maybe I'll have them bronzed.   46

☜ Opening the Dialogue

1. "A Giant Step" focuses on the author's progress toward overcoming a
physical disability, but it also traces a more subtle evolution. Beginning in
paragraph 11, Gates reproduces a conversation he had with a doctor
when he was fourteen; a few paragraphs later, he quotes an exchange
between his mother and the doctor. How do these two uses of dialogue
add meaning to the essay's title? What do you think is the "giant step" to
which Gates refers?

2. List the personal details Gates supplies about himself. Given the nature
of these details, and the fact that Gates today is a professor at Harvard
and a respected scholar, do you think the doctor was justified in calling
him an overachiever? Do you think he would have considered Gates an
overachiever if Gates had been white? If he had come from a large city?

3. At the end of his essay, when Gates looks at his shoes in the trash can,
what do you think he sees?

☜ Keeping a Notebook

In what sense, if any, do you think belonging to a racial minority could
(or should) be considered a handicap?

⊛ Working Together

Working in groups, compile a list of all the specific conditions—not necessarily physical disabilities—that handicap people in American society. Then, rank these handicaps according to their relative severity and the relative difficulty of overcoming each. In class discussion, compare your lists with those of other groups, and try to reach a consensus about what conditions actually constitute the most severe handicaps, and why.

⊛ Writing an Essay

Write a narrative essay in which you identify a characteristic or condition that you believe has handicapped you, focusing either on an incident that made you aware of your handicap or on a time when you were able (or unable) to overcome it.

ELIZABETH WONG

The Struggle to Be
an All-American Girl

Born in 1958, Elizabeth Wong grew up in Chinatown in Los Angeles. She received a B.A. from the University of California in 1980 and worked for ten years as a news reporter before leaving journalism to write plays.

Her first play, *Letters to a Student Revolutionary*, premiered Off Broadway at the Pan Asian Repertory Theatre in 1991 and won the 1990 Playwrights' Forum Award and the 1992 Margo Jones New Play Citation. Wong's latest play, *Kimchee and Chitlins*, is a satire on the black boycott of Korean grocers in New York. She has been commissioned by the Pan Asian Repertory Theatre to write a play based on the Chinese epic *The Three Kingdoms*. Awarded a 1992–93 fellowship with Touchstone Television in Los Angeles, Wong is a member of New York City's Circle Repertory Theatre Playwrights' Project.

First published in the Los Angeles *Times*, the following essay is a wistful account of Wong's early rejection of her Chinese heritage. "It's been ages since I wrote this essay," she says, "eons since I reread it, and light years from the embarrassment and resentment I used to feel about 'my Chineseness.' Nowadays, I don't think about dying my hair blonde or getting my eyelids redone. I like who I am, the way I am, although my mother will always beg to differ. The self-confidence thing? The writer thing?—It all started with this very essay. I'm glad I wrote it."

Note as you read how Wong uses specific descriptive detail and dialogue to bring vividness to her childhood story.

I T 'S STILL THERE, the Chinese school on Yale Street where my brother   1
and I used to go. Despite the new coat of paint and the high wire fence,
the school I knew ten years ago remains remarkably, stoically the same.

Every day at 5 P.M., instead of playing with our fourth- and fifth-   2
grade friends or sneaking out to the empty lot to hunt ghosts and animal
bones, my brother and I had to go to Chinese school. No amount of
kicking, screaming, or pleading could dissuade my mother, who was solidly determined to have us learn the language of our heritage.

Forcibly, she walked us the seven long, hilly blocks from our home   3
to school, depositing our defiant tearful faces before the stern principal.
My only memory of him is that he swayed on his heels like a palm tree,
and he always clasped his impatient twitching hands behind his back. I
recognized him as a repressed maniacal child killer, and knew that if we
ever saw his hands we'd be in big trouble.

We all sat in little chairs in an empty auditorium. The room smelled   4
like Chinese medicine, an imported faraway mustiness. Like ancient mothballs or dirty closets. I hated that smell. I favored crisp new scents. Like
the soft French perfume that my American teacher wore in public school.

There was a stage far to the right, flanked by an American flag and   5
the flag of the Nationalist Republic of China, which was also red, white
and blue but not as pretty.

Although the emphasis at the school was mainly language—speak-   6
ing, reading, writing—the lessons always began with an exercise in politeness. With the entrance of the teacher, the best student would tap a
bell and everyone would get up, kowtow, and chant, "Sing san ho," the
phonetic for "How are you, teacher?"

Being 10 years old, I had better things to learn than ideographs   7
copied painstakingly in lines that ran right to left from the tip of a *moc but*,
a real ink pen that had to be held in an awkward way if blotches were to
be avoided. After all, I could do the multiplication tables, name the satellites of Mars, and write reports on *Little Women* and *Black Beauty*. Nancy
Drew, my favorite book heroine, never spoke Chinese.

The language was a source of embarrassment. More times than not,   8
I had tried to disassociate myself from the nagging loud voice that followed me wherever I wandered in the nearby American supermarket outside Chinatown. The voice belonged to my grandmother, a fragile
woman in her seventies who could outshout the best of the street ven-

dors. Her humor was raunchy, her Chinese rhythmless, patternless. It was quick, it was loud, it was unbeautiful. It was not like the quiet, lilting romance of French or the gentle refinement of the American South. Chinese sounded pedestrian. Public.

In Chinatown, the comings and goings of hundreds of Chinese on   9
their daily tasks sounded chaotic and frenzied. I did not want to be thought of as mad, as talking gibberish. When I spoke English, people nodded at me, smiled sweetly, said encouraging words. Even the people in my culture would cluck and say that I'd do well in life. "My, doesn't she move her lips fast," they would say, meaning that I'd be able to keep up with the world outside Chinatown.

My brother was even more fanatical than I about speaking English.   10
He was especially hard on my mother, criticizing her, often cruelly, for her pidgin speech—smatterings of Chinese scattered like chop suey in her conversation. "It's not 'What it is,' Mom," he'd say in exasperation. "It's 'What *is* it, what *is* it, what *is* it!'" Sometimes Mom might leave out an occasional "the" or "a," or perhaps a verb of being. He would stop her in mid-sentence: "Say it again, Mom. Say it right." When he tripped over his own tongue, he'd blame it on her: "See, Mom, it's all your fault. You set a bad example."

What infuriated my mother most was when my brother cornered   11
her on her consonants, especially "r." My father had played a cruel joke on Mom by assigning her an American name that her tongue wouldn't allow her to say. No matter how hard she tried, "Ruth" always ended up "Luth" or "Roof."

After two years of writing with a *moc but* and reciting words with   12
multiples of meanings, I finally was granted a cultural divorce. I was permitted to stop Chinese school.

I thought of myself as multicultural. I preferred tacos to egg rolls; I   13
enjoyed Cinco de Mayo more than Chinese New Year.

At last, I was one of you; I wasn't one of them.   14

Sadly, I still am.   15

⟪⟫ Opening the Dialogue

1. Identify specific differences between Wong's Chinese and American worlds. In general terms, how would you characterize the difference be-

tween these two worlds? Do you think most Americans live in two worlds?

2. Much of Wong's essay focuses on language. Do you think the conversational exchange in paragraph 10 is sufficient to illustrate Wong's negative feelings about the Chinese language? What additional details could she add to make her reaction seem more understandable?

3. Wong's narrative is called " The Struggle to Be an All-American Girl," but a more appropriate title might be " The Struggle Not to Be a Chinese-American Girl." What do you see as the difference between these two struggles?

⟨€⟩ Keeping a Notebook

In the last lines of her essay Wong says, "At last, I was one of you; I wasn't one of them. Sadly, I still am." Who are the *you* and *them* to whom she refers? What does she mean by *sadly?* What do you think she gains (and loses) by being "one of you"?

⟨€⟩ Working Together

In paragraph 7 Wong asserts her "all-American" status: "Nancy Drew, my favorite book heroine, never spoke Chinese." Working in groups, compile a list of heroes and heroines—actual or fictional—whom you believe appeal to young Americans regardless of their racial, ethnic, or regional backgrounds. In class discussion, decide what specific characteristics give these individuals their universal appeal. What values do they reinforce? Would you characterize any of them as "all-American"?

⟨€⟩ Writing an Essay

Despite the introduction of multicultural material into textbooks and curricula, a great deal of what is taught in American public schools today focuses on the shared experiences of all Americans. Do you believe this emphasis is desirable? Write a narrative in which you tell what cultural perspectives were emphasized in the schools you attended and evaluate the suitability of those perspectives for you.

AUDRE LORDE

The Fourth of July

Audre Lorde was born in New York City in 1934, her parents
having immigrated from Grenada in the Caribbean. (In later life,
Lorde made her home in St. Croix and often used her adopted African name, Gamba Adisa.) A writer from an early age, Lorde had
a poem accepted by *Seventeen* magazine while she was still in high
school. Before her death in 1992, she had published more than fifteen collections of poetry and essays as well as an autobiography,
Zami: A New Spelling of My Name (1982), from which the following
selection is taken. Her essay collection *A Burst of Light* won the
American Book Award in 1989, and she was named poet laureate
of New York in 1991. Her last book was *Undersong: Chosen Poems,
Old and New.*

Describing herself as "a black-lesbian-feminist-warrior-mother,"
Lorde explained in an interview shortly before her death how she
found her voice as a writer: "I came to writing early. . . . Like all
of us, I started as a coward, inarticulate, very shy. After a year of
college, I went to Mexico, taught, wrote, traveled. In Mexico I
saw something different. It was the first time I'd seen dark-
skinned people, people of color, everywhere. I'd always had the
feeling that I was strange, different, that there was something
wrong with me. In Mexico, I learned to walk upright, to say the
things I felt."

As you read "The Fourth of July," Lorde's remembrance of a family trip to Washington, D.C., shortly after World War II, consider how her narrative conveys the conflict between wanting to
speak up and feeling an inability to do so.

THE FIRST TIME I went to Washington, D.C., was on the edge of the
summer when I was supposed to stop being a child. At least that's what

they said to us all at graduation from the eighth grade. My sister Phyllis graduated at the same time from high school. I don't know what she was supposed to stop being. But as graduation presents for us both, the whole family took a Fourth of July trip to Washington, D.C., the fabled and famous capital of our country.

It was the first time I'd ever been on a railroad train during the day.   2
When I was little, and we used to go to the Connecticut shore, we always went at night on the milk train, because it was cheaper.

Preparations were in the air around our house before school was   3
even over. We packed for a week. There were two very large suitcases that my father carried, and a box filled with food. In fact, my first trip to Washington was a mobile feast; I started eating as soon as we were comfortably ensconced in our seats, and did not stop until somewhere after Philadelphia. I remember it was Philadelphia because I was disappointed not to have passed by the Liberty Bell.

My mother had roasted two chickens and cut them up into dainty   4
bite-size pieces. She packed slices of brown bread and butter and green pepper and carrot sticks. There were little violently yellow iced cakes with scalloped edges called "marigolds," that came from Cushman's Bakery. There was a spice bun and rock-cakes from Newton's, the West Indian bakery across Lenox Avenue from St. Mark's School, and iced tea in a wrapped mayonnaise jar. There were sweet pickles for us and dill pickles for my father, and peaches with the fuzz still on them, individually wrapped to keep them from bruising. And, for neatness, there were piles of napkins and a little tin box with a washcloth dampened with rose water and glycerine for wiping sticky mouths.

I wanted to eat in the dining car because I had read all about them,   5
but my mother reminded me for the umpteenth time that dining car food always cost too much money and besides, you never could tell whose hands had been playing all over that food, nor where those same hands had been just before. My mother never mentioned that Black people were not allowed into railroad dining cars headed south in 1947. As usual, whatever my mother did not like and could not change, she ignored. Perhaps it would go away, deprived of her attention.

I learned later that Phyllis's high school senior class trip had been   6
to Washington, but the nuns had given her back her deposit in private, explaining to her that the class, all of whom were white, except Phyllis, would be staying in a hotel where Phyllis "would not be happy," meaning,

Daddy explained to her, also in private, that they did not rent rooms to Negroes. "We will take you to Washington, ourselves," my father had avowed, "and not just for an overnight in some measly fleabag hotel."

American racism was a new and crushing reality that my parents   7
had to deal with every day of their lives once they came to this country. They handled it as a private woe. My mother and father believed that they could best protect their children from the realities of race in america and the fact of american racism by never giving them name, much less discussing their nature. We were told we must never trust white people, but *why* was never explained, nor the nature of their ill will. Like so many other vital pieces of information in my childhood, I was supposed to know without being told. It always seemed like a very strange injunction coming from my mother, who looked so much like one of those people we were never supposed to trust. But something always warned me not to ask my mother why she wasn't white, and why Auntie Lillah and Auntie Etta weren't, even though they were all that same problematic color so different from my father and me, even from my sisters, who were some-where in-between.

In Washington, D.C., we had one large room with two double beds   8
and an extra cot for me. It was a back-street hotel that belonged to a friend of my father's who was in real estate, and I spent the whole next day after Mass squinting up at the Lincoln Memorial where Marian Anderson had sung after the D.A.R. refused to allow her to sing in their auditorium because she was Black. Or because she was "Colored," my father said as he told us the story. Except that what he probably said was "Negro," because for his times, my father was quite progressive.

I was squinting because I was in that silent agony that characterized   9
all of my childhood summers, from the time school let out in June to the end of July, brought about by my dilated and vulnerable eyes exposed to the summer brightness.

I viewed Julys through an agonizing corolla of dazzling whiteness   10
and I always hated the Fourth of July, even before I came to realize the travesty such a celebration was for Black people in this country.

My parents did not approve of sunglasses, nor of their expense.   11

I spent the afternoon squinting up at monuments to freedom and   12
past presidencies and democracy, and wondering why the light and heat were both so much stronger in Washington, D.C., than back home in

New York City. Even the pavement on the streets was a shade lighter in color than back home.

Late that Washington afternoon my family and I walked back   13
down Pennsylvania Avenue. We were a proper caravan, mother bright and father brown, the three of us girls step-standards in-between. Moved by our historical surroundings and the heat of the early evening, my father decreed yet another treat. He had a great sense of history, a flair for the quietly dramatic and the sense of specialness of an occasion and a trip.

"Shall we stop and have a little something to cool off, Lin?"   14

Two bocks away from our hotel, the family stopped for a dish of   15
vanilla ice cream at a Breyer's ice cream and soda fountain. Indoors, the soda fountain was dim and fan-cooled, deliciously relieving to my scorched eyes.

Corded and crisp and pinafored, the five of us seated ourselves one   16
by one at the counter. There was I between my mother and father, and my two sisters on the other side of my mother. We settled ourselves along the white mottled marble counter, and when the waitress spoke at first no one understood what she was saying, and so the five of us just sat there.

The waitress moved along the line of us closer to my father and   17
spoke again. "I said I kin give you to take out, but you can't eat here. Sorry." Then she dropped her eyes looking very embarrassed, and suddenly we heard what it was she was saying all at the same time, loud and clear.

Straight-backed and indignant, one by one, my family and I got   18
down from the counter stools and turned around and marched out of the store, quiet and outraged, as if we had never been Black before. No one would answer my emphatic questions with anything other than a guilty silence. "But we hadn't done anything!" This wasn't right or fair! Hadn't I written poems about Bataan and freedom and democracy for all?

My parents wouldn't speak of this injustice, not because they had   19
contributed to it, but because they felt they should have anticipated it and avoided it. This made me even angrier. My fury was not going to be acknowledged by a like fury. Even my two sisters copied my parents' pretense that nothing unusual and anti-american had occurred. I was left to write my angry letter to the president of the united states all by myself,

although my father did promise I could type it out on the office type-writer next week, after I showed it to him in my copybook diary.

   The waitress was white, and the counter was white, and the ice   20
cream I never ate in Washington, D.C., that summer I left childhood was
white, and the white heat and the white pavement and the white stone
monuments of my first Washington summer made me sick to my stomach
for the whole rest of that trip and it wasn't much of a graduation present
after all.

Opening the Dialogue

1. In addition to her identity as an African American, Lorde also identifies
her economic status. How does she do so? Why do you think she makes
a point of communicating her status?

2. Color imagery—particularly the use of *black* and *white*—is prominent in
"The Fourth of July." What different connotations do these words have in
the essay? What emotional associations does the word *white* have at the
end of the essay that it does not have at the beginning?

3. In paragraph 5 Lorde comments, "As usual, whatever my mother did
not like and could not change, she ignored. Perhaps it would go away,
deprived of her attention." How is Lorde's attitude different from her
mother's? Which attitude do you believe was appropriate in the late
1940s, given the racial climate of the times?

Keeping a Notebook

Why do you think Lorde does not begin *american* and *united states* with
capital letters? Does this usage offend you, or do you believe it is justified? Do you have a similar reaction to Lorde's beginning *white* with a
lower-case letter but using an upper-case letter for *Black*?

Working Together

By contrasting the real and the ideal Washington, D.C., Lorde also contrasts the "two nations" of American society. Working in groups, list all

the details Lorde uses to characterize the real Washington and all those that depict the ideal Washington. In class discussion, consider which Washington—and which America—is the central focus of Lorde's essay.

🕲 Writing an Essay

Lorde's trip to Washington is presented as a post-graduation milestone, an experience that serves as a sobering turning point for her. Write a narrative essay about a similar turning point in your own life—for example, a time when you learned that not everyone viewed you as you viewed yourself.

ROGELIO R. GOMEZ

Foul Shots

In 1956, Rogelio Gomez's father moved his family to Chicago from their home in Castana Coahuila, Mexico, to pursue his vision of the "American dream." But their struggle in a foreign and sometimes hostile country quickly tinged that dream with nightmare. Speaking no English, six-year-old Rogelio was "nothing but eyes then before a strange reality." He was labeled learning-disabled after he failed the first grade and grew up haunted by the stigma of retardation: "It placed before me an unconscious quest for self-actualization. Eyes and ears eventually became synchronized when I learned English; it was language—its ability to address reality—that inspired me." Gomez's struggle to find a voice in a society that denigrated his native language is integral to his life and work.

After moving with his family to Texas as a teenager, Gomez earned a B.A. in history from the University of Texas at San Antonio. In 1990, when he received an M.A. in English, Gomez expressed his appreciation for his father's courage in pursuing his dream of a better life. "He wanted to give his Mexican children a better chance. His gift to me is that I now have a voice, one that can speak, effectively, where so many others remain muted by social disadvantages. . . . I thank him as my father, admiring him as a man. His is an American story."

In "Foul Shots," published in 1991, Gomez examines the shame and anger he felt as a teenager confronted by barriers of race and social class. As you read, think about how he makes a single incident in his life symbolic of a larger, more universal issue.

NOW AND THEN I can still see their faces, snickering and laughing, 1
their eyes mocking me. And it bothers me that I should remember. Time

52

and maturity should have diminished the pain, because the incident happened more than 20 years ago. Occasionally, however, a smug smile triggers the memory, and I think, "I should have done something." Some act
of defiance could have killed and buried the memory of the incident.
Now it's too late.

In 1969, I was a senior on the Luther Burbank High School basket- 2
ball team. The school is on the south side of San Antonio, in one of the
city's many barrios. After practice one day our coach announced that we
were going to spend the following Saturday scrimmaging with the ball
club from Winston Churchill High, located in the city's rich, white north
side. After the basketball game, we were to select someone from the
opposing team and "buddy up"—talk with him, have lunch with him
and generally spend the day attempting friendship. By telling us that
this experience would do both teams some good, I suspect our well-
intentioned coach was thinking about the possible benefits of integration
and of learning to appreciate the differences of other people. By integrating us with this more prosperous group, I think he was also trying to
inspire us.

But my teammates and I smiled sardonically at one another, and 3
our sneakers squeaked as we nervously rubbed them against the waxed
hardwood floor of our gym. The prospect of a full day of unfavorable
comparisons drew from us a collective groan. As "barrio boys," we were
already acutely aware of the differences between us and them. Churchill
meant "white" to us: It meant shiny new cars, two-story homes with fire-
places, pedigreed dogs and manicured hedges. In other words, everything that we did not have. Worse, travelling north meant putting up a
front, to ourselves as well as to the Churchill team. We felt we had to
pretend that we were cavalier about it all, tough guys who didn't care
about "nothin.' "

It's clear now that we entered the contest with negative images of 4
ourselves. From childhood, we must have suspected something was inherently wrong with us. The evidence wrapped itself around our collective psyche like a noose. In elementary school, we were not allowed to
speak Spanish. The bladed edge of a wooden ruler once came crashing
down on my knuckles for violating this dictum. By high school, however,
policies had changed, and we could speak Spanish without fear of physical reprisal. Still, speaking our language before whites brought on spasms
of shame—for the supposed inferiority of our language and culture—and

guilt at feeling shame. That mixture of emotions fueled our burning sense of inferiority.

After all, our mothers in no way resembled the glamorized models 5 of American TV mothers—Donna Reed baking cookies in high heels. My mother's hands were rough and chafed, her wardrobe drab and worn. And my father was preoccupied with making ends meet. His silence starkly contrasted with the glib counsel Jim Anderson offered in "Father Knows Best." And where the Beaver worried about trying to understand some difficult homework assignment, for me it was an altogether different horror, when I was told by my elementary school principal that I did not have the ability to learn.

After I failed to pass the first grade, my report card read that I had 6 a "learning disability." What shame and disillusion it brought my parents! To have carried their dream of a better life from Mexico to America, only to have their hopes quashed by having their only son branded inadequate. And so somewhere during my schooling I assumed that saying I had a "learning disability" was just another way of saying that I was "retarded." School administrators didn't care that I could not speak English.

As teen-agers, of course, my Mexican-American friends and I did 7 not consciously understand why we felt inferior. But we might have understood if we had fathomed our desperate need to trounce Churchill. We viewed the prospect of beating a white, north-side squad as a particularly fine coup. The match was clearly racial, our need to succeed born of a defiance against prejudice. I see now that we used the basketball court to prove our "blood." And who better to confirm us, if not those whom we considered better? In retrospect, I realize the only thing confirmed that day was that we saw ourselves as negatively as they did.

After we won the morning scrimmage, both teams were led from 8 the gym into an empty room where everyone sat on a shiny linoleum floor. We were supposed to mingle—rub the colors together. But the teams sat separately, our backs against concrete walls. We faced one another like enemies, the empty floor between us a no man's land. As the coaches walked away, one reminded us to share lunch. God! The mere thought of offering them a taco from our brown bags when they had refrigerated deli lunches horrified us.

Then one of their players tossed a bag of Fritos at us. It slid across 9 the slippery floor and stopped in the center of the room. With hearts beating anxiously, we Chicanos stared at the bag as the boy said with a sneer, "Y'all probably like 'em"—the "Frito Bandito" commercial being popular then. And we could see them, smiling at each other, giggling, jabbing their elbows into one another's ribs at the joke. The bag seemed to grow before our eyes like a monstrous symbol of inferiority.

We won the afternoon basketball game as well. But winning had   10 accomplished nothing. Though we had wanted to, we couldn't change their perception of us. It seems, in fact, that defeating them made them meaner. Looking back, I feel these young men needed to put us "in our place," to reaffirm the power they felt we had threatened. I think, more-over, that they felt justified, not only because of their inherent sense of superiority, but because our failure to respond to their insult underscored our worthlessness in their eyes.

Two decades later, the memory of their gloating lives on in me.   11 When a white person is discourteous, I find myself wondering what I should do, and afterward, if I've done the right thing. Sometimes I argue when a deft comment would suffice. Then I reprimand myself, for I am no longer a boy. But my impulse to argue bears witness to my ghosts. For, invariably, whenever I feel insulted I'm reminded of that day at Churchill High. And whenever the past encroaches upon the present, I see myself rising boldly, stepping proudly across the years and crushing, underfoot, a silly bag of Fritos.

☺ Opening the Dialogue

1. What does Gomez realize now about himself, his friends, and his neighborhood that he did not realize in 1969? What phrases does he use to introduce these insights to readers?

2. Paragraphs 4 through 7 interrupt the narrative. What purpose do these paragraphs serve? Could they have been placed elsewhere? *Should* they have been?

3. Why does Gomez see the bag of Fritos as a "monstrous symbol of inferiority" (paragraph 9)? Do you think he is overreacting, or do you believe it really has the significance he attributes to it? What item might have similarly offensive connotations for you? Why?

ⓔ Keeping a Notebook

In paragraph 5 Gomez compares his parents to the model mothers and fathers in contemporary television shows. What stereotype does he define? Are parents on television still depicted as they were when Gomez was younger? How do you think your own parents compare with those depicted on television today?

ⓔ Working Together

To what extent do you associate various sports with particular classes, races, ethnic groups, genders, or geographical regions? Working in groups, identify each sport that your group agrees is associated with a particular category. In class discussion, examine the positive and negative effects of these perceptions.

ⓔ Writing an Essay

Gomez's biggest regret about the incident he recounts in "Foul Shots" is expressed in paragraph 1 when he says, " 'I should have done something.' " Write a narrative about an incident about which you have similar regrets—a time when you, or someone else, "should have done something" but did not.

Maya Angelou

Graduation

A woman of amazingly varied talents, Maya Angelou was born
Marguerite Johnson in the black section of the small town of
Stamps, Arkansas, in 1928. Sexually assaulted at the age of eight,
Angelou has said that "for a number of years, I was mute. . . . I
wrote because I read."

As a young woman Angelou worked as an "exotic dancer," a
singer, and an actress. She has written and directed for the stage
and television and is the author of several books of poetry. Angelou is particularly well known for her series of autobiographical
works, the first of which, *I Know Why the Caged Bird Sings* (1970), is
the source of the following selection. In 1993, she read her poem
"On the Pulse of Morning," composed at President Clinton's request, during his inaugural ceremony.

A long-time civil rights activist and currently a professor at Wake
Forest University, Angelou asserts that "we should be about the
business of eradicating all the ugly 'isms' from our textbooks,
from our classrooms, from our homes—so we don't carry into the
twenty-first century the blight of racism, sexism, AIDSism.
Young children who are 5 or 7, who will be 15 and 17 and capable of being queer-bashers or white-haters or black-haters or people who are threats to the lives of Asians, can be informed
now . . . so that by the time they do reach their teens, they are
not impaled by hate and ignorance."

As you read about this 1940 graduation ceremony, consider the
extent to which the existence since the 1950s of integrated
schools has affected the fight against racism, hatred, and ignorance.

THE CHILDREN IN STAMPS trembled visibly with anticipation. Some   1
adults were excited too, but to be certain the whole young population
had come down with graduation epidemic. Large classes were graduating
from both the grammar school and the high school. Even those who were
years removed from their own day of glorious release were anxious to
help with preparations as a kind of dry run. The junior students who were
moving into the vacating classes' chairs were tradition-bound to show
their talents for leadership and management. They strutted through the
school and around the campus exerting pressure on the lower grades.
Their authority was so new that occasionally if they pressed a little too
hard it had to be overlooked. After all, next term was coming, and it
never hurt a sixth grader to have a play sister in the eighth grade, or a
tenth-year student to be able to call a twelfth grader Bubba. So all was
endured in a spirit of shared understanding. But the graduating classes
themselves were the nobility. Like travelers with exotic destinations on
their minds, the graduates were remarkably forgetful. They came to
school without their books, or tablets or even pencils. Volunteers fell
over themselves to secure replacements for the missing equipment.
When accepted, the willing workers might or might not be thanked, and
it was of no importance to the pregraduation rites. Even teachers were
respectful of the now quiet and aging seniors, and tended to speak to
them, if not as equals, as beings only slightly lower than themselves.
After tests were returned and grades given, the student body, which acted
like an extended family, knew who did well, who excelled, and what pit-
eous ones had failed.

    Unlike the white high school, Lafayette County Training School   2
distinguished itself by having neither lawn, nor hedges, nor tennis court,
nor climbing ivy. Its two buildings (main classrooms, the grade school
and home economics) were set on a dirt hill with no fence to limit either
its boundaries or those of bordering farms. There was a large expanse to
the left of the school which was used alternately as a baseball diamond or
basketball court. Rusty hoops on swaying poles represented the permanent recreational equipment, although bats and ball as could be borrowed from the P.E. teacher if the borrower was qualified and if the diamond wasn't occupied.

    Over this rocky area relieved by a few shady tall persimmon trees   3
the graduating class walked. The girls often held hands and no longer

bothered to speak to the lower students. There was a sadness about them, as if this old world was not their home and they were bound for higher ground. The boys, on the other hand, had become more friendly, more outgoing. A decided change from the closed attitude they projected while studying for finals. Now they seemed not ready to give up the old school, the familiar paths and classrooms. Only a small percentage would be continuing on to college—one of the South's A & M (agricultural and mechanical) schools, which trained Negro youths to be carpenters, farmers, handymen, masons, maids, cooks and baby nurses. Their future rode heavily on their shoulders, and blinded them to the collective joy that had pervaded the lives of the boys and girls in the grammar school graduating class.

Parents who could afford it had ordered new shoes and ready-made   4
clothes for themselves from Sears and Roebuck or Montgomery Ward. They also engaged the best seamstresses to make the floating graduating dresses and to cut down secondhand pants which would be pressed to a military slickness for the important event.

Oh, it was important, all right. Whitefolks would attend the cere-   5
mony, and two or three would speak of God and home, and the Southern way of life, and Mrs. Parsons, the principal's wife, would play the graduation march while the lower-grade graduates paraded down the aisles and took their seats below the platform. The high school seniors would wait in empty classrooms to make their dramatic entrance.

In the Store[1] I was the person of the moment. The birthday girl.   6
The center. Bailey had graduated the year before, although to do so he had had to forfeit all pleasures to make up for his time lost in Baton Rouge.

My class was wearing butter-yellow piqué dresses, and Momma   7
launched out on mine. She smocked the yoke into tiny crisscrossing puckers, then shirred the rest of the bodice. Her dark fingers ducked in and out of the lemony cloth as she embroidered raised daisies around the hem. Before she considered herself finished she had added a crocheted cuff on the puff sleeves, and a pointy crocheted collar.

I was going to be lovely. A walking model of all the various styles   8

---

[1]A general store owned by Angelou's grandmother, whom she and her brother, Bailey, called "Momma."

of fine hand sewing and it didn't worry me that I was only twelve years old and merely graduating from the eighth grade. Besides, many teachers in Arkansas Negro schools had only that diploma and were licensed to impart wisdom.

The days had become longer and more noticeable. The faded   9
beige of former times had been replaced with strong and sure colors. I began to see my classmates' clothes, their skin tones, and the dust that waved off pussy willows. Clouds that lazed across the sky were objects of great concern to me. Their shiftier shapes might have held a message that in my new happiness and with a little bit of time I'd soon decipher. During that period I looked at the arch of heaven so religiously my neck kept a steady ache. I had taken to smiling more often, and my jaws hurt from the unaccustomed activity. Between the two physical sore spots, I suppose I could have been uncomfortable, but that was not the case. As a member of the winning team (the graduating class of 1940) I had outdistanced unpleasant sensations by miles. I was headed for the freedom of open fields.

Youth and social approval allied themselves with me and we tram-   10
meled memories of slights and insults. The wind of our swift passage remodeled my features. Lost tears were pounded to mud and then to dust. Years of withdrawal were brushed aside and left behind, as hanging ropes of parasitic moss.

My work alone had awarded me a top place and I was going to be   11
one of the first called in the graduating ceremonies. On the classroom blackboard, as well as on the bulletin board in the auditorium, there were blue stars and white stars and red stars. No absences, no tardinesses, and my academic work was among the best of the year. I could say the preamble to the Constitution even faster than Bailey. We timed ourselves often: "WethepeopleoftheUnitedStatesinordertoformamoreperfectunion . . ." I had memorized the Presidents of the United States from Washington to Roosevelt in chronological as well as alphabetical order.

My hair pleased me too. Gradually the black mass had lengthened   12
and thickened, so that it kept at last to its braided pattern, and I didn't have to yank my scalp off when I tried to comb it.

Louise and I had rehearsed the exercises until we tired out ourselves. Henry Reed was class valedictorian. He was a small, very black   13
boy with hooded eyes, a long, broad nose and an oddly shaped head. I had admired him for years because each term he and I vied for the best

grades in our class. Most often he bested me, but instead of being disappointed I was pleased that we shared top places between us. Like many Southern Black children, he lived with his grandmother, who was as strict as Momma and as kind as she knew how to be. He was courteous, respectful and soft-spoken to elders, but on the playground he chose to play the roughest games. I admired him. Anyone, I reckoned, sufficiently afraid or sufficiently dull could be polite. But to be able to operate at a top level with both adults and children was admirable.

His valedictory speech was entitled "To Be or Not to Be." The rigid tenth-grade teacher had helped him write it. He'd been working on the dramatic stresses for months.   14

The weeks until graduation were filled with heady activities. A group of small children were to be presented in a play about buttercups and daisies and bunny rabbits. They could be heard throughout the building practicing their hops and their little songs that sounded like silver bells. The older girls (nongraduates, of course) were assigned the task of making refreshments for the night's festivities. A tangy scent of ginger, cinnamon, nutmeg and chocolate wafted around the home economics building as the budding cooks made samples for themselves and their teachers.   15

In every corner of the workshop, axes and saws split fresh timber as the woodshop boys made sets and stage scenery. Only the graduates were left out of the general bustle. We were free to sit in the library at the back of the building or look in quite detachedly, naturally, on the measures being taken for our event.   16

Even the minister preached on graduation the Sunday before. His subject was, "Let your light so shine that men will see your good works and praise your Father, Who is in Heaven." Although the sermon was purported to be addressed to us, he used the occasion to speak to backsliders, gamblers and general ne'er-do-wells. But since he had called our names at the beginning of the service we were mollified.   17

Among Negroes the tradition was to give presents to children going only from one grade to another. How much more important this was when the person was graduating at the top of the class. Uncle Willie and Momma had sent away for a Mickey Mouse watch like Bailey's. Louise gave me four embroidered handkerchiefs. (I gave her crocheted doilies.) Mrs. Sneed, the minister's wife, made me an undershirt to wear for graduation, and nearly every customer gave me a nickel or maybe even a   18

dime with the instruction "Keep on moving to higher ground," or some
such encouragement.

Amazingly the great day finally dawned and I was out of bed before   19
I knew it. I threw open the back door to see it more clearly, but Momma
said, "Sister, come away from that door and put your robe on."

I hoped the memory of that morning would never leave me. Sun-   20
light was itself young, and the day had none of the insistence maturity
would bring it in a few hours. In my robe and barefoot in the backyard,
under cover of going to see about my new beans, I gave myself up to the
gentle warmth and thanked God that no matter what evil I had done in
my life He had allowed me to live to see this day. Somewhere in my
fatalism I had expected to die, accidentally, and never have the chance to
walk up the stairs in the auditorium and gracefully receive my hard-
earned diploma. Out of God's merciful bosom I had won reprieve.

Bailey came out in his robe and gave me a box wrapped in Christ-   21
mas paper. He said he had saved his money for months to pay for it. It felt
like a box of chocolates, but I knew Bailey wouldn't save money to buy
candy when we had all we could want under our noses.

He was as proud of the gift as I. It was a soft-leather-bound copy of   22
a collection of poems by Edgar Allan Poe, or, as Bailey and I called him,
"Eap." I turned to "Annabel Lee" and we walked up and down the garden
rows, the cool dirt between our toes, reciting the beautifully sad lines.

Momma made a Sunday breakfast although it was only Friday.   23
After we finished the blessing, I opened my eyes to find the watch on my
plate. It was a dream of a day. Everything went smoothly and to my
credit. I didn't have to be reminded or scolded for anything. Near evening I was too jittery to attend to chores, so Bailey volunteered to do all
before his bath.

Days before, we had made a sign for the Store, and as we turned   24
out the lights Momma hung the cardboard over the doorknob. It read
clearly: CLOSED. GRADUATION.

My dress fitted perfectly and everyone said that I looked like a sun-   25
beam in it. On the hill, going toward the school, Bailey walked behind
with Uncle Willie, who muttered, "Go on, Ju." He wanted him to walk
ahead with us because it embarrassed him to have to walk so slowly. Bailey said he'd let the ladies walk together, and the men would bring up the
rear. We all laughed, nicely.

Little children dashed by out of the dark like fireflies. Their crepe-   26 paper dresses and butterfly wings were not made for running and we heard more than one rip, dryly, and the regretful "uh uh" that followed.

The school blazed without gaiety. The windows seemed cold and 27 unfriendly from the lower hill. A sense of ill-fated timing crept over me, and if Momma hadn't reached for my hand I would have drifted back to Bailey and Uncle Willie, and possibly beyond. She made a few slow jokes about my feet getting cold, and tugged me along to the now-strange building.

Around the front steps, assurance came back. There were my fel- 28 low "greats," the graduating class. Hair brushed back, legs oiled, new dresses and pressed pleats, fresh pocket handkerchiefs and little hand-bags, all homesewn. Oh, we were up to snuff, all right. I joined my com-rades and didn't even see my family go in to find seats in the crowded auditorium.

The school band struck up a march and all classes filed in as had 29 been rehearsed. We stood in front of our seats, as assigned, and on a signal from the choir director, we sat. No sooner had this been accom-plished than the band started to play the national anthem. We rose again and sang the song, after which we recited the pledge of allegiance. We remained standing for a brief minute before the choir director and the principal signaled to us, rather desperately I thought, to take our seats. The command was so unusual that our carefully rehearsed and smooth-running machine was thrown off. For a full minute we fumbled for our chairs and bumped into each other awkwardly. Habits change or solidify under pressure, so in our state of nervous tension we had been ready to follow our usual assembly pattern: the American national anthem, then the pledge of allegiance, then the song every Black person I knew called the Negro national anthem. All done in the same key, with the same pas-sion and most often standing on the same foot.

Finding my seat at last, I was overcome with a presentiment of 30 worse things to come. Something unrehearsed, unplanned, was going to happen, and we were going to be made to look bad. I distinctly remem-ber being explicit in the choice of pronoun. It was "we," the graduating class, the unit, that concerned me then.

The principal welcomed "parents and friends" and asked the Baptist 31 minister to lead us in prayer. His invocation was brief and punchy, and for a second I thought we were getting on the high road to right action. When the principal came back to the dais, however, his voice had changed. Sounds always affected me profoundly and the principal's voice was one of my favorites. During assembly it melted and lowed weakly into the audience. It had not been in my plan to listen to him, but my curiosity was piqued and I straightened up to give him my attention.

He was talking about Booker T. Washington, our "late great   32 leader," who said we can be as close as the fingers on the hand, etc. . . . Then he said a few vague things about friendship and the friendship of kindly people to those less fortunate than themselves. With that his voice nearly faded, thin, away. Like a river diminishing to a stream and then to a trickle. But he cleared his throat and said, "Our speaker tonight, who is also our friend, came from Texarkana to deliver the commencement address, but due to the irregularity of the train schedule, he's going to, as they say, 'speak and run.' " He said that we understood and wanted the man to know that we were most grateful for the time he was able to give us and then something about how we were willing always to adjust to another's program, and without more ado—"I give you Mr. Edward Donleavy."

Not one but two white men came through the door off-stage. The   33 shorter one walked to the speaker's platform, and the tall one moved to the center seat and sat down. But that was our principal's seat, and already occupied. The dislodged gentleman bounced around for a long breath or two before the Baptist minister gave him his chair, then with more dignity than the situation deserved, the minister walked off the stage.

Donleavy looked at the audience once (on reflection, I'm sure that   34 he wanted only to reassure himself that we were really there), adjusted his glasses and began to read from a sheaf of papers.

He was glad "to be here and to see the work going on just as it was   35 in the other schools."

At the first "Amen" from the audience I willed the offender to im-   36 mediate death by choking on the word. But Amens and Yes, sir's began to fall around the room like rain through a ragged umbrella.

He told us of the wonderful changes we children in Stamps had in   37 store. The Central School (naturally, the white school was Central) had already been granted improvements that would be in use in the fall. A well-known artist was coming from Little Rock to teach art to them. They were going to have the newest microscopes and chemistry equipment for their laboratory. Mr. Donleavy didn't leave us long in the dark over who made these improvements available to Central High. Nor were we to be ignored in the general betterment scheme he had in mind.

He said that he had pointed out to people at a very high level that one of the first-line football tacklers at Arkansas Agricultural and Mechanical College had graduated from good old Lafayette County Training School. Here fewer Amen's were heard. Those few that did break through lay dully in the air with the heaviness of habit.

He went on to praise us. He went on to say how he had bragged that "one of the best basketball players at Fisk sank his first ball right here at Lafayette County Training School."

The white kids were going to have a chance to become Galileos and Madame Curies and Edisons and Gauguins, and our boys (the girls weren't even in on it) would try to be Jesse Owenses and Joe Louises.

Owens and the Brown Bomber were great heroes in our world, but what school official in the white-goddom of Little Rock had the right to decide that those two men must be our only heroes? Who decided that for Henry Reed to become a scientist he had to work like George Washington Carver, as a bootblack, to buy a lousy microscope? Bailey was obviously always going to be too small to be an athlete, so which concrete angel glued to what county seat had decided that if my brother wanted to become a lawyer he had to first pay penance for his skin by picking cotton and hoeing corn and studying correspondence books at night for twenty years?

The man's dead words fell like bricks around the auditorium and too many settled in my belly. Constrained by hard-learned manners I couldn't look behind me, but to my left and right the proud graduating class of 1940 had dropped their heads. Every girl in my row had found something new to do with her handkerchief. Some folded the tiny squares into love knots, some into triangles, but most were wadding them, then pressing them flat on their yellow laps.

On the dais, the ancient tragedy was being replayed. Professor Parsons sat, a sculptor's reject, rigid. His large heavy body seemed devoid of will or willingness, and his eyes said he was no longer with us. The other teachers examined the flag (which was draped stage right) or their notes, or the windows which opened on our now-famous playing diamond.

Graduation, the hush-hush magic time of frills and gifts and congratulations and diplomas, was finished for me before my name was called. The accomplishment was nothing. The meticulous maps, drawn in three colors of ink, learning and spelling decasyllabic words, memorizing the whole of *The Rape of Lucrece*—it was for nothing. Donleavy had exposed us.

We were maids and farmers, handymen and washerwomen, and   45 anything higher that we aspired to was farcical and presumptuous.

Then I wished that Gabriel Prosser and Nat Turner had killed all   46 whitefolks in their beds and that Abraham Lincoln had been assassinated before the signing of the Emancipation Proclamation, and that Harriet Tubman had been killed by that blow on her head and Christopher Columbus had drowned in the *Santa Maria.*[2]

It was awful to be a Negro and have no control over my life. It was   47 brutal to be young and already trained to sit quietly and listen to charges brought against my color with no chance of defense. We should all be dead. I thought I should like to see us all dead, one on top of the other. A pyramid of flesh with the whitefolks on the bottom, as the broad base, then the Indians with their silly tomahawks and teepees and wigwams and treaties, the Negroes with their mops and recipes and cotton sacks and spirituals sticking out of their mouths. The Dutch children should all stumble in their wooden shoes and break their necks. The French should choke to death on the Louisiana Purchase (1803) while silkworms ate all the Chinese with their stupid pigtails. As a species, we were an abomination. All of us.

Donleavy was running for election, and assured our parents that if   48 he won we could count on having the only colored paved playing field in that part of Arkansas. Also—he never looked up to acknowledge the grunts of acceptance—also, we were bound to get some new equipment for the home economics building and the workshop.

He finished, and since there was no need to give any more than the   49 most perfunctory thank-you's, he nodded to the men on the stage, and the tall white man who was never introduced joined him at the door. They left with the attitude that now they were off to something really

---

[2]Prosser and Turner led unsuccessful slave rebellions. Tubman was an escaped slave who helped hundreds of other slaves to freedom and worked as a Union spy during the Civil War.

important. (The graduation ceremonies at Lafayette County Training School had been a mere preliminary.)

The ugliness they left was palpable. An uninvited guest who wouldn't leave. The choir was summoned and sang a modern arrangement of "Onward, Christian Soldiers," with new words pertaining to graduates seeking their place in the world. But it didn't work. Elouise, the daughter of the Baptist minister, recited "Invictus," and I could have cried at the impertinence of "I am the master of my fate, I am the captain of my soul." 50

My name had lost its ring of familiarity and I had to be nudged to go and receive my diploma. All my preparations had fled. I neither marched up to the stage like a conquering Amazon, nor did I look in the audience for Bailey's nod of approval. Marguerite Johnson, I heard the name again, my honors were read, there were noises in the audience of appreciation, and I took my place on the stage as rehearsed. 51

I thought about colors I hated: ecru, puce, lavender, beige and black. 52

There was shuffling and rustling around me, then Henry Reed was giving his valedictory address. "To Be or Not to Be." Hadn't he heard the whitefolks? We couldn't *be*, so the question was a waste of time. Henry's voice came out clear and strong. I feared to look at him. Hadn't he got the message? There was no "nobler in the mind" for Negroes because the world didn't think we had minds, and they let us know it. "Outrageous fortune"? Now, that was a joke. When the ceremony was over I had to tell Henry Reed some things. That is, if I still cared. Not "rub," Henry, "erase." "Ah, there's the erase." Us. 53

Henry had been a good student in elocution. His voice rose on tides of promise and fell on waves of warnings. The English teacher had helped him to create a sermon winging through Hamlet's soliloquy. To be a man, a doer, a builder, a leader, or to be a tool, an unfunny joke, a crusher of funky toadstools. I marveled that Henry could go through with the speech as if we had a choice. 54

I had been listening and silently rebutting each sentence with my eyes closed; then there was a hush, which in an audience warns that something unplanned is happening. I looked up and saw Henry Reed, the conservative, the proper, the A student, turn his back to the audience and turn to us (the proud graduating class of 1940) and sing, nearly speaking, 55

"Lift ev'ry voice and sing
Till earth and heavy ring
Ring with the harmonies of Liberty. . ."

It was the poem written by James Weldom Johnson. It was the music composed by J. Rosamond Johnson. It was the Negro national anthem. Out of habit we were singing it.

Our mothers and fathers stood in the dark hall and joined the   56
hymn of encouragement. A kindergarten teacher led the small children onto the stage and the buttercups and daisies and bunny rabbits marked time and tried to follow:

"Stony the road we trod
Bitter the chastening rod
Felt in the days when hope, unborn, had died.
Yet with a steady beat
Have not our weary feet
Come to the place for which our fathers sighed?"

Each child I knew had learned that song with his ABC's and along   57
with "Jesus Loves Me This I Know." But I personally had never heard it before. Never heard the words, despite the thousands of times I had sung them. Never thought they had anything to do with me.

On the other hand, the words of Patrick Henry had made such an   58
impression on me that I had been able to stretch myself tall and trembling and say, "I know not what course others may take, but as for me, give me liberty or give me death."

And now I heard, really for the first time: 59

"We have come over a way that with tears
has been watered,
We have come, treading our path through
the blood of the slaughtered."

While echoes of the song shivered in the air, Henry Reed bowed   60
his head, said "Thank you," and returned to his place in the line. The tears that slipped down many faces were not wiped away in shame.

We were on top again. As always, again. We survived. The depths   61 had been icy and dark, but now a bright sun spoke to our souls. I was no longer simply a member of the proud graduating class of 1940; I was a proud member of the wonderful, beautiful Negro race.

Oh, Black known and unknown poets, how often have your auctioned pains sustained us? Who will compute the lonely nights made less lonely by your songs, or the empty pots made less tragic by your tales? 62

If we were a people much given to revealing secrets, we might raise monuments and sacrifice to the memories of our poets, but slavery cured us of that weakness. It may be enough, however, to have it said that we survive in exact relationship to the dedication of our poets (include preachers, musicians and blues singers). 63

☜ Opening the Dialogue

1. Much of the first half of Angelou's essay focuses on building a sense of anticipation. Identify details that establish the approaching graduation as a momentous event. Why is this buildup essential to the essay?

2. Angelou creates a sense of intimacy in describing her ethnic and regional culture by giving each character in her narrative a distinct personality, carefully established through dialogue and physical description. How do these descriptions of setting and character help to establish the essay's central conflict?

3. Angelou's memoir reveals that she has learned a good deal in terms of both formal and informal education. In what ways are the two kinds of education interrelated in this essay? How does this connection enrich the meaning of the essay's title?

☜ Keeping a Notebook

In paragraph 61 Angelou observes, "We were on top again. As always, again. We survived." She attributes this triumph to the "known and unknown poets" of her race who have sustained her. Who are the "poets" whose dedication has helped *you* to survive? In what way have these individuals—literary or musical artists, religious leaders, family members—inspired you?

🤹 Working Together

Like Elizabeth Wong (p. 42), Angelou sees completing school as the beginning of a new life. Working in groups, examine how Wong's and Angelou's views of leaving their schools are alike and how they are different. In class discussion, consider to what extent their different views of their cultural identities determine their different perspectives.

🤹 Writing an Essay

Angelou's essay has a definite, almost musical rhythm, with its building excitement, deflation, and upward movement to the point where she is "on top" again. Select an incident from your own personal history in which you trace a similar pattern of raised and lowered expectations as you tell your story.

MARY CLEARMAN BLEW

The Unwanted Child

America's western myths are full of stories of men whose challenges to the vastness of mountain and plain are ingrained in our collective idea of the American "character." But the stories of the women of this romantic and unforgiving landscape can show us even more profoundly how the American character is reflected in the sacrifices of family relationships, in the way values are articulated and transformed from generation to generation.

Born at the end of the Depression to a ranching family, Mary Clearman Blew has spent her life on the high, dry plains of Montana. "I am bone-deep in landscape," she says. "In this dome of sky and river and undeflected sunlight, in this illusion of timelessness, I can almost feel my body, blood, and breath in the broken line of the bluffs and the pervasive scent of ripening sweet clover and dust, almost feel the sagging fence line of ancient cedar posts stapled across my vitals."

Blew's 1991 memoir, *All But the Waltz: Essays on a Montana Family*, from which the following is excerpted, examines what she describes as "that romantic and despairing mythology which has racked and scarred the lives of so many men and women in the West." In "The Unwanted Child," Blew, now a college writing instructor, describes the hard choices she faced as a young married student in the 1950s. Notice how the opening and closing sections of her essay help tie together the complex narrative of multiple incidents that comes in between.

DECEMBER 1958. I lie on my back on an examination table in a Missoula clinic while the middle-aged doctor whose name I found in the Yellow Pages inserts his speculum and takes a look. He turns to the sink and washes his hands. 1

71

" Yes, you're pregnant," he says. "Congratulations, Mommy."   2

His confirmation settles over me like a fog that won't lift. Myself I   3
can manage for, but for myself and *it?*

After I get dressed, he says, "I'll want to see you again in a month,   4
Mommy."

If he calls me Mommy again, I will break his glasses and grind them   5
in his face, grind them until he has no face. I will kick him right in his
obscene fat paunch. I will bury my foot in his disgusting flesh.

I walk through the glass doors and between the shoveled banks of   6
snow to the parking lot where my young husband waits in the car.

"You're not, are you?" he says.   7

"Yes."   8

"Yes, you're not?"   9

"Yes, I am! Jeez!"   10

His feelings are hurt. But he persists: "I just don't think you are. I   11
just don't see how you could be."

He has a theory on the correct use of condoms, a theory consider-   12
ably more flexible than the one outlined by the doctor I visited just before our marriage three months ago, and which he has been arguing with
increasing anxiety ever since I missed my second period. I stare out the
car window at the back of the clinic while he expounds on his theory for
the zillionth time. What difference does it make now? Why can't he shut
up? If I have to listen to him much longer, I will kill him, too.

At last, even his arguments wear thin against the irrefutable fact. As   13
he turns the key in the ignition his eyes are deep with fear.

"But I'll stand by you," he promises.   14

Why get married at eighteen?   15

When you get married, you can move into married student hous-   16
ing. It's a shambles, it's a complex of converted World War II barracks
known as the Strips, it's so sorry the wind blows through the cracks
around the windows and it lacks hot-water heaters and electric stoves,
but at least it's not the dormitory, which is otherwise the required residence of all women at the University of Montana. Although no such regulations apply to male students, single women must be signed in and
ready for bed check by ten o'clock on weeknights and one on weekends.
No alcohol, no phones in rooms. Women must not be reported on cam-

pus in slacks or shorts (unless they can prove they are on their way to a physical education class), and on Sundays they may not appear except in heels, hose, and hat. A curious side effect of marriage, however, is that the responsibility for one's virtue is automatically transferred from the dean of women to one's husband. Miss Maurine Clow never does bed checks or beer checks in the Strips.

When you get married, you can quit making out in the back seat of   17
a parked car and go to bed in a bed. All young women in 1958 like sex. Maybe their mothers had headaches or hang-ups, but *they* are normal, healthy women with normal, healthy desires, and they know the joy they will find in their husbands' arms will—well, be better than making out, which, though none of us will admit it, is getting to be boring. We spend hours shivering with our clothes off in cars parked in Pattee Canyon in subzero weather, groping and being groped and feeling embarrassed when other cars crunch by in the snow, full of onlookers with craning necks, and worrying about the classes we're not attending because making out takes so much time. We are normal, healthy women with normal, healthy desires if we have to die to prove it. Nobody has ever said out loud that she would like to go to bed and *get it over with* and get on with something else.

There's another reason for getting married at eighteen, but it's   18
more complicated.

By getting married I have eluded Dean Maurine Clow only to fall   19
into the hands of in-laws.

"We have to tell the folks," my husband insists. "They'll want to   20
know."

His letter elicits the predictable long-distance phone call from   21
them. I make him answer it. While he talks to them I rattle dishes in the kitchen, knowing exactly how they look, his momma and his daddy in their suffocating Helena living room hung with mounted elk antlers and religious calendars, their heads together over the phone, their faces wreathed in big grins at his news.

" They want to talk to you," he says finally. Then "Come on!"   22
I take the phone with fear and hatred. "Hello?"   23
"Well!!!" My mother-in-law's voice carols over the miles. "I guess   24
this is finally the end of college for you!"

A week after Christmas I lean against the sink in my mother's   25
kitchen at the ranch and watch her wash clothes.

She uses a Maytag washing machine with a wringer and a monoto-   26
nous, daylong chugging motor which, she often says, is a damn sight
better than a washboard. She starts by filling the tub with boiling water
and soap flakes. Then she agitates her whites for twenty minutes, fishes
them out with her big fork, and feeds them sheet by sheet into the
wringer. After she rinses them by hand, she reverses the wringer and
feeds them back through, creased and steaming hot, and carries them out
to the clothesline to freeze dry. By this time the water in the tub has
cooled off enough for the coloreds. She'll keep running through her loads
until she's down to the blue jeans and the water is thick and greasy. My
mother has spent twenty-five years of Mondays on the washing.

I know I have to tell her I'm pregnant.   27

She's talking about college, she's quoting my grandmother, who   28
believes that every woman should be self-sufficient. Even though I'm
married now, even though I had finished only one year at the University
of Montana before I got married, my grandmother has agreed to go on
lending me what I need for tuition and books. Unlike my in-laws, who
have not hesitated to tell me I should go to work as a typist or a waitress
to support my husband through college (after all, he will be supporting
me for the rest of my life), my grandmother believes I should get my own
credentials.

My mother and grandmother talk about a teaching certificate as if   29
it were a gold ring which, if I could just grab it, would entitle the two of
them to draw a long breath of relief. Normally I hate to listen to their
talk. They don't even know you can't get a two-year teaching certificate
now, you have to go the full four years.

But beyond the certificate question, college has become something   30
that I never expected and cannot explain: not something to grab and have
done with but a door opening, a glimpse of an endless passage and professors who occasionally beckon from far ahead—like lovely, elderly
Marguerite Ephron, who lately has been leading four or five of us
through the *Aeneid*. Latin class has been my sanctuary for the past few
months; Latin has been my solace from conflict that otherwise has left me
as steamed and agitated as my mother's whites, now churning away in the
Maytag; Latin in part because it is taught by Mrs. Ephron, always serene,
endlessly patient, mercilessly thorough, who teaches at the university

while Mr. Ephron works at home, in a basement full of typewriters with special keyboards, on the translations of obscure clay tablets.

So I've been accepting my grandmother's money under false pre-   31
tenses. I'm not going to spend my life teaching around Fergus County the way she did, the way my mother would have if she hadn't married my father. I've married my husband under false pretenses, too; he's a good fly-fishing Helena boy who has no idea in the world of becoming a Mr. Ephron. But, subversive as a foundling in a fairy tale, I have tried to explain none of my new aspirations to my mother or grandmother or, least of all, my husband and his parents, who are mightily distressed as it is by my borrowing money for my own education.

"—and it's all got to be paid back, you'll be starting your lives in   32
debt!"

"—the important thing is to get *him* through, *he's* the one who's got   33
to go out and face the world!"

"—what on earth do you think you'll do with your education?"   34

And now all the argument is pointless, the question of teaching   35
certificate over quest for identity, the importance of my husband's future over mine, the relentless struggle with the in-laws over what is most mine, my self. I'm done for, knocked out of the running by the application of a faulty condom theory.

"Mom," I blurt, "I'm pregnant."   36

She gasps. And before she can let out that breath, a frame of mem-   37
ory freezes with her in it, poised over her rinse tub, looking at me through the rising steam and the grinding wringer. Right now I'm much too miserable to wonder what she sees when she looks at me: her oldest daughter, her bookish child, the daydreamer, the one she usually can't stand, the one who takes everything too seriously, who will never learn to take no for an answer. Thin and strong and blue-jeaned, bespectacled and crop-haired, this girl could pass for fifteen right now and won't be able to buy beer in grocery stores for years without showing her driver's license. This girl who is too miserable to look her mother in the face, who otherwise might see in her mother's eyes the years of blight and disappointment. She does hear what her mother says:

"Oh, Mary, no!"   38

My mother was an unwanted child. The fourth daughter of a   39
homesteading family racked by drought and debt, she was only a year old

when the sister nearest her age died of a cancerous tumor. She was only two years old when the fifth and last child, the cherished boy, was born. She was never studious like her older sisters nor, of course, was she a boy, and she was never able to find her own ground to stand on until she married.

Growing up, I heard her version often, for my mother was given to   40 a kind of continuous oral interpretation of herself and her situation. Standing over the sink or stove, hoeing the garden, running her sewing machine with the permanent angry line deepening between her eyes, she talked. Unlike the stories our grandmothers told, which, like fairy tales, narrated the events of the past but avoided psychological speculation ("Great-great-aunt Somebody-or-other was home alone making soap when the Indians came, so she waited until they got close enough, and then she threw a ladle of lye on them . . . "), my mother's dwelt on the motives behind the darkest family impulses.

"Ma never should have had me. It was her own fault. She never   41 should have had me if she didn't want me."

"But then you wouldn't have been born!" I interrupted, horrified at   42 the thought of not being.

"Wouldn't have mattered to me," she said. "I'd never have known   43 the difference."

What I cannot remember today is whom my mother was telling her   44 story to. Our grandmothers told their stories to my little sisters and me, to entertain us, but my mother's bitter words flowed past us like a river current past small, ignored onlookers who eavesdropped from its shores. I remember her words, compulsive, repetitious, spilling out over her work—for she was always working—and I was awed by her courage. What could be less comprehensible than not wanting to be? More fearsome than annihilation?

Nor can I remember enough about the circumstances of my   45 mother's life during the late 1940s and the early 1950s to know why she was so angry, why she was so compelled to deconstruct her childhood. Her lot was not easy. She had married into a close-knit family that kept to itself. She had her husband's mother on her hands all her life, and on top of the normal isolation and hard work of a ranch wife of those years, she had to provide home schooling for her children.

And my father's health was precarious, and the ranch was failing.   46 The reality of that closed life along the river bottom became more and more attenuated by the outward reality of banks and interest rates and the shifting course of agribusiness. She was touchy with money worries. She saw the circumstances of her sisters' lives grow easier as her own grew harder. Perhaps these were reasons enough for rage.

I recall my mother in her middle thirties through the telescoped 47 eye of the child which distorts the intentions of parents and enlarges them to giants. Of course she was larger than life. Unlike my father, with his spectrum of ailments, she was never sick. She was never hospitalized in her life for any reason but childbirth, never came down with anything worse than a cold. She lugged the armloads of wood and buckets of water and slops and ashes that came with cooking and washing and ironing in a kitchen with a wood range and no plumbing; she provided the endless starchy meals of roast meat and potatoes and gravy; she kept salads on her table and fresh or home-canned vegetables at a time when iceberg lettuce was a town affectation.

She was clear-skinned, with large gray eyes that often seemed fixed 48 on some point far beyond our familiar slopes and cutbanks. And even allowing for the child's telescoped eye, she was a tall woman who thought of herself as oversized. She was the tallest of her sisters. "*As big as Doris* is what they used to say about me!"

Bigness to her was a curse. "You big ox!" she would fling at me over 49 some altercation with my little sister. True to the imperative that is handed down through the generations, I in turn bought my clothes two sizes too large for years.

All adult ranch women were fat. I remember hardly a woman out of 50 her teens in those years who was not fat. The few exceptions were the women who had, virtually, become a third sex by taking on men's work in the fields and corrals; they might stay as skinny and tough in their Levi's as hired hands.

But women who remained women baked cakes and cream pies and 51 breads and sweet rolls with the eggs from their own chickens and the milk and butter and cream from the cows they milked, and they ate heavily from appetite and from fatigue and from the monotony of their isolation. They wore starched cotton print dresses and starched aprons and walked ponderously beside their whiplash husbands. My mother, unless she was going to be riding or helping in the hayfields, always wore those shapeless, starched dresses she sewed herself, always cut from the same pattern, always layered over with an apron.

What was she so angry about? Why was her forehead kneaded per-   52
manently into a frown? It was a revelation for me one afternoon when she
answered a knock at the screen door, and she smiled, and her voice lifted
to greet an old friend of hers and my father's from their single days. Color
rose in her face, and she looked pretty as she told him where he could
find my father. Was that how outsiders always saw her?

Other ranch women seemed cheerful enough on the rare occasions   53
when they came in out of the gumbo. Spying on them as they sat on
benches in the shade outside the horticulture house at the county fair or
visited in the cabs of trucks at rodeos, I wondered if these women, too,
were angry when they were alone with only their children to observe
them. What secrets lay behind those vast placid, smiling faces, and what
stories could their children tell?

My mother believed that her mother had loved her brother best   54
and her older sisters next best. "He was always The Boy and they were
The Girls, and Ma was proud of how well they did in school," she explained again and again to the walls, the stove, the floor she was mop-
ping, "and I was just Doris. I was average."

Knowing how my grandmother had misjudged my mother, I felt   55
guilty about how much I longed for her visits. I loved my grandmother
and her fresh supply of stories about the children who went to the
schools she taught, the games they played, and the books they read.
School for me was an emblem of the world outside our creek-bottom
meadows and fenced mountain slopes. At eight, I was still being taught at
home; our gumbo road was impassable for most of the school months,
and my father preferred that we be kept safe from contact with "them
damn town kids," as he called them. Subversively I begged my grandmother to repeat her stories again and again, and I tried to imagine what
it must be like to see other children every day and to have a real desk and
real lessons. Other than my little sister, my playmates were mostly cats.
But my grandmother brought with her the breath of elsewhere.

My mother's resentment whitened in intensity during the weeks   56
before a visit from my grandmother, smoldered during the visit itself, and
flared up again as soon as my grandmother was safely down the road to
her next school. "I wonder if she ever realizes she wouldn't even have any
grandchildren if I hadn't got married and had some kids! *The Girls* never
had any kids! Some people should never have kids! Some people should
never get married!"

With a child's logic, I thought she was talking about me. I thought   57
I was responsible for her anger. I was preoccupied for a long time with a
story I had read about a fisherman who was granted three wishes; he had
used his wishes badly, but I was sure I could do better, given the chance.
I thought a lot about how I would use three wishes, how I would use their
potential for lifting me out of the present.

"What would you wish for, if you had three wishes?" I prodded my   58
mother.

She turned her faraway gray eyes on me, as though she had not   59
been ranting about The Girls the moment before. "I'd wish you'd be
good," she said.

That was what she always said, no matter how often I asked her.   60
With everything under the sun to wish for, that unfailing answer was a
perplexity and a worry.

I was my grandmother's namesake, and I was a bookworm like my   61
mother's older sisters. Nobody could pry my nose out of a book to do my
chores, even though I was marked to be the outdoor-working child, even
though I was supposed to be my father's boy.

Other signs that I was not a boy arose to trouble us both and ac-   62
count, I thought, for my mother's one wish.

"Mary's getting a butt on her just like a girl," she remarked one   63
night as I climbed out of the tub. Alarmed, I craned my neck to see what
had changed about my eight-year-old buttocks.

"Next thing, you'll be mooning in the mirror and wanting to pluck   64
your eyebrows like the rest of 'em," she said.

"I will not," I said doubtfully.   65

I could find no way through the contradiction. On the one hand, I   66
was a boy (except that I also was a bookworm), and my chores were always in the barns and corrals, never the kitchen. *You don't know how to cook
on a wood stove?* my mother-in-law was to cry in disbelief. *And you grew up
on a ranch?*

To act like a boy was approved; to cry or show fear was to invite   67
ridicule. *Sissy! Big bellcalf!* On the other hand, I was scolded for hanging
around the men, the way ranch boys did. I was not a boy (my buttocks,
my vanity). What was I?

"Your dad's boy," my mother answered comfortingly when I asked   68
her. She named a woman I knew. "Just like Hazel. Her dad can't get along
without her."

Hazel was a tough, shy woman who rode fences and pulled calves   69
and took no interest in the country dances or the "running around" her
sisters did on weekends. Hazel never used lipstick or permed her hair; she
wore it cut almost like a man's. Seen at the occasional rodeo or bull sale
in her decently pressed pearl-button shirt and new Levi's, she stuck close
to her dad. Like me, Hazel apparently was not permitted to hang around
the men.

What Hazel did not seem interested in was any kind of fun, and a   70
great resolve arose in me that, whatever I was, I was going to have . . .
whatever it was. I would get married, even if I wasn't supposed to.

But my mother had another, darker reason to be angry with me,   71
and I knew it. The reason had broken over me suddenly the summer I was
seven and had been playing, on warm afternoons, in a rain barrel full of
water. Splashing around, elbows and knees knocking against the side of
the barrel, I enjoyed the rare sensation of being wet all over. My little
sister, four, came and stood on tiptoe to watch. It occurred to me to boost
her into the barrel with me.

My mother burst out of the kitchen door and snatched her back.   72
"What are you trying to do, kill her?" she shouted.   73
I stared back at her, wet, dumbfounded.   74
Her eyes blazed over me, her brows knotted at their worst. "And   75
after you'd drowned her, I suppose you'd have slunk off to hide some-
where until it was all over!"

It had never crossed my mind to kill my sister, or that my mother   76
might think I wanted to. (Although I had, once, drowned a setting of
baby chicks in a rain barrel.) But that afternoon, dripping in my underpants, goose-bumped and ashamed, I watched her carry my sister into the
house and then I did go off to hide until it was, somehow, all over, for she
never mentioned it at dinner.

The chicks had been balls of yellow fuzz, and I had been three. I   77
wanted them to swim. I can just remember catching a chick and holding
it in the water until it stopped squirming and then laying it down to catch
a fresh one. I didn't stop until I had drowned the whole dozen and laid
them out in a sodden yellow row.

What the mind refuses to allow to surface is characterized by a   78
suspicious absence. Of detail, of associations. Memories skirt the edge of

nothing. There is for me about this incident that suspicious absence. What is being withheld?

Had I, for instance, given my mother cause to believe I might harm   79
my sister? Children have done such harm, and worse. What can be submerged deeper, denied more vehemently, than the murderous impulse? At four, my sister was a tender, trusting little girl with my mother's wide gray eyes and brows. A younger sister of an older sister. A good girl. Mommy's girl.

What do I really know about my mother's feelings toward her own   80
dead sister? Kathryn's dolls had been put away; my mother was never allowed to touch them.

"I'll never, never love one of my kids more than another!" she   81
screamed at my father in one of her afternoons of white rage. The context is missing.

During the good years, when cattle prices were high enough to pay   82
the year's bills and a little extra, my mother bought wallpaper out of a catalog and stuck it to her lumpy walls. She enameled her kitchen white, and she sewed narrow strips of cloth she called "drapes" to hang at the sides of her windows. She bought a stiff tight cylinder of linoleum at Sears, Roebuck in town and hauled it home in the back of the pickup and unrolled it in a shiny flowered oblong in the middle of her splintery front room floor.

Occasionally I would find her sitting in her front room on her "dav-   83
enport," which she had saved for and bought used, her lap full of sewing and her forehead relaxed out of its knot. For a moment there was her room around her as she wanted it to look: the clutter subdued, the new linoleum mopped and quivering under the chair legs that held down its corners, the tension of the opposing floral patterns of wallpaper, drapes, and slipcovers held in brief, illusory harmony by the force of her vision.

How hard she tried for her daughters! Over the slow thirty miles of   84
gumbo and gravel we drove to town every summer for dentist appointments at a time when pulling teeth was still a more common remedy than filling them, when our own father and his mother wore false teeth before they were forty.

During the good years, we drove the thirty miles for piano lessons.   85
An upright Kimball was purchased and hauled home in the back of the

pickup. Its carved oak leaves and ivories dominated the front room, where she found time to "sit with us" every day as we practiced. With a pencil she pointed out the notes she had learned to read during her five scant quarters in normal school, and made us read them aloud. "F sharp!" she would scream over the throb of the Maytag in the kitchen as one of us pounded away.

She carped about bookworms, but she located the dim old Carnegie library in town and got library cards for us even though, as country kids, we weren't strictly entitled to them. After that, trips home from town with sacks of groceries included armloads of library books. Against certain strictures, she could be counted on. When, in my teens, I came home with my account of the new book the librarian kept in her desk drawer and refused to check out to me, my mother straightened her back as I knew she would. "She thinks she can tell one of my kids what she can read and what she can't read?"   86

On our next visit to the library, she marched up the stone steps and into the mote-filled sanctum with me.   87

The white-haired librarian glanced up inquiringly.   88

"You got *From Here to Eternity*?"[1]   89

The librarian looked at me, then at my mother. Without a word she reached into her drawer and took out a heavy volume. She stamped it and handed it to my mother, who handed it to me.   90

How did she determine that books and dentistry and piano lessons were necessities for her daughters, and what battles did she fight for them as slipping cattle prices put even a gallon of white enamel paint or a sheet of new linoleum beyond her reach?   91

Disaster followed disaster on the ranch. An entire season's hay crop lost to a combination of ancient machinery that would not hold together and heavy rains that would not let up. A whole year's calf crop lost because the cows had been pastured in timber that had been logged, and when they ate the pine needles from the downed tops, they spontaneously aborted. As my father grew less and less able to face the reality of the downward spiral, what could she hope to hold together with her pathetic floral drapes and floral slipcovers?   92

Bundled in coats and overshoes in the premature February dark, our white breaths as one, my mother and I huddle in the shadow of the chicken house. By moon-   93

[1]A 1951 novel by James Jones, considered particularly "adult" in its day.

light we watch the white-tailed deer that have slipped down out of the timber to feed from the haystack a scant fifty yards away. Cautiously I raise my father's rifle to my shoulder. I'm not all that good a marksman, I hate the inevitable explosive crack, but I brace myself on the corner of the chicken house and sight carefully and remember to squeeze. Ka-crack!

Eight taupe shapes shoot up their heads and spring for cover. A single mound   94
remains in the snow near the haystack. By the time my mother and I have climbed through the fence and trudged up to the haystack, all movement from the doe is reflexive. "Nice and fat," says my mother.

Working together with our butcher knives, we lop off her scent glands and slit her   95
and gut her and save the heart and liver in a bucket for breakfast. Then, each taking a leg, we drag her down the field, under the fence, around the chicken house, and into the kitchen, where we will skin her out and butcher her.

We are two mid-twentieth-century women putting meat on the table for the next   96
few weeks. Neither of us has ever had a hunting license, and if we did, hunting season is long closed, but we're serene about what we're doing. "Eating our hay, aren't they?" says my mother. "We're entitled to a little venison. The main thing is not to tell anybody what we're doing."

And the pregnant eighteen-year-old? What about her?   97

In June of 1959 she sits up in the hospital bed, holding in her arms   98
a small warm scrap whose temples are deeply dented from the forceps.
She cannot remember birthing him, only the long hours alone before the
anesthetic took over. She feels little this morning, only a dull worry about
the money, money, money for college in the fall.

The in-laws are a steady, insistent, increasingly frantic chorus of   99
disapproval over her plans. *But, Mary! Tiny babies have to be kept warm!* her
mother-in-law keeps repeating, pathetically, ever since she was told
about Mary's plans for fall quarter.

But, Mary! How can you expect to go to college and take good care of a hus-   100
band and a baby?

Finally, *We're going to put our foot down!*   101

She knows that somehow she has got to extricate herself from   102
these sappy folks. About the baby, she feels only a mild curiosity. Life
where there was none before. The rise and fall of his tiny chest. She has
him on her hands now. She must take care of him.

Why not an abortion?   103

Because the thought never crossed her mind. Another suspicious   104 absence, another void for memory to skirt. What she knew about abortion was passed around the midnight parties in the girls' dormitory: *You drink one part turpentine with two parts sugar.* Or was it the other way around? *. . . two parts turpentine to one part sugar. You drink gin in a hot bath . . .*

She has always hated the smell of gin. It reminds her of the pine 105
needles her father's cattle ate, and how their calves were born shallow-breathed and shriveled, and how they died. She knows a young married woman who begged her husband to hit her in the stomach and abort their fourth child.

Once, in her eighth month, the doctor had shot her a look across 106
his table. "If you don't want this baby," he said, "I know plenty of people who do."

"I want it," she lied. 107

No, but really. What is to become of this eighteen-year-old and 108
her baby?

Well, she's read all the sentimental literature they shove on the 109
high school girls. She knows how the plot is supposed to turn out.

Basically, she has two choices. 110

One, she can invest all her hopes for her own future in this sleeping 111
scrap. *Son, it was always my dream to climb to the stars. Now the tears of joy spring at the sight of you with your college diploma . . .*

Even at eighteen, this lilylicking is enough to make her sick. 112

Or two, she can abandon the baby and the husband and become 113
really successful and really evil. This is the more attractive version of the plot, but she doesn't really believe in it. Nobody she knows has tried it. It seems as out of reach from ordinary daylight Montana as Joan Crawford or the Duchess of Windsor or the moon. As she lies propped up in bed with the sleeping scrap in her arms, looking out over the dusty downtown rooftops settling into noon in the waning Eisenhower years, she knows very well that Joan Crawford will never play the story of her life.

What, then? What choice is left to her? 114

What outcome could possibly be worth all this uproar? Her hus- 115
band is on the verge of tears these days; he's only twenty himself, and he had no idea what trouble he was marrying into, his parents pleading and arguing and threatening, even his brothers and their wives chiming in with their opinions, even the minister getting into it, even the neighbors; and meanwhile his wife's grandmother firing off red-hot letters from her side, meanwhile his wife's mother refusing to budge an inch—united,

those two women are as formidable as a pair of rhinoceroses, though of course he has no idea in the world what it took to unite them.

All this widening emotional vortex over whether or not one Mon-   116
tana girl will finish college. What kind of genius would she have to be to justify it all? Will it be enough that, thirty years later, she will have read approximately 16,250 freshman English essays out of an estimated lifetime total of 32,000?

Will it be enough, over the years, that she remembers the frozen   117
frame of her mother's face over the rinse tub that day after Christmas in 1958 and wonders whether she can do as much for her son as was done for her? Or that she often wonders whether she really lied when she said, *I want it?*

Will it be enough? What else is there?   118

✿ Opening the Dialogue

1. Is the unwanted child to whom Blew refers in her title her mother, herself, or her own son? Which is really the focus of her essay?

2. Do you find Blew's attitude toward her newborn son shocking? Unnatural? On the other hand, are her in-laws' expectations of her justified?

3. Does Blew identify herself, explicitly or implicitly, as a member of any particular racial, ethnic, or regional group? How would you categorize her?

4. Blew says, near the end of her essay, that she knows "how the plot is supposed to turn out." She offers two possible choices, neither of which she finds satisfactory. What options, if any, would she have today that she did not have in 1959? Do you think a young woman with Blew's background and values would—or should—make different choices today?

✿ Keeping a Notebook

Why do you think access to education is so vitally important to Blew (as well as to Angelou and Gates)? What does it represent for her? Have you ever felt, like Blew, that education was something you "never expected and cannot explain: not something to grab and have done with but a door opening, a glimpse of an endless passage . . . "?

🕮 Working Together

Working in groups, decide what each of the following kinds of material contributes to Blew's essay: descriptions of housework and ranch life, information about money problems, mentions of doctor's visits, comments about stories (fairy tales, "sentimental literature," the family's storytelling tradition), and descriptions of her mother's and her own physical appearances. In class discussion, consider which of these are essential to the essay's impact, and why.

🕮 Writing an Essay

Blew discusses a variety of factors that limited her and held her back, keeping her personal and educational goals out of reach; she also identifies her mother and grandmother as forces that gave her the emotional and economic support to persevere. What do you see as the greatest obstacles in the lives of young people like yourself today? What support systems are available to help you overcome these obstacles? Write a narrative about the life of a typical person from your community, identifying the challenges that confront this individual and the resources that are available to help him or her.

Writing about Culture and Personal History

1. Trace the history of your family's immigration into the United States (or migration to the part of the country in which you now live). You may focus on the obstacles one member of your family faced as he or she emigrated, resettled, and began to participate in American (or community) society.

2. Do you consider yourself a "blended" American (Italian American or African American, for example) or simply an American? Tell about an incident that helped define your national or ethnic identity.

3. Write a narrative about a milestone, such as a graduation, wedding, birth, or death. Focus on explaining why this event was important to you.

4. Tell the story of your formal education, including episodes of frustration or disappointment as well as moments of triumph.

5. Interview your oldest living relative, and use the information he or she provides to help you write his or her life story.

CHAPTER 3

CULTURE AND ENVIRONMENT
DESCRIBING ONE'S WORLD

The Malaysian officials took our boat and my father's map. Then they took us to Pilau Bidang Island, where we stayed for a year until we were allowed to emigrate to the United States. Life on the island was difficult. We lived in a small ramshackle house made of wood and plastic sheeting. At night the house would get so hot that my family and I would go outside and sleep on the ground. When it rained, the water ran through holes in the plastic and dripped on us as we slept. Every week we were given a small bag of rice, a few dented cans of vegetables, and some orange powder that we mixed with water to drink. Once a month we were given a chicken and some cabbage. Some of the men made canoes from scraps so that they could go fishing. Once they caught two large sea turtles and killed them for their meat. The men did not know that the people of Pilau Bidang honored the turtle. To punish the fishermen, the islanders burned their canoes.

Tran Nguyen, student

Culture and Environment

Writing situations in a variety of academic disciplines call for description: Biology laboratory reports describe an organism's physiology, psychology case studies describe subjects, anthropology field studies describe artifacts, technical proposals describe facilities, and art history papers describe paintings. Because it presents detailed word pictures of people, places, and objects, **description**—telling what something looks like, sounds like, tastes like, and smells like—is a natural choice for writing about culture and environment. For example, writers can describe a family member or ancestor or a place that has special meaning to them. They can use description to characterize a particular community—an ethnic neighborhood, a rural area, or a group united by special interests.

They can also describe an artist, a writer, or a musician who is important to them—or even a work of art, literature, or music. Sometimes description can be an end in itself, recreating the sights and sounds of a place for readers; at other times, description can give a particular experience meaning or significance.

Many of the writers whose works appear in this chapter explore their own cultural backgrounds to give readers a sense of the people and places that helped make them what they are today. Jeanne Wakatsuki Houston, for example, describes a place that links her to her past (p. 98). In the process she examines what relocation meant to Japanese Americans and how they balanced their ideas about the United States with the conditions they encountered when they lived in detention camps. Like Houston, Ishmael Reed describes a place—his neighborhood—that has meaning to him (p. 105). As he does so, he explains why he abandoned the suburbs for a culturally diverse inner city neighborhood. No matter what specific themes they explore, the writers in this chapter all use description to convey a unique vision of their culture and environment.

In your writing, description can help you examine your family, your community, your values, and your history. You can describe family members who epitomize your cultural heritage, or you can describe people—people you know, historical or contemporary figures, even fictional characters—who have played a part in shaping your cultural identity. You can also use description to define the character of your family or neighborhood and determine whether it has remained the same or changed over the years. Finally, you can describe items such as documents, photographs, or furnishings that connect you to the history of your family or community.

Note in the following essay how the student uses description to sketch a figure she sees as central to her own sense of cultural heritage.

STUDENT VOICE: MOLLY WARD

Finding Azariel

When people talk about their ethnic backgrounds, I think of Azariel Smith, my great-great-great-grandfather. To me, Azariel's

journey west to begin farming is comparable to the journeys of immigrants who came to America from all over the world to find a
better life. When people ask me what I am (and it is painfully obvious that I am nothing interesting), I say I am part English and part
German. But I think to myself, I am part Azariel.

Although my ethnic background does not provide me with a   2
rich ethnic heritage from which to draw ideas and traditions, I do
feel connected to my family. Azariel and his journey are the beginnings of what I consider my heritage. When I was little, all I knew
of him was that his comb factory in Pennsylvania had burned
down, forcing him, along with his wife and children, to migrate to
Somerset, Michigan. Now I know that his descendents are my ancestors; they give me my roots.

When I was nine years old, my family visited Somerset. It was   3
hardly a town—it seemed more like an expanded network of corn-
fields, cow pastures, and uncultivated pockets of vegetation. Scattered among the fields were about twenty buildings. Most of them
were old brick farmhouses, each accompanied by a rusting silo and
a faded barn. This was Somerset, where Azariel Smith had settled
his family. I was not impressed.

After visiting my great-grandmother's brick house, which had   4
been the center of the Smith family from the middle part of this
century, my family and I took a walk, past the marshy plot of land
that my mother remembered as a pond for swimming, to the Con-
gregationalist church. A simple white building with a stained-glass
window, it still wore the curtains my great-grandmother had made
for it before she died. Along with my brother, who was four, I sat

on hard pews inside while my mother told us stories about all her cousins, uncles, and aunts.

Soon baffled and bored in this strange world of meaningless   5
names that were supposed to be our family and stiff from sitting on the hard benches, my brother and I wandered out to the ancient cemetery behind the church. There, on the oldest-looking gravestone of them all, was the name "Azariel Smith." Beside him was the grave of his wife, Mary. We looked around, reading the names on the stones, and soon I realized that all the gravestones bore the name "Smith." I asked my mother whether all these people were my relatives, and she said they were. I stood with my bare feet in the soil where my ancestors lay, and I felt that I belonged.

My brother hopped from stone to stone but stopped when he   6
came to Azariel's. It was far too large and ancient for him to cross.

🌿 Describing One's World

Whereas a narrative tells a story, a **description** tells what something looks like, feels like, tastes like, sounds like, or smells like. Thus a descriptive essay is primarily concerned with creating a verbal picture of what we experience. Descriptive essays do not always have to rely on sense impressions, however. Sometimes they use statistics or other data to describe complex subjects such as the behavior of groups of people.

A description can be either *objective*—providing factual information about the subject without any personal reactions—or *subjective*—conveying a writer's impressionistic responses to the subject. When writers objectively describe something, they reveal its shape, its size, its color, and other physical features. A subjective description does this too, but it also expresses the emotional impact of the object on the writer. Such a description could, for example, tell how the size and shape of a building made a writer feel insignificant or reminded her of something she had experienced as a child. Notice in the following paragraph from "Finding Azariel" (p. 90) how Molly Ward uses a combination of objective and subjective elements to convey her impression of the church she visited when she was a child:

> After visiting my great-grandmother's brick house, which had been the center of the Smith family from the middle part of this century, my family and I took a walk, past the marshy plot of land that my mother remembered as a pond for swimming, to the Congregationalist church. A simple white building with a stained-glass window, it still wore the curtains my great-grandmother had made for it before she died. Along with my brother, who was four, I sat on hard pews inside while my mother told us stories about all her cousins, uncles, and aunts.

CREATING A DOMINANT IMPRESSION

The main purpose of a descriptive essay is to *create a dominant impression* about a subject. The dominant impression of a descriptive essay is the main idea or concept that draws together all the details of the essay. This impression may be something the writer observes—such as the cultural diversity of a neighborhood—or something the writer feels—such as the emotional impact of a mural on the side of a building. Whatever the case, the dominant impression of a descriptive essay helps the writer form an impression of the subject. In "Silent Dancing" (p. 116), for example, Judith Ortiz Cofer wishes to convey the idea of how far some Puerto Rican women have moved from the immigrant past represented by their mothers and other members of their families. To do so, she describes the differences between her mother, her eighteen-year-old cousin, and her brother's girlfriend:

> The three women in red sitting on the couch are my mother, my eighteen-year-old cousin, and her brother's girlfriend. The *novia* is just up from the Island, which is apparent in her body language. She sits up formally, her dress pulled over her knees. She is a pretty girl, but her posture makes her look insecure, lost in her full-skirted

dress, which she has carefully tucked around her to make room for my gorgeous cousin, her future sister-in-law. My cousin has grown up in Paterson and is in her last year of high school. She doesn't have a trace of what Puerto Ricans call *la mancha* (literally, the stain: the mark of the new immigrant—something about the posture, the voice, or the humble demeanor that makes it obvious to everyone the person has just arrived on the mainland). My cousin is wearing a tight, sequined cocktail dress. Her brown hair has been lightened with peroxide around the bangs, and she is holding a cigarette expertly between her fingers, bringing it up to her mouth in a sensuous arc of her arm as she talks animatedly. My mother, who has come up to sit between the two women, both only a few years younger than herself, is somewhere between the poles they represent in our culture.

SELECTING DETAILS

As you plan and write your description, *select details that support your dominant impression.* Effective descriptions use language that enables readers to see, hear, feel, smell, or taste what they are describing. If your purpose is to enable readers to see what you have seen, it is not enough simply to tell them about your subject. You must paint a verbal picture that lets them see what you have seen. The same is true for other sense impressions. Everything you will describe has its own individual characteristics, and it is up to you to select the concrete words that will make your experience come alive for your readers—for example, the "three women in red," the girl "lost in her full-skirted dress," and the "tight, sequined cocktail dress" described by Judith Ortiz Cofer.

However, the inclusion of concrete details is not enough. You must be sure that the details you include are exactly the ones that you need to bring your subject into focus. For this reason, you should ask yourself what your readers already know about your subject and what they need to know. In "My Neighborhood," for example, Ishmael Reed does not assume that his readers are necessarily familiar with the appearance of an urban black neighborhood. Therefore, when he discusses Oakland, he includes many evocative details ("I've grown accustomed to the common sights here—teenagers moving through the neighborhood carrying radios blasting music by Grandmaster Flash and Prince, men hovering over cars with tools and rags in hand, decked-out female church delegations visiting the sick").

SELECTING AN ORGANIZING PRINCIPLE

When planning a descriptive essay, you should *decide on an organizing principle* that reinforces your dominant impression. The details in a descriptive essay can be organized *spatially*, from top to bottom, near to far, right to left, or inside to outside. They can also be organized *in order of importance*, from the most important to the least important, or vice versa. Finally, they can be organized according to *sensory impressions*, from sight, to smell, to touch, and so on.

In "Manzanar, U.S.A." (p. 98), Jeanne Wakatsuki Houston wants to convey the desolation of the relocation camp in which she and her family lived for the duration of World War II. After selecting the details she wishes to discuss—the dryness, the isolation, the dust, the fruit trees, the small houses, the high school yearbook—she decides on an organizing principle that will reinforce her dominant impression. She begins her essay by describing the fruit trees that stood near Block 28. Next, she focuses on the house in which she and her family lived, and then she moves on to consider all of Block 28. She ends by describing the pictures of her classmates in her high school yearbook. By moving from near to far and back again, Houston brackets her negative, bleak description of the camp with details that suggest a promising future—trees and children. The contrast between promise and reality conveys a sharp sense of how the relocation camp limited the lives of those who lived there.

USING VIVID LANGUAGE

All effective descriptions rely on language that conveys an image as clearly as possible. As you write and revise, be sure to *use vivid language* to create a clear, focused picture.

Objective descriptions rely on language that is exact and relatively free of emotional associations. Naturally, no word will convey the same impression to every reader, but objective descriptions should be as unambiguous as possible. One way to avoid ambiguity is to use concrete language, avoiding words that are so general that they communicate no real meaning. Consider the differences between the following pairs of descriptions:

The farmhouses were old.	Most of them were old brick farm-houses, each accompanied by a rusting silo and a faded barn. (Molly Ward)
The grass is dry.	The grass turns brittle and brown, and it cracks beneath your feet. (N. Scott Momaday)
The little girls were dressed nicely.	Almost any day it was possible to . . . see little girls being photo-graphed in the tiaras and ruffled hoop skirts and maribou-trimmed illusion capes they would wear. . . . (Joan Didion)

Subjective descriptions also use concrete, specific language, but they are more likely to rely on the emotional associations of words than objective descriptions are. Writers of subjective descriptions will deliberately use words that stimulate a reader's imagination. Often, they will use *figures of speech*—imaginative comparisons—to create vivid impressions and provoke strong reactions. The following examples illustrate the three most common figures of speech:

SIMILE—A comparison of two seemingly unlike things using *like* or *as*:

There seemed to be a preference for strictest grey or black [dresses], but the effect remained lush, tropical, like a room full of perfectly groomed mangoes. (Joan Didion)

METAPHOR—A comparison—without *like* or *as*—that equates two things that may at first glance seem dissimilar:

The old woman's mouth becomes a cavernous black hole I fall into. (Judith Ortiz Cofer)

PERSONIFICATION –The attribution of human characteristics or qualities to things that are not human:

At a distance in July or August the steaming foliage seems almost to writhe in fire. (N. Scott Momaday)

REVIEW CHECKLIST: DESCRIBING ONE'S WORLD

✓ Create a dominant impression that reinforces the main point of your essay.

✓ Select details that support your dominant impression.

✓ Select an organizing principle that reinforces your dominant impression.

✓ Use vivid language.

JEANNE WAKATSUKI HOUSTON

Manzanar, U.S.A.

Americans were horrified and outraged when the Japanese air force attacked the U.S. naval base at Pearl Harbor in Hawaii on December 7, 1941. Public anger at the "treachery" of the surprise attack ran deep, and the U.S. government, fearing disloyalty and sabotage, summarily revoked the civil rights of all people of Japanese descent living in proximity to West Coast military bases. Over 110,000 people were arrested and imprisoned in "internment camps" for the duration of World War II, most of them losing their homes and personal property. Fully 64 percent of these prisoners were American citizens, confined for no other reason than their Japanese heritage.

Jeanne Wakatsuki, a second-generation Japanese American, or *nisei*, was only seven years old when she and her family were imprisoned in the Manzanar internment camp in 1942. By the time they were released after the war ended in 1945, her family, she has said, had "collapsed as an organized unit. Whatever dignity or filial strength we may have known before December 1941 was lost, and we did not recover it until many years after the war."

Speaking about the effect of her imprisonment, she made the following statement: "It [took] me twenty-five years to reach the point where I could talk openly about Manzanar. . . . To tell what I knew and felt about it would mean telling something about my family before the war, and the years that followed the war, and about my father's past, as well as my own way of seeing things now. Writing it has been a way of coming to terms with the impact these years have had on my entire life."

Houston was born in California in 1935. She studied journalism and sociology at San Jose State College, where she met her husband, James D. Houston, with whom she wrote her memoir, *Farewell to Manzanar* (1973). She has spent most of her life on the West Coast and still lives in Santa Cruz.

Notice as you read how Houston knits together a variety of incidents to narrate this crucial phase in her life.

I N SPANISH, Manzanar means "apple orchard." Great stretches of　1 Owens Valley were once green with orchards and alfalfa fields. It has been a desert ever since its water started flowing south into Los Angeles, sometime during the twenties. But a few rows of untended pear and apple trees were still growing there when the camp opened, where a shallow water table had kept them alive. In the spring of 1943 we moved to Block 28, right up next to one of the old pear orchards. That's where we stayed until the end of the war, and those trees stand in my memory for the turning of our life in camp, from the outrageous to the tolerable.

Papa pruned and cared for the nearest trees. Late that summer we　2 picked the fruit green and stored it in a root cellar he had dug under our new barracks. At night the wind through the leaves would sound like the surf had sounded in Ocean Park, and while drifting off to sleep I could almost imagine we were still living by the beach.

Mama had set up this move. Block 28 was also close to the camp　3 hospital. For the most part, people lived there who had to have easy access to it. Mama's connection was her job as dietician. A whole half of one barracks had fallen empty when another family relocated. Mama hustled us in there almost before they'd snapped their suitcases shut.

For all the pain it caused, the loyalty oath finally did speed up the　4 relocation program. One result was a gradual easing of the congestion in the barracks. A shrewd house-hunter like Mama could set things up fairly comfortably—by Manzanar standards—if she kept her eyes open. But you had to move fast. As soon as the word got around that so-and-so had been cleared to leave, there would be a kind of tribal restlessness, a nervous rise in the level of neighborhood gossip as wives jockeyed for position to see who would get the empty cubicles.

In Block 28 we doubled our living space—four rooms for the　5 twelve of us. Ray and Woody walled them with sheetrock. We had ceilings this time, and linoleum floors of solid maroon. You had three colors to choose from—maroon, black, and forest green—and there was plenty of it around by this time. Some families would vie with one another for the most elegant floor designs, obtaining a roll of each color from the supply shed, cutting it into diamonds, squares, or triangles, shining it with heating oil, then leaving their doors open so that passers-by could admire the handiwork.

Papa brought his still with him when we moved. He set it up be-   6 hind the door, where he continued to brew his own sake and brandy. He wasn't drinking as much now, though. He spent a lot of time outdoors. Like many of the older Issei[1] men, he didn't take a regular job in camp. He puttered. He had been working hard for thirty years and, bad as it was for him in some ways, camp did allow him time to dabble with hobbies he would never have found time for otherwise.

Once the first year's turmoil cooled down, the authorities started   7 letting us outside the wire for recreation. Papa used to hike along the creeks that channeled down from the base of the Sierras. He brought back chunks of driftwood, and he would pass long hours sitting on the steps carving myrtle limbs into benches, table legs, and lamps, filling our rooms with bits of gnarled, polished furniture.

He hauled stones in off the desert and built a small rock garden   8 outside our doorway, with succulents and a patch of moss. Near it he laid flat steppingstones leading to the stairs.

He also painted watercolors. Until this time I had not known he   9 could paint. He loved to sketch the mountains. If anything made that country habitable it was the mountains themselves, purple when the sun dropped and so sharply etched in the morning light the granite dazzled almost more than the bright snow lacing it. The nearest peaks rose ten thousand feet higher than the valley floor, with Whitney, the highest, just off to the south. They were important for all of us, but especially for the Issei. Whitney reminded Papa of Fujiyama, that is, it gave him the same kind of spiritual sustenance. The tremendous beauty of those peaks was inspirational, as so many natural forms are to the Japanese (the rocks outside our doorway could be those mountains in miniature). They also represented those forces in nature, those powerful and inevitable forces

---

[1]A Japanese person who emigrated to the United States after the 1907 exclusion proclamation and so was unable to become an American citizen.

that cannot be resisted, reminding a man that sometimes he must simply endure that which cannot be changed.

Subdued, resigned, Papa's life—all our lives—took on a pattern   10
that would hold for the duration of the war. Public shows of resentment pretty much spent themselves over the loyalty oath crises. *Shikata ga nai* again became the motto, but under altered circumstances. What had to be endured was the climate, the confinement, the steady crumbling away of family life. But the camp itself had been made livable. The government provided for our physical needs. My parents and older brothers and sisters, like most of the internees, accepted their lot and did what they could to make the best of a bad situation. "We're here," Woody would say. "We're here, and there's no use moaning about it forever."

Gardens had sprung up everywhere, in the firebreaks, between the   11
rows of barracks—rock gardens, vegetable gardens, cactus and flower gardens. People who lived in Owens Valley during the war still remember the flowers and lush greenery they could see from the highway as they drove past the main gate. The soil around Manzanar is alluvial and very rich. With water siphoned off from the Los Angeles–bound aqueduct, a large farm was under cultivation just outside the camp, providing the mess halls with lettuce, corn, tomatoes, eggplant, string beans, horseradish, and cucumbers. Near Block 28 some of the men who had been professional gardeners built a small park, with mossy nooks, ponds, waterfalls and curved wooden bridges. Sometimes in the evenings we could walk down the raked gravel paths. You could face away from the barracks, look past a tiny rapids toward the darkening mountains, and for a while not be a prisoner at all. You could hang suspended in some odd, almost lovely land you could not escape from yet almost didn't want to leave.

As the months at Manzanar turned to years, it became a world unto   12
itself, with its own logic and familiar ways. In time, staying there seemed far simpler than moving once again to another, unknown place. It was as if the war were forgotten, our reason for being there forgotten. The present, the little bit of busywork you had right in front of you, became the most urgent thing. In such a narrowed world, in order to survive, you learn to contain your rage and your despair, and you try to re-create, as well as you can, your normality, some sense of things continuing. The fact that America had accused us, or excluded us, or imprisoned us, or whatever it might be called, did not change the kind of world we wanted.

Most of us were born in this country; we had no other models. Those parks and gardens lent it an oriental character, but in most ways it was a totally equipped American small town, complete with schools, churches, Boy Scouts, beauty parlors, neighborhood gossip, fire and police departments, glee clubs, softball leagues, Abbott and Costello movies, tennis courts, and traveling shows. (I still remember an Indian who turned up one Saturday billing himself as a Sioux chief, wearing bear claws and head feathers. In the firebreak he sang songs and danced his tribal dances while hundreds of us watched.)

In our family, while Papa puttered, Mama made her daily rounds to   13
the mess halls, helping young mothers with their feeding, planning diets for the various ailments people suffered from. She wore a bright yellow, long-billed sun hat she had made herself and always kept stiffly starched. Afternoons I would see her coming from blocks away, heading home, her tiny figure warped by heat waves and that bonnet a yellow flower wavering in the glare.

In their disagreement over serving the country, Woody and Papa   14
had struck a kind of compromise. Papa talked him out of volunteering; Woody waited for the army to induct him. Meanwhile he clerked in the co-op general store. Kiyo, nearly thirteen by this time, looked forward to the heavy winds. They moved the sand around and uncovered obsidian arrowheads he could sell to old men in camp for fifty cents apiece. Ray, a few years older, played in the six-man touch football league, sometimes against Caucasian teams who would come in from Lone Pine or Independence. My sister Lillian was in high school and singing with a hillbilly band called The Sierra Stars—jeans, cowboy hats, two guitars, and a tub bass. And my oldest brother, Bill, led a dance band called The Jive Bombers—brass and rhythm, with cardboard fold-out music stands lettered J. B. Dances were held every weekend in one of the recreation halls. Bill played trumpet and took vocals on Glenn Miller arrangements of such tunes as *In the Mood, String of Pearls,* and *Don't Fence Me In.* He didn't sing *Don't Fence Me In* out of protest, as if trying quietly to mock the authorities. It just happened to be a hit song one year, and they all wanted to be an up-to-date American swing band. They would blast it out into recreation barracks full of bobby-soxed, jitter-bugging couples:

> *Oh, give me land, lots of land,*
> *Under starry skies above.*

Don't fence me in.
Let me ride through the wide
Open country that I love.

Pictures of the band, in their bow ties and jackets, appeared in the   15
high school yearbook for 1943–1944, along with pictures of just about
everything else in camp that year. It was called *Our World.* In its pages
you see school kids with armloads of books, wearing cardigan sweaters
and walking past rows of tarpapered shacks. You see chubby girl yell
leaders, pompons flying as they leap with glee. You read about the school
play, called *Growing Pains,* ". . . the story of a typical American home, in
this case that of the McIntyres. They see their boy and girl tossed into
the normal awkward growing up stage, but can offer little assistance or
direction in their turbulent course . . ." with Shoji Katayama as George
McIntyre, Takudo Ando as Terry McIntyre, and Mrs. McIntyre played
by Kazuko Nagai.

All the class pictures are in there, from the seventh grade through   16
twelfth, with individual head shots of seniors, their names followed by
the names of the high schools they would have graduated from on the
outside: Theodore Roosevelt, Thomas Jefferson, Herbert Hoover, Sacred
Heart. You see pretty girls on bicycles, chicken yards full of fat pullets,
patients back-tilted in dental chairs, lines of laundry, and finally, two
large blowups, the first of a high tower with a searchlight, against a Sierra
backdrop, the next a two-page endsheet showing a wide path that curves
among rows of elm trees. White stones border the path. Two dogs are
following an old woman in gardening clothes as she strolls along. She is
in the middle distance, small beneath the trees, beneath the snowy peaks.
It is winter. All the elms are bare. The scene is both stark and comforting.
This path leads toward one edge of camp, but the wire is out of sight, or
out of focus. The tiny woman seems very much at ease. She and her tiny
dogs seem almost swallowed by the landscape, or floating in it.

Opening the Dialogue

1. Houston begins and ends her essay with images of trees. What function do trees serve in the essay? What do they come to signify for her?

2. Do you think those held in Manzanar should have done more to resist their imprisonment? What might they have done? Why do you think they did not act?

3. Houston does not describe Manzanar in totally negative terms. In fact, she seems to look back nostalgically on some of the things she experienced there. How do you account for her ambivalence?

☜ Keeping a Notebook

Japanese Americans who signed an oath pledging loyalty to the government of the United States were allowed to leave Manzanar. (Some, in fact, enlisted in the U.S. Army and served with distinction.) For various reasons—not the least of which was the idea that their patriotism was being questioned—many refused to sign the loyalty oath. Would you sign such an oath? What factors would influence your decision?

☜ Working Together

Make a list of the various strategies that people used to make conditions in Manzanar bearable. Review the entries on the list in order to determine the most productive strategies. In class discussion, consider exactly what you would—and would not—be willing to do to make life better in Manzanar.

☜ Writing an Essay

Write an essay in which you describe a place that, like Manzanar, has both positive and negative associations. Begin your essay as Houston does, with an image that sums up your ambivalent feelings about the place you will describe.

Ishmael Reed

My Neighborhood

One of the most innovative voices in contemporary American literature, Ishmael Reed was born Emmett Coleman in 1938 in Chattanooga, Tennessee. He grew up in a working class neighborhood of Buffalo, New York, similar to the one he describes in the following essay.

"My Neighborhood," originally published in *California* magazine, explores the relationships between people and place that give our neighborhoods their unique cultures. Reed's choice of neighborhood reflects his deep belief in the importance of multicultural inclusion. He explained recently, "[Multiculturalism has] been portrayed as a racist movement on the part of African Americans but is simply a mosaic of the different ethnic groups and their contributions to American culture. It's people writing about their backgrounds, nothing wrong with it. . . . There is even a hunger to learn about their backgrounds among the people classified as white. The cat is out of the bag and won't be put back in."

Reed has enjoyed a prolific and successful career as an educator, poet, playwright, essayist, and editor, and he is the recipient of many literary prizes. He is author of several satirical novels, including *Mumbo Jumbo* and *Flight to Canada*, and numerous essay collections, including *Writin' is Fightin'*. (Another essay by Reed appears on p. 439.) Reed's iconoclastic prose has been characterized as "Afro-American history played in the rhythms of improvised jazz." Note how the wealth of descriptive detail in this essay has been orchestrated to create a dynamic portrait of Reed's world.

MY STEPFATHER is an evolutionist. He worked for many years at the   1
Chevrolet division of General Motors in Buffalo, a working-class auto

and steel town in upstate New York, and was able to rise from relative
poverty to the middle class. He believes that each succeeding generation
of Afro-Americans will have it better than its predecessor. In 1979 I
moved into the kind of neighborhood that he and my mother spent about
a third of their lives trying to escape. According to the evolutionist inte-
grationist ethic, this was surely a step backward, since "success" was seen
as being able to live in a neighborhood in which you were the only black
and joined your neighbors in trying to keep out "them."

My neighborhood, bordered by Genoa, Market Street, and 48th   2
and 55th streets in North Oakland, is what the media refer to as a "predominantly black neighborhood." It's the kind of neighborhood I grew
up in before leaving for New York City in 1962. My last New York residence was an apartment in a brownstone, next door to the building in
which poet W. H. Auden lived. There were trees in the backyard, and I
thought it was a swell neighborhood until I read in Robert Craft's biography of [the composer] Stravinsky that "when Stravinsky sent his chauffeur to pick up his friend Auden, the chauffeur would ask, 'Are you sure
Mr. Auden lives in this neighborhood?'" By 1968 my wife and I were able
to live six months of the year in New York and the other six in California.
This came to an end when one of the people I sublet the apartment to
abandoned it. He had fled to England to pursue a romance. He didn't pay
the rent, and so we were evicted long distance.

My first residence in California was an apartment on Santa Ynez   3
Street, near Echo Park Lake in Los Angeles, where I lived for about six
months in 1967. I was working on my second novel, and Carla Blank, my
wife, a dancer, was teaching physical education at one of Eddie
Rickenbacker's camps, located on an old movie set in the San Bernardino
Mountains. Carla's employers were always offering me a cabin where
they promised I could write without interruption. I never took them up
on the offer, but for years I've wondered about what kind of reception I
would have received had they discovered that I am black.

During my breaks from writing I would walk through the shopping   4
areas near Santa Ynez, strolling by vending machines holding newspapers whose headlines screamed about riots in Detroit. On some weekends we'd visit novelist Robert Gover (*The One Hundred Dollar Misunderstanding*) and his friends in Malibu. I remember one of Gover's friends, a
scriptwriter for the *Donna Reed Show*, looking me in the eye and telling me
that if he were black he'd be "on a Detroit rooftop, sniping at cops," as he

reclined, glass of scotch in hand, in a comfortable chair whose position gave him a good view of the rolling Pacific.

My Santa Ynez neighbors were whites from Alabama and Missis-   5
sippi, and we got along fine. Most of them were elderly, left behind by white flight to the suburbs, and on weekends the street would be lined with cars belonging to relatives who were visiting. While living here I observed a uniquely Californian phenomenon. Retired men would leave their houses in the morning, enter their cars, and remain there for a good part of the day, snoozing, reading newspapers, or listening to the radio.

I didn't experience a single racial incident during my stay in this   6
Los Angeles neighborhood of ex-southerners. Once, however, I had a strange encounter with the police. I was walking through a black work-ing-class neighborhood on my way to the downtown Los Angeles library. Some cops drove up and rushed me. A crowd gathered. The cops snatched my briefcase and removed its contents: books and notebooks having to do with my research of voodoo. The crowd laughed when the cops said they thought I was carrying a purse.

In 1968 my wife and I moved to Berkeley, where we lived in one   7
Bauhaus box after another until about 1971, when I received a three-book contract from Doubleday. Then we moved into the Berkeley Hills, where we lived in the downstairs apartment of a very grand-looking house on Bret Harte Way. There was a Zen garden with streams, waterfalls, and bridges outside, along with many varieties of flowers and plants. I didn't drive, and Carla was away at Mills College each day, earning a master's degree in dance. I stayed holed up in that apartment for two years, during which time I completed my third novel, *Mumbo Jumbo*.

During this period I became exposed to some of the racism I hadn't   8
detected on Santa Ynez or in the Berkeley flats. As a black male working at home, I was regarded with suspicion. Neighbors would come over and warn me about a heroin salesman they said was burglarizing the neigh-borhood, all the while looking over my shoulder in an attempt to pry into what I was up to. Once, while I was eating breakfast, a policeman entered through the garden door, gun drawn. "What on earth is the problem, officer?" I asked. He said they got word that a homicide had been com-mitted in my apartment, which I recognized as an old police tactic used to gain entry into somebody's house. Walking through the Berkeley Hills on Sundays, I was greeted by unfriendly stares and growling, snarling dogs. I remember one pest who always poked her head out of her window

whenever I'd walk down Bret Harte Way. She was always hassling me about parking my car in front of her house. She resembled Miss Piggy. I came to think of this section of Berkeley as "Whitetown."

Around 1974 the landlord raised the rent on the house in the hills,   9 and we found ourselves again in the Berkeley flats. We spent a couple of peaceful years on Edith Street, and then moved to Jayne Street, where we encountered another next-door family of nosy, middle-class progressives. I understand that much time at North Berkeley white neighborhood association meetings is taken up with discussion of and fascination with blacks who move through the neighborhoods, with special concern given those who tarry, or who wear dreadlocks. Since before the Civil War, vagrancy laws have been used as political weapons against blacks. Appropriately, there has been talk of making Havana—where I understand a woman can get turned in by her neighbors for having too many boyfriends over—Berkeley's sister city.

In 1976 our landlady announced that she was going to reoccupy   10 the Jayne Street house. I facetiously told a friend that I wanted to move to the most right-wing neighborhood he could think of. He mentioned El Cerrito. There, he said, your next-door neighbor might even be a cop. We moved to El Cerrito. Instead of the patronizing nosiness blacks complain about in Berkeley, I found the opposite on Terrace Drive in El Cerrito. The people were cold, impersonal, remote. But the neighborhood was quiet, serene even—the view was Olympian, and our rented house was secluded by eucalyptus trees. The annoyances were minor. Occasionally a car would careen down Terrace Drive full of white teenagers, and one or two would shout, "Hey, nigger!" Sometimes as I walked down The Arlington toward Kensington Market, the curious would stare at me from their cars, and women I encountered would give me nervous, frightened looks. Once, as I was walking to the market to buy magazines, a white child was sitting directly in my path. We were the only two people on the street. Two or three cars actually stopped, and their drivers observed the scene through their rearview mirrors until they were assured I wasn't going to abduct the child.

At night the Kensington Market area was lit with a yellow light,   11 especially eerie during a fog. I always thought that this section of Kensington would be a swell place to make a horror movie—the residents would make great extras—but whatever discomfort I felt about traveling through this area at 2 A.M. was mixed with the relief that I had just navi-

gated safely through Albany, where the police seemed always to be lurk-
ing in the shadows, prepared to ensnare blacks, hippies, and others they
didn't deem suitable for such a neighborhood.

In 1979 our landlord, a decent enough fellow in comparison to   12
some of the others we had had (who made you understand why the communists shoot the landlords first when they take over a country), announced he was going to sell the house on Terrace Drive. This was the
third rented house to be sold out from under us. The asking price was
way beyond our means, and so we started to search for another home,
only to find that the ones within our price range were located in North
Oakland, in a "predominantly black neighborhood." We finally found a
huge Queen Anne Victorian, which seemed to be about a month away
from the wrecker's ball if the termites and the precarious foundation
didn't do it in first, but I decided that I had to have it. The oldest house
on the block, it was built in 1906, the year the big earthquake hit Northern California, but left Oakland unscathed because, according to Bret
Harte, "there are some things even the earth can't swallow." If I was ap-
prehensive about moving into this neighborhhood—on television all
black neighborhoods resemble the commotion of the station house on
Hill Street Blues—I was later to learn that our neighbors were just as appre-
hensive about us. Were we hippies? Did I have a job? Were we going to
pay as much attention to maintaining our property as they did to theirs?
Neglected, the dilapidated monstrosity I'd got myself into would blight
the entire block.

While I was going to college I worked as an orderly in a psychiatric   13
hospital, and I remember a case in which a man was signed into the institution, after complaints from his neighbors that he mowed the lawn at
four in the morning. My neighbors aren't that finicky, but they keep very
busy pruning, gardening, and mowing their laws. Novelist Toni Cade
Bambara wrote of the spirit women in Atlanta who plant by moonlight
and use conjure to reap gorgeous vegetables and flowers. A woman on
this block grows roses the size of cantaloupes.

On New Year's Eve, famed landscape architect John Roberts ac-   14
companied me on my nightly walk, which takes me from 53rd Street to
Aileen, Shattuck, and back to 53rd Street. He was able to identify plants
and trees that had been imported from Asia, Africa, the Middle East, and
Australia. On Aileen Street he discovered a banana tree! And Arthur
Monroe, a painter and art historian, traces the "Tabby" garden design—

in which seashells and plates are mixed with lime, sand, and water to form decorative borders, found in this Oakland neighborhood, and others—to the influence of Islamic slaves brought to the Gulf Coast.

I won over my neighbors, I think, after I triumphed over a dozen 15 generations of pigeons that had been roosting in the crevices of this house for many years. It was a long and angry war, and my five year old constantly complained to her mother about Daddy's bad words about the birds. I used everything I could get my hands on, including chicken wire and mothballs, and I would have tried the clay owls if the only manufacturer hadn't gone out of business. I also learned never to underestimate the intelligence of pigeons; just when you think you've got them whipped, you'll notice that they've regrouped on some strategic rooftop to prepare for another invasion. When the house was free of pigeons and their droppings, which had spread to the adjoining properties, the lady next door said, "Thank you."

Every New Year's Day since then our neighbors have invited us to 16 join them and their fellow Louisianans for the traditional Afro-American good luck meal called Hoppin' John. This year the menu included black-eyed peas, ham, corn bread, potato salad, chitterlings, greens, fried chicken, yams, head cheese, macaroni, rolls, sweet potato pie, and fruit-cake. I got up that morning weighing 214 pounds and came home from the party weighing 220.

We've lived on 53rd Street for three years now. Carla's dance and 17 theater school, which she operates with her partner, Jody Roberts—Roberts and Blank Dance/Drama—is already five years old. I am working on my seventh novel and a television production of my play *Mother Hubbard*. The house has yet to be restored to its 1906 glory, but we're working on it.

I've grown accustomed to the common sights here—teenagers 18 moving through the neighborhood carrying radios blasting music by Grandmaster Flash and Prince, men hovering over cars with tools and rags in hand, decked-out female church delegations visiting the sick. Unemployment up, one sees more men drinking from sacks as they walk through Market Street or gather in Helen McGregor Plaza, on Shattuck and 52nd Street, near a bench where mothers sit with their children, waiting for buses. It may be because the bus stop is across the street from Children's Hospital (exhibiting a brand-new antihuman, postmodern wing), but there seem to be a lot of sick black children these days. The criminal courts and emergency rooms of Oakland hospitals, both medical and psychiatric, are also filled with blacks.

White men go from door to door trying to unload spoiled meat. 19 Incredibly sleazy white contractors and hustlers try to entangle people into shady deals that sometimes lead to the loss of a home. Everybody knows of someone, usually a widow, who has been gypped into paying thousands of dollars more than the standard cost for, say, adding a room to a house. It sure ain't El Cerrito. In El Cerrito the representatives from the utilities were very courteous. If they realize they're speaking to someone in a black neighborhood, however, they become curt and sarcastic. I was trying to arrange for the gas company to come out to fix a stove when the woman from Pacific Gas and Electric gave me some snide lip. I told her, "Lady, if you think what you're going through is an inconvenience, you can imagine my inconvenience paying the bills every month." Even she had to laugh.

The clerks in the stores are also curt, regarding blacks the way the 20 media regard them, as criminal suspects. Over in El Cerrito the cops were professional, respectful—in Oakland they swagger about like candidates for a rodeo. In El Cerrito and the Berkeley Hills you could take your time paying some bills, but in this black neighborhood if you miss paying a bill by one day, "reminders" printed in glaring and violent typefaces are sent to you, or you're threatened with discontinuance of this or that service. Los Angeles police victim Eulia Love, who was shot in the aftermath of an argument over an overdue gas bill, would still be alive if she had lived in El Cerrito or the Berkeley Hills.

I went to a bank a few weeks ago that advertised easy loans on 21 television, only to be told that I would have to wait six months after opening an account to be eligible for a loan. I went home and called the same bank, this time putting on my Clark Kent voice, and was informed that I could come in and get the loan the same day. Other credit unions and banks, too, have different lending practices for black and white neighborhoods, but when I try to tell white intellectuals that blacks are prevented from developing industries because the banks find it easier to lend money to communist countries than to American citizens, they call me paranoid. Sometimes when I know I am going to be inconvenienced by merchants or creditors because of my 53rd Street address, I give the address of my Berkeley studio instead. Others are not so fortunate.

Despite the inconveniences and antagonism from the outside 22 world one has to endure for having a 53rd Street address, life in this neighborhood is more pleasant than grim. Casually dressed, well-groomed elderly men gather at the intersections to look after the small children as they walk to and from school, or just to keep an eye on the neighborhood. My next-door neighbor keeps me in stitches with his informed commentary on any number of political comedies emanating from Washington and Sacramento. Once we were discussing pesticides, and the man who was repairing his porch told us that he had a great garden and didn't have to pay all that much attention to it. As for pesticides, he said, the bugs have to eat, too.

There are people on this block who still know the subsistence skills   23
many Americans have forgotten. They can hunt and fish (and if you don't fish, there is a man who covers the neighborhood selling fresh fish and yelling, "Fishman," recalling a period of ancient American commerce when you didn't have to pay the middleman). They are also loyal Americans—they vote, they pay taxes—but you don't find the extreme patriots here that you find in white neighborhoods. Although Christmas, Thanksgiving, New Year's, and Easter are celebrated with all get-out, I've never seen a flag flying on Memorial Day, or on any holiday that calls for the showing of the flag. Blacks express their loyalty in concrete ways. For example, you rarely see a foreign car in this neighborhood. And this 53rd Street neighborhood, as well as black neighborhoods like it from coast to coast, will supply the male children who will bear the brunt of future jungle wars, just as they did in Vietnam.

We do our shopping on a strip called Temescal, which stretches   24
from 46th to 51st streets. Temescal, according to Oakland librarian William Sturm, is an Aztec word for "hothouse," or "bathhouse." The word was borrowed from the Mexicans by the Spanish to describe similar hothouses, early saunas, built by the California Indians in what is now North Oakland. Some say the hothouses were used to sweat out demons; others claim the Indians used them for medicinal purposes. Most agree that after a period of time in the steam, the Indians would rush en masse into the streams that flowed through the area. One still runs underneath my backyard—I have to mow the grass there almost every other day.

Within these five blocks are the famous Italian restaurant Bertola's,   25
"Since 1932"; Siam restaurant; La Belle Creole, a French-Caribbean restaurant; Asmara, an Ethiopian restaurant; and Ben's Hof Brau, where white and black senior citizens, dressed in the elegance of a former time,

congregate to talk or to have an inexpensive though quality breakfast
provided by Ben's hardworking and courteous staff.

The Hof Brau shares its space with Vern's market, where you can   26
shop to the music of DeBarge. To the front of Vern's is the Temescal
Delicatessen, where a young Korean man makes the best po' boy sandwiches north of Louisiana, and near the side entrance is Ed Fraga's Auto-
motive. The owner is always advising his customers to avoid stress, and
he says goodbye with a "God bless you." The rest of the strip is taken up
by the Temescal Pharmacy, which has a resident health advisor and a
small library of health literature; the Aikido Institute; an African book-
store; and the internationally known Genova deli, to which people from
the surrounding cities travel to shop. The strip also includes the Clausen
House thrift shop, which sells used clothes and furniture. Here you can
buy novels by J.D. Salinger and John O'Hara for ten cents each.

Space that was recently occupied by the Buon Gusto Bakery is now   27
for rent. Before the bakery left, an Italian lady who worked there introduced me to a crunchy, cookie-like treat called "bones," which she said
went well with Italian wine. The Buon Gusto had been a landmark since
the 1940s, when, according to a guest at the New Year's Day Hoppin'
John supper, North Oakland was populated by Italians and Portuguese.
In those days a five-room house could be rented for $45 a month, she
said.

The neighborhood is still in transition. The East Bay Negro Histor-   28
ical Society, which was located around the corner on Grove Street, included in its collection letters written by nineteenth-century macho man
Jack London to his black nurse. They were signed, "Your little white
pickaninny." It's been replaced by the New Israelite Delight restaurant,
part of the Israelite Church, which also operates a day care center. The
restaurant offers homemade Louisiana gumbo and a breakfast that includes grits.

Unlike the other California neighborhoods I've lived in, I know   29
most of the people on this block by name. They are friendly and cooperative, always offering to watch your house while you're away. The day
after one of the few whites who lives on the block—a brilliant muckrak-
ing journalist and former student of mine—was robbed, neighbors gathered in front of his house to offer assistance.

In El Cerrito my neighbor was indeed a cop. He used pomade on   30
his curly hair, sported a mustache, and there was a grayish tint in his

brown eyes. He was a handsome man, with a smile like a movie star's. His was the only house on the block I entered during my three-year stay in that neighborhood, and that was one afternoon when we shared some brandy. I wanted to get to know him better. I didn't know he was dead until I saw people in black gathered on his doorstep.

I can't imagine that happening on 53rd Street. In a time when dour   31 thinkers view alienation and insensitivity toward the plight of others as characteristics of the modern condition, I think I'm lucky to live in a neighborhood where people look out for one another.

A human neighborhood.   32

✪ Opening the Dialogue

1. In paragraph 1 Reed says that his stepfather believes that each generation of African Americans will have it better than the previous generation. Do you think Reed's stepfather is correct?

2. Why do you suppose Reed decides to move to the city even though he never experienced a racial incident in the suburbs? Why does he move into a neighborhood of the sort his parents have always sought to escape?

3. By saying that Oakland is a "human place," Reed implies that the suburban neighborhoods in which he lived are somehow lacking in humanity. Do you believe his assessment is accurate, or do you think he judges the suburbs too harshly?

✪ Keeping a Notebook

Do you think Reed is painting an accurate picture of his inner-city neighborhood—especially in light of recent racial unrest in some cities? What details do you think he might be ignoring? What motive could he have for downplaying the negative features of his neighborhood?

✪ Working Together

Divide into groups. Half the groups should list the advantages of living in the city and the disadvantages of living in the suburbs. The other half should list the disadvantages of living in the city and the advantages of living in the suburbs. Then, in class discussion, debate what one gains and what one loses in each environment.

⟨ℰ⟩ Writing an Essay

Write an essay in which you describe a neighborhood that you consider to be particularly urban or suburban. Make sure you include specific details.

JUDITH ORTIZ COFER

Silent Dancing

Judith Ortiz Cofer was born in Hormigueros, Puerto Rico, in 1952 and, as she relates in the following poignant essay, moved to New Jersey as a small child. A poet, novelist, and essayist, she has taken the crosscurrents of these two cultures as her literary inspiration: "Writing began for me as a fascination with a language I was not born into. As a native Spanish speaker growing up in the United States, I first perceived of language, especially the English language, as a barrier, a challenge to be met with the same kind of closed-eye bravado that prompted me to jump into the deep end of the pool before taking my first swimming lesson. The analogy is not so ludicrous—during my first weeks in the third grade in a Paterson, New Jersey, public school, I felt as disconnected with the world of language as I did when I sank in slow motion to the bottom of that swimming pool. But I managed to surface and breathe the air of the real world, just as I took in words my first year in America—breathlessly, and yes, almost desperately, for I needed to be able to communicate almost as much as I needed to breathe."

"Silent Dancing" is the title essay of a collection published in 1991. It was chosen by Joyce Carol Oates for inclusion in *The Best American Essays* for 1991. (Another essay by Cofer appears on p. 220.) Educated at the University of Georgia, Florida Atlantic University, and Oxford University, Cofer is a member of the English department at the University of Georgia and is the author of a novel, *The Line of the Sun*, and the poetry collections *Terms of Survival* and *Reaching for the Mainland*. Note in the following essay how she alternates description of a specific family party with more general details of her early life.

W E HAVE A HOME MOVIE *of this party. Several times my mother and I have* 1
watched it together, and I have asked questions about the silent revelers coming in and
out of focus. It is grainy and of short duration, but it's a great visual aid to my memory
of life at that time. And it is in color—the only complete scene in color I can recall from
those years.

We lived in Puerto Rico until my brother was born in 1954. Soon 2
after, because of economic pressures on our growing family, my father
joined the United States Navy. He was assigned to duty on a ship in
Brooklyn Yard—a place of cement and steel that was to be his home base
in the States until his retirement more than twenty years later. He left the
Island first, alone, going to New York City and tracking down his uncle
who lived with his family across the Hudson River in Paterson, New Jersey. There my father found a tiny apartment in a huge tenement that had
once housed Jewish families but was just being taken over and transformed by Puerto Ricans, overflowing from New York City. In 1955 he
sent for us. My mother was only twenty years old, I was not quite three,
and my brother was a toddler when we arrived at El Building, as the place
had been christened by its newest residents.

My memories of life in Paterson during those first few years are all 3
in shades of gray. Maybe I was too young to absorb vivid colors and details, or to discriminate between the slate blue of the winter sky and the
darker hues of the snow-bearing clouds, but that single color washes over
the whole period. The building we lived in was gray, as were the streets,
filled with slush the first few months of my life there. The coat my father
had bought for me was similar in color and too big; it sat heavily on my
thin frame.

I do remember the way the heater pipes banged and rattled, star- 4
tling all of us out of sleep until we got so used to the sound that we automatically shut it out or raised our voices above the racket. The hiss from
the valve punctuated my sleep (which has always been fitful) like a non-
human presence in the room—a dragon sleeping at the entrance of my
childhood. But the pipes were also a connection to all the other lives
being lived around us. Having come from a house designed for a single
family back in Puerto Rico—my mother's extended-family home—it was
curious to know that strangers lived under our floor and above our heads,
and that the heater pipe went through everyone's apartment. (My first

spanking in Paterson came as a result of playing tunes on the pipes in my room to see if there would be an answer.) My mother was as new to this concept of beehive life as I was, but she had been given strict orders by my father to keep the doors locked, the noise down, ourselves to ourselves.

It seems that Father had learned some painful lessons about preju-   5
dice while searching for an apartment in Paterson. Not until years later did I hear how much resistance he had encountered with landlords who were panicking at the influx of Latinos into a neighborhood that had been Jewish for a couple of generations. It made no difference that it was the American phenomenon of ethnic turnover which was changing the urban core of Paterson, and that the human flood could not be held back with an accusing finger.

"You Cuban?" one man had asked my father, pointing at his name   6
tag on the navy uniform—even though my father had the fair skin and light brown hair of his northern Spanish background, and the name Ortiz is as common in Puerto Rico as Johnson is in the United States.

"No," my father had answered, looking past the finger into his   7
adversary's angry eyes. "I'm Puerto Rican."

"Same shit." And the door closed.   8

My father could have passed as European, but we couldn't. My   9
brother and I both have our mother's black hair and olive skin, and so we lived in El Building and visited our great-uncle and his fair children on the next block. It was their private joke that they were the German branch of the family. Not many years later that area too would be mainly Puerto Rican. It was as if the heart of the city map were being gradually colored brown—*café con leche* brown. Our color.

The movie opens with a sweep of the living room. It is "typical" immigrant Puerto Rican   10
decor for the time: the sofa and chairs are square and hard-looking, upholstered in bright
colors (blue and yellow in this instance) and covered with the transparent plastic that
furniture salesmen then were so adept at convincing women to buy. The linoleum on the
floor is light blue; where it had been subjected to spike heels, as it was in most places, there
were dime-size indentations all over it that cannot be seen in this movie. The room is full
of people dressed up: dark suits for the men, red dresses for the women. When I have asked
my mother why most of the women are in red that night, she has shrugged and said, "I
don't remember. Just a coincidence." She doesn't have my obsession for assigning sym-
bolism to everything.

The three women in red sitting on the couch are my mother, my eighteen-year-old   11
cousin, and her brother's girlfriend. The novia *is just up from the Island, which is*
apparent in her body language. She sits up formally, her dress pulled over her knees. She
is a pretty girl, but her posture makes her look insecure, lost in her full-skirted dress,
which she has carefully tucked around her to make room for my gorgeous cousin, her
future sister-in-law. My cousin has grown up in Paterson and is in her last year of high
school. She doesn't have a trace of what Puerto Ricans call la mancha *(literally,*
the stain: the mark of the new immigrant—something about the posture, the voice, or the
humble demeanor that makes it obvious to everyone the person has just arrived on the
mainland). My cousin is wearing a tight, sequined, cocktail dress. Her brown hair has
been lightened with peroxide around the bangs, and she is holding a cigarette expertly
between her fingers, bringing it up to her mouth in a sensuous arc of her arm as she talks
animatedly. My mother, who has come up to sit between the two women, both only a
few years younger than herself, is somewhere between the poles they represent in our
culture.

It became my father's obsession to get out of the barrio, and thus we were   12
never permitted to form bonds with the place or with the people who
lived there. Yet El Building was a comfort to my mother, who never got
over yearning for *la isla*. She felt surrounded by her language: the walls
were thin, and voices speaking and arguing in Spanish could be heard all
day. *Salsas* blasted out of radios, turned on early in the morning and left
on for company. Women seemed to cook rice and beans perpetually—
the strong aroma of boiling red kidney beans permeated the hallways.

Though Father preferred that we do our grocery shopping at the   13
supermarket when he came home on weekend leaves, my mother insisted
that she could cook only with products whose labels she could read.
Consequently, during the week I accompanied her and my little brother
to La Bodega—a hole-in-the-wall grocery store across the street from El
Building. There we squeezed down three narrow aisles jammed with various products. Goya and Libby's—those were the trademarks that were
trusted by her *mamá*, so my mother bought many cans of Goya beans,
soups, and condiments, as well as little cans of Libby's fruit juices for us.
And she also bought Colgate toothpaste and Palmolive soap. (The final *e*
is pronounced in both these products in Spanish, so for many years I
believed that they were manufactured on the Island. I remember my surprise at first hearing a commercial on television in which "Colgate"
rhymed with "ate.") We always lingered at La Bodega, for it was there

that Mother breathed best, taking in the familiar aromas of the foods she knew from Mamá's kitchen. It was also there that she got to speak to the other women of El Building without violating outright Father's dictates against fraternizing with our neighbors.

Yet Father did his best to make our "assimilation" painless. I can still   14 see him carrying a real Christmas tree up several flights of stairs to our apartment, leaving a trail of aromatic pine. He carried it formally, as if it were a flag in a parade. We were the only ones in El Building that I knew of who got presents on both Christmas and *dia de Reyes*, the day when the Three Kings brought gifts to Christ and to Hispanic children.

Our supreme luxury in El Building was having our own television   15 set. It must have been a result of Father's guilt feelings over the isolation he had imposed on us, but we were among the first in the barrio to have one. My brother quickly became an avid watcher of Captain Kangaroo and Jungle Jim, while I loved all the series showing families. By the time I started first grade, I could have drawn a map of Middle America as exemplified by the lives of characters in *Father Knows Best, The Donna Reed Show, Leave It to Beaver, My Three Sons,* and (my favorite) *Bachelor Father,* where John Forsythe treated his adopted teenage daughter like a princess because he was rich and had a Chinese houseboy to do everything for him. In truth, compared to our neighbors in El Building, *we* were rich. My father's navy check provided us with financial security and a standard of living that the factory workers envied. The only thing his money could not buy us was a place to live away from the barrio—his greatest wish. Mother's greatest fear.

In the home movie the men are shown next, sitting around a card table set up in one   16 *corner of the living room, playing dominoes. The clack of the ivory pieces was a familiar sound. I heard it in many houses on the Island and in many apartments in Paterson. In* Leave It to Beaver, *the Cleavers played bridge in every other episode; in my childhood, the men started every social occasion with a hotly debated round of dominoes. The women would sit around and watch, but they never participated in the games.*

Here and there you can see a small child. Children were always brought to   17 *parties and, whenever they got sleepy, were put to bed in the host's bedroom. Babysitting was a concept unrecognized by the Puerto Rican women I knew: a responsible mother did not leave her children with any stranger. And in a culture where children are not considered intrusive, there was no need to leave the children at home. We went where our mother went.*

Of my preschool years I have only impressions: the sharp bite of the wind   18
in December as we walked with our parents toward the brightly lit stores
downtown; how I felt like a stuffed doll in my heavy coat, boots, and
mittens; how good it was to walk into the five-and-dime and sit at the
counter drinking hot chocolate. On Saturdays our whole family would
walk downtown to shop at the big department stores on Broadway.
Mother bought all our clothes at Penney's and Sears, and she liked to buy
her dresses at the women's specialty shops like Lerner's and Diana's. At
some point we'd go into Woolworth's and sit at the soda fountain to eat.

We never ran into other Latinos at these stores or when eating out,   19
and it became clear to me only years later that the women from El Building shopped mainly in other places—stores owned by other Puerto
Ricans or by Jewish merchants who had philosophically accepted our
presence in the city and decided to make us their good customers, if not
real neighbors and friends. These establishments were located not downtown but in the blocks around our street, and they were referred to generically as La Tienda, El Bazar, La Bodega, La Botánica. Everyone knew
what was meant. These were the stores where your face did not turn a
clerk to stone, where your money was as green as anyone's else's.

One New Year's Eve we were dressed up like child models in the   20
Sears catalogue: my brother in a miniature man's suit and bow tie, and I
in black patent-leather shoes and a frilly dress with several layers of crin-
oline underneath. My mother wore a bright red dress that night, I remember, and spike heels; her long black hair hung to her waist. Father,
who usually wore his navy uniform during his short visits home, had put
on a dark civilian suit for the occasion: we had been invited to his uncle's
house for a big celebration. Everyone was excited because my mother's
brother Hernan—a bachelor who could indulge himself with luxuries—
had bought a home movie camera, which he would be trying out that
night.

Even the home movie cannot fill in the sensory details such a gath-   21
ering left imprinted in a child's brain. The thick sweetness of women's
perfumes mixing with the ever-present smells of good cooking in the
kitchen: meat and plantain *pasteles,* as well as the ubiquitous rice dish
made special with pigeon peas—*gandules*—and seasoned with precious
sofrito sent up from the Island by somebody's mother or smuggled in by a
recent traveler. *Sofrito* was one of the items that women hoarded, since it
was hardly ever in stock at La Bodega. It was the flavor of Puerto Rico.

The men drank Palo Viejo rum, and some of the younger ones got   22
weepy. The first time I saw a grown man cry was at a New Year's Eve
party: he had been reminded of his mother by the smells in the kitchen.
But what I remember most were the boiled *pasteles,* plantain or yucca rec-
tangles stuffed with corned beef or other meats, olives, and many other
savory ingredients, all wrapped in banana leaves. Everybody had to fish
one out with a fork. There was always a "trick" *pastel*—one without stuff-
ing—and whoever got that one was the "New Year's Fool."

There was also the music. Long-playing albums were treated like   23
precious china in these homes. Mexican recordings were popular, but the
songs that brought tears to my mother's eyes were sung by the melancholy Daniel Santos, whose life as a drug addict was the stuff of legend.
Felipe Rodríguez was a particular favorite of couples, since he sang about
faithless women and brokenhearted men. There is a snatch of one lyric
that has stuck in my mind like a needle on a worn groove: *De piedra ha de
ser mi cama, de piedra la cabezera . . . la mujer que a mi me quiera . . . ha de quererme
de veras. Ay, Ay, Ay, corazón, porque no amas . . .* I must have heard it a thousand times since the idea of a bed made of stone, and its connection to
love, first troubled me with its disturbing images.

The five-minute home movie ends with people dancing in a circle—the   24
creative filmmaker must have set it up, so that all of them could file past
him. It is both comical and sad to watch silent dancing. Since there is no
justification for the absurd movements that music provides for some of
us, people appear frantic, their faces embarrassingly intense. It's as if you
were watching sex. Yet for years, I've had dreams in the form of this home
movie. In a recurring scene, familiar faces push themselves forward into
my mind's eye, plastering their features into distorted close-ups. And I'm
asking them: "Who is *she?* Who is the old woman I don't recognize? Is she
an aunt? Somebody's wife? Tell me who she is."

"See the beauty mark on her cheek as big as a hill on the lunar   25
landscape of her face—well, that runs in the family. The women on
your father's side of the family wrinkle early; it's the price they pay for
that fair skin. The young girl with the green stain on her wedding dress
is *la novia*—just up from the Island. See, she lowers her eyes when she
approaches the camera, as she's supposed to. Decent girls never look at
you directly in the face. *Humilde,* humble, a girl should express humility

in all her actions. She will make a good wife for your cousin. He should consider himself lucky to have met her only weeks after she arrived here. If he marries her quickly, she will make him a good Puerto Rican—style wife; but if he waits too long, she will be corrupted by the city, just like your cousin there."

"She means me. I do what I want. This is not some primitive   26
island I live on. Do they expect me to wear a black mantilla on my head and go to mass every day? Not me. I'm an American woman, and I will do as I please. I can type faster than anyone in my senior class at Central High, and I'm going to be a secretary to a lawyer when I graduate. I can pass for an American girl anywhere—I've tried it. At least for Italian, anyway—I never speak Spanish in public. I hate these parties, but I wanted the dress. I look better than any of these *humildes* here. *My* life is going to be different. I have an American boyfriend. He is older and has a car. My parents don't know it, but I sneak out of the house late at night sometimes to be with him. If I marry him, even my name will be American. I hate rice and beans—that's what makes these women fat."

"Your *prima* is pregnant by that man she's been sneaking around   27
with. Would I lie to you? I'm your *tía política*, your great-uncle's common-law wife—the one he abandoned on the Island to go marry your cousin's mother. I was not invited to this party, of course, but I came anyway. I came to tell you that story about your cousin that you've always wanted to hear. Do you remember the comment your mother made to a neighbor that has always haunted you? The only thing you heard was your cousin's name, and then you saw your mother pick up your doll from the couch and say: "It was as big as this doll when they flushed it down the toilet." This image has bothered you for years, hasn't it? You had nightmares about babies being flushed down the toilet, and you wondered why anyone would do such a horrible thing. You didn't dare ask your mother about it. She would only tell you that you had not heard her right, and yell at you for listening to adult conversations. But later, when you were old enough to know about abortions, you suspected.

"I am here to tell you that you were right. Your cousin was grow-   28
ing an *americanito* in her belly when this movie was made. Soon after,

she put something long and pointy into her pretty self, thinking maybe she could get rid of the problem before breakfast and still make it to her first class at the high school. Well, *niña*, her screams could be heard downtown. Your aunt, her *mamá*, who had been a midwife on the Island, managed to pull the little thing out. Yes, they probably flushed it down the toilet. What else could they do with it—give it a Christian burial in a little white casket with blue bows and ribbons? Nobody wanted that baby—least of all the father, a teacher at her school with a house in West Paterson that he was filling with real children, and a wife who was a natural blonde.

"Girl, the scandal sent your uncle back to the bottle. And guess   29 where your cousin ended up? Irony of ironies. She was sent to a village in Puerto Rico to live with a relative on her mother's side: a place so far away from civilization that you have to ride a mule to reach it. A real change in scenery. She found a man there—women like that cannot live without male company—but believe me, the men in Puerto Rico know how to put a saddle on a woman like her. *La gringa*, they call her. Ha, ha, ha. *La gringa* is what she always wanted to be . . . "

The old woman's mouth becomes a cavernous black hole I fall into. And   30 as I fall, I can feel the reverberations of her laughter. I hear the echoes of her last mocking words: *la gringa, la gringa!* And the conga line keeps moving silently past me. There is no music in my dream for the dancers.

When Odysseus visits Hades to see the spirit of his mother, he   31 makes an offering of sacrificial blood, but since all the souls crave an audience with the living, he has to listen to many of them before he can ask questions. I, too, have to hear the dead and the forgotten speak in my dream. Those who are still part of my life remain silent, going around and around in their dance. The others keep pressing their faces forward to say things about the past.

My father's uncle is last in line. He is dying of alcoholism, shrunken   32 and shriveled like a monkey, his face a mass of wrinkles and broken arteries. As he comes closer I realize that in his features I can see my whole family. If you were to stretch that rubbery flesh, you could find my father's face, and deep within *that* face—my own. I don't want to look into those eyes ringed in purple. In a few years he will retreat into silence, and take a long, long time to die. *Move back, Tío*, I tell him. *I don't want to hear*

what you have to say. Give the dancers room to move. Soon it will be midnight. Who
is the New Year's Fool this time?

✺ Opening the Dialogue

1. In her essay Cofer alternates between passages of plain text and passages in italics. How are the focuses of these two types of passages different? How does each enrich the other? Are both necessary?

2. Do you think this essay is about the past? About assimilation? About family? About Puerto Rico? Or is it about something else?

3. Cofer says that it was her father's greatest wish and her mother's greatest fear to move out of the barrio. In view of what life in the inner cities— and in the United States as a whole—is like now, whose attitude do you think makes more sense?

✺ Keeping a Notebook

In what ways are the women described by Cofer like the women in your family? In what ways are they different?

✺ Working Together

Working in groups, list the advantages and disadvantages for Cofer's family of remaining in the barrio. In class discussion, consider whether or not the advantages outweigh the disadvantages.

✺ Writing an Essay

Write an essay in which you describe some members of your family who, although no longer alive, still exert a strong influence on you. You may, if you wish, alternate between passages recreating a remembered conversation or a specific event, such as a family dinner, and physical description of the family members.

N. Scott Momaday

The Way to Rainy Mountain

N. Scott Momaday (b. 1934) is a Kiowa who grew up on reservations in the Southwest. His Kiowa name, "Tsoai-talee," shows how intrinsic the power of place is to Native Americans. It means "Rock-Tree Boy" and refers to Tsoai (the Rock-Tree), or Devil's Tower, the Wyoming monolith that looms above the Black Hills and figures prominently in Kiowa legend. Much of Momaday's work reflects the struggle to reconcile the power of Native American tradition with the immediacy of the modern world.

Momaday believes strongly that Native Americans can best interpret their own heritage: "Surely the non-native's view of the Native, across five centuries, ought at last to be qualified by the Native American's view of himself; it is patently a more authentic and accurate view," he said recently. "In so many books . . . [the Native American] is presented as a museum piece. He is not flesh and blood so much as he is ink on paper, paint on canvas, light on film, the lifeless sum of his own artifacts. What is surely needed is an idea of the Native American as the recorder of his own changing image."

The author of a memoir, *The Way to Rainy Mountain* (from which the following is taken), as well as several novels (including *The Ancient Child* and the Pulitzer Prize–winning *House of Dawn*), Momaday is also a poet and painter. He is currently Regents Professor of English at the University of Arizona.

Note how Momaday links his description of the land to his description of his grandmother, creating a dominant impression that interrelates the two.

A SINGLE KNOLL rises out of the plain in Oklahoma, north and west   1
of the Wichita Range. For my people, the Kiowas, it is an old landmark,
and they gave it the name Rainy Mountain. The hardest weather in the
world is there. Winter brings blizzards, hot tornadic winds arise in the
spring, and in summer the prairie is an anvil's edge. The grass turns brittle
and brown, and it cracks beneath your feet. There are green belts along
the rivers and creeks, linear groves of hickory and pecan, willow and
witch hazel. At a distance in July or August the steaming foliage seems
almost to writhe in fire. Great green-and-yellow grasshoppers are everywhere in the tall grass, popping up like corn to sting the flesh, and tor-
toises crawl about on the red earth, going nowhere in the plenty of time.
Loneliness is an aspect of the land. All things in the plain are isolate; there
is no confusion of objects in the eye, but *one* hill or *one* tree or *one* man. To
look upon that landscape in the early morning, with the sun at your back,
is to lose the sense of proportion. Your imagination comes to life, and
this, you think, is where Creation was begun.

I returned to Rainy Mountain in July. My grandmother had died in   2
the spring, and I wanted to be at her grave. She had lived to be very old
and at last infirm. Her only living daughter was with her when she died,
and I was told that in death her face was that of a child.

I like to think of her as a child. When she was born, the Kiowas   3
were living that last great moment of their history. For more than a hundred years they had controlled the open range from the Smoky Hill River
to the Red, from the headwaters of the Canadian to the fork of the Arkansas and Cimarron. In alliance with the Comanches, they had ruled the
whole of the southern Plains. War was their sacred business, and they
were among the finest horsemen the world has ever known. But warfare
for the Kiowas was preeminently a matter of disposition rather than of
survival, and they never understood the grim, unrelenting advance of the
U.S. Cavalry. When at last, divided and ill-provisioned, they were driven
onto the Staked Plains in the cold rains of autumn, they fell into panic. In
Palo Duro Canyon they abandoned their crucial stores to pillage and had
nothing then but their lives. In order to save themselves, they surrendered to the soldiers at Fort Sill and were imprisoned in the old stone
corral that now stands as a military museum. My grandmother was spared
the humiliation of those high gray walls by eight or ten years, but she

must have known from birth the affliction of defeat, the dark brooding of old warriors.

Her name was Aho, and she belonged to the last culture to evolve   4
in North America. Her forebears came down from the high country in western Montana nearly three centuries ago. They were a mountain people, a mysterious tribe of hunters whose language has never been positively classified in any major group. In the late seventeenth century they began a long migration to the south and east. It was a long journey toward the dawn, and it led to a golden age. Along the way the Kiowas were befriended by the Crows, who gave them the culture and religion of the Plains. They acquired horses, and their ancient nomadic spirit was suddenly free of the ground. They acquired Tai-me, the sacred Sun Dance doll, from that moment the object and symbol of their worship, and so shared in the divinity of the sun. Not least, they acquired the sense of destiny, therefore courage and pride. When they entered upon the southern Plains, they had been transformed. No longer were they slaves to the simple necessity of survival; they were a lordly and dangerous society of fighters and thieves, hunters and priests of the sun. According to their origin myth, they entered the world through a hollow log. From one point of view, their migration was the fruit of an old prophecy, for indeed they emerged from a sunless world.

Although my grandmother lived out her long life in the shadow of   5
Rainy Mountain, the immense landscape of the continental interior lay like memory in her blood. She could tell of the Crows, whom she had never seen, and of the Black Hills, where she had never been. I wanted to see in reality what she had seen more perfectly in the mind's eye, and traveled fifteen hundred miles to begin my pilgrimage.

Yellowstone, it seemed to me, was the top of the world, a region of   6
deep lakes and dark timber, canyons and waterfalls. But, beautiful as it is, one might have the sense of confinement there. The skyline in all directions is close at hand, the high wall of the woods and deep cleavages of shade. There is a perfect freedom in the mountains, but it belongs to the eagle and the elk, the badger and the bear. The Kiowas reckoned their stature by the distance they could see, and they were bent and blind in the wilderness.

Descending eastward, the highland meadows are a stairway to the   7
plain. In July the inland slope of the Rockies is luxuriant with flax and

buckwheat, stonecrop and larkspur. The earth unfolds and the limit of the land recedes. Clusters of trees and animals grazing far in the distance cause the vision to reach away and wonder to build upon the mind. The sun follows a longer course in the day, and the sky is immense beyond all comparison. The great billowing clouds that sail upon it are shadows that move upon the grain like water, dividing light. Farther down, in the land of the Crows and Blackfeet, the plain is yellow. Sweet clover takes hold of the hills and bends upon itself to cover and seal the soil. There the Kiowas paused on their way; they had come to the place where they must change their lives. The sun is at home on the plains. Precisely there does it have the certain character of a god. When the Kiowas came to the land of the Crows, they could see the dark lees of the hills at dawn across the Bighorn River, the profusion of light on the grain shelves, the oldest deity ranging after the solstices. Not yet would they veer southward to the caldron of the land that lay below; they must wean their blood from the northern winter and hold the mountains a while longer in their view. They bore Tai-me in procession to the east.

A dark mist lay over the Black Hills, and the land was like iron. At the top of a ridge I caught sight of Devil's Tower upthrust against the gray sky as if in the birth of time the core of the earth had broken through its crust and the motion of the world was begun. There are things in nature that engender an awful quiet in the heart of man; Devil's Tower is one of them. Two centuries ago, because they could not do otherwise, the Kiowas made a legend at the base of the rock. My grandmother said:

"Eight children were there at play, seven sisters and their brother. Suddenly the boy was struck dumb; he trembled and began to run upon his hands and feet. His fingers became claws, and his body was covered with fur. Directly there was a bear where the boy had been. The sisters were terrified; they ran, and the bear after them. They came to the stump of a great tree, and the tree spoke to them. It bade them climb upon it, and as they did so, it began to rise into the air. The bear came to kill them, but they were just beyond its reach. It reared against the tree and scored the bark all around with its claws. The seven sisters were borne into the sky, and they became the stars of the Big Dipper."

From that moment, and so long as the legend lives, the Kiowas have kinsmen in the night sky. Whatever they were in the mountains, they could be no more. However tenuous their well-being, however much they had suffered and would suffer again, they had found a way out of the wilderness.

My grandmother had a reverence for the sun, a holy regard that   9
now is all but gone out of mankind. There was a wariness in her, and an ancient awe. She was a Christian in her later years, but she had come a long way about, and she never forgot her birthright. As a child she had been to the Sun Dances; she had taken part in those annual rites, and by them she had learned the restoration of her people in the presence of Tai-me. She was about seven when the last Kiowa Sun Dance was held in 1887 on the Washita River above Rainy Mountain Creek. The buffalo were gone. In order to consummate the ancient sacrifice—to impale the head of a buffalo bull upon the medicine tree—a delegation of old men journeyed into Texas, there to beg and barter for an animal from the Goodnight herd. She was ten when the Kiowas came together for the last time as a living Sun Dance culture. They could find no buffalo; they had to hang an old hide from the sacred tree. Before the dance could begin, a company of soldiers rode out from Fort Sill under orders to disperse the tribe. Forbidden without cause the essential act of their faith, having seen the wild herds slaughtered and left to rot upon the ground, the Kiowas backed away forever from the medicine tree. That was July 20, 1890, at the great bend of the Washita. My grandmother was there. Without bitterness, and for as long as she lived, she bore a vision of deicide.

Now that I can have her only in memory, I see my grandmother in   1(
the several postures that were peculiar to her: standing at the wood stove on a winter morning and turning meat in a great iron skillet; sitting at the south window, bent above her beadwork, and afterwards, when her vision had failed, looking down for a long time into the fold of her hands; going out upon a cane, very slowly as she did when the weight of age came upon her; praying. I remember her most often at prayer. She made long, rambling prayers out of suffering and hope, having seen many things. I was never sure that I had the right to hear, so exclusive were they of all mere custom and company. The last time I saw her she prayed standing by the side of her bed at night, naked to the waist, the light of a kerosene lamp moving upon her dark skin. Her long, black hair, always drawn and braided in the day, lay upon her shoulders and against her

breasts like a shawl. I do not speak Kiowa, and I never understood her prayers, but there was something inherently sad in the sound, some merest hesitation upon the syllables of sorrow. She began in a high and descending pitch, exhausting her breath to silence; then again and again—and always the same intensity of effort, of something that is, and is not, like urgency in the human voice. Transported so in the dancing light among the shadows of her room, she seemed beyond the reach of time. But that was illusion; I think I knew then that I should not see her again.

⟨€⟩ Opening the Dialogue

1. How would you describe Momaday's attitude toward his grandmother? Do you think he paints a realistic picture of her?

2. How would you describe Momaday's relationship to Native American culture? How involved is he with traditional customs?

3. Do you think it is possible for Native Americans to hold on to their traditions while participating in contemporary American culture? Do you think it is harder for them do to so than for members of other ethnic or racial groups? Why?

⟨€⟩ Keeping a Notebook

Which family members do you believe most strongly represent your own ethnic or cultural background? Which of their character traits best reflect your group's traditional values?

⟨€⟩ Working Together

Like Judith Ortiz Cofer, Momaday sees a family member as a window to the past. Working in groups, list the attributes that both Momaday and Cofer emphasize in the family members they describe. In class discussion determine how these descriptions convey the writers' respective attitudes toward their ethnic roots.

✪ Writing an Essay

Think of a place that you identify with a member of your family or with your culture. Write a letter to your future children in which you describe your memories of this place.

JOAN DIDION

Miami: The Cuban Presence

Born in 1934 in Sacramento, California, Joan Didion comes from a long line of pioneers (her great-great-grandmother was a member of the original Donner party), a heritage that, in Didion's words, has left her with an "ineptness for tolerating the complexities of postindustrial life."

Didion was a nervous child, afraid of everything from atom bombs to rattlesnakes. Her mother gave her a notebook, suggesting she "stop whining" and start writing; at the age of five Didion wrote her first story. During her senior year at the University of California at Berkeley, she won *Vogue* magazine's Prix de Paris contest and began a career as an elegant prose stylist and one of the most celebrated of the "new journalists."

Praised for her distinctive literary voice and the precision and control of her writing, Didion is, according to the *New York Times Magazine*, "a gifted reporter" and "a prescient witness, finding in her own experiences parallels of the times. The voice is always precise, the tone unsentimental, the view unabashedly subjective. She takes things personally."

A common theme in Didion's novels (*Run River, Play It As It Lays, A Book of Common Prayer*, and *Democracy*), as well as her essays and nonfiction (collected in *Slouching Toward Bethlehem, The White Album*, and *After Henry*), is the disorder in society, the fact that, in the poet Yeats's words, "things fall apart; the center cannot hold." For years her favorite subject was her native California, but in the last ten years she has broadened her perspective, examining in two recent works of nonfiction (*Salvador* and *Miami*) the ambiguous relationship between the culture of the United States and the Spanish cultures of Central and South America.

Didion has contributed many short stories, articles, and reviews to magazines and has collaborated on several screenplays with her husband, novelist John Gregory Dunne.

As you read, notice how Didion steps into the background, choosing details with a reporter's objective eye.

O N THE ONE HUNDRED AND FIFTIETH ANNIVERSARY of the founding   1
of Dade County, in February of 1986, the *Miami Herald* asked four prominent amateurs of local history to name "the ten people and the ten events that had the most impact on the county's history." Each of the four submitted his or her own list of "The Most Influential People in Dade's History," and among the names mentioned were Julia Tuttle ("pioneer businesswoman"), Henry Flagler ("brought the Florida East Coast Railway to Miami"), Alexander Orr, Jr. ("started the research that saved Miami's drinking water from salt"), Everest George Sewell ("publicized the city and fostered its deepwater seaport"), Carl Fisher ("creator of Miami Beach"), Hugh M. Anderson ("to whom we owe Biscayne Boulevard, Miami Shores, and more"), Charles H. Crandon ("father of Dade County's park system"), Glenn Curtiss ("developer and promoter of the area's aviation potential"), and James L. Knight ("whose creative management enabled the *Miami Herald* to become a force for good"), this last nominee the choice of a retired *Herald* editorial writer.

There were more names. There were John Pennekamp ("conceived   2
Dade's metropolitan form of government and fathered the Everglades National Park") and Father Theodore Gibson ("inspirational spokesman for racial justice and social change"). There were Maurice Ferre ("Mayor for twelve years") and Majorie Stoneman Douglas ("indefatigable environmentalist") and Dr. Bowman F. Ashe ("first and longtime president of the University of Miami"). There was David Fairchild, who "popularized tropical plants and horticulture that have made the county a more attractive place to live." There was William A. Graham, "whose Miami Lakes is a model for real estate development," Miami Lakes being the area developed by William A. Graham and his brother, Senator Bob Graham, at the time of Dade's one hundred and fiftieth anniversay the governor of Florida, on three thousand acres their father had just west of the Opa-Locka Airport.

There was another Graham, Ernest R., the father of Bob and Wil- 3
liam A., nominated for his "experiments with sugarcane culture and dairy-
ing." There was another developer, John Collins, as in Collins Avenue,
Miami Beach. There were, as a dual entry, Richard Fitzpatrick, who
"owned four square miles between what is now Northeast 14th Street and
Coconut Grove," and William F. English, who "platted the village of
Miami." There was Dr. James M. Jackson, an early Miami physician.
There was Napoleon Bonaparte Broward, the governor of Florida who
initiated the draining of the Everglades. There appeared on three of the
four lists the name of the developer of Coral Gables, George Merrick.
There appeared on one of the four lists the name of the coach of the
Miami Dolphins, Don Shula.

On none of these lists of "The Most Influential People in Dade's 4
History" did the name Fidel Castro appear, nor for that matter did the
name of any Cuban, although the presence of Cubans in Dade County
did not go entirely unnoted by the *Herald* panel. When it came to naming
the Ten Most Important "Events," as opposed to "People," all four panel-
ists mentioned the arrival of the Cubans, but at slightly off angles
("Mariel Boatlift of 1980" was the way one panelist saw it), and as if this
arrival had been just another of those isolated disasters or innovations
which deflect the course of any growing community, on an approximate
par with the other events mentioned, for example the Freeze of 1895, the
Hurricane of 1926, the opening of the Dixie Highway, the establishment
of Miami International Airport, and the adoption, in 1957, of the metropolitan form of government, "enabling the Dade County Commission to
provide urban services to the increasingly populous unincorporated
area."

This set of mind, in which the local Cuban community was seen as 5
a civil challenge determinedly met, was not uncommon among Anglos to
whom I talked in Miami, many of whom persisted in the related illusions
that the city was small, manageable, prosperous in a predictable broad-
based way, southern in a progressive sunbelt way, American, and belonged to them. In fact 43 percent of the population of Dade County was
by that time "Hispanic," which meant mostly Cuban. Fifty-six percent of
the population of Miami itself was Hispanic. The most visible new buildings on the Miami skyline, the Arquitectonica buildings along Brickell
Avenue, were by a firm with a Cuban founder. There were Cubans in the
board rooms of the major banks, Cubans in the clubs that did not admit

Jews or blacks, and four Cubans in the most recent mayoralty campaign, two of whom, Raul Masvidal and Xavier Suarez, had beaten out the incumbent and all other candidates to meet in a runoff, and one of whom, Xavier Suarez, a thirty-six-year-old lawyer who had been brought from Cuba to the United States as a child, was by then mayor of Miami.

The entire tone of the city, the way people looked and talked and   6
met one another, was Cuban. The very image the city had begun presenting of itself, what was then its newfound glamour, its "hotness" (hot colors, hot vice, shady dealings under the palm trees), was that of prerevolutionary Havana, as perceived by Americans. There was even in the way women dressed in Miami a definable Havana look, a more distinct emphasis on the hips and décolletage, more black, more veiling, a generalized flirtatiousness of style not then current in American cities. In the shoe departments at Burdines and Jordan Marsh there were more platform soles than there might have been in another American city, and fewer displays of the running-shoe ethic. I recall being struck, during an afternoon spent at La Liga Contra el Cancer, a prominent exile charity which raises money to help cancer patients, by the appearance of the volunteers who had met that day to stuff envelopes for a benefit. Their hair was sleek, of a slightly other period, immaculate page boys and French twists. They wore Bruno Magli pumps, and silk and linen dresses of considerable expense. There seemed to be a preference for strictest gray or black, but the effect remained lush, tropical, like a room full of perfectly groomed mangoes.

This was not, in other words, an invisible 56 percent of the popula-   7
tion. Even the social notes in *Diario Las Americas* and in *El Herald*, the daily Spanish edition of the *Herald* written and edited for *el exilio*, suggested a dominant culture, one with money to spend and a notable willingness to spend it in public. La Liga Contra el Cancer alone sponsored, in a single year, two benefit dinner dances, one benefit ball, a benefit children's fashion show, a benefit telethon, a benefit exhibition of jewelry, a benefit presentation of Miss Universe contestants, and a benefit showing, with Saks Fifth Avenue and chicken *vol-au-vent*, of the Adolfo (as it happened, a Cuban) fall collection. One morning *El Herald* would bring news of the gala at the Pavillon of the Amigos Latinamericanos del Museo de Ciencia y Planetarium; another morning, of an upcoming event at the Big Five Club, a Miami club founded by former members of five fashionable clubs in pre-revolutionary Havana: a *coctel*, or cocktail party, at which tables

would be assigned for yet another gala, the annual "Baile Imperial de las Rosas" of the American Cancer Society, Hispanic Ladies Auxiliary. Some members of the community were honoring Miss America Latina with dinner dancing at the Doral. Some were being honored themselves, at the Spirit of Excellence Awards Dinner at the Omni. Some were said to be enjoying the skiing at Vail; others to prefer Bariloche, in Argentina. Some were reported unable to attend (but sending checks for) the gala at the Pavillon of the Amigos Latinamericanos del Museo de Ciencia y Planetarium because of a scheduling conflict, with *el coctel de* Paula Hawkins.

Fete followed fete, all high visibility. Almost any day it was possible to drive past the limestone arches and fountains which marked the boundaries of Coral Gables and see little girls being photographed in the tiaras and ruffled hoop skirts and maribou-trimmed illusion capes they would wear at their *quinces,* the elaborate fifteenth-birthday parties at which the community's female children came of official age. The favored facial expression for a *quince* photograph was a classic smolder. The favored backdrop was one suggesting Castilian grandeur, which was how the Coral Gables arches happened to figure. Since the idealization of the virgin implicit in the *quince* could exist only in the presence of its natural foil, *machismo,* there was often a brother around, or a boyfriend. There was also a mother, in dark glasses, not only to protect the symbolic virgin but to point out the better angle, the more aristocratic location. The *quinceañera* would pick up her hoop skirts and move as directed, often revealing the scuffed Jellies she had worn that day to school. A few weeks later there she would be, transformed in *Diario Las Americas,* one of the morning battalion of smoldering fifteen-year-olds, each with her arch, her fountain, her borrowed scenery, the gift if not exactly the intention of the late George Merrick, who built the arches when he developed Coral Gables.

Neither the photographs of the Cuban *quinceañeras* nor the notes about the *coctel* at the Big Five were apt to appear in the newspapers read by Miami Anglos, nor, for that matter, was much information at all about the daily life of the Cuban majority. When, in the fall of 1986, Florida International University offered an evening course called "Cuban Miami: A Guide for Non-Cubans," the *Herald* sent a staff writer, who covered the classes as if from a distant beat. "Already I have begun to make some sense out of a culture that, while it totally surrounds us, has remained inacces-

8

9

sible and alien to me," the *Herald* writer was reporting by the end of the first meeting, and, by the end of the fourth: "What I see day to day in Miami, moving through mostly Anglo corridors of the community, are just small bits and pieces of that other world, the tip of something much larger than I'd imagined. . . . We may frequent the restaurants here, or wander into the occasional festival. But mostly we try to ignore Cuban Miami, even as we rub up against this teeming, incomprehensible presence."

Only thirteen people, including the *Herald* writer, turned up for the   10
first meeting of "Cuban Miami: A Guide for Non-Cubans" (two more appeared at the second meeting, along with a security guard, because of telephone threats prompted by what the *Herald* writer called "somebody's twisted sense of national pride"), an enrollment which tended to suggest a certain willingness among non-Cubans to let Cuban Miami remain just that, Cuban, the "incomprehensible presence." In fact there had come to exist in South Florida two parallel cultures, separate but not exactly equal, a key distinction being that only one of the two, the Cuban, exhibited even a remote interest in the activities of the other. "The American community is not really aware of what is happening in the Cuban community," an exile banker named Luis Botifoll said in a 1983 *Herald* Sunday magazine piece about ten prominent local Cubans. "We are clannish, but at least we know who is who in the American establishment. They do not." About another of the ten Cubans featured in this piece, Jorge Mas Canosa, the *Herald* had this to say: "He is an advisor to U.S. Senators, a confidant of federal bureaucrats, a lobbyist for anti-Castro U.S. policies, a near unknown in Miami. When his political group sponsored a luncheon speech in Miami by Secretary of Defense Caspar Weinberger, almost none of the American business leaders attending had ever heard of their Cuban host."

The general direction of this piece, which appeared under the   11
cover line "THE CUBANS: *They're ten of the most powerful men in Miami. Half the population doesn't know it,*" was, as the *Herald* put it, "to challenge the widespread presumption that Miami's Cubans are not really Americans, that they are a foreign presence here, an exile community that is trying to turn South Florida into North Cuba. . . . The top ten are not separatists; they have achieved success in the most traditional ways. They are the solid, bedrock citizens, hard-working humanitarians who are role models for a

community that seems determined to assimilate itself into American society."

This was interesting. It was written by one of the few Cubans then 12 on the *Herald* staff, and yet it described, however unwittingly, the precise angle at which Miami Anglos and Miami Cubans were failing to connect: Miami Anglos were in fact interested in Cubans only to the extent that they could cast them as aspiring immigrants, "determined to assimilate," a "hard-working" minority not different in kind from other groups of resident aliens. (But had I met any Haitians, a number of Anglos asked when I said that I had been talking to Cubans.) Anglos (who were, significantly, referred to within the Cuban community as "Americans") spoke of cross-culturalization, and of what they believed to be a meaningful second-generation preference for hamburgers, and rock and roll. They spoke of "diversity," and of Miami's "Hispanic flavor," an approach in which 56 percent of the population was seen as decorative, like the Coral Gables arches.

Fixed as they were on this image of the melting pot, of immigrants 13 fleeing a disruptive revolution to find a place in the American sun, Anglos did not on the whole understand that assimilation would be considered by most Cubans a doubtful goal at best. Nor did many Anglos understand that living in Florida was still at the deepest level construed by Cubans as a temporary condition, an accepted political option shaped by the continuing dream, if no longer the immediate expectation, of a vindicatory return. *El exilio* was for Cubans a ritual, a respected tradition. *La revolución* was also a ritual, a trope fixed in Cuban political rhetoric at least since José Martí, a concept broadly interpreted to mean reform, or progress, or even just change. Ramón Grau San Martín, the president of Cuba during the autumn of 1933 and again from 1944 until 1948, had presented himself as a revolutionary, as had his 1948 successor, Carlos Prío. Even Fulgencio Batista had entered Havana life calling for *la revolución,* and had later been accused of betraying it, even as Fidel Castro was now.

This was a process Cuban Miami understood, but Anglo Miami did 14 not, remaining as it did arrestingly innocent of even the most general information about Cuba and Cubans. Miami Anglos, for example, still had trouble with Cuban names, and Cuban food. When the Cuban novelist Guillermo Cabrera Infante came from London to lecture at Miami-Dade Community College, he was referred to by several Anglo faculty members to whom I spoke as "Infante." Cuban food was widely seen not as a minute variation on that eaten throughout both the Caribbean and the Mediterranean but as "exotic," and full of garlic. A typical Thursday food section of the *Herald* included recipes for Broiled Lemon-Curry Cornish Game Hens, Chicken Tetrazzini, King Cake, Pimiento Cheese, Raisin Sauce for Ham, Sautéed Spiced Peaches, Shrimp Scampi, Easy Beefy Stir-Fry, and four ways to use dried beans ("Those cheap, humble beans that have long sustained the world's poor have become the trendy set's new pet"), none of them Cuban.

This was all consistent, and proceeded from the original construc-   15
tion, that of the exile as an immigration. There was no reason to be curious about Cuban food, because Cuban teenagers preferred hamburgers. There was no reason to get Cuban names right, because they were complicated, and would be simplified by the second generation, or even by the first. "Jorge L. Mas" was the way Jorge Más Canosa's business card read. "Raul Masvidal" was the way Raúl Masvidal y Jury ran for mayor of Miami. There was no reason to know about Cuban history, because history was what immigrants were fleeing. Even the revolution, the reason for the immigration, could be covered in a few broad strokes: "Batista," "Castro," "26 Julio," this last being the particular broad stroke that inspired the Miami Springs Holiday Inn, on July 26, 1985, the thirty-second anniversary of the day Fidel Castro attacked the Moncada Barracks and so launched his six-year struggle for power in Cuba, to run a bar special on Cuba Libres, thinking to attract local Cubans by commemorating their holiday. "It was a mistake," the manager said, besieged by outraged exiles. "The gentleman who did it is from Minnesota."

There was in fact no reason, in Miami as well as in Minnesota, to   16
know anything at all about Cubans, since Miami Cubans were now, if not Americans, at least aspiring Americans, and worthy of Anglo attention to the exact extent that they were proving themselves, in the *Herald*'s words, "role models for a community that seems determined to assimilate itself into American society"; or, as Vice President George Bush put it in a 1986 Miami address to the Cuban American National Foundation, "the most eloquent testimony I know to the basic strength and success of America, as well as to the basic weakness and failure of Communism and Fidel Castro."

The use of this special lens, through which the exiles were seen as   17
a tribute to the American system, a point scored in the battle of the

ideologies, tended to be encouraged by those outside observers who dropped down from the northeast corridor for a look and a column or two. George Will, in *Newsweek,* saw Miami as "a new installment in the saga of America's absorptive capacity," and Southwest Eighth Street as the place where "these exemplary Americans," the seven Cubans who had been gotten together to brief him, "initiated a columnist to fried bananas and black-bean soup and other Cuban contributions to the tanginess of American life." George Gilder, in *The Wilson Quarterly,* drew pretty much the same lesson from Southwest Eighth Street, finding it "more effervescently thriving than its crushed prototype," by which he seemed to mean Havana. In fact Eighth Street was for George Gilder a street that seemed to "percolate with the forbidden commerce of the dying island to the south . . . the Refrescos Cawy, the Competidora and El Cuño cigarettes, the *guayaberas,* the Latin music pulsing from the storefronts, the pyramids of mangoes and tubers, gourds and plantains, the iced coconuts served with a straw, the new theaters showing the latest anti-Castro comedies."

There was nothing on this list, with the possible exception of   18
the "anti-Castro comedies," that could not most days be found on Southwest Eighth Street, but the list was also a fantasy, and a particularly gringo fantasy, one in which Miami Cubans, who came from a culture which had represented western civilization in this hemisphere since before there was a United States of America, appeared exclusively as vendors of plantains, their native music "pulsing" behind them. There was in any such view of Miami Cubans an extraordinary element of condescension, and it was the very condescension shared by Miami Anglos, who were inclined to reduce the particular liveliness and sophistication of local Cuban life to a matter of shrines on the lawn and love potions in the *botánicas,* the primitive exotica of the tourist's Caribbean.

Cubans were perceived as most satisfactory when they appeared to   19
most fully share the aspirations and manners of middle-class Americans, at the same time adding "color" to the city on appropriate occasions, for example at their *quinces* (the *quinces* were one aspect of Cuban life almost invariably mentioned by Anglos, who tended to present them as evidence of Cuban extravagance, *i.e.,* Cuban irresponsibility, or childishness), or on the day of the annual Calle Ocho Festival, when they could, according to the *Herald,* "samba" in the streets and stir up a paella for two

thousand (10 cooks, 2,000 mussels, 220 pounds of lobster and 440 pounds of rice), using rowboat oars as spoons. Cubans were perceived as least satisfactory when they "acted clannish," "kept to themselves," "had their own ways," and, two frequent flash points, "spoke Spanish when they didn't need to" and "got political"; complaints, each of them, which suggested an Anglo view of what Cubans should be at significant odds with what Cubans were.

✇ Opening the Dialogue

1. Didion finds Cuban Americans reluctant to assimilate. Do you see this as a positive or a negative trait? Do you think Cuban Americans are correct in assuming that living in Florida is at best a temporary condition, or is this a form of self-deception?

2. In what ways do Cuban Americans share the aspirations of other middle class Americans? In what ways are their aspirations different?

3. Cuban Americans are among the most affluent groups in the United States, with a yearly income well above that of the average American. To what extent can they be held up as examples of the success of the American free enterprise system? To what extent is this a "gringo fantasy"?

✇ Keeping a Notebook

What neighborhood in your city or town has a distinct ethnic flavor? What gives it that flavor? In what ways does this neighborhood reflect the various groups who live there?

✇ Working Together

Working in groups, identify the different groups—ethnic as well as special interest—that are represented at your school. In what way does each make its presence felt? What do you feel the presence of different groups contributes to the educational environment of your school?

☺ Writing an Essay

Didion says that the Anglo idea of what Cubans should be is significantly at odds with what Cubans actually are. Write an essay in which you describe a group to which you belong to someone who is not familiar with it.

MICHAEL NAVA

Gardenland, Sacramento, California

Michael Nava was born in 1950 and grew up in the "Gardenland" neighborhood described in the following essay. Mexican-American and openly gay, Nava began to write poetry at the age of fourteen. He explains, "I began writing when I was fourteen because there was no safe place in my family to express my feelings. As I write in the essay, I am filled with all the words I never spoke as a child. In 'Gardenland' I am trying to speak those words, to honor the child I was, and to try to understand some of the forces that have made me the man I have become."

After receiving his law degree from Stanford University in 1981, Nava began work as a deputy city attorney for the city of Los Angeles, but after three years he quit to focus seriously on writing. Since then he has published a series of increasingly successful mystery novels featuring a gay Mexican-American hero. (These include *The Little Death, Goldenboy,* and *How Town.*) "Mystery readers tend to be a bit more intelligent and tolerant than average," Nava says. "Give them a good mystery and they'll take the rest."

More than conventional thrillers, Nava's mysteries are marked by their compassion and insight. He has often acknowledged the profound effect his homosexuality has had on his writing: "It went against the grain of everything I knew. I had to say to myself, 'I am a homosexual, and I am still a good human being,' notwithstanding what the Catholic Church, or my classmates, or my family members say. That act of compassion toward myself compels me to be compassionate toward others."

Note how Nava's selection of detail reveals himself as much as it does the world in which he grew up.

I GREW UP in a neighborhood of Sacramento called Gardenland, a poor   1
community, almost entirely Mexican, where my maternal family, the
Acunas, had lived since the 1920s. Sacramento's only distinction used to
be that it was the state capital. Today, because it frequently appears on
lists of the country's most livable cities, weary big-town urbanites have
turned it into a boomtown rapidly becoming unlivable. But when I was a
child, in the late fifties and early sixties, the only people who lived in
Sacramento were the people who'd been born there.

Downtown the wide residential neighborhoods were lined with   2
oaks shading turreted, run-down Victorian mansions, some partitioned
into apartments, others still of a piece, but all of them exuding a shadowy
small-town melancholy. The commercial district was block after block of
shabby brick buildings housing small businesses. The city's skyline was
dominated by the gold-domed capitol, a confectioner's spun-sugar dream
of a building. It was set in a shady park whose grass seemed always to
glisten magically, as if hidden under each blade of grass were an Easter
egg.

Sacramento's only other landmarks of note were its two rivers, the   3
American and the Sacramento. They came together in muddy confluence
beneath the slender iron joints of railroad bridges. Broad and shallow, the
rivers passed as slowly as thought between the thick and tumble of their
banks.

A system of levees fed into the rivers. One of these tributaries was   4
called the Bannon Slough. Gardenland was a series of streets carved out
of farmland backed up against the slough. It flowed south, curving east
behind a street called Columbus Avenue, creating Gardenland's southern
and eastern boundaries. The northern boundary was a street called El
Camino. Beyond El Camino was middle-class tract housing. To the west,
beyond Bowman Street, were fields and then another neighborhood that
may just as well have existed on another planet for all I knew of it.

What I knew were the nine streets of Gardenland: Columbus, Jef-   5
ferson, Harding, Cleveland, El Camino, Peralta, Wilson, Haggin, and
Bowman; an explorer, an odd lot of presidents, an unimaginative Spanish
phrase, and three inexplicable proper names, one in Spanish, two in English. It was as if the streets had been named out of a haphazard perusal
of a child's history text. There were two other significant facts about the
streets in Gardenland; they all dead-ended into the levee and their names

were not continued across El Camino Boulevard into the Anglo suburb, called Northgate. Gardenland's streets led, literally, nowhere.

Unlike El Camino, where little square houses sat on little square 6
lots, Gardenland had not been subdivided to maximum utility. Broad uncultivated fields stretched between and behind the ramshackle houses. Someone's "front yard" might consist of a quarter acre of tall grass and the remnants of an almond orchard. The fields were littered with abandoned farming implements and the foundations of long-gone houses. For a dreamy boy like me, these artifacts were magical. Finding my own world often harsh, I could imagine from these rusted pieces of metal and fragments of walls a world in which I would have been a prince.

But princes were hard to come by in Gardenland. Almost everyone 7
was poor, and most residents continued to farm after a fashion, keeping vegetable gardens and flocks of chickens. There were neither sidewalks nor streetlights, and the roads, cheaply paved, were always crumbling and narrow as country lanes. At night, the streets and fields were lit by moonlight and the stars burned with millennial intensity above the low roofs of our houses.

The best way to think of Gardenland is not as an American suburb 8
at all, but rather as a Mexican village, transported perhaps from Guanajuato, where my grandmother's family originated, and set down lock, stock, and chicken coop in the middle of California.

My cousin Josephine Robles had divided her tiny house in half and 9
ran a beauty shop from one side. Above her porch was a wooden sign that said in big blue letters GARDENLAND and, in smaller print below, BEAUTY SALON. Over the years the weather took its toll and the bottom half faded completely, leaving only the word GARDENLAND in that celestial blue, like a road sign to a cut-rate Eden.

By the time I was born, in 1954, my family had lived in Gardenland for at 10
least twenty-five years. Virtually all I know of my grandfather's family, the Acunas, was that they were Yaqui Indians living in northern Mexico near the American border at Yuma, Arizona. My grandmother's family, the Trujillos, had come out of central Mexico in 1920, escaping the displacements caused by the Mexican Revolution of 1910. I have dim memories of my great-grandparents, Ygnacio and Phillipa Trujillo, doll-like, white-haired figures living in a big, dark two-story house in east Sacramento.

My grandparents settled on Haggin Avenue in a house they built   11
themselves. My cousins, the Robles, lived two doors down. My family
also eventually lived on Haggin Avenue, next door to my grandparents.
Our house was the pastel plaster box that became standard suburban architecture in California in the fifties and sixties but it was the exception
in Gardenland.

Most houses seemed to have begun as shacks to which rooms were   12
added to accommodate expanding families. They were not built with privacy in mind but simply as shelter. We lived in a series of such houses
until our final move to Haggin Avenue. In one of them, the living room
was separated from the kitchen by the narrow rectangular bedroom in
which my brothers and sisters and I slept. Adults were always walking
through it while we were trying to sleep. This made for jittery children,
but no one had patience for our complaints. It was enough that we had a
place to live.

By the standards of these places, my grandparents' house was luxu-   13
rious. It was a four-bedroom, L-shaped building that they had built themselves. My grandmother put up the original three rooms while my grandfather was in the navy during World War II. My aunt Socorro told me
that my grandmother measured the rooms by having her children lie
head to toe across a plot of ground. She bought the cement for the foundations, mixed and troweled it, and even installed pipes for plumbing.
Later, when my grandfather returned, they added a series of long, narrow
rooms paneled in slats of dark-stained pine, solid and thick walled.

Massive, dusty couches upholstered in a heavy maroon fabric,   14
oversize beds soft as sponges, and a leather-topped dining room table
furnished the house. Like the rusted combines in the field, these things
seemed magical in their antiquity. I would slip into the house while my
grandparents were both at work and wander through it, opening drawers
and inspecting whatever presented itself to my attention. It was in this
fashion that I opened a little-used closet and found it full of men's clothes
that obviously were not my grandfather's. Later I learned that they had
belonged to my uncle Raymond who had been killed in a car accident. In
a subsequent exploration I found pictures of his funeral, including a picture taken of him in his casket, a smooth-faced, dark-skinned, pretty boy
of fifteen.

Another time, I found a voluminous red petticoat in a cedar chest.   15
Without much hesitation, I put it on and went into my grandmother's

bedroom where I took out her face powder and lipstick. I applied these in the careful manner of my grandmother, transforming myself in the dressing mirror beneath the grim gaze of a crucified Christ. Looking back, I don't think I was trying to transform myself into a girl, but only emulating the one adult in my family who loved me without condition. Because she was the soul of kindness, it never occurred to me, as a child, that my grandmother might be unhappy. Only looking back do I see it.

She and my grandfather slept in separate rooms at opposite ends of   16
their house. In the evening, my grandfather would sit on a couch in front of the television quietly drinking himself into a stupor while my grandmother did needlework at the kitchen table. They barely spoke. I would sit with my grandmother, looking at pictures in the *Encyclopedia Americana*, comfortable with the silence, which, to her, must have been a deafening indictment of a failed marriage.

In my parents' house, the marriage of my mother and stepfather   17
was as noisily unhappy as my grandparents' was quietly miserable. In each shabby house where we lived I would be awakened by their fights. I learned to turn myself into a stone, or become part of the bed or the walls so as to abate the terror I felt. No one ever spoke of it. There was only one house in which my family lived together peaceably but it only existed as a blueprint that had come somehow into my stepfather's possession.

In the evening, he would take it down from a shelf and unroll it on   18
the kitchen table. Together we would study it, laying claim to rooms, planning alterations. At the time, we lived in a tiny one-bedroom cinderblock house. My brother and I slept on a bunk bed in an alcove off the kitchen. At night, I could hear mice scampering across the cement floor, terrifying me when I woke up having to pee and pick my way through the darkness to the bathroom.

When we finally moved from the cinder-block house, it was to an-   19
other, bigger version of that house rather than to the dream house of the blueprint. One night, my mother's screaming woke me. I hurried into the bedroom she and my stepfather occupied and found him beating her. When I tried to stop him, he threw me across the room. The next morning my mother told me he was sorry, but it was too late. Where I lived no longer mattered to me because I learned to live completely within myself in rooms of rage and grief. Now I think these rooms were not so different from the rooms we all occupied, my unhappy family and I.

Although not literally cut off from the outside world, Gardenland was   20
little touched by it. We were tribal in our outlook and our practices. Anglos were generically called "paddies," whether or not they were Irish. All
fair-skinned people were mysterious but also alike. Even TV, that great
equalizer, only emphasized our isolation since we never saw anyone who
looked remotely like us, or lived as we did, on any of the popular shows
of the day. At school, the same homogeneity prevailed. Until I was nine
I attended a neighborhood grade school where virtually every other child
was like me, dark eyed and dark skinned, answering to names like Juarez,
Delgadillo, Robles, Martinez. My own name, Michael Angel, was but an
Anglicized version of Miguel Angel, a name I shared with at least three
other of my classmates.

I had a remarkable amount of freedom as a child. As I said, we even-   21
tually lived on the same street as other members of my maternal family
and I roamed their houses as unself-consciously as a Bedouin child might
move among the tents of his people. I ate in whatever house I found myself at mealtime and the meals were the same in each of my relatives'
houses—rice, beans, lettuce and tomato salad, stewed or fried meat, tortillas, salsa. My grandparents did not lock their doors at night—who did?
what was there to steal?—so that I could slip into their house quietly and
make my bed on their sofa when my parents were fighting.

But most of the time I spent outdoors, alone or with my friends. In   22
spring, the field behind my house was overrun with thistles. We neighborhood kids put in long days cutting trails through them and hacking
out clearings that became our forts. Tiring of the fields, we'd lurk in abandoned houses, empty barns, and chicken coops. When all other amuse-
ments failed, there was always Bannon Slough, a muddy brown creek that
flowed between thickly wooded banks. It was too filthy to swim in. Instead, in the steep shadows of bridges and railroad trestles we taught each
other how to smoke and to swear.

Just as often I would be off by myself. Early on, I looked for ways   23
to escape my family. I found it in the stillness of the grass and the slap of
the slough's brown water against the shore. There I discovered my own
capacity for stillness. Lying on the slope of the levee, I could hear my
own breath in the wind and feel my skin in the warm blades of grass that
pressed against my neck. In those moments, Gardenland *was* Eden, and I
felt the wonder and loneliness of the first being.

For, like Adam, I was lonely. Being everyone's child, I was no one's   24 child. I could disappear in the morning and stay out until dusk and my absence went unnoticed. Children barely counted as humans in our tribe. We were more like livestock and our parents' main concern was that the head count at night matched the head count in the morning.

My loneliness became as much a part of me as my brown hair and   25
the mole above my lip, something unremarkable. When I came out, I missed that sense of joining a community of others like me that so many of my friends describe. My habits of secrecy and loneliness were too deeply ingrained. I had become like my grandfather, who, in a rare moment of self-revelation, told me he was a "lone wolf"; the most unsociable of an unsociable tribe. Though I've changed as I've grown older, I still sometimes wonder if one reason I write is because I am filled with all the words I never spoke as a child.

Two things opened up for me the narrow passage through which I finally   26
escaped Gardenland for good. The first was books. I learned to read early and, once started, could not get enough of books. In this affinity, I was neither encouraged nor discouraged by my family. Education beyond its most basic functions, learning how to read and write, to do sums, had absolutely no interest for them. My love of reading became simply another secret part of me.

There wasn't a library in Gardenland. Instead, a big white van   27
pulled up to the corner of Wilson and El Camino, the city Bookmobile. Inside, patrons squeezed into a narrow passageway between tall shelves of books. The children's books occupied the bottom shelves. At the exit, a woman checked out books from a standing desk. The Bookmobile came once a week and I was a regular customer, always taking my limit of books.

Everything about the process pleased me. I was proud of my library   28
card, a yellow piece of cardboard with my name typed on it, which I carried in a cowhide wallet that was otherwise empty. I liked taking books from the shelves, noting their heft and volume, the kind of type, whether they were illustrated, and I studied the record of their circulation, the checkout dates stamped in blue on stiff white cards in paper pockets on the inside covers. I loved the books as much as I loved reading. To me, they were organic things, as alive in their way as I was.

Like so many other bright children growing up in the inarticulate   29
world of the poor, books fueled my imagination, answered my questions,

led me to new ones, and helped me conceive of a world in which I would not feel so set apart. Yet I do not believe that my brains alone, even aided by my bookish fantasies, would have been enough to escape Gardenland. For this, I needed the kind of courage that arises out of desperation.

I found this courage in my homosexuality. Early on, I acquired a   30
taste for reading history, particularly ancient history. I suppose that pictures of ruined Greek cities reminded me of the crumbling, abandoned
houses in the fields of Gardenland. But I was also fascinated by pictures
of the nude male statues. There was something about the smooth, headless torsos, the irisless eyes of ephebes that made me stop my idle flipping
through pages and touch the paper where these things were depicted. By
the time I was twelve I understood that my fascination was rooted in my
sexual nature. One day, walking to school, clutching my books to my
chest, girl-style, I heard myself say, "I'm a queer."

It was absolutely clear to me that Gardenland could not accommo-   31
date this revelation. Gardenland provided the barest of existences for its
people. What made it palatable was the knowledge that everyone was
about the same, united in ethnicity and poverty and passivity. The only
rituals were the rituals of family, and family was everything there. But I
knew that I was not the same as everyone else. And I was certain that my
family, already puzzled by my silent devotion to books, would reject me
entirely if it became known exactly what thoughts occupied my silence.

Had I been a different child I would have run away from home.   32
Instead, I ran away without leaving home. I escaped to books, to sexual
fantasy, to painful, unrequited crushes on male classmates. No one ever
knew. I turned myself into an outsider, someone at the margins of a community that was itself outcast. Paradoxically, by doing this, I learned the
peasant virtues of my hometown, endurance and survival. As a member of
yet another embattled community, those virtues I absorbed as a child
continue to serve me.

✆ Opening the Dialogue

1. According to Nava, Gardenland was cut off from the outside world.
What do you think were the disadvantages of this cultural isolation? Can
you think of any advantages?

2. The fact that Nava read books marked him as different. In what ways do you think reading isolated him from his community? What does this situation suggest about the values of his community?

3. Nava is Chicano, and he is also gay. Which of these two cultures do you think defines his identity more clearly?

☉ Keeping a Notebook

Should Nava have run away from home? Do you think his failure to leave showed cowardice or courage?

☉ Working Together

In his concluding paragraph Nava says that he was an outsider in a community that was itself an outcast. Working in groups, consider what things he learned in his hometown that prepared him for survival in the outside world. In class discussion, consider whether his experiences ultimately helped him or hurt him.

☉ Writing an Essay

Write about a time when you felt like an outsider. Include descriptions of yourself as well as the community from which you felt alienated.

Writing about Culture and Environment

1. Many of the essays in this chapter describe a person or place that helped the writer come to terms with his or her cultural roots. Describe a person—an entertainer or a civic leader, for example—who enabled you to realize the importance of your culture.

2. Michael Nava describes a place about which he has ambivalent feelings. Write an essay in which you, like Nava, describe a place about which you have mixed feelings. Make certain your description is balanced so that it clearly conveys your ambivalent feelings about your subject.

3. In "Silent Dancing" Judith Ortiz Cofer describes a home movie she and her mother watch. Locate a home movie, a videotape, or a photo album featuring pictures of one of your relatives. Write an essay in which you describe what you observe.

4. Suppose that you, like Jeanne Wakatsuki Houston and her family, are living in Manzanar. Write an anonymous letter to a local newspaper describing the conditions that exist in the camp. Assume that the people who will read your letter know little about what is occurring.

5. N. Scott Momaday powerfully describes his grandmother, who serves as a link between him and his family's traditions. Describe your own grandparents and explain how they provide a connection to your family's unique cultural identity.

CHAPTER 4

CULTURE AND
CUSTOM
EXPLAINING
PROCESSES

CARMEN LOMAS GARZA · CASCARONES (1989)

I made the decision to convert to Judaism shortly before my Bar Mitzvah. I had been raised as a Jew, but my mother was not Jewish, so technically neither was I. I wanted to give my Jewishness some sort of external legitimacy. I rode to a nearby *mikvah*—a ceremonial bath of pure water—with my father, my rabbi, and two witnesses who were family friends. In the waiting room outside the *mikvah* my rabbi asked me a few questions about why I wanted to become a Jew. The questions were not difficult. Soon he was satisfied, and the five of us entered the *mikvah*. At this point we removed our clothes and entered the bath, which was a small pool of warm, clear water about chest deep. Then my rabbi asked me to recite as many verses as I could of the *Sh'ma*, a prayer. When I finished, he told me to submerge myself in the water. I could feel his hand on my head, gently holding me down while they said several other short prayers. It was somewhat frightening to be held under water, but it did not last long. That was the ceremony. Later, my rabbi and the witnesses signed my certificate saying that I had been ritually converted.

Claude Platton, student

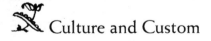 Culture and Custom

A **process** structure—a series of steps presented in a fixed order—has many applications in academic writing. It can, for example, be used to explain how legislation is proposed and passed, the process by which language changes, and numerous scientific and technical procedures. When they write about the American experience, writers can use process explanation to accomplish a variety of purposes. A process essay can explain the process of learning a vital survival skill—such as how to speak English, how to perform a job-related task, or how to master urban public transportation. Process essays can communicate an ethnic group's unique sense of its culture by explaining how its members create a craft, perform a dance, prepare a meal, or participate in a religious ceremony or cultural ritual. Writers can use process to help their readers understand the complexity of applying for permission to leave a country or becoming a citizen of another. Process can also have more subtle purposes. For example, writers may wish to identify the stages of a spiritual or intellectual enlightenment, explain a process of cultural assimilation, trace the steps toward identifying with a particular political or social movement, or describe the process of an individual's initiation into adulthood or a group's change of status.

The writers whose essays appear in this chapter use process to explore culture and custom as they attempt to come to terms with the place they, and others like them, occupy in American society. For example, they present the steps in a coming-of-age ritual, explain tribal marriage customs, recall a holiday celebration, and tell how to make a quilt that reflects America's complex heritage. As they write about these specific topics, the writers address themes central to all Americans—for Malcolm X (p. 163), trying to define his own racial identity; for Mourning Dove (p. 170), trying to explain social customs that shape her culture; for Ramón Pérez (p. 177), attempting to understand an alien culture by observing its rituals as he recalls those of his own culture; and for Whitney Otto (p. 182), finding common ground in American history. In much the same way, an essay that explains a process can help you describe customs that characterize your own cultural and national identity.

The following student essay explains the process by which a familiar custom is carried out—a process that helps the student to understand who she is.

STUDENT VOICE: HEIDI WENGERD

The Mennonite Footwashing Ceremony

Imagine for a moment a Sunday morning church service where   1 congregational singing is done in a cappella four-part harmony, where the people enjoy fellowship after the church service at a carry-in dinner, and where the strong support and love of a closely knit group of people is evident. Chances are you are imagining life in the Mennonite Church.

Mennonites are a Protestant denomination differing from others   2
in three major respects. The first is baptism. Mennonite institutions do not baptize infants, which makes us an Anabaptist denomination. Instead, the baptism ritual is performed when the child is old enough to make the decision to embrace Christianity voluntarily. A second strong Mennonite belief is pacifism. Mennonites strive to live peacefully and in harmony with their fellow humans in order to promote a world of peace and equality for all. Community is also important to the Mennonite tradition. We believe as a church body that we need to support and uplift one another, and to be humble enough to put others' needs before our own. We try to surround those in our community who are hurting and provide them with a support system on which they can lean. One of the rituals Mennonites practice that honors our heritage of humbleness is that of footwashing.

The traditional footwashing ceremony is based on the biblical   3
text in which Jesus washes his disciples' feet during the Last Supper and then instructs them: "Do you understand what I have done for you? Now that I, your Lord and Teacher, have washed your feet, you also should wash one another's feet" (John 13:12–14, New International Version). Footwashing is practiced today in most Mennonite churches across the country at various times throughout the year. My church incorporates the ceremony into our biannual communion service, in the spring and fall of each year.

The ceremony begins with ushers bringing chairs, towels, and   4 basins of water into the church sanctuary and placing them at the ends of every fifth or sixth pew. Our pastor begins the formal ceremony by reading the Bible and a statement written specifically for this ritual.

Men are asked to file to the basement, while the women stay in   5
the sanctuary. This is the only ceremony in which men and women are separated.

Once the men have left, the women remove their shoes, divide   6
into pairs (usually with other women on their pew), and line up by the basins. One partner kneels by the basin while the other sits on a chair. The kneeling woman takes each foot of her partner one at a time, holds it above the basin, splashes water on it, and dries it with a towel. The women then reverse positions.

At the end of the ritual, partners embrace and verbally bless   7
each other. They then return to their pews and sit quietly until the men return.

The ritual is the same for the men, who have basins, chairs, and   8
towels set up for them in the basement.

After the men return, a congregational hymn is sung with a mes-   9
sage of servanthood. A blessing is given by the pastor, and this concludes the formal ceremony.

This ritual has been a part of my life for as long as I can recall. It   10
is a way to remember to be humble; it is a time to reflect on the rich legacy the Mennonite heritage offers to those who are a part of it. It is a way to enact and follow the teachings of Jesus Christ; it is a time to strengthen the ties of our community of believers. It is a way to say, "This is who we are."

Explaining Processes

A **process** essay tells how a particular task or operation is accomplished, or how it is habitually carried out. A process essay can also describe how something—a machine, a system, an organization—works. Process, like narrative, relates events in chronological sequence, but a process, unlike a narrative, is made up of a series of steps that always occur or are performed in the same order. A process essay can take the form of an *explanation*, whose purpose is to help readers to understand how something works or how a process is carried out, or it can be written as a set of *instructions* designed to enable readers to perform the process themselves.

In their simplest form, process essays explain how to complete a physical task—how to perform CPR or bake a cake, for example. But process essays are more than recipes. Often they describe complex (even abstract) processes, and they can be persuasive as well as informative.

USING CHRONOLOGICAL SEQUENCE

When you write process essays, you should *follow strict chronological sequence,* presenting steps in the exact order in which they are performed and avoiding the flashbacks used in narrative essays. You should show how each step in the process logically follows the one before it, so that the entire sequence is clear. Avoid digressions or detours that do not contribute to the flow of the sequence. (If several steps occur simultaneously, or if some steps overlap in time, be careful to make this clear.) Be sure to avoid repetition, asides, and backtracking, which can confuse readers or slow them down.

USING VERB TENSES

You should also be sure to *use consistent verb tenses*—generally either past tense (to describe a process that has occurred in the past) or present tense (to describe a process that occurs regularly). Thus Mourning Dove, in "Marriage Customs among the Salishan" (p. 170), uses past tense to describe traditional tribal customs: "For an important marriage the chief *presided,* aided by his wife. He *passed* a pipe around the room. . . . " To describe a ritual that occurs regularly, however, Heidi Wengerd uses present tense in "The Mennonite Footwashing Ceremony" (p. 156): "Once the men have left, the women *remove* their shoes, *divide* into pairs . . . and *line up* by the basins."

USING STATEMENTS AND COMMANDS

When you write a process explanation, your goal is to enable readers to understand the process you describe. Therefore, you should generally *use clear declarative statements*, as Heidi Wengerd does in the following sentence: "The ceremony begins with ushers bringing chairs, towels, and basins into the church sanctuary and placing them at the ends of every fifth or sixth pew."

When you write a set of instructions, however, *use imperative statements (commands)*. In this case, readers expect to be able not only to understand or visualize but also to perform the process; your purpose is to tell them exactly what they must do to duplicate your steps. Therefore, in "How to Make an American Quilt" (p. 182), Whitney Otto tells us to "*Take* material from clothing that belongs to some family member or friend or lover. . . . "

USING TRANSITIONS

As you write and revise process essays, *choose transitions carefully*, being sure you have enough transitions so readers can follow (and, if necessary, duplicate) the process. Also be sure you have selected the transitions that will most accurately define the relationships among the steps in the process. Malcolm X does this when he describes the process of having his hair chemically straightened in "My First Conk" (p. 163):

He made me sit down, and he tied the string of the new rubber apron tightly around my neck, *and* combed up my bush of hair. *Then*, from the big vaseline jar, he took a handful and massaged it hard through my hair and into the scalp. He *also* thickly vaselined my neck, ears and forehead.

KEY TRANSITIONS: PROCESS

First (second, third, and so on)	Meanwhile
After that	While
Then	Before
Next	Now
At the same time	Finally

BEING THOROUGH AND PRECISE

In addition to using careful sequencing, consistent verb tense, and appropriate transitions to clarify the order of steps and the relationships among them, you should carefully *revise your process essays for completeness and precision of detail.* Process essays that describe a set of physical tasks, for instance, should include a list of the materials needed to perform the process. This list should appear early in the essay, as it does in "My First Conk," where Malcolm X explains that he purchased "a can of Red Devil lye, two eggs, and two medium-sized white potatoes" at one location and "a large jar of vaseline, a large bar of soap, a large-toothed comb and a fine-toothed comb, one of those rubber hoses with a metal spray head, a rubber apron and a pair of gloves" at another. Similarly, Whitney Otto begins "How to Make an American Quilt" with "What you need:" followed by "You need a large wooden frame and enough chairs to accommodate it."

As you write and revise always keep your audience's needs in mind. Remember that your goal is for readers to understand exactly how the process works (and, in some cases, to duplicate it). For this reason, it is important that you include specific details: exact measurements for distances and sizes, and exact descriptions of colors and shapes. For the same reason, it is important that no steps be omitted. (In a long or complex process essay, related steps can be grouped into stages.) In addition, an essay that gives instructions for a process readers may perform themselves should include explanations, reminders, and warnings to protect readers from frustration or failure—or even danger. Thus Whitney Otto warns, "When you choose your colors, make them sympathetic to one another," and Malcolm X's friend reminds him, "'Never use a metal spoon; the lye will turn it black.' "

REVIEW CHECKLIST: EXPLAINING PROCESSES

✓ Follow strict chronological sequence.

✓ Use consistent verb tenses.

✓ Use declarative statements for explanations and imperative statements for instructions.

✓ Choose transitions carefully.

✓ Be thorough and precise.

MALCOLM X

My First Conk

Revered as liberator, denounced as racist, Malcolm X lived a life as paradoxical as his legacy. He was born Malcolm Little in 1925 in Omaha, Nebraska. According to Malcolm's autobiography, his father, an avid supporter of black separatism, was brutally murdered by white supremacists when Malcolm was a child. The emotional and financial strain led to his mother's institutionalization, and her eight children were placed separately in foster homes. Despite these harrowing difficulties, Malcolm was an excellent student in high school and dreamed of becoming a lawyer, a dream that dissolved in anger and despair when a white teacher advised carpentry instead and told him to "be realistic about being a nigger." He quit school soon after.

After becoming a pimp and a drug dealer, Malcolm turned to robbery to support his own drug addiction; in 1946, three months before his twenty-first birthday, he was sentenced to ten years in prison. There, Malcolm began studying the teachings of Elijah Mohammed, founder of the radical black separatist Nation of Islam. Abandoning the "slave name" of Little, he adopted Malcolm X; upon his release in 1952 he became an articulate and aggressive spokesman for black separatism and espoused a radical agenda in the fight for civil rights, insisting that blacks must fight racism with "any means necessary."

Malcolm X eventually became estranged from Elijah Mohammed and, after a pilgrimage to Mecca, underwent a cathartic transformation. As he explained in *The Autobiography of Malcolm X*, "Since I learned the *truth* in Mecca, my dearest friends have come to include all kinds—some Christians, Jews, Buddhists, Hindus, agnostics, and even atheists! I have friends who are called capitalists, Socialists, and Communists! Some of my friends are moderates,

conservatives, and extremists—some are even Uncle Toms! My
friends today are black, brown, red, yellow, and *white!"*

Perceiving him as a threat, members of the Nation of Islam con-
spired to kill him, and on February 21, 1965, Malcolm X was assassinated at the Audubon Ballroom in Harlem.

The following selection is from *The Autobiography of Malcolm X* by
Alex Haley, published posthumously to critical acclaim. In 1985
Charles Nichols wrote: "[It] is probably the most influential book
read by this generation of Afro-Americans. . . . Paradoxically, the
book, designed to be an indictment of American and European
bigotry and exploitation, is a triumphant affirmation of the possibilities of the human spirit."

In this excerpt, notice how Malcolm X describes a process in a
way that suggests a larger political and social meaning.

SHORTY SOON DECIDED that my hair was finally long enough to be   1
conked. He had promised to school me in how to beat the barbershops'
three- and four-dollar price by making up congolene, and then conking
ourselves.

I took the little list of ingredients he had printed out for me, and   2
went to a grocery store, where I got a can of Red Devil lye, two eggs, and
two medium-sized white potatoes. Then at a drugstore near the pool-
room, I asked for a large jar of vaseline, a large bar of soap, a large-
toothed comb and a fine-toothed comb, one of those rubber hoses with
a metal spray-head, a rubber apron and a pair of gloves.

"Going to lay on that first conk?" the drugstore man asked me. I   3
proudly told him, grinning, "Right!"

Shorty paid six dollars a week for a room in his cousin's shabby   4
apartment. His cousin wasn't at home. "It's like the pad's mine, he spends
so much time with his woman," Shorty said. "Now, you watch me—"

He peeled the potatoes and thin-sliced them into a quart-sized   5
Mason fruit jar, then started stirring them with a wooden spoon as he
gradually poured in a little over half the can of lye. "Never use a metal
spoon; the lye will turn it black," he told me.

A jelly-like, starchy-looking glop resulted from the lye and pota-   6
toes, and Shorty broke in the two eggs, stirring real fast—his own conk
and dark face bent down close. The congolene turned pale-yellowish.
"Feel the jar," Shorty said. I cupped my hand against the outside, and
snatched it away. "Damn right, it's hot, that's the lye," he said. "So you
know it's going to burn when I comb it in—it burns bad. But the longer
you can stand it, the straighter the hair."

He made me sit down, and he tied the string of the new rubber   7
apron tightly around my neck, and combed up my bush of hair. Then,
from the big vaseline jar, he took a handful and massaged it hard all
through my hair and into the scalp. He also thickly vaselined my neck,
ears and forehead. "When I get to washing out your head, be sure to tell
me anywhere you feel any little stinging." Shorty warned me, washing his
hands, then pulling on the rubber gloves, and tying on his own rubber
apron. "You always got to remember that any congolene left in burns a
sore into your head."

The congolene just felt warm when Shorty started combing it in.   8
But then my head caught fire.

I gritted my teeth and tried to pull the sides of the kitchen table   9
together. The comb felt as if it was raking my skin off.

My eyes watered, my nose was running. I couldn't stand it any   10
longer; I bolted to the washbasin. I was cursing Shorty with every name I
could think of when he got the spray going and started soap-lathering my
head.

He lathered and spray-rinsed, lathered and spray-rinsed, maybe   11
ten or twelve times, each time gradually closing the hot-water faucet,
until the rinse was cold, and that helped some.

"You feel any stinging spots?"   12

"No," I managed to say. My knees were trembling.   13

"Sit back down, then. I think we got it all out okay."   14

The flame came back as Shorty, with a thick towel, started drying   15
my head, rubbing hard. "*Easy, man, easy!*" I kept shouting.

"The first time's always worst. You get used to it better before long.   16
You took it real good, homeboy. You got a good conk."

When Shorty let me stand up and see in the mirror, my hair hung   17
down in limp, damp strings. My scalp still flamed, but not as badly; I
could bear it. He draped the towel around my shoulders, over my rubber
apron, and began again vaselining my hair.

I could feel him combing, straight back, first the big comb, then   18
the fine-tooth one.

Then, he was using a razor, very delicately, on the back of my   19
neck. Then, finally, shaping the sideburns.

My first view in the mirror blotted out the hurting. I'd seen some   20
pretty conks, but when it's the first time, on your *own* head, the transformation, after the lifetime of kinks, is staggering.

The mirror reflected Shorty behind me. We both were grinning   21
and sweating. And on top of my head was this thick, smooth sheen of
shining red hair—real red—as straight as any white man's.

How ridiculous I was! Stupid enough to stand there simply lost in   22
admiration of my hair now looking "white," reflected in the mirror in
Shorty's room. I vowed that I'd never again be without a conk, and I never
was for many years.

This was my first really big step toward self-degradation: when I   23
endured all of that pain, literally burning my flesh to have it look like a
white man's hair. I had joined that multitude of Negro men and women
in America who are brainwashed into believing that the black people are
"inferior"—and white people "superior"—that they will even violate and
mutilate their God-created bodies to try to look "pretty" by white standards.

Look around today, in every small town and big city, from two-bit   24
catfish and soda-pop joints into the "integrated" lobby of the Waldorf-
Astoria, and you'll see conks on black men. And you'll see black women
wearing these green and pink and purple and red and platinum-blonde
wigs. They're all more ridiculous than a slapstick comedy. It makes you
wonder if the Negro has completely lost his sense of identity, lost touch
with himself.

You'll see the conk worn by many, many so-called "upper class"   25
Negroes, and, as much as I hate to say it about them, on all too many
Negro entertainers. One of the reasons that I've especially admired some
of them, like Lionel Hampton and Sidney Poitier, among others, is that
they have kept their natural hair and fought to the top. I admire any
Negro man who has never had himself conked, or who has had the sense
to get rid of it—as I finally did.

I don't know which kind of self-defacing conk is the greater   26
shame—the one you'll see on the heads of the black so-called "middle
class" and "upper class," who ought to know better, or the one you'll see

on the heads of the poorest, most downtrodden, ignorant black men. I mean the legal-minimum-wage ghetto-dwelling kind of Negro, as I was when I got my first one. It's generally among these poor fools that you'll see a black kerchief over the man's head, like Aunt Jemima; he's trying to make his conk last longer, between trips to the barbershop. Only for special occasions is this kerchief-protected conk exposed—to show off how "sharp" and "hip" its owner is. The ironic thing is that I have never heard any woman, white or black, express any admiration for a conk. Of course, any white woman with a black man isn't thinking about his hair. But I don't see how on earth a black woman with any race pride could walk down the street with any black man wearing a conk—the emblem of his shame that he is black.

To my own shame, when I say all of this I'm talking first of all about   27
myself—because you can't show me any Negro who ever conked more faithfully than I did. I'm speaking from personal experience when I say of any black man who conks today, or any white-wigged black woman, that if they gave the brains in their heads just half as much attention as they do their hair, they would be a thousand times better off.

☜ Opening the Dialogue

1. Seeing how prevalent processed hair and colored wigs are makes Malcolm X "wonder if the Negro has completely lost his sense of identity, lost touch with himself" (paragraph 24). Today such blatant attempts to "look white" have largely been abandoned. Why do you think this is so?

2. Do you believe straightening hair or making other attempts to erase physical characteristics identified with particular racial or ethnic groups is on the same level as wearing a corporate uniform—that is, simply a pragmatic attempt to "blend in"? Or do you see it as something more—for example, an explicit denial of racial identity, or even an expression of racial self-hatred?

3. Since the time Malcolm X wrote his essay, African Americans have begun adopting styles that affirm their heritage—for instance, wearing African dress and accessories, using urban black vernacular, adopting hairstyles such as dreadlocks and cornrows, and wearing T-shirts and baseball caps whose pictures and slogans are identified with black issues

and heroes. Do you see this development as positive, or do you think such expressions of African-American identity have a negative side?

4. How are standards of beauty established in a culture? Who sets the standards? Who represents the ideal?

☺ Keeping a Notebook

Do you believe such a thing as a neutral or "American" style of appearance and dress exists? If so, what individuals or institutions define this "average" appearance? What advantages do you believe are gained by someone who has such an appearance? Do you think attaining such a neutral or average appearance is more important for some groups—for example, adolescents—than for others?

☺ Working Together

Working in groups, decide under what circumstances, if any, you would alter your appearance to eliminate distinctively ethnic, racial, or regional characteristics:

- To get a job or promotion
- To "fit in" in a new neighborhood or school
- To avoid discrimination
- To make yourself more appealing to a boyfriend or girlfriend
- To win elective office

Then, decide to what extent you would be willing to go to achieve this appearance:

- Conform to a dress code
- Cut, dye, straighten, or curl your hair
- Invest in a new wardrobe
- Wear colored contact lenses
- Undergo plastic surgery
- Wear a wig
- Take speech classes

In class discussion, try to balance the reasons for making such changes against the reasons for refusing to do so. What principles are involved? Do these principles change according to the extent of the changes or the motivation for making them? To what extent should people have to conform? How should the rights of the individual be balanced against the demands of an employer or a society?

⊛ Writing an Essay

Explain a process you went through to change your appearance in some way. What prompted this change? How did people react? Was it worth it?

Mourning Dove
(Christine Quintasket)

Marriage Customs among the Salishan

Mourning Dove (Christine Quintasket) was the first Native American woman to publish a novel, *Cogewea* (1927). By her own account, she was born about 1885 in a canoe while her mother was crossing the Idaho River. She grew up on the Colville Reservation in eastern Washington state, and when she died in 1936 (of "exhaustion from manic depressive psychosis"), she left no children, no debt, no savings.

Her legacy is the collection of manuscripts and rough drafts that were edited by Jay Miller into a remarkable autobiography, *Mourning Dove*, in 1990. Quintasket's life was difficult, emotionally and financially. She worked primarily as a seasonal laborer and never enjoyed a stable home or support in her ambition to write. Determined to fight the deeply ingrained stereotype of Native Americans as stoic and unemotional, she offered her clearest statement of her goals as a writer in an interview in 1916: "It is all wrong, this saying that Indians do not feel as deeply as whites. We do feel, and by and by some of us are going to be able to make our feelings appreciated, and then will the true Indian character be revealed."

Fiercely protective of her privacy, she originally chose "Morning Dove" as her pen name as symbolic of the dawning of her career, but in light of the obstacles she faced, found "Mourning Dove" and its tragic overtones more appropriate. Working by night after exhausting days spent picking apples or cleaning other people's homes, Quintasket kept secret her ambition to write a novel sympathetic to Native Americans. When word of its publication became known, she faced deep suspicion and hostility from both family and neighbors—and in fact was accused of having merely lent her name to a white man's work.

Quintasket, who saw herself as a mediator between the white and Native American worlds, perceived literacy as the means to reconciliation. Her autobiography is a valuable contribution to the history of her people and an account of a difficult life made meaningful by the overwhelming need to write.

The following account of Salishan marriage customs is a good example of how process description can be used to present an anthropological perspective on personal culture.

[AMONG THE SALISHAN PEOPLE] if a man wanted a girl to be his wife, he 1
did not go directly to her and begin courting, because she was very well chaperoned. He first came to visit her parents on the pretext of a social call, returning several times if he felt welcomed and encouraged. He gave the father presents of robes and ponies. A few days later he came back and gave other gifts to the grandparents, chaperon, and other near relatives with influence on the girl. Finally, he sent his mother or other close female relative to ask the father of the girl for her to be his wife.

Usually there was a great deal of consultation among the relatives 2
until all were satisfied with the match. Then the parents gave their consent. Sometimes the chief of the tribe was consulted alone by the mother or chaperon, or they took the wife of the chief into their confidence to ask the advice of her husband on the alliance. For the marriage of important people, the whole community had to reach a satisfied consensus.

Everyone was concerned with the character of the groom and the 3
quality of his family before they reached an agreement. Usually the girl had the final right to approve or reject this man; however, her parents felt they knew what was best for her and the family. Sometimes they would force a marriage the bride did not want or like, but if she had been properly raised and knew her place in society, she went along with the wisdom of her elders.

Parents decided when a girl was available for marriage. A com- 4
moner was usually married early, before age twenty, because she became a burden to her poor parents due to the extra work of feeding both her and the chaperon, who received no compensation other than food and

clothing. The daughter of a chief usually married around twenty because her parents could afford to take care of her longer. . . .

A marriage was seldom conducted in public unless the girl was a   5
princess. Then the ceremony took place with the whole village as witnesses, resting comfortably in a circle under the shade of the council lodge or a sunshade of boughs. A marriage between commoners was held in the tipi home of the bride, with just their families gathered together for the occasion.

The groom arrived on the day of the marriage with his family, who   6
set up camp next to that of the bride. At the proper time, he walked into the lodge of the girl with his relatives following, and all of them sat on one side. The girl and her family sat across the fire from them.

For an important marriage the chief presided, aided by his wife. He   7
passed a pipe around the room so each could share a smoke in common. In this way the families were publicly united to banish any past or future disagreements and thus stood as "one united." The chief then gave the couple an oration of his advice, pointing out the good characteristics of each, and then offered his congratulations to them for a happy future.

The father of the girl took her by the hand and led her to meet the   8
groom at the back of the tent or middle rear of the gathering. In this manner he gave his daughter in marriage to the man. The husband then removed the virgin's cape from his wife's shoulders so all could now view her form. This declared them married for all to see. They then sat upon the finest robes with their most prominent guests. Food was then provided by both sets of parents, a wedding feast shared by everyone to rejoice in the uniting of the two families.

The first night the couple slept at the home of the bride. The hus-   9
band removed the buckskin bloomers worn by the girl, and the work of the chaperon was finished.

The next day the couple left to live at the camp of the husband's   10
people, often moving into his parents' home. A newly married couple usually did not live alone until they had children, making their old home too small for all of them. Yet if the groom was of poor family, they might move in with the family of the bride and stay there for several years until they had collected enough material to set up their own household.

When a bride moved in with her mother-in-law, she took over all   11
the hard work of the tipi. The older woman retired from heavy work,

content to sit, rest, or sleep while the daughter-in-law worked continuously. If the new bride was inclined to be lazy or was unwilling to get up mornings after the old woman called, the mother-in-law would beat her legs and feet. A new wife seldom talked back to her in-laws. Sometimes her sisters-in-law also abused her in an overbearing way, but her husband usually would not come to her rescue because ancient teachings held that she had to learn her own place in the new family.

If a man tired of a woman soon after marriage or left her for another   12
woman, she might continue to live with his parents if she had made a place for herself, faithfully doing all the housework and food preparation in the hope that her husband would return to her some day. Next to the dog, the native woman had no equal in taking abuse from "her man." On other occasions a woman who was abandoned would return to her own parents to stay until she was ready to remarry. Then she would appear in public with her face decorated with red paint to challenge [encourage] another marriage proposal. A woman who was abandoned was considered lawfully divorced and thus honorably entitled to another husband.

If she truly loved the man and felt ashamed at the desertion, she   13
might hang herself from a tree branch, throw herself into the river, or plunge onto a sharp weapon. Her suicide would be blamed on her abandoner.

A woman who committed adultery disgraced her family and was   14
either lawfully killed by a male relative, who shot her with an arrow, or offered the chance to commit suicide to save her family from adverse criticism, reproach, or gossip. Her "feelings" were never considered, only the lawful resentment of her community.

An Indian woman would have only one husband at a time, and if   15
she married too many times she was marked by lost decency and became known as "Mrs. Many Husbands."

If a woman had been previously married, a man courted her in a   16
different way. He might visit her family several times without speaking directly to her. He would look at her beauty and watch her skills at cooking, cleaning, and sewing. If he was satisfied, he took some small pebbles and threw them near her when no one else was paying attention. If she was in favor of him, she tossed some pebbles back to him to encourage the proposal. Then he left and held conferences with his own relatives. Meanwhile, she was doing the same with her close kin. If everyone

agreed, the man then went to wait for her at the place where her camp got water. When she came, he would quietly ask for the marriage. If she accepted, he walked into her tipi just before bedtime and sat on her bed. If she allowed this, that was a public declaration of their marriage. Everyone else in the tipi gave each other an understanding look and offered congratulations and advice for their future happiness.

A husband could have as many wives as he could support, so polyg-   17
amy was a mark of wealth. These wives seldom lived together in one tipi; each usually had her own home. Often the youngest was the favorite who lived with his parents so that his mother could keep a watchful eye on her and also have a strong helper. Other wives had separate homes or lived with relatives, receiving meat and visits from the husband in turn. In return, each made him moccasins, clothing, and other artistic gifts as a dutiful wife. She showed these to the co-wives, who advised and helped each other as the need arose. As long as all were satisfied with their influential status as the lawful wives of an important man, all went smoothly.

When a man died, his wife mourned for a period of at least one   18
year. A longer period of mourning meant that she truly loved him and held him with regard in her heart. She did not look after her appearance, remaining unkempt in old clothing till she was ready to remarry. Whenever she appeared in public wearing good clothing and red face paint, men knew she was ready to marry again. Often a dead husband's brother or another close male relative had first claim on the status of husband so as to perpetuate the alliance between the two families. If such a man wanted his former sister-in-law, he came forward and proposed; otherwise he made himself scarce so the woman could arrange another marriage.

If a woman decided she did not want to be the wife of a man who   19
held such a "mortgage right" to her, she went to him and asked permission to marry someone of her own choice. Such a personal request was usually granted. Sometimes mutual consent was involved, and both people found themselves at liberty to choose the spouse each wanted.

If a woman married someone else without asking permission of the   20
"mortgage-holder," however, her former in-laws had the right to duel with the new husband, fighting with either bow and arrows, a long spear, or a rough-and-tumble wrestling match with a stone knife, the opponents slashing each other until one of them was badly wounded or killed. The best man would win the woman, who followed him out of fear or grati-

tude that she was loved or wanted strongly enough that men would fight over her.

Much of this devotion, concern, and love was missed by white peo- 21 ple, who often failed to understand the native perspective. A man never openly showed affection to a woman in public unless he intended to make light and sport of her character. Even though legally married to a woman, he never showed the true feeling of his heart, as a white man does in kissing and embracing a woman. An Indian who did this would shame the woman and call her character into serious question. It was told that in primitive times an Indian man never kissed a woman in any love-making. He did embrace her close to his heart in his affections, but never in a physical sense unless they were quite alone. A faithful woman was satisfied that her spouse loved her by the very nature of his stoicism.

◉ Opening the Dialogue

1. To some extent, social class influences the customs Mourning Dove describes. How does class determine differences among marriage customs in our society?

2. "Marriage Customs among the Salishan" describes practices on a reservation in Washington state in the early part of the twentieth century. What does the essay reveal about the role of women in this place and time? What do marriage customs reveal about the status of women in our society?

3. Which seems to be most important in Salishan society—the individual, the family, or the community? Which do you believe *should* be of primary importance?

◉ Keeping a Notebook

What aspects of the customs Mourning Dove describes strike you as most "foreign"? Which of the customs associated with marriage in our society would a Salishan find most alien?

❧ Working Together

Working in groups, compile a list of marriage customs with which you are familiar. In class discussion, determine which customs are unique to a particular culture and which (perhaps in a slightly different form) are practiced in several cultures. What can you conclude about the universality of marriage customs?

❧ Writing an Essay

Write a set of guidelines delineating the unwritten rules of courtship and marriage in the community with whose customs you are most familiar. You may interpret *community* to mean members of your age group, school, ethnic group, or neighborhood.

RAMÓN PÉREZ

The Day of the Dead

Ramón "Tianguis" Pérez was born in San Pablo Macuiltianguis (hence his nickname), a small village in the state of Oaxaca, Mexico. He moved to Mexico City in the late 1970s and became involved in the revolutionary movement led by Florencio "Guero" Modranos. After the movement collapsed following the death of Modranos, Pérez drifted through a series of menial jobs and crossed the border several times to live in Texas, Oregon, and California as an "illegal alien," or undocumented immigrant.

The following selection is taken from Pérez's memoir, *Diaro de un Mojado (Diary of an Undocumented Immigrant,* 1991, translated by Dick J. Reavis.) In the United States and Mexico, Pérez has worked as a carpenter, busman, newspaper reporter, and laborer. He and his wife now live in Xalapa, Vera Cruz, Mexico, where Pérez is a photographer. *Diary of an Undocumented Immigrant* is his only book to date.

Note how Pérez uses his explanation of the Day of the Dead ceremony to make a point about differences between Mexican culture and practices in the United States.

I T IS THE DAY before Halloween. I receive a letter from my parents in   1
Mexico saying that they are fine and that one of our cows has given birth
to a beautiful calf. In the letter, they remind me that the Day of the Dead
is coming up; they tell me that they understand that I can't be with them,
and they wish me the best in celebrating it. I write back a long letter to
them, telling them about my job . . . and about the nostalgia I feel for the
All Souls Day and Day of the Dead festivals in our village.

Anybody would miss our celebration. I can almost hear the tolling   2
of the bell from the church tower, while up and down the streets the

cross is carried by someone who, because of the gravity of the ceremony, appears to be a walking statue. With a missal in his hands the cantor walks alongside, repeating the Our Father, keeping rhythm with his steps. One the other side of the cross goes whoever is responsible for carrying the vase of holy water. He dips a yellow *zempoalxochitl,* or dead man's flower, into the vase, withdrawing the flower to make the sign of the cross on every door. Behind these three figures follows a crowd of those who like to accompany the cross, many of them children. All of them must be respectful; it is forbidden to laugh or play. To make sure that gravity and order are kept, the *Ta ruehda,* or keeper of the church keys, goes along, supported by his helpers who are armed with the *Yetih shquia,* a type of quirt made from the penis of a bull. It is an effective tool for punishments, but it also gives rise to mischief. Some of the companions of the cross always try to provoke a punishment, by laughing behind the backs of innocents, for example. When that happens, the hand that holds the quirt cuts through the air until it cracks on the shoulders or back of the individual who is suspected, who can accuse someone else if he wants.

One time a friend of mine named Ignacio was infatuated with one   3
of the girls in the village, but he hadn't made his feelings known, even though she was waiting for him to tell her. On the feast of All Saints Day—the day prior to Day of the Dead—Ignacio followed the cross to her house. When it got there, he brought punishment on himself several times, in order to show the girl that he was really *macho.* The next day Ignacio went walking in the streets, his back striped with the bruises the whip had left, and the young woman took that opportunity to offer help in healing his wounds.

After they've prayed for the dead, the householders give the com-   4
panions of the cross shots of *mezcal,* baked sweet potatoes, oranges, chewing gum, whatever they can afford to give. Then the man carrying the cross leads the procession on to the next house. The cantor and carrier both tire, and have to be replaced every few hours, and the companions of the cross tire, too, but new followers join the procession. After all of the houses have been visited, the cross returns to its place in the church until the next year.

In my parents' house, the altar is probably completely adorned with   5
zempoalxochitl flowers, turkey crest flowers and rat flowers, and with bunches of bananas of all kinds, with oranges, lemons, candies, *mezcal,*

tortillas, red *mole,* tamales, cookies, soft drinks, water, chocolate, beer, breads made in the shape of people, and in the middle of it all, a cooked chicken. Everything is arranged around the images of the saints so that at the appointed hour, the dead can come and savor these delicacies, because they won't be served like this again until next year.

During one of these festivals, I remember talking to my short little   6 grandmother. We had asked her how she knew that the dead come back on their day. She said that she'd known of a case of a daughter who had told her dying mother that if she returned from the grave, she wanted her to make a sign. The two had agreed that the sign would be a noise made by shaking their kitchen table. When the mother died, the daughter anxiously awaited All Souls Day to prepare the altar and to wait for her mother's return at midnight. My grandmother said that the daughter saw her mother come into the door, accompanied by other spirits walking single file, each of them with a candle in hand. As they'd agreed, the mother went to the table and shook it. As she and the spirits walked out, each handed a candle to the daughter. When the sun came up the next morning, relatives of the daughter found her dead in the doorway. The candles in her hands had turned into a bundle of bones.

"Why did the daughter die?" we'd asked my grandmother.   7

"Her mother took her with her, so that the daughter wouldn't con-   8 tinue suffering in this world," was the answer that my grandmother gave.

In our village, the festivals of the dead last two or three days, dur-   9 ing which no one works. But here in the United States there's no great celebration, as my parents imagine. I tell them in my letter that people work as usual during what is called Halloween, and that at night, the people dress up like warlocks, or hunchbacks or pirates, or in short, any disguise that seems frightening, so that they can get together with friends, dance and drink beer. That kind of celebration seems simple and cold, to my point of view.

Of course, I also tell them that the children dress in disguises and   10 go from door to door saying "Trick or Treat," which is about like saying, "Candy or I'll harm you," and the owners of houses keep on hand a good store of sweets to give the children. I spend Halloween night with the landlady, giving candy to the children who come by. She tells me that the children have sometimes done damage on Halloween, breaking windows and writing on walls.

She recalls for me Day of the Dead celebrations in Querétaro,   11 where she was born, and from which she and her husband emigrated some forty years ago. Her husband had come to Texas as a *bracero*. When his employer arranged permanent immigration papers for him, he went back to Querétaro to bring her. Since then, she's returned only once, in 1965, when her father died. She still has relatives in Mexico, but everyone has lost touch. "Now," she says, "it won't be long before it will be our turn to rest forever."

"You still seem pretty hale," I say, merely not to confirm what she's predicted.   12

"Ah, what of it? Our time is coming! My husband could go any day,   13 and me, too. All we've got is the house, and we're thinking about selling it, if we can find someone who will let us live here as renters until the end."

"Have you liked the United States?" I ask her, to change the sub-   14 ject.

"Well, I don't know what to tell you. One gets used to wherever   15 one has to in order to make a living. From what I remember of my village, we were poor. Here, we're not rich but at least we have the house and we've raised our children and that's what God has permitted us to do."

Groups of children come by and the landlady gives each of them a   16 fistful of candy. Most of the children are accompanied by their parents.

"Poor things," the landlady says as she watches some children go   17 off, candy-filled bags in their hands. "Today the parents go with their children for fear that somebody is going to poison them, as has happened on some Halloweens. There are people who are sick in the head who've put poison or pins in the candies, and some children have died because of this. All of a sudden there are crazy people all over the United States," she says.

🕉 Opening the Dialogue

1. In paragraph 2 Pérez comments, "Anybody would miss our celebration." Later in his essay he dismisses Halloween, saying, "That kind of celebration seems simple and cold, to my point of view" (paragraph 9). Does Pérez convince you that the Mexican Day of the Dead is intrinsically more meaningful and significant than Halloween?

2. In what way do you think the differences between Halloween and the Day of the Dead might mirror the differences between American and Mexican attitudes toward horror and death?

3. Over the years, has Halloween become more associated with violence and crime in American society? In your neighborhood? Do you, like Pérez's landlady, see a link between the way Halloween is celebrated today and the emergence of what she calls "crazy people all over the United States" (paragraph 17)?

Keeping a Notebook

What rituals from your childhood do you miss the most? What is it about them that makes you miss them? For example, are they associated with special times, keepsakes, people, or places?

Working Together

Is there a uniquely "American" way of celebrating a particular holiday, or do celebrations vary from culture to culture or from community to community? Choose one holiday celebrated by everyone in your group, and compile a list of all the things each person associates with the celebration. In class discussion, consider whether in a multicultural society there can be a truly "American" way of celebrating a holiday.

Writing an Essay

Assuming the point of view of an individual far from home, perhaps in a foreign country, write a nostalgic explanation of how a cherished holiday is observed in your family or community. Include details about the sounds and smells of the holiday as well as the sights.

WHITNEY OTTO

How to Make an American Quilt

Five years after earning a B.A in history from the University of
California at Irvine, Whitney Otto returned to graduate school.
"Not to learn to write," she has said, "but to support a habit. Writ-
ing schools provide you with time, community, and support."
Born and raised in California, Otto was working in San Francisco
when she began studying for an M.F.A. degree. "I figured out that
I needed help to be able to write. I thought that graduate school
would enable me [to have] the 'silence' I need to write."

A short story written for a workshop became *How to Make an American Quilt* (1991), considered by the *New York Times Book Review* "a
remarkable first novel. . . . It is a tribute to an art form that allowed women self-expression even when society did not. Above
all, though, it is an affirmation of the strength and power of individual lives, and the way they cannot help fitting together."

The quilting instructions that begin each chapter of the novel
bind together the fictional stories of the women in the quilting
group. Soon after *How to Make an American Quilt* was published,
Otto commented: "I suppose some people think that this is going
to be a sweet or instructional book. But it had occurred to me
that quilting was a good way to write about women's lives. We
are always having to juggle and piece together separate parts to
make a whole. The art is the whole of the thing."

Note that Otto's description of quilt making is written in the
form of instructions, using imperative verbs.

W HAT YOU NEED: 1
     You need a large wooden frame and enough space to accommodate   2
it. Put comfortable chairs around it, allowing for eight women of varying
ages, weight, coloring, and cultural orientation. It is preferable that this
large wood frame be located in a room in a house in Atwater or Los Banos
or a small town outside Bakersfield called Grasse. It should be a place that
gets a thick, moist blanket of tule fog in the winter and be hot as blazes
in the summer. Fix plenty of lemonade. Cookies are a nice complement.
     When you choose your colors, make them sympathetic to one an-   3
other. Consider the color wheel of grammar school—primary colors,
phenomena of light and dark; avoid antagonism of hues—it detracts from
the pleasure of the work. Think of music as you orchestrate the shades
and patterns; pretend that you are a conductor in a lush symphony hall,
imagine the audience saying *Ooh* and *Ahh* as they applaud your work.
     Patterns with tiny, precise designs always denote twentieth-century 4
taste.
     Your needles must be finely honed so you do not break the weave   5
of your fabric. The ones from England are preferable. And plenty of
good-quality thread, both to bind the pieces and adorn the quilt. Embroidery thread is required for the latter. You will need this to hold the work
together for future generations. Unless you are interested in selling your
quilt at an art fair or gallery, in which case the quilt will still need to be
held together for generations of people you will never meet.
     The women who circle the frame should be compatible. . . . When   6
you have assembled the group, once a week for better than thirty-five
years, give or take some latecomers, you will be ready to begin the traditional, free-form *Crazy Quilt.*
     The *Crazy Quilt* was a fad of the nineteenth century and as such is 7
not truly considered Art, yet still it has its devotees. It is comprised of
remnants of material in numerous textures, colors; actually, you could not
call the squares of a *Crazy Quilt* squares, since the stitched-together
pieces are of all sizes and shapes. This is the pattern with the least amount
of discipline and the greatest measure of emotion. Considering the eight
quilters surrounding the frame in the room of the house in the small town
outside Bakersfield called Grasse, considering the more than thirty-five
years it will reveal, perhaps some emerging images will be lambs or yellow roses or mermaids, entwined wedding rings or hearts in states of dis-

repair. You will find this work to be most revealing, not only in the material contributions to the quilt, but in who enjoys sewing them and who does not. This random piecing together.

What you should understand when undertaking the construction   8
of a quilt is that it is comprised of spare time as well as excess material. Something left over from a homemade dress or a man's shirt or curtains for the ktichen window. It utilizes that which would normally be thrown out, "waste," and eliminates the extra, the scraps. And out of that which is left comes a new, useful object.

Take material from clothing that belongs to some family member   9
or friend or lover (if you find yourself to be that sort of a girl). Bind them together carefully. Wonder at the disparity of your life. Finger the patches representing "lover" and meditate on the meaning of illicit love in early American society. Failing that, consider the meaning of the affair in today's time frame.

The Roanoke Island Company, founded by Sir Walter Raleigh in   10
1585, completely disappeared—all 117 men, women, and children—by 1590 with no one knowing exactly what took place during that five-year period, and a single word carved into a tree the only viable clue: CROATOAN. No historian has figured out what that means. This you will find as the genesis and recurring theme in America as founded by the English: that we are a people fraught with mysteries and clues; there are things that cannot be fathomed.

Do not forget that the Norse, Spanish, French, Italians, and god   11
knows who else arrived before the English, relative latecomers to this place, and that the Indians stood on the shores, awaiting them all. These same Indians were exploited by the English, who were lazy and preferred to spend their time smoking tobacco on the banks of the James River rather than till the soil, expecting "someone else" to do it for them. Killing themselves by the end of the first winter because, as they emphatically told the Indians, *We are not farmers. We are explorers,* then demanded their provisions. Some say this is where the seeds of slavery were sown. An institution the English were not devious enough to come up with on their own, instead adopting it from the Spanish, who had been dealing in African flesh for a number of years. But that is another story.

Consider that women came across the Atlantic from the beginning   12
and were not allowed to vote until 1920. A quick calculation leaves you

wondering about those hundreds of years in between. You are curious about their power, their spheres of influence. Most historians agree that the first president voted in by the women was a washout, a different sort of man than Washington, Lincoln, Jefferson, and so on. Men can take credit for those presidents.

Recall that women who came to newly colonized America often   13
outlived their husbands and that it was not uncommon, in those early Virginia days, for them to be widowed and inherit, remarry, be widowed and inherit, remarry, and so on. This, you would think, may have been a frightening cycle to a number of men in the area, never knowing when their number was up, so to speak. But with so few careers open to women at the time, they simply made the best with what they had to work with. Not unlike fashioning a quilt from scraps, if you think about it. And there weren't that many of them, proportionally speaking. With that sort of social arrangement, you find yourself wondering if all these husband deaths were strictly due to natural causes; but to conjecture such a thought, without historical verification, would be to assume the worst about the early settlers. No reputable historian would suggest such a thing: duplicitous, untrustworthy, murderous women. Not just any women, but *wives.*

She used whatever material she had at hand and if she was too   14
overburdened with work she could ask her husband, sweetly, with sugar in her voice, to please, please look into acquiring an indentured servant. England, experiencing a bit of an economic crisis, had a surplus of unemployed citizens it was not much interested in caring for, and Virginia, Tidewater, and Maryland took on the look of an acceptable repository. Ah, but that is to confuse convicts with indentures and, really, they are not the same. An indentured servant is more like a slave, whereas a convict is more like a caged man. Different. You see.

Later, a turn in England's financial fortunes led to a drop-off of peo-   15
ple interested in coming to America as servants, what with renewed opportunity at home (and that unholy Atlantic crossing), and an attempt to fill the resulting American employment gap paved the way for African-American slavery. But that is another story.

The nineteenth century brought an explosion of ideas to the con-   16
cept of the quilt, of a woman's political voice. Not to mention the domestic conflicts of the Revolutionary War, followed by the Civil War (with

one or two small—by comparison—skirmishes in between). Ignore the
fact that the Revolution still left some unequal and the Civil War had a
rather specific definition of brother against brother, neglecting to include
color or gender. That, too, is another story.

Your concern might be trying to reduce your chosen quilt topic to   17
more manageable dimensions. For example, the Revolutionary War could
be defined as a bloody betrayal. One can almost hear the voice of Mother
England crying, "But you are mine. An extension of me. You promised to
be faithful, to send back your riches and keep me in a style to which I
have become accustomed." America's answer something like: "I need my
space. It isn't that I am not fond of you. We can still maintain a friendly
trading relationship."

There is the Civil War, which is a conflict of the blood tie. No one   18
fights dirtier or more brutally than blood; only family knows its own
weakness, the exact placement of the heart. The tragedy is that one can
still love with the force of hatred. Feel infuriated that once you are born
to another, that kinship lasts through life and death, immutable, un-
changing, no matter how great the misdeed or betrayal. Blood cannot be
denied, and perhaps that is why we fight tooth and claw, because we
cannot, being only human, put asunder what God has joined together.

Women were witness to Abraham Lincoln's assassination. Find   19
some quality silk and cotton in red, white, and blue. Cut white stars in the
evening as you sit on your summer porch. Appliqué the letters that spell
out your name, your country, your grief. Stitch across the quilt a flag held
in the beak of a dove. Ponder the fact that you could not vote for the man
but will defy any male citizen who will not allow you your measure of
sorrow at the president's sudden death. Say something in cloth about the
Union lasting, preserved. Listen to the men expound their personal satisfaction in glory of the vote. Listen to them express surprise that you, too,
would like to vote and be heard. They might say, *This is not your concern,*
and conclude that perhaps you are too idle at home and should consider
having another child.

Save your opinions for your quilt. Put your heart and voice into it.   20
Cast your ballot; express your feelings regarding industrialization, emancipation, women's suffrage, your love of family.

Send away for silk ribbon printed with black-lined photolitho-   21
graphs. Try your hand at doing these ink drawings yourself. Experiment
with the colors newly available from nineteenth-century factories: pea-

cock blue, scarlet, jade green, eggplant, and amber. Save a scrap of vel-
vet. For texture.

As the nineteenth century draws to a close, be sure to express your   22
gratitude for the "improvements" in your life; you can drive your own
buggy, attend college, or work in a textile factory in Lowell, Massachusetts. And do not forget the popular magazines like *Peterson's* or *Godey's
Lady's Book*, which encourage the decorative quilt over the story quilt (the
quilt with a voice), as it can safely be displayed outside the bedroom
without offense. Place it in the parlor. Simply to work a pattern and color
with no ulterior thought is the mark of a woman of leisure and reflects
well on her husband.

You want to keep these things in mind: history and family. How   23
they are often inseparable. In the twentieth century you may feel that all
those things that went before have little to do with you, that you are
made immune to the past by the present day: All those dead people and
conflicts and ideas—why, they are only stories we tell one another. History and politics and conflict and rebellion and family and betrayal.

Think about it.   24

✥ Opening the Dialogue

1. In addition to writing instructions for how to make a quilt, Otto is also
writing about larger issues—community cooperation, historical docu-
mentation, family unity, women's solidarity, and preservation of values
and traditions. Why do you suppose she chooses quilt making as a metaphor for these issues? Is it an appropriate one?

2. Otto says, "Save your opinions for your quilt. Put your heart and voice
into it. Cast your ballot. . . . " (paragraph 20). Is the idea of quilt making
as a political statement a reasonable one? Could it be considered counterproductive, or even reactionary? Is Otto telling women to channel their
political energies into domestic pursuits? Or is she saying something else?

3. In paragraph 23 Otto says, "You want to keep these things in mind:
history and family. How they are often inseparable." Whom do you think
she is addressing here (and throughout the selection)? Do you see family
and history as connected in your life?

⟨€⟩ Keeping a Notebook

What associations does the idea of making a quilt have for you? For example, what kind of people do you envision as engaged in this activity? Do you see quilt making as rooted in a particular time and place? What other processes have similar associations for you?

⟨€⟩ Working Together

"Think about it" Otto says (paragraph 24), referring to the question of whether or not the events of history really have anything to do with our lives today. Working in groups, decide on some specific historical events—wars, elections, famines, natural disasters, terrorist acts, political changes—that you believe have had a direct impact on the way you live. In class discussion, try to agree on the relative importance of these events. What conclusions can you draw about those historical events deemed most important? To what extent does when and where the events occurred affect your assessment of their relative importance?

⟨€⟩ Writing an Essay

How would you make an American quilt? What colors, fabrics, pictures, and patterns would you use? What group would you assemble to work on the project? How would you intertwine family, community, cultural, and national history? What would you use to bind the quilt pieces together? What would you call your quilt?

Writing about Culture and Custom

1. Write a set of instructions explaining how to become a "typical" student at your college. Focus on the clothing and possessions such a student would have to acquire and the behavior and customs he or she would need to adopt in order to belong to your college's dominant culture.

2. Explain a ritual or ceremony important to members of your religious or ethnic group, as Mourning Dove and Ramón Pérez do. Direct your explanation to an audience who is unfamiliar with the ceremony you describe. Try to do more than just describe the process; provide insight as well.

3. Create a recipe for a dish familiar to people in the region in which you live. Write your essay as a set of instructions, but expand your instructions with anecdotes and background information that will help to explain the significance of the dish in your geographic area.

4. Trace the process by which you became a member of a particular community within your town or school (a social clique, a political group, or a social action organization, for example). How difficult was it to become accepted?

5. For Malcolm X, straightening his hair served as a coming-of-age ritual, a rite of passage through which he confronted his culture. Identify the stages you went through as you developed your ethnic or racial identity.

CHAPTER 5

PERCEPTIONS OF CULTURE
DISCOVERING THROUGH EXAMPLES

CHARLES ALSTON, "WALKING" (1958)

At the time my parents left, Poland was still a country under Communist rule. Many of the things that they now take for granted in the United States were impossible to obtain in their native land. It was unheard of, for example, to own a private house, so large families were forced to live in single-roomed apartment complexes that were very cramped and often in bad condition. Entering a store, you would always find the shelves empty. Food was rationed. Meat was hard to find, and candy and fresh fruits were considered luxuries. Because it was a rare occurrence to see candy in stores and because of the great demand for it, children would savor every single lick of a lollipop, often tenderly rewrapping it to save it for a later time. In order to get bread, shoppers would have to leave before sunrise and stand in long lines for hours, frequently to be told there was none left when they finally got into the store.

Urszula Kathie Bujnowska,

student

Perceptions of Culture

Examples are a vital part of virtually all academic writing. In essay exams, business letters, literary analyses, and research papers, effective examples can support your generalizations. Because **exemplification** can illustrate and particularize unfamiliar concepts, it is an ideal strategy for writing about diverse cultures. Thus writers whose subject is the American experience can illustrate the complexity of immigration laws or make concrete the problems associated with assimilation. They can also use exemplification to spell out the economic difficulties they have faced or to show exactly how they learned about prejudice. Because exemplification can help explain an abstract idea that readers might find strange or alien, writers often use it to examine cultural rituals and customs or to discuss how certain institutions—such as a church or a settlement house—have helped to maintain the cultural identity of a community.

The writers whose works are collected in this chapter use examples for a variety of purposes. Virtually all of them use examples to shed light on general or abstract concepts. In his essay "In Search of Bruce Lee's Grave" (p. 205), for example, Shanlon Wu describes his need to discover Asian heroes in the United States. Certainly this is a difficult concept to convey, especially to readers who may not feel the need to identify with Asian male role models. Wu is able, however, to convey the importance of finding Asian heroes by examining his obsession with Bruce Lee. This analysis, more than any general discussion, makes his search for a strong Asian male image concrete and understandable.

In "The Media's Image of Arabs" (p. 210), Jack Shaheen uses a number of specific, carefully chosen examples to convince readers that his conclusions are reasonable. It is one thing to assert that the media portray Arabs unfairly; it is far more effective to illustrate this statement, as Shaheen does, with a range of examples drawn from television and movies. These examples serve as the evidence that validates Shaheen's position and convinces readers that his points are worth considering.

Other writers in this chapter use examples—anecdotes, for instance—calculated to draw readers into their essays as well as to clarify concepts or to convince. Notice in the following paragraph from "Just Walk on By" (p. 199) how Brent Staples uses several disturbing examples to focus attention on the point he is making:

> In that first year, my first away from my hometown, I was to become thoroughly familiar with the language of fear. At dark, shadowy intersections in Chicago, I could cross in front of a car stopped at a traffic light and elicit the *thunk, thunk, thunk, thunk* of the driver—black, white, male, or female—hammering down the door locks. On less traveled streets after dark, I grew accustomed to but never comfortable with people who crossed to the other side of the street rather than pass me. Then there were the standard unpleasantries with police, doormen, bouncers, cab drivers, and others whose business it is to screen out troublesome individuals *before* there is any nastiness.

In your own writing, exemplification can help you convey your ideas and experiences to readers. For instance, you can use a series of examples to show readers how certain character traits make a member of your family interesting and unique. You can also use exemplification to illustrate how your school's culturally diverse curriculum makes it a good place to get an education, or how instances of cultural misunderstanding create tensions in your neighborhood. In addition, you can present examples that support your position about a political, ethical, or social issue—for example, that non-native speakers should have access to bilingual education programs. Finally, you can use exemplification to illustrate the distinctive character of a particular group's language, food, or dress.

Notice in the following essay how the writer uses examples to support her impressions.

STUDENT VOICE: MIRIAM CASIMIR

Look at Me

Being one of the few black students at a predominantly white   1
college has not been easy. Often I am really unhappy about the
way certain people at school react toward me. Lately, I have felt
the stigma of being black more and more.

One recent thing that made me feel especially uncomfortable   2
was people's reaction to my newly braided hair, which I see as a
sign of my Afrocentrism. It amazed me how my fellow African
Americans looked at me with admiration while my white counter-
parts stared at me in total bewilderment—or was it disapproval? I
often wondered who it was they saw when they looked at me. Did
they see the black man who snatched their pocketbook? Or was it
the drug dealer who shot the police officer who lived down the
street? Or maybe it was the black prostitute who sells her body to
support her habit?

Many times I have felt them stare at me. At school I felt their   3
stares during the time I braided my hair. Outside of school I felt

their gaze just about every day of my life. Many times I have seen in my own life what Brent Staples refers to as his ability to "alter public space in ugly ways." I remember one particular time when my family and I were at a restaurant that had very few blacks in it (aside from the ones in the kitchen). My sister and I were waiting in line to use the ladies' room when the woman directly in front of us shifted her pocketbook when she saw us behind her. My sister, who is quick to rectify injustices, said, "Don't bother moving it on account of me." The woman said with a sickening sweetness, "Oh, Oh, that's not why I moved it." But we could see her embarrassment, so we knew what had motivated her. How could this woman think that my sister, a sophomore in dental school, and I, a college freshman, would want to take something out of her pocketbook? Couldn't she *see* that we were intelligent young women? Couldn't she *see* that we were not felons?

I have come to realize through trial and error that some white   4
folks will never see me for anything other than just what Paule Marshall in her book *Brown Girl, Brownstones* calls a "negro, some flat, one-dimensional, bas-relief figure." I have given up trying to "prove" that I am "okay." I have come to the realization that I am who I am: a young, black, bursting-with-potential woman. I don't have to apologize for my color. I won't listen when well-meaning but ignorant people say things about my people like "You can't help your color" or "It's just a lack of proper training or education."

My people, the African Americans, are beautiful. Our strength,   5
determination, and integrity have sustained us from slavery to freedom. I will wear my color as a badge of honor. I'll consider being

black a privilege. Finally, when I get my hair braided again, I won't wonder "Why do they stop and stare?" I'll know the reason.

Discovering through Examples

An example is a concrete instance of a general or abstract idea. **Exemplification** is a way of supporting, explaining, and developing ideas that enables writers to spell out in concrete terms exactly what they mean. Without examples most essays would be no more than collections of general statements that readers would have great difficulty understanding. This is because abstract concepts—such as love, prejudice, or patriotism—can best be explained by means of examples, which connect writers' general ideas to their readers' experience. Since examples are so useful, almost every essay in this book—regardless of pattern—uses them to illustrate, support, and enliven general discussions.

Before you begin your essay, gather as many examples as you can. Personal experiences, class discussions, observations, conversations, and reading (textbooks, newspapers, magazines) can all serve as sources of useful examples. Your goal should be to collect examples that are varied and interesting. As you do so, you should look for material that is provocative, unusual, and even controversial. These are the kinds of examples that readers are likely to find not only convincing but also engaging and memorable. In addition, you should try to gather examples that are representative and relevant to your topic.

USING ENOUGH EXAMPLES

As you write and revise, be sure you *use a sufficient number of examples.* No rule determines exactly how many examples to use in an essay. In some cases, using several brief examples provides the best way to appeal to your readers. In others, a single *extended example* is enough to establish your credibility. The number of examples you need depends to a large extent on the audience you are addressing and the point you are trying to make.

In "Just Walk on By," Brent Staples uses several related examples drawn from his own experience to advance the somewhat shocking idea that a lone African-American male is an object of fear to many Americans. The cumulative effect of several brief, provocative examples enables Staples to convince readers of something that a single example, no matter how compelling, could not—that the attitude he describes is widely held.

In some cases, though, a single extended example is sufficient— and perhaps more effective than several short ones. Because an extended example can be so compelling, it may be all that is necessary for a writer to make a point. Moreover, several short examples might not have the emotional impact or the depth of a single extended example, and possibly might even distract readers. In her essay "Look at Me" (p. 193), Miriam Casimir focuses on an extended example to support her point. By describing a white woman's reaction to her sister and herself, she illustrates the subtle but far-reaching prejudice that many African Americans face daily.

The most common method of structuring an exemplification essay is by combining short and long examples. In "The Myth of the Latin Woman" (p. 220), for instance, Judith Ortiz Cofer combines both types of examples and gains the advantages of each. Mixing three extended examples of prejudice with brief vignettes about her childhood, she effectively illustrates her point that Anglos constantly make unfounded and offensive assumptions about Puerto Rican women.

Using Representative Examples

Be careful to *select examples that represent the full range of your topic.* Examples that pertain to one aspect of a topic or that support one point of view at the expense of all others can be misleading and dishonest. Writers know that to be convincing they must cite examples that fairly represent all aspects of the topic about which they are writing. In "The Media's Image of Arabs," for example, Jack Shaheen wants to support his point that the American media stereotype Arabs. In order to convince readers that his assertion is valid, he includes a variety of familiar examples, primarily from popular movies and television programs. By doing so, he avoids the charge that he is using atypical or skewed examples to make his case. (Of course, Shaheen could have strengthened his essay even more by including examples from other media, such as magazines and newspapers, as well.)

USING RELEVANT EXAMPLES

It is not enough to use representative examples; you should also *use relevant examples.* Occasionally, especially when presenting brief examples, you may unintentionally include some that are not germane to your topic. Because such irrelevant digressions can confuse or distract your readers, you should edit carefully to identify and delete any irrelevant details. Imagine how confusing it would be, for example, if Jack Shaheen included in his essay a discussion of the Arab-Israeli conflict, or if Miriam Casimir included in her essay a digression about the 1964 Civil Rights Act. As you read the essays in this section, notice how the writers limit their examples to those that directly address the points they are making. (Jack Shaheen, for example, discusses *only* how Arabs are portrayed by the media, and Miriam Casimir recounts *only* the experiences that support her assertions about race and fear.)

USING TRANSITIONS TO IDENTIFY EXAMPLES

When you revise, *include transitional words and phrases* that help readers to understand your essay and keep examples distinct from one another.

KEY TRANSITIONS: EXEMPLIFICATION

For example	Thus
For instance	The first (second, third) example
Namely	Another example
Specifically	

If you are dealing with just a few examples, it often makes sense to arrange them in order of increasing importance—that is, to begin with the least important example and move toward the most significant one. If you do this, your transitions should indicate the progression: "One important example . . ."; "The most important example . . . " At other times you may want to begin and end with your strongest examples and include other examples in between. However you arrange examples, though, the transitional words and phrases you select should move readers easily from one example to the next.

REVIEW CHECKLIST: DISCOVERING THROUGH EXAMPLES

✓ Use a sufficient number of examples.
✓ Use representative examples.
✓ Use relevant examples.
✓ Include transitional words and phrases.

BRENT STAPLES

Just Walk on By

Brent Staples, the youngest member of the *New York Times* editorial board, has been described as a "black at the very heart of white power, perhaps one of the most successful blacks of his generation."

His beginnings were not auspicious. The son of a truck driver, Staples was born in 1951 in Chester, Pennsylvania, a place he has characterized as "an angry, heavily black, heavily poor, industrial city southwest of Philadelphia." (As he describes in another essay on p. 301, his brother succumbed tragically to this violent environment.)

He was recruited by Widener College's only African-American professor, went on to earn a Ph.D. from the University of Chicago, and after seven years as a reporter for the *Chicago Sun-Times* won a spot as one of only two African-American members of the *New York Times* editorial board.

When he was hired, Staples was assertive about his role as a journalist. "I did not want to do black issues. . . . Why should the color of my skin limit what I want to do intellectually? I write on intellectual politics and culture. We have a Scotsman on the black beat."

In addition to writing essays and editorials, Staples is the author of magazine articles, book and theatre reviews, and *Parallel Time: A Memoir.*

As you read "Just Walk on By," one of Staples's most frequently anthologized essays, notice how he has organized his examples, beginning with the extended example about his first "victim."

M

Y FIRST VICTIM was a woman—white, well dressed, probably in   1
her early twenties. I came upon her late one evening on a deserted street
in Hyde Park, a relatively affluent neighborhood in an otherwise mean,
impoverished section of Chicago. As I swung onto the avenue behind
her, there seemed to be a discreet, uninflammatory distance between us.
Not so. She cast back a worried glance. To her, the youngish black
man—a broad six feet two inches with a beard and billowing hair, both
hands shoved into the pockets of a bulky military jacket—seemed men-
acingly close. After a few more quick glimpses, she picked up her pace
and was soon running in earnest. Within seconds she disappeared into a
cross street.

That was more than a decade ago. I was 22 years old, a graduate   2
student newly arrived at the University of Chicago. It was in the echo of
that terrified woman's footfalls that I first began to know the unwieldly
inheritance I'd come into—the ability to alter public space in ugly ways.
It was clear that she thought herself the quarry of a mugger, a rapist, or
worse. Suffering a bout of insomnia, however, I was stalking sleep, not
defenseless wayfarers. As a softy who is scarcely able to take a knife to a
raw chicken—let alone hold it to a person's throat—I was surprised, embarrassed, and dismayed all at once. Her flight made me feel like an ac-
complice in tyranny. It also made it clear that I was indistinguishable
from the muggers who occasionally seeped into the area from the surrounding ghetto. That first encounter, and those that followed, signified
that a vast, unnerving gulf lay between nighttime pedestrians—particularly women—and me. And I soon gathered that being perceived as dangerous is a hazard in itself. I only needed to turn a corner into a dicey
situation, or crowd some frightened, armed person in a foyer somewhere,
or make an errant move after being pulled over by a policeman. Where
fear and weapons meet—and they often do in urban America—there is
always the possibility of death.

In that first year, my first away from my hometown, I was to be-   3
come thoroughly familiar with the language of fear. At dark, shadowy
intersections in Chicago, I could cross in front of a car stopped at a traffic
light and elicit the *thunk, thunk, thunk, thunk* of the driver—black, white,
male, or female—hammering down the door locks. On less traveled
streets after dark, I grew accustomed to but never comfortable with people who crossed to the other side of the street rather than pass me. Then

there were the standard unpleasantries with police, doormen, bouncers, cab drivers, and others whose business it is to screen out troublesome individuals *before* there is any nastiness.

I moved to New York nearly two years ago and I have remained an 4 avid night walker. In central Manhattan, the near-constant crowd cover minimizes tense one-on-one street encounters. Elsewhere—visiting friends in SoHo, where sidewalks are narrow and tightly spaced buildings shut out the sky—things can get very taut indeed.

Black men have a firm place in New York mugging literature. Nor- 5 man Podhoretz in his famed (or infamous) 1963 essay, "My Negro Prob- lem—And Ours," recalls growing up in terror of black males; they "were tougher than we were, more ruthless," he writes—and as an adult on the Upper West Side of Manhattan, he continues, he cannot constrain his nervousness when he meets black men on certain streets. Similarly, a de- cade later, the essayist and novelist Edward Hoagland extols a New York where once "Negro bitterness bore down mainly on other Negroes." Where some see mere panhandlers, Hoagland sees "a mugger who is clearly screwing up his nerve to do more than just *ask* for money." But Hoagland has "the New Yorker's quick-hunch posture for broken-field maneuvering," and the bad guy swerves away.

I often witness that "hunch posture," from women after dark on the 6 warrenlike streets of Brooklyn where I live. They seem to set their faces on neutral and, with their purse straps strung across their chests bandolier style, they forge ahead as though bracing themselves against being tack- led. I understand, of course, that the danger they perceive is not a hallu- cination. Women are particularly vulnerable to street violence, and young black males are drastically overrepresented among the perpetra- tors of that violence. Yet these truths are no solace against the kind of alienation that comes of being ever the suspect, against being set apart, a fearsome entity with whom pedestrians avoid making eye contact.

It is not altogether clear to me how I reached the ripe old age of 22 7 without being conscious of the lethality nighttime pedestrians attributed to me. Perhaps it was because in Chester, Pennsylvania, the small, angry industrial town where I came of age in the 1960s, I was scarcely notice- able against a backdrop of gang warfare, street knifings, and murders. I grew up one of the good boys, had perhaps a half-dozen fist fights. In retrospect, my shyness of combat has clear sources.

Many things go into the making of a young thug. One of those 8

things is the consummation of the male romance with the power to intimidate. An infant discovers that random flailings send the baby bottle
flying out of the crib and crashing to the floor. Delighted, the joyful babe
repeats those motions again and again, seeking to duplicate the feat. Just
so, I recall the points at which some of my boyhood friends were finally
seduced by the perception of themselves as tough guys. When a mark
cowered and surrendered his money without resistance, myth and reality
merged—and paid off. It is, after all, only manly to embrace the power to
frighten and intimidate. We, as men, are not supposed to give an inch of
our lane on the highway; we are to seize the fighter's edge in work and in
play and even in love; we are to be valiant in the face of hostile forces.

Unfortunately, poor and powerless young men seem to take all this   9
nonsense literally. As a boy, I saw countless tough guys locked away; I
have since buried several, too. They were babies, really—a teenage
cousin, a brother of 22, a childhood friend in his mid-twenties—all gone
down in episodes of bravado played out in the streets. I came to doubt
the virtues of intimidation early on. I chose, perhaps even unconsciously,
to remain a shadow—timid, but a survivor.

The fearsomeness mistakenly attributed to me in public places   10
often has a perilous flavor. The most frightening of these confusions occurred in the late 1970s and early 1980s when I worked as a journalist in
Chicago. One day, rushing into the office of a magazine I was writing for
with a deadline story in hand, I was mistaken for a burglar. The office
manager called security and, with an ad hoc posse, pursued me through
the labyrinthine halls, nearly to my editor's door. I had no way of proving
who I was. I could only move briskly toward the company of someone
who knew me.

Another time I was on assignment for a local paper and killing time   11
before an interview. I entered a jewelry store on the city's affluent Near
North Side. The proprietor excused herself and returned with an enormous red Doberman pinscher straining at the end of a leash. She stood,
the dog extended toward me, silent to my questions, her eyes bulging
nearly out of her head. I took a cursory look around, nodded, and bade
her good night. Relatively speaking, however, I never fared as badly as
another black male journalist. He went to nearby Waukegan, Illinois, a
couple of summers ago to work on a story about a murderer who was
born there. Mistaking the reporter for the killer, police hauled him from
his car at gunpoint and but for his press credentials would probably have

tried to book him. Such episodes are not uncommon. Black men trade tales like this all the time.

In "My Negro Problem—And Ours," Podhoretz writes that the hatred he feels for blacks makes itself known to him through a variety of avenues—one being his discomfort with that "special brand of paranoid touchiness" to which he says blacks are prone. No doubt he is speaking here of black men. In time, I learned to smother the rage I felt at so often being taken for a criminal. Not to do so would surely have led to madness—via that special "paranoid touchiness" that so annoyed Podhoretz at the time he wrote the essay. 12

I began to take precautions to make myself less threatening. I move about with care, particularly late in the evening. I give a wide berth to nervous people on subway platforms during the wee hours, particularly when I have exchanged business clothes for jeans. If I happen to be entering a building behind some people who appear skittish, I may walk by, letting them clear the lobby before I return, so as not to seem to be following them. I have been calm and extremely congenial on those rare occasions when I've been pulled over by the police. 13

And on late-evening constitutionals along streets less traveled by, I employ what has proved to be an excellent tension-reducing measure: I whistle melodies from Beethoven and Vivaldi and the more popular classical composers. Even steely New Yorkers hunching toward nighttime destinations seem to relax, and occasionally they even join in the tune. Virtually everybody seems to sense that a mugger wouldn't be warbling bright, sunny selections from Vivaldi's *Four Seasons*. It is my equivalent of the cowbell that hikers wear when they know they are in bear country. 14

☉ Opening the Dialogue

1. Does Staples provide enough examples to convince you that whites overreact in the presence of African-American men, or do you think he is the one who is overreacting?

2. Staples says that both white men and white women feel intimidated by African-American men. Do you agree? What are the political and social implications of such a reaction?

3. As many incidents across the nation have shown, African Americans

have legitimate reasons to fear whites—including those in power such as police officers. Should Staples have made this point?

⟨€⟩ Keeping a Notebook

Do you think the fear Staples attributes to whites is based on their personal experiences with African-American males? What other reasons could whites have for feeling the way they do?

⟨€⟩ Working Together

List other strategies Staples could use to lessen the fear he says he inspires in whites. Does your group believe Staples *should* take such steps? In class discussion examine possible ways that African Americans and whites could cooperate to reduce the racial tensions that Staples describes.

⟨€⟩ Writing an Essay

Write an essay in which you discuss whether you think the racial situation in the United States is better or worse than the way Staples portrays it in his essay. Use examples from your own experience and from current events to support your thesis.

SHANLON WU

In Search of Bruce Lee's Grave

Shanlon Wu's parents came to the United States from China in . the late 1940s as graduate students and were stranded when the Communist Revolution prevented their return to their homeland. Wu, an only child, was born in 1959 in Manhattan. The following essay is his first published work. In it Wu relates how his adolescent adoration of a martial arts expert bemused his intellectual parents, and he explains how the lack of Asian-American heroes affected his own self-image as a young Chinese-American man.

Wu holds a B.A. degree in English literature from Vassar College, an M.F.A. degree in creative writing from Sarah Lawrence College, and a law degree from Georgetown University. He lives in the Washington, D.C., area, where he works for the U.S. Attorney's office.

Wu is presently at work on a novel about Chinese graduate students stranded, like his parents, in the United States following the Chinese revolution. Although Wu's work reflects a strong interest in the Chinese-American experience, he emphasizes that his writing is not limited to one subject: "I write stories about anything I want. Writing reconciles for me the different forces that I always feel pulling at me. On days when I feel like a Chinese, like an American, like an artist, and like a lawyer all at once, writing gives me coherence."

Notice the variety of examples Wu uses to make his point about the scarcity of "powerful Asian male images."

IT'S SATURDAY MORNING in Seattle, and I am driving to visit Bruce Lee's   1
grave. I have been in the city for only a couple of weeks and so drive two
blocks past the cemetery before realizing that I've passed it. I double back

205

and turn through the large wrought-iron gate, past a sign that reads: "Open to 9 P.M. or dusk, whichever comes first."

It's a sprawling cemetery, with winding roads leading in all direc- 2
tions. I feel silly trying to find his grave with no guidance. I think that my search for his grave is similar to my search for Asian heroes in America.

I was born in 1959, an Asian-American in Westchester County, 3
N.Y. During my childhood there were no Asian sports stars. On television, I can recall only that most pathetic of Asian characters, Hop Sing, the Cartwright family houseboy on "Bonanza." But in my adolescence there was Bruce.

I was 14 years old when I first saw "Enter the Dragon," the grand- 4
daddy of martial-arts movies. Bruce had died suddenly at the age of 32 of cerebral edema, an excess of fluid in the brain, just weeks before the release of the film. Between the ages of 14 and 17, I saw "Enter the Dragon" 22 times before I stopped counting. During those years I collected Bruce Lee posters, putting them up at all angles in my bedroom. I took up Chinese martial arts and spent hours comparing my physique with his.

I learned all I could about Bruce: that he had married a Caucasian, 5
Linda; that he had sparred with Kareem Abdul-Jabbar; that he was a buddy of Steve McQueen and James Coburn, both of whom were his pallbearers.

My parents, who immigrated to America and had become profes- 6
sors at Hunter College, tolerated my behavior, but seemed puzzled at my admiration of an "entertainer." My father jokingly tried to compare my obsession with Bruce to his boyhood worship of Chinese folk-tale heroes.

"I read them just like you read American comic books," he said. 7

But my father's heroes could not be mine; they came from an an- 8
cient literary tradition, not comic books. He and my mother had grown up in a land where they belonged to the majority. I could not adopt their childhood and they were wise enough not to impose it upon me.

Although I never again experienced the kind of blind hero worship 9
I felt for Bruce, my need to find heroes remained strong.

In college, I discovered the men of the 442d Regimental Combat 10
Team, a United States Army all-Japanese unit in World War II. Allowed to fight only against Europeans, they suffered heavy casualties while their families were put in internment camps. Their motto was "Go for Broke."

I saw them as Asians in a Homeric epic, the protagonists of a   11
Shakespearean tragedy; I knew no Eastern myths to infuse them with.
They embodied my own need to prove myself in the Caucasian world. I
imagined how their American-born flesh and muscle must have resembled mine: epicanthic folds set in strong faces nourished on milk and
beef. I thought how much they had proved where there was so little to
prove.

After college, I competed as an amateur boxer in an attempt to find   12
my self-image in the ring. It didn't work. My fighting was only an attempt
to copy Bruce's movies. What I needed was instruction on how to live. I
quit boxing after a year and went to law school.

I was an anomaly there: a would-be Asian litigator. I had always   13
liked to argue and found I liked doing it in front of people even more.
When I won the first-year moot court competition in law school, I asked
an Asian classmate if he thought I was the first Asian to win. He laughed
and told me I was probably the only Asian to even compete.

The law-firm interviewers always seemed surprised that I wanted to   14
litigate.

"Aren't you interested in Pacific Rim trade?" they asked.   15

"My Chinese isn't good enough," I quipped.   16

My pat response seemed to please them. It certainly pleased me. I   17
thought I'd found a place of my own—a place where the law would insu-
late me from the pressure of defining my Asian maleness. I sensed the
possibility of merely being myself.

But the pressure reasserted itself. One morning, the year after grad-   18
uating from law school, I read the obituary of Gen. Minoru Genda—the
man who planned the Pearl Harbor attack. I'd never heard of him and had
assumed that whoever did that planning was long since dead. But the
general had been alive all those years—rising at 4 every morning to do
his exercises and retiring every night by 8. An advocate of animal rights,
the obituary said.

I found myself drawn to the general's life despite his association   19
with the Axis powers. He seemed a forthright, graceful man who died
unhumbled. The same paper carried a front-page story about Congress's
failure to pay the Japanese-American internees their promised reparation
money. The general, at least, had not died waiting for reparations.

I was surprised and frightened by my admiration for General   20

Genda, by my still-strong hunger for images of powerful Asian men. That hunger was my vulnerability manifested, a reminder of my lack of place.

 The hunger is eased this gray morning in Seattle. After asking di-   21
rections from a policeman—Japanese—I easily locate Bruce's grave. The headstone is red granite with a small picture etched into it. The picture is very Hollywood—Bruce wears dark glasses—and I think the calligraphy looks a bit sloppy. Two tourists stop but leave quickly after glancing at me.

 I realize I am crying. Bruce's grave seems very small in comparison   22
to his place in my boyhood. So small in comparison to my need for heroes. Seeing his grave, I understand how large the hole in my life has been and how desperately I'd sought to fill it.

 I had sought an Asian hero to emulate. But none of my choices   23
quite fit me. Their lives were defined through heroic tasks—they had villains to defeat and wars to fight—while my life seemed merely a struggle to define myself.

 But now I see how that very struggle has defined me. I must be my   24
own hero even as I learn to treasure those who have gone before.

 I have had my powerful Asian male images: Bruce, the men of the   25
442d and General Genda; I may yet discover others. Their lives beckon like fireflies on a moonless night, and I know that they—like me—may have been flawed by foolhardiness and even cruelty. Still, their lives were real. They were not houseboys on "Bonanza."

◉ Opening the Dialogue

1. How have Asians been stereotyped in the United States? What qualities are associated with Asian males? With Asian females? Are these characteristics largely positive or negative?

2. Do you think Wu has given the right examples to support his contention that Asian Americans have few heroes to emulate? Where else might he have looked for heroes?

3. Would a school curriculum that stressed the contributions of figures from various minority cultures have helped Wu find heroes? Do you think enhancing the self-esteem of students is a legitimate role of education?

⟨⟩ Keeping a Notebook

Ask your parents what heroes they had when they were your age and what heroes they admire today. In groups, make lists of the qualities these heroes have. Then, in class discussion, decide in what ways these heroes reflect the hopes of your parents' generation.

⟨⟩ Working Together

List possible objections to Bruce Lee's serving as a role model for young Asian Americans. In class discussion decide on other individuals who might be more appropriate role models. Must these role models all be Asian or Asian-American?

⟨⟩ Writing an Essay

Write an essay in which you discuss what role models today's college students admire and what these heroes reveal about American culture.

JACK G. SHAHEEN

The Media's Image of Arabs

Jack Shaheen (b. 1935) grew up in the small steel town of Clairton, Pennsylvania. The working class immigrant community was a diverse cultural mix (Shaheen's own family was originally from Lebanon). It was, he says, an environment of "ethnic and racial sharing. I grew up prejudice-free because of the mix of people."

Shaheen credits his mother, a cashier at the local movie theater, for helping him recognize the danger of sterotypes. As Shaheen, a self-described "movie buff," absorbed the often racist world Hollywood portrayed, his mother taught him how to think critically about cultural images: "She sensitized me to the danger of stereotypes, in both the real and imaginary worlds."

After earning degrees from the Carnegie Institute of Technology and Penn State, Shaheen traveled in the Middle East and taught for three years at the American University in Beirut. The contrast he found between reality and media portrayals of Arab people led him to focus on what he calls "the Don Quixote quest for fair play. Not only for Arabs, but for all people."

"Every group has its bad guys," he says, "but they're a small number. To selectively frame a group according to its minority is a terrible injustice. The American government was helped in its internment of Japanese Americans by the way they were portrayed in newspapers and in the movies. The Nazis were able to destroy millions of Jews because German media had perpetuated such vicious stereotypes. I have to ask myself who benefits when a group is stereotyped."

Shaheen has taught mass communications at Southern Illinois

University at Edwardsville for over two decades. He is the author of *The TV Arab, The Nuclear War Films,* and numerous essays—including the following, which has been reprinted from *Newsweek.*

Notice how Shaheen selects examples that support his thesis about the dangers of negative stereotyping.

AMERICA'S BOGYMAN is the Arab. Until the nightly news brought us 1
TV pictures of Palestinian boys being punched and beaten, almost all portraits of Arabs seen in America were dangerously threatening. Arabs were either billionaires or bombers—rarely victims. They were hardly ever seen as ordinary people practicing law, driving taxis, singing lullabies or healing the sick. Though TV news may portray them more sympathetically now, the absence of positive media images nurtures suspicion and stereotype. As an Arab-American, I have found that ugly caricatures have had an enduring impact on my family.

I was sheltered from prejudicial portraits at first. My parents came 2
from Lebanon in the 1920s; they met and married in America. Our home in the steel city of Clairton, Pa., was a center for ethnic sharing—black, white, Jew and gentile. There was only one major source of media images then, at the State movie theater where I was lucky enough to get a part-time job as an usher. But in the late 1940s, Westerns and war movies were popular, not Middle Eastern dramas. Memories of World War II were fresh, and the screen heavies were the Japanese and the Germans. True to the cliché of the times, the only good Indian was a dead Indian. But when I mimicked or mocked the bad guys, my mother cautioned me. She explained that stereotypes blur our vision and corrupt the imagination. "Have compassion for all people, Jackie," she said. "This way, you'll learn to experience the joy of accepting people as they are, and not as they appear in films. Stereotypes hurt."

Mother was right. I can remember the Saturday afternoon when 3
my son, Michael, who was seven, and my daughter, Michele, six, suddenly called out: "Daddy, Daddy, they've got some bad Arabs on TV." They were watching that great American morality play, TV wrestling. Akbar the Great, who liked to hear the cracking of bones, and Abdullah

the Butcher, a dirty fighter who liked to inflict pain, were pinning their foes with "camel locks." From that day on, I knew I had to try to neutralize the media caricatures.

It hasn't been easy. With my children, I have watched animated   4
heroes Heckle and Jeckle pull the rug from under "Ali Boo-Boo, the Desert Rat," and Laverne and Shirley stop "Sheik Ha-Mean-Ie" from conquering "the U.S. and the world." I have read comic books like the "Fantastic Four" and "G.I. Combat" whose characters have sketched Arabs as "lowlifes" and "human hyenas." Negative stereotypes were everywhere. A dictionary informed my youngsters that an Arab is a "vagabond, drifter, hobo and vagrant." Whatever happened, my wife wondered, to Aladdin's good genie?

To a child, the world is simple: good versus evil. But my children   5
and others with Arab roots grew up without ever having seen a humane Arab on the silver screen, someone to pattern their lives after. Is it easier for a camel to go through the eye of a needle than for a screen Arab to appear as a genuine human being?

Hollywood producers must have an instant Ali Baba kit that con-   6
tains scimitars, veils, sunglasses and such Arab clothing as *chadors* and *kufiyahs*. In the mythical "Ay-rabland," oil wells, tents, mosques, goats and shepherds prevail. Between the sand dunes, the camera focuses on a mock-up of a palace from "Arabian Nights"—or a military air base. Recent movies suggest that Americans are at war with Arabs, forgetting the fact that out of 32 Arab nations, America is friendly with 19 of them. And in "Wanted Dead or Alive," a movie that starred Gene Simmons, the leader of the rock group Kiss, the war comes home when an Arab terrorist comes to the United States dressed as a rabbi and, among other things, conspires with Arab-Americans to poison the people of Los Angeles. The movie was released last year.

The Arab remains American culture's favorite whipping boy. In his   7
memoirs, Terrel Bell, Ronald Reagan's first secretary of education, writes about an "apparent bias among mid-level, right-wing staffers at the White House" who dismissed Arabs as "sand niggers." Sadly, the racial slurs continue. At a recent teacher's conference, I met a woman from Sioux Falls, S.D., who told me about the persistence of discrimination. She was in the process of adopting a baby when an agency staffer warned her that the infant had a problem. When she asked whether the child was mentally ill,

or physically handicapped, there was silence. Finally, the worker said:
"The baby is Jordanian."

To me, the Arab demon of today is much like the Jewish demon of   8
yesterday. We deplore the false portrait of Jews as a swarthy menace. Yet
a similar portrait has been accepted and transferred to another group of
Semites—the Arabs. Print and broadcast journalists have started to challenge this stereotype. They are now revealing more humane images of
Palestinian Arabs, a people who traditionally suffered from the myth that
Palestinian equals terrorist. Others could follow that lead and retire the
stereotypical Arab to a media Valhalla.

It would be a step in the right direction if movie and TV producers   9
developed characters modeled after real-life Arab-Americans. We could
then see a White House correspondent like Helen Thomas, whose father
came from Lebanon, in "The Golden Girls," a heart surgeon patterned
after Dr. Michael DeBakey on "St. Elsewhere," or a Syrian-American
playing tournament chess like Yasser Seirawan, the Seattle grandmaster.

Politicians, too, should speak out against the cardboard caricatures.   10
They should refer to Arabs as friends, not just as moderates. And religious
leaders could state that Islam like Christianity and Judaism maintains that
all mankind is one family in the care of God. When all imagemakers
rightfully begin to treat Arabs and all other minorities with respect and
dignity, we may begin to unlearn our prejudices.

☜ Opening the Dialogue

1. Is the kind of media treatment Shaheen describes ever justified? Under
what circumstances, if any, could the media legitimately vilify a particular group?

2. Do you agree with Shaheen's contention that the Arab is "American
culture's favorite whipping boy" (paragraph 7)? Do you think he is overstating his case? Can you think of other groups—not necessarily racial or
ethnic groups—that are treated as badly by the media?

3. Many negative stories come out of the Middle East each week. Is
Shaheen implying that journalists should stop reporting these stories because they convey negative stereotypes? Or is he saying something else?

✎ Keeping a Notebook

What images do you associate with Arabs who live in the Middle East? What is the source of these images? Do you have the same impressions of Arab Americans? How do you account for any differences that might exist between the two images?

✎ Working Together

After watching the national news on a different network for each of three consecutive nights, work in groups to record the way Arabs are portrayed in newscasts. Then, in class discussion, consider to what extent your observations support Shaheen's contentions in the first paragraph of his essay.

✎ Writing an Essay

Write an essay in which you discuss how your ethnic group or culture is treated by the media. Make sure you present examples from a variety of different media to support your conclusion that the media either treat your group with dignity or create negative stereotypes.

DAVID MURA

Bashed in the U.S.A.

David Mura (b. 1953) grew up in the middle class Jewish suburb
of Skokie, Illinois, and had no sense of himself as a *sansei*, or third-
generation Japanese American, until he reached adolescence:
"That's when I really became conscious of a certain feeling of
being an outsider, and that [feeling] was never identified in terms
of issues of race by the people around me, my family, or myself.
When this happens, there's a tendency, if you're the only person
experiencing it, to ask, 'What's wrong with me?' "

Mura's effort to explore his sense of alienation from the white majority conflicted with his parents' efforts to assimilate. His Japanese-American parents had been imprisoned in internment camps
during World War II, but like many of their generation, they
chose not to talk about the experience. As Mura says, "They
came out determined to prove the camps were a mistake, and families worked hard to be 'Americans' without calling attention to
being Japanese Americans, or, as in my parents' case, they tried to
ignore it. . . . My dad wanted to mainstream and work the family
into a middle class white suburb. I think he was a very angry man
while I was growing up, but he didn't realize why. . . . It at least
partly had something to do with relocation camps and race."

In 1984, Mura received a fellowship that allowed him to spend a
year in Japan. His experiences there were a revelation and became the source of a widely acclaimed memoir, *Turning Japanese:
Memoirs of a Sansei* (1991). "Japan was in every way a watershed for
me," he says. "It was a reaffirmation of pride of being that hyphen-
ate: Japanese-American. And despite the title [of the book], I'm
not Japanese. I'm Japanese-American. My struggle with identity is
here, not in Japan."

Mura is also the author of a volume of poetry, *After We Lost Our Way* (1990). As you read his essay, notice the many different kinds of examples he presents to support his contention that racism against Asians in America is a serious problem.

I AM A *SANSEI*, a third-generation Japanese American. A couple of years   1
ago, I asked a white friend what he felt about me the first time we met. He insisted he had learned not to stereotype people, that he had gone past racist classifications. Fine, I said, but what stereotypes came up? Finally, after a half-hour of my questioning, he relented. "I guess I thought you'd be too powerful for me," he said.

"What does that mean?" I asked.   2

"Well, my father always said that the Japanese lost the war but they   3
were going to win the war after the war."

My friend's remarks brought up a question that still plagues Japan-   4
ese Americans: Are you Japanese or American? Behind this question lie certain troubling racist assumptions.

In 1942, in the months after Pearl Harbor, Congressional hearings   5
were held concerning the Japanese Americans and Japanese aliens on the West Coast. Although Earl Warren, then the Governor of California, acknowledged that there appeared to be no fifth-column activity, he argued that this was merely proof that such activity was planned.

Taking a somewhat different tack, Senator Tom Stewart of Ten-   6
nessee maintained, "A Jap is a Jap wherever you find him. They do not believe in God and have no respect for an oath of allegiance."

As the son of internment camp prisoners, even now I feel the need   7
to point out that no Japanese American was ever convicted of espionage. A 1982 study commissioned by Congress concluded that the causes for the internment were wartime hysteria, racism and lack of political leadership. The Congress acknowledged this in 1988 when it awarded damage payments to Japanese Americans who had been detained.

And yet, I know that the circular logic of Earl Warren and Tom   8
Stewart is still present. Witness last year's best seller, "The Coming War with Japan." In defending their title, George Friedman and Meredith Lebard argued that they did not have to prove that Japan was preparing for war, they merely needed to prove that such an act would be in its interest.

Japan's economic success will "inevitably give way to a more natu-   9
ral, and more fierce, national sensibility," they wrote. "Pacifism is not native to Japan, nor is national modesty." Implicit in this is the idea that the
Japanese cannot change or accept foreign beliefs. (One wonders where
pacifism *is* native?) Yet in a recent poll, only 10 percent of Japanese sur-
veyed said they would fight for their country.

There are those who argue that charges of Japan bashing are exag-   10
gerated or even completely off the mark. In Michael Crichton's best
seller, "Rising Sun," such claims are used by the Japanese to their own
advantage and serve mainly as a smoke screen for the "real" issues.

Obviously, I look at Japan bashing from a different perspective.   11
When I see people taking a sledgehammer to a Japanese car on TV, I
wonder what would happen if my daughter and I happened to walk by.
Would they care if we were Japanese or Japanese American?

To someone like Michael Crichton, I would ask: If the whiff of   12
racism is not in the air, how does one explain the anti-Japan slogans
painted on the walls of the Japanese American community center in Nor-
walk, Calif., in November? Or the message, "all Japs must die," written on
the door of a Wellesley College Chinese American student in February?
Or the Thai American man in Torrance, Calif., who was beaten in March
by a white man who asked him if he was Japanese?

A conclusion reached through racism is not necessarily incorrect. A   13
case can be made that the U.S. has legitimate trade differences with
Japan and that Japan's success has hurt our economy. Where racism
comes in is in the force of emotions and in the inability to distinguish
between Japanese and Japanese Americans. It gives people a scapegoat.
Since the scapegoated group is considered less human and less worthy, it
cannot possibly do better than one's own group. Unless the group has
some unfair advantage. Unless it cheats.

In Senator Ernest Hollings's remarks that anyone who doubts U.S.   14
power and skill should remember that we dropped an atomic bomb on
Japan, in Lee Iacocca's angrily protectionist commercials, the underlying
premise is that Americans are always the best. They only lose when the
playing field isn't level.

Asian Americans are the largest group at the University of Califor-   15
nia, Berkeley, and at U.C.L.A. Their success has engendered resentment.
They are grinds; they work too hard. They have an unfair advantage.
Sounds a little like the complaints against the Japanese, doesn't it?

Such feelings were behind the Asian Exclusion Act of 1882, the 16
Alien Land Law of 1913 and the internment of my parents and other Japanese Americans. They also have a lot to do with the recent rise in hate
crimes against Asian Americans documented by the U.S. Commission on
Civil Rights in February.

Perhaps if Americans had a better knowledge of the Japanese and 17
Japanese Americans, such resentment would not flourish so easily. Unfor-
tunately, most Americans still base their image of Asians and Asian
Americans on stereotypes.

The success of "Rising Sun," with its picture of the Japanese as du- 18
plicitous and cruel, as the most racist people on earth, is merely another
example of Orientalism. (Yes, the Japanese are racist, but Mr. Crichton's
picture of racism in the U.S. is much less troubled than mine or Toni
Morrison's or Louise Erdrich's[1].) Did resentment and fear cause some
Americans to see Kristi Yamaguchi, who won a gold medal in figure skat-
ing at the Winter Olympics, as less American than her teammates?

Often, when white Americans tell me they are not racist, I reply 19
that I grew up thinking of myself as less than 100 percent American. In
certain ways I hated the way I looked and felt ashamed of my heritage. If
I took racist values from society, I ask them, how is it they did not?

To dig out the roots of racial resentment, Americans must come to 20
terms with their subjective vision of race. If someone of another color
gets a job you're applying for, is your resentment more than if a person of
your own color won the job? When you hear the word American, whose
face flashes before your mind?

🕲 Opening the Dialogue

1. Mura sees anti-Japanese sentiment in the United States as part of a
general anti-Asian bias. Do you agree?

2. In a letter to the editor responding to Mura's essay, a reader charged
that Mura "exhibits an insecurity and an inferiority complex" common in
some Japanese Americans. Do you think the essay reveals such insecur-

---

[1]Highly regarded novelists and critics; Morrison is African American and Erdrich is Native
American.

ity? Why, for example, does Mura question his "white friend" so persistently about his image of him as a Japanese?

3. Is Mura correct when he says, in paragraph 17, "if Americans had a better knowledge of the Japanese and Japanese Americans, such resentment would not flourish so easily"? Do you think increased knowledge is all that is needed to eliminate negative stereotypes, or do you think Mura is underestimating the problem?

🖘 Keeping a Notebook

A good deal of the negative feeling some Americans have toward the Japanese is a result of the economic competition between the United States and Japan. How much of this negative feeling do you think is justified? How much is simply a refusal to face problems that exist in the United States?

🖘 Working Together

Working in groups, list your emotional responses to the following events: the bombing of Pearl Harbor; the dropping of the atomic bomb on Japan; the internment of Japanese Americans during World War II; payment of reparations to Japanese Americans who were interned; the recent economic success of Japan. Then, in class discussion, examine how your responses to these events color your thinking about Japanese and Japanese Americans.

🖘 Writing an Essay

Write a letter to a fictional U.S. college that has limited the number of Japanese Americans it will admit. Using material from Mura's essay as well as examples of your own, explain to the dean of admissions why this policy is wrong and how it reinforces racist stereotypes of Japanese and Japanese Americans.

JUDITH ORTIZ COFER

The Myth of the Latin Woman: I Just Met a Girl Named Maria

In the following essay (a longer version of which appears in her collection *The Latin Deli*), Judith Ortiz Cofer ponders the destructive stereotype of the "hot-blooded" Latina that results when the sexual signals and cultural cues of two societies are misunderstood or misinterpreted.

Born in Puerto Rico in 1952 and raised in the United States, Cofer herself has struggled to reconcile the two cultures: "One of the things I've discovered about myself as a bilingual person is that the very term 'bilingual' tells you I have two worlds. At least now, they're very strictly separated, but when I was growing up it was a constant shift back and forth. I think my brain developed a sense of my world and my reality as being composed of two halves. But I'm not divided in them. I accept them, and I think they have basically been the difference that has allowed me to write things that are not like anybody else's."

Cofer is an award-winning poet and teaches English and creative writing at the University of Georgia. "My aim as a teacher," she recently explained, "is to expose students of whatever age to model works of literature that are interesting and accessible, but at the same time I want them to find their own individual voices. My aim is to convince those who want to write that their own lives are the raw material. I show them how they can begin to understand themselves and the world around them by writing about it, as I have done."

As you read the following essay, notice how Cofer chooses carefully from her experiences to present examples that clearly illustrate her view of how Latin women are stereotyped.

O N A BUS TRIP to London from Oxford University where I was earning some graduate credits one summer, a young man, obviously fresh from a pub, spotted me and as if struck by inspiration went down on his knees in the aisle. With both hands over his heart he broke into an Irish tenor's rendition of "Maria" from *West Side Story*. My politely amused fellow passengers gave his lovely voice the round of gentle applause it deserved. Though I was not quite as amused, I managed my version of an English smile: no show of teeth, no extreme contortions of the facial muscles—I was at this time of my life practicing reserve and cool. Oh, that British control, how I coveted it. But "Maria" had followed me to London, reminding me of a prime fact of my life: you can leave the island, master the English language, and travel as far as you can, but if you are a Latina, especially one like me who so obviously belongs to Rita Moreno's gene pool, the island travels with you.

This is sometimes a very good thing—it may win you that extra   2
minute of someone's attention. But with some people, the same things can make *you* an island—not a tropical paradise but an Alcatraz, a place nobody wants to visit. As a Puerto Rican girl living in the United States and wanting like most children to "belong," I resented the stereotype that my Hispanic appearance called forth from many people I met.

Growing up in a large urban center in New Jersey during the 1960s,   3
I suffered from what I think of as "cultural schizophrenia." Our life was designed by my parents as a microcosm of their *casas* on the island. We spoke in Spanish, ate Puerto Rican food bought at the *bodega*, and practiced strict Catholicism at a church that allotted us a one-hour slot each week for mass, performed in Spanish by a Chinese priest trained as a missionary for Latin America.

As a girl I was kept under strict surveillance by my parents, since   4
my virtue and modesty were, by their cultural equation, the same as their honor. As a teenager I was lectured constantly on how to behave as a proper *senorita*. But it was a conflicting message I received, since the Puerto Rican mothers also encouraged their daughters to look and act like women and to dress in clothes our Anglo friends and their mothers found too "mature" and flashy. The difference was, and is, cultural; yet I often felt humiliated when I appeared at an American friend's party wearing a dress more suitable to a semi-formal than to a playroom birthday

celebration. At Puerto Rican festivities, neither the music nor the colors we wore could be too loud.

I remember Career Day in our high school, when teachers told us   5
to come dressed as if for a job interview. It quickly became obvious that to the Puerto Rican girls "dressing up" meant wearing their mother's ornate jewelry and clothing, more appropriate (by mainstream standards) for the company Christmas party than as daily office attire. That morning I had agonized in front of my closet, trying to figure out what a "career girl" would wear. I knew how to dress for school (at the Catholic school I attended, we all wore uniforms), I knew how to dress for Sunday mass, and I knew what dresses to wear for parties at my relatives' homes. Though I do not recall the precise details of my Career Day outfit, it must have been a composite of these choices. But I remember a comment my friend (an Italian American) made in later years that coalesced my impressions of that day. She said that at the business school she was attending, the Puerto Rican girls always stood out for wearing "everything at once." She meant, of course, too much jewelry, too many accessories. On that day at school we were simply made the negative models by the nuns, who were themselves not credible fashion experts to any of us. But it was painfully obvious to me that to the others, in their tailored skirts and silk blouses, we must have seemed "hopeless" and "vulgar." Though I now know that most adolescents feel out of step much of the time, I also know that for the Puerto Rican girls of my generation that sense was intensified. The way our teachers and classmates looked at us that day in school was just a taste of the cultural clash that awaited us in the real world, where prospective employers and men on the street would often misinterpret our tight skirts and jingling bracelets as a "come-on."

Mixed cultural signals have perpetuated certain stereotypes—for   6
example, that of the Hispanic woman as the "hot tamale" or sexual firebrand. It is a one-dimensional view that the media have found easy to promote. In their special vocabulary, advertisers have designated "sizzling" and "smoldering" as the adjectives of choice for describing not only the foods but also the women of Latin America. From conversations in my house I recall hearing about the harassment that Puerto Rican women endured in factories where the "boss-men" talked to them as if sexual innuendo was all they understood, and worse, often gave them the choice of submitting to their advances or being fired.

It is custom, however, not chromosomes, that leads us to choose   7
scarlet over pale pink. As young girls, it was our mothers who influenced
our decisions about clothes and colors—mothers who had grown up on a
tropical island where the natural environment was a riot of primary colors, where showing your skin was one way to keep cool as well as to look
sexy. Most important of all, on the island, women perhaps felt freer to
dress and move more provocatively since, in most cases, they were protected by the traditions, mores, and laws of a Spanish/Catholic system of
morality and machismo whose main rule was: *You may look at my sister, but
if you touch her I will kill you.* The extended family and church structure
could provide a young woman with a circle of safety in her small pueblo
on the island; if a man "wronged" a girl, everyone would close in to save
her family honor.

My mother has told me about dressing in her best party clothes on   8
Saturday nights and going to the town's plaza to promenade with her
girlfriends in front of the boys they liked. The males were thus given an
opportunity to admire the women and to express their admiration in the
form of *piropos:* erotically charged street poems they composed on the
spot. (I have myself been subjected to a few *piropos* while visiting the island, and they can be outrageous, although custom dictates that they
must never cross into obscenity.) This ritual, as I understand it, also en-
tails a show of studied indifference on the woman's part; if she is "decent,"
she must not acknowledge the man's impassioned words. So I do understand how things can be lost in translation. When a Puerto Rican girl
dressed in her idea of what is attractive meets a man from the mainstream
culture who has been trained to react to certain types of clothing as a
sexual signal, a clash is likely to take place. I remember the boy who took
me to my first formal dance leaning over to plant a sloppy, over-eager
kiss painfully on my mouth; when I didn't respond with sufficient passion,
he remarked resentfully: "I thought you Latin girls were supposed to mature early," as if I were expected to *ripen* like a fruit or vegetable, not just
grow into womanhood like other girls.

It is surprising to my professional friends that even today some   9
people, including those who should know better, still put others "in their
place." It happened to me most recently during a stay at a classy metropolitan hotel favored by young professional couples for weddings. Late
one evening after the theater, as I walked toward my room with a col-

league (a woman with whom I was coordinating an arts program), a middle-aged man in a tuxedo, with a young girl in satin and lace on his arm, stepped directly into our path. With his champagne glass extended toward me, he exclaimed "Evita!"[1]

Our way blocked, my companion and I listened as the man half-recited, half-bellowed "Don't Cry for Me, Argentina." When he finished, the young girl said: "How about a round of applause for my daddy?" We complied, hoping this would bring the silly spectacle to a close. I was becoming aware that our little group was attracting the attention of the other guests. "Daddy" must have perceived this too, and he once more barred the way as we tried to walk past him. He began to shout-sing a ditty to the tune of "La Bamba"—except the lyrics were about a girl named Maria whose exploits rhymed with her name and gonorrhea. The girl kept saying "Oh, Daddy" and looking at me with pleading eyes. She wanted me to laugh along with the others. My companion and I stood silently waiting for the man to end his offensive song. When he finished, I looked not at him but at his daughter. I advised her calmly never to ask her father what he had done in the army. Then I walked between them and to my room. My friend complimented me on my cool handling of the situation, but I confessed that I had really wanted to push the jerk into the swimming pool. This same man—probably a corporate executive, well-educated, even worldly by most standards—would not have been likely to regale an Anglo woman with a dirty song in public. He might have checked his impulse by assuming that she could be somebody's wife or mother, or at least *somebody* who might take offense. But, to him, I was just an Evita or a Maria: merely a character in his cartoon-populated universe.

Another facet of the myth of the Latin woman in the United States is the menial, the domestic—Maria the housemaid or countergirl. It's true that work as domestics, as waitresses, and in factories is all that's available to women with little English and few skills. But the myth of the Hispanic menial—the funny maid, mispronouncing words and cooking up a spicy storm in a shiny California kitchen—has been perpetuated by the media in the same way that "Mammy" from *Gone with the Wind* became America's idea of the black woman for generations. Since I do not wear my diplo-

10

11

---

[1] A musical about Eva Duarte de Peron, the former first lady of Argentina.

mas around my neck for all to see, I have on occasion been sent to that "kitchen" where some think I obviously belong.

One incident has stayed with me, though I recognize it as a minor   12
offense. My first public poetry reading took place in Miami, at a restaurant where a luncheon was being held before the event. I was nervous and excited as I walked in with notebook in hand. An older woman motioned me to her table, and thinking (foolish me) that she wanted me to autograph a copy of my newly published slender volume of verse, I went over. She ordered a cup of coffee from me, assuming that I was the waitress. (Easy enough to mistake my poems for menus, I suppose.) I know it wasn't an intentional act of cruelty. Yet of all the good things that happened later, I remember that scene most clearly, because it reminded me of what I had to overcome before anyone would take me seriously. In retrospect I understand that my anger gave my reading fire. In fact, I have almost always taken any doubt in my abilities as a challenge, the result most often being the satisfaction of winning a convert, of seeing the cold, appraising eyes warm to my words, the body language change, the smile that indicates I have opened some avenue for communication. So that day as I read, I looked directly at that woman. Her lowered eyes told me she was embarrassed at her faux pas, and when I willed her to look up at me, she graciously allowed me to punish her with my full attention. We shook hands at the end of the reading and I never saw her again. She has probably forgotten the entire incident, but maybe not.

Yet I am one of the lucky ones. There are thousands of Latinas   13
without the privilege of an education or the entrees into society that I have. For them life is a constant struggle against the misconceptions perpetuated by the myth of the Latina. My goal is to try to replace the old stereotypes with a much more interesting set of realities. Every time I give a reading, I hope the stories I tell, the dreams and fears I examine in my work, can achieve some universal truth that will get my audience past the particulars of my skin color, my accent, or my clothes.

I once wrote a poem in which I called all Latinas "God's brown   14
daughters." This poem is really a prayer of sorts, offered upward, but also, through the human-to-human channel of art, outward. It is a prayer for communication and for respect. In it, Latin women pray "in Spanish to an Anglo God/ with a Jewish heritage," and they are "fervently hoping/ that if not omnipotent,/ at least He be bilingual."

✪ Opening the Dialogue

1. Cofer gives a number of examples of how problems occur when a person from one culture misunderstands the signals sent by a person from another culture. Can you think of additional examples—perhaps from newspaper accounts—that support her conclusion?

2. Do the mixed signals Cofer describes cross lines other than ethnic or racial ones—for example, lines separating people of different ages or genders? Give examples from your own experience, if possible.

3. Do you believe it is realistic for people to expect to maintain their traditional ethnic cultures in the United States? Why or why not?

✪ Keeping a Notebook

In paragraph 3 Cofer says that she lived in two completely different worlds—one a microcosm of her family's life in Puerto Rico, and the other the Anglo world that existed outside her home in New Jersey. Do you, like Cofer, ever feel as if you live in two worlds? In what ways do your two worlds clash with each other?

✪ Working Together

Working in groups, list the cultural misconceptions that are frequently associated with particular minority groups; have each group of students focus on a different ethnic or racial minority. In class discussion, examine the potential dangers of these myths.

✪ Writing an Essay

Should Cofer—as well as other ethnic Americans—stop complaining about being stereotyped and make more of an effort to assimilate into mainstream culture? Write an essay in which you give examples to support your position.

Writing about Perceptions of Culture

1. A number of the essays in this chapter allude to the way some of the media perpetuate negative stereotypes. Write an essay in which you use examples to illustrate the way films, television shows, or newspapers characterize persons with disabilities, gay men and lesbians, the elderly, women, or the rural poor. Be sure to discuss whether you think these portrayals are accurate or whether you believe they misrepresent reality.

2. Write an exemplification essay in which you discuss how certain words and phrases—possibily in another language—remind you of your regional or cultural roots.

3. In her essay Judith Ortiz Cofer illustrates how problems occur when signals sent by a person of one culture are misinterpreted by a person from another culture. Write an essay in which you discuss an instance of this kind of misunderstanding. You may discuss an example from your own experience or one about which you have read.

4. Focus on a recent news story that was of special interest to members of a group with whose values you identify. Write an essay in which you give examples to explain why this event was so important.

5. Many of the essays in this chapter deal with the problems that people from other cultures have in being accepted as individuals in the United States. Which essays do you believe suggest the most serious problem? Use a series of examples to show which cultural group faces the greatest challenges and why.

CHAPTER 6

SOCIETY AND CULTURE
EXPLORING CAUSAL
CONNECTIONS

YUN GEE, 'WHERE IS MY MOTHER' (1926–27)

A desire for better education for their children was what first made my parents consider the possibility of packing their belongings and traveling over six thousand miles westward in 1976. But emerging political, economic, and religious problems also encouraged us to leave. The Shah's oil policies had increased inflation, and rural speculators hoping to make their fortunes in the cities had brought about a housing shortage. The Shah had also taken away much of the clergy's power, and the government had taken over the management of the curriculum for students of religion. Political protests had increased dramatically. If we had stayed in Iran, we would have been risking our lives, and I would have been drafted into the army in 1980, at the age of nine, to fight in the war against Iraq. In many ways, my family really had no choice but to leave.

Peyman Markazi, student

Society and Culture

Cause and effect—searching for causes or predicting effects—is a useful strategy in many academic assignments. Writers may, for example, analyze the causes that led to an economic recession, to an earthquake, to an individual's behavior change, to a political victory, or to a literary movement. As they seek to discover how events influence their world, they may consider the effects of tribal wars on political systems, the ways in which world events affect a poet's writing, or how a scientific discovery improves people's lives. When writers explore the American experience, they can examine the causes of cultural or regional differences; consider the contributions of a particular region or culture to American literature, art, or music; predict the likely effects of living in an ethnically homogeneous neighborhood or attending racially integrated schools; describe the impact of a historical or political event; assess the benefits of an educational or professional opportunity; identify the key events or ideas that have influenced a respected public figure; or examine the reasons behind a person's (or a group's) migration to the United States (or movement from one region of the United States to another).

The writers whose essays are collected in this chapter use cause and effect to examine larger social, political, and economic forces—issues and events that affect them not only as individuals but also as members of a particular culture. As they do so, they examine both obvious and subtle causes and consider positive and negative effects. Thus Marita Golden speculates about the causes and observes the immediate effects on the African-American community of the death of Martin Luther King, Jr.; Gary Soto considers the effects of a life of poverty on his savings habits; Mary Crow Dog and Richard Erdoes illustrate the negative effects of the Indian boarding schools on their pupils; Melanie Scheller examines the impact of rural poverty—specifically, the absence of indoor plumbing— on her life; and Gene Oishi confronts the forces that led him to deny his heritage. As they examine these and other issues, the writers here explore larger themes: the positive and negative aspects of assimilating into a dominant culture, the search for a cultural or racial identity, and the struggle to come to terms with forces (within themselves and in outside institutions) that define and limit their aspirations.

When you write an essay in which you explore causal connections, you may focus on particular topics and issues such as those just discussed. You may also use cause and effect to examine your own cultural identity—to discover who you are, and why. In the process, you may learn about the forces that shape other cultures as well as your own.

In the essay that follows, a student uses cause and effect to explore the experiences that motivated her to learn Tagalog, the native language of her Filipino parents.

STUDENT VOICE: RUEL ESPEJO

Learning Tagalog

Like many young adults my age, I have spent nearly eighteen   1

years trying to be like everyone else. For me, a first-generation

American, this has meant becoming less Filipino and more Ameri-

can. At the same time, though, the particular circumstances of my life have tugged at me, making me want to hold on to my heritage. Little by little, my parents have helped me to realize that I do not want to leave my culture behind. Because I want to hold on to that culture, I have decided to learn Tagalog, my parents' native language.

Sometimes, late at night, my mother would tell me about her childhood back in the Philippines. I loved listening to her accent become thicker and thicker as she went on about her experiences and the beautiful island she called home. It was through her old stories that I grew to know my grandfather. I could see that he was her hero and that she wished I could see him. I also learned about all the traditional roles that my mother reacted against—she was the first feminist I ever met. Once in a while, though, she would try to describe something—the landscape or a native fruit—in the hybrid language we call "Taglish" (half Tagalog, half English), only to give up, saying, "Well, someday I'll take you home. . . ." After these stories, I went to sleep disappointed. I knew that even if I went to the Philippines with her, I would never truly understand what she was talking about.

My father would go through the same routine with me almost every day. He would struggle to tell me something, only to be frustrated by his mixed-up words. His inability to express himself embarrassed him, but we'd laugh it off. Gradually, though, as a result of these conversations, I began to see how lacking my relationships with him and with my mother were because of our communication gap. I know that first-generation Americans often reject their parents' culture and embrace American culture, and I know how easy it has been for me to lose touch with my background because I have always been surrounded by all things American. I also know that this rejection results in more than just your ordinary generation gap—it results in a cultural gap, too. But only now do I realize how unfair and wrong this situation is.

I had often read about assimilation, about cultural groups giving   4
up what makes them unique in order to be accepted. But until I really thought about my parents and our communication barrier, it never occurred to me that I was living it. I always thought that I knew a lot about the Filipino culture; my parents exposed me to it early, and they even taught me some of the traditional dances. But lately I have begun to feel it slipping away. I don't want to lose it forever, and so I have decided to learn Tagalog.

My favorite English teacher has a method of learning new words   5
she calls "Eighty Flashes." She says that the more you expose yourself to a word, either by sight or by usage, the better you'll learn it. In other words, if you use something every day, it will become the norm. Through this technique, I can learn to communicate more fully with my parents and stay in touch with my background. The easiest way to prevent assimilation is to make Filipino culture the norm—and to do that, I will have to use something from it every day. By learning and speaking Tagalog, I can keep my culture alive. I am proud of being a Filipino American, and I want to celebrate it every day. I don't want to end up being one of those completely assimilated "first generationers" I've read about so often.

Without ever telling me what to do, my parents opened up my   6
eyes to my ignorance. Because of them, I have come to realize that

I need to keep on being Filipino as well as American, and because of them I have discovered exactly how to do so. When I can speak Tagalog, I will no longer have to watch my father or mother struggle to explain something to me. I will be able to meet them halfway, on a sort of language bridge. The feeling of alienation between us will disappear, and in its place will be a mutual understanding.

I know that it will take years to learn Tagalog, and I know that   7 it won't be easy. But because my desire to be close to my parents is stronger than my need to "fit in," and because being close to my parents means being close to my culture, I will take the time and effort to learn our native language. My goal is like any other young person's: to realize my whole self. And by learning and speaking my language, I will be doing just that.

Exploring Causal Connections

Cause-and-effect essays search for causes or predict (or describe) effects; sometimes a single essay does both. When you explore causal connections, you look for relationships; these relationships, however, are not sequential (as in narrative or process essays) but causal. Cause-and-effect essays by their nature depend on the development of a logical sequence of events. Any slip in logic—for example, omitting an event that serves as a direct link in a *causal chain* (p. 235)—is therefore more noticeable in cause-and-effect essays than it might be in most other types of writing.

IDENTIFYING CAUSES AND EFFECTS

When you write an essay that examines causal connections, you should *clearly identify causes and effects,* using key words and phrases—such as *cause, change, shape, bring about, create, lead to, effect, result, impact,* and *out-come*—to make your focus on causality clear.

You should also use language to make clear to your readers whether your focus is on finding causes or predicting effects. When, in "In Search of Hiroshi" (p. 250), Gene Oishi asks, "What was it that made me so afraid, so ashamed, and . . . so guilty?" his question reveals that his focus is on a search for *causes.* Similarly, in "Civilize Them with a Stick" (p. 263), Mary Crow Dog and Richard Erdoes make their essay's focus on *effects* just as clear through their use of the word *affected* in the first sentence: "It is almost impossible to explain to a sympathetic white person what a typical old Indian boarding school was like; how it affected the Indian child suddenly dumped into it. . . . "

CONSIDERING ALL SIGNIFICANT CAUSES AND EFFECTS

As you write and revise, check to be sure you *consider all significant causes and effects.* You do not want to examine every conceivable cause and effect or get sidetracked by irrelevant details, but you do not want to overlook a relevant cause or effect, either. Your goal is to present all causes and effects your readers will need to understand the logic of your causal analysis and appreciate its complexity.

When discussing causes, you should consider *subtle* as well as *obvious* causes and *minor* as well as *major* ones—as long as they are relevant to your discussion. Rather than settling for easy answers, Marita Golden in "A Day in April" (p. 244) considers subtle factors that contributed to Martin Luther King's death: "We knew no one man had killed the prophet. Rather, the combined weight of racism and an absence of moral courage had crushed him. A constitution ignored, laws denied, these were the weapons. America pulled the trigger."

When discussing effects, you may consider both *positive* and *negative* results, both *immediate* and *long-term* consequences, and both *personal* and *global* impact. Thus Golden's essay, while stressing the immediate negative effects of King's death—grief, fear, tension, anger, violence—also suggests a more positive long-term effect on the author and people like her: a stronger " 'commitment to the struggle' " of civil rights. Melanie Scheller's "On the Meaning of Plumbing and Poverty" (p. 238), while presenting the largely negative effects of her early years without indoor plumbing, considers the process globally (as it affected other poor families in the rural South) as well as personally (as it affected her own family). Mary Crow Dog and Richard Erdoes see the Indian boarding schools as a plague on the Indian race as well as a setting for personal tragedy.

ARRANGING CAUSES AND EFFECTS

When you plan and draft your essay, remember to *arrange causes and effects logically.* First, decide whether you will treat causes, effects, or both. If your emphasis is on causes, begin with the effect—"I insisted that the experience be seen through the eyes of . . . Hiroshi"—and proceed to examine its causes. If your focus is on effects, begin with the cause—"I spent much of my childhood living in houses without indoor plumbing"—and move on to consider its effects.

If you treat both causes and effects, you can proceed chronologically from cause to effect. In arranging causes and effects within your essay you can use *emphatic order,* beginning with the most significant cause or effect and working toward the least important; or, if you want to build interest, you can begin with the least significant and move toward the most important.

You can also organize your essay as a *causal chain,* a sequence in which each effect is also a cause. For example, you might decide to examine the forces that influenced your career choice. You could begin with the cause—a role model in your community. This individual—a female police officer who is a member of your ethnic group—inspires in you an interest in the field of criminal justice, a decision that leads you to enter college and choose a major. Then, after several years of college and exposure to a variety of courses, your focus shifts to the field of public policy. This interest in turn steers you to the decision to pursue a master's degree. Thus your original role model led you to an interest in a particular field, which led you to seek a college education, which led you on another career path, which led you to an advanced degree.

CHOOSING TRANSITIONS

When you write and revise cause-and-effect essays, *select transitions that make causal connections clear.*

KEY TRANSITIONS: CAUSE AND EFFECT

Because	So
As a result	Then
Consequently	Since
Accordingly	Therefore

In the opening paragraph of "Learning Tagalog" (p. 230), Ruel Espejo uses a transitional word to clarify the connection between cause (her desire to remain in touch with Filipino culture) and effect (learning Tagalog): "*Because* I want to hold on to that culture, I have decided to learn Tagalog, my parents' native language." Later, in paragraph 4, she uses another transition to emphasize the link between cause and effect: "I don't want to lose it forever, and *so* I have decided to learn Tagalog." In her essay's final paragraph, Ruel once again uses a transitional word to make her causal connections clear: "But *because* my desire to be close to my parents is stronger than my need to 'fit in,' and *because* being close to my parents means being close to my culture, I will take the time and effort to learn our native language."

In addition to using words and phrases such as those listed here, you should include transitional expressions to move your readers from one cause or effect to the next ("Another cause"; "The final effect") and to distinguish between more important and less important causes or effects ("The most important effect"; "A minor cause"). In some cases, particularly in long or complex essays, you may decide to include a short transitional *paragraph* to move readers from causes to effects or from effects to causes.

DISTINGUISHING CAUSALITY
FROM SEQUENCE

When you write and revise, be very careful to *distinguish causality from sequence*. The fact that one event *follows* another does not mean that the second is the *result* of the first. When you confuse causality with sequence—that is, when you assume that because event A *precedes* event B, event A *causes* event B—you commit a logical fallacy formally called *post hoc, ergo propter hoc*. It may be true, for example, that a family fleeing Haiti as its economy worsens is seeking to emigrate because of the country's extreme poverty. The actual cause of the family's flight, however, may well be fear of political repression. Although Haiti's economic decline may *precede* an exodus of its citizens, the economy is not necessarily the cause of their departure.

REVIEW CHECKLIST: EXPLORING CAUSAL CONNECTIONS
✓ Clearly identify causes and effects.
✓ Consider all significant causes and effects.
✓ Arrange causes and effects logically.
✓ Select transitions that make causal connections clear.
✓ Distinguish causality from sequence.

MELANIE SCHELLER

On the Meaning of
Plumbing and Poverty

In the following essay Melanie Scheller, winner of the 1990
North Carolina Writers' Network Creative Journalism Contest,
writes ruefully of growing up as "poor white trash" in rural North
Carolina.

One of six children of a widowed mother, Scheller moved with
her family from one dilapidated farmhouse to another during the
1960s. None of her childhood homes had an indoor bathroom,
and the hardships of poverty were compounded by the scorn of
her peers. Indoor plumbing, a convenience most Americans take
for granted, became an obsession.

"My family was visibly and undeniably poor," she writes. "My
clothes were obviously hand-me-downs. I got free lunches at
school. I went to the health department for immunizations.
Surely it was equally obvious that we didn't have a flush toilet.
But like an alcoholic who believes no one will know he has a
problem as long as he doesn't drink in public, I convinced myself
that no one knew my family's little secret. It was a form of denial
that would color my relationships with the outside world for
years to come."

Scheller has written extensively on health and wellness topics for
national consumer publications, and she published a children's
book, *My Grandfather's Hat*, in 1992. She holds graduate degrees in
education and public health administration from the University
of North Carolina at Chapel Hill.

Notice in this essay how Scheller explores the effects of her own
childhood poverty in order to lead her readers to see a larger
point.

S EVERAL YEARS AGO I spent some time as a volunteer on the geriatric   1
ward of a psychiatric hospital. I was fascinated by the behavior of one of
the patients, an elderly woman who shuffled at regular intervals to the
bathroom, where she methodically flushed the toilet. Again and again
she carried out her sacred mission as if summoned by some supernatural
force, until the flush of the toilet became a rhythmic counterpoint for the
ward's activity. If someone blocked her path or if, God forbid, the bathroom was in use when she reached it, she became agitated and confused.

Obviously, that elderly patient was a sick woman. And yet I felt a   2
certain kinship with her, for I too have suffered from an obsession with
toilets. I spent much of my childhood living in houses without indoor
plumbing, and while I don't feel compelled to flush a toilet at regular
intervals, I sometimes feel that toilets, or the lack thereof, have shaped
my identity in ways that are painful to admit.

I'm not a child of the Depression, but I grew up in an area of the   3
South that had changed little since the days of the New Deal. My mother
was a widow with six children to support, not an easy task under any
circumstances, but especially difficult in rural North Carolina during the
1960s. To her credit, we were never seriously in danger of going hungry.
Our vegetable garden kept us stocked with tomatoes and string beans.
We kept a few chickens and sometimes a cow. Blackberries were free for
the picking in the fields nearby. Neighbors did their good Christian duty
by bringing us donations of fresh fruit and candy at Christmastime. But a
roof over our heads—that wasn't so easily improvised.

Like rural Southern gypsies, we moved from one dilapidated   4
Southern farmhouse to another in a constant search for a decent place to
live. Sometimes we moved when the rent increased beyond the 30 or 40
dollars my mother could afford. Or the house burned down, not an unusual occurrence in substandard housing. One year when we were gathered together for Thanksgiving dinner, a stranger walked in without
knocking and announced that we were being evicted. The house had
been sold without our knowledge and the new owner wanted to start
remodeling immediately. We tried to finish our meal with an attitude of
thanksgiving while he worked around us with his tape measure.

Usually we rented from farm families who'd moved from the old   5
home place to one of the brick boxes that are now the standard in rural

Southern architecture. The old farmhouse wasn't worth fixing up with a septic tank and flush toilet, but it was good enough to rent for a few dollars a month to families like mine. The idea of tenants' rights hadn't trickled down yet from the far reaches of the liberal North. It never occurred to us to demand improvements in the facilities. The ethic of the land said we should take what we could get and be grateful for it.

Without indoor plumbing, getting clean is a tiring and time-   6 consuming ritual. At one point I lived in a five-room house with six or more people, all of whom congregated in the one heated room to eat, do homework, watch television, dress and undress, argue, wash dishes. During cold weather we dragged mattresses from the unheated rooms and slept huddled together on the floor by the woodstove. For my bathing routine, I first pinned a sheet to a piece of twine strung across the kitchen. That gave me some degree of privacy from the six other people in the room. At that time our house had an indoor cold-water faucet, from which I filled a pot of water to heat on the kitchen stove. It took several pots of hot water to fill the metal washtub we used.

Since I was a teenager and prone to sulkiness if I didn't get special   7 treatment, I got to take the first bath while the water was still clean. The others used the water I left behind, freshened up with hot water from the pot on the stove. Then the tub had to be dragged to the door and the bath water dumped outside. I longed to be like the woman in the Calgon bath oil commercials, luxuriating in a marble tub full of scented water with bubbles piled high and stacks of thick, clean towels nearby.

People raised in the land of the bath-and-a-half may wonder why I   8 make such a fuss about plumbing. Maybe they spent a year in the Peace Corps, or they back-packed across India, or they worked at a summer camp and, gosh, using a latrine isn't all that bad. And of course it's *not* that bad. Not when you can catch the next plane out of the country, or pick up your duffel bag and head for home, or call mom and dad to come and get you when things get too tedious. A sojourn in a Third World country, where everyone shares the same primitive facilities, may cause some temporary discomfort, but the experience is soon converted into amusing anecdotes for cocktail-party conversation. It doesn't corrode your self-esteem with a sense of shame the way a childhood spent in chronic, unrelenting poverty can.

In the South of my childhood, not having indoor plumbing was the   9 indelible mark of poor white trash. The phrase "so poor they didn't have a pot to piss in" said it all. Poor white trash were viciously stereotyped, and never more viciously than on the playground. White-trash children had cooties—everybody knew that. They had ringworm and pinkeye—don't get near them or you might catch it. They picked their noses. They messed in their pants. If a white-trash child made the mistake of catching a softball during recess, the other children made an elaborate show of wiping it clean before they would touch it.

Once a story circulated at school about a family whose infant   10
daughter had fallen into the "slop jar" and drowned. When I saw the smirks and heard the laughter with which the story was told, I felt sick and afraid in the pit of my stomach. A little girl had died, but people were laughing. What had she done to deserve that laughter? I could only assume that using a chamber pot was something so disgusting, so shameful, that it made a person less than human.

My family was visibly and undeniably poor. My clothes were obvi-   11
ously hand-me-downs. I got free lunches at school. I went to the health department for immunizations. Surely it was equally obvious that we didn't have a flush toilet. But like an alcoholic who believes no one will know he has a problem as long as he doesn't drink in public, I convinced myself that no one knew my family's little secret. It was a form of denial that would color my relationships with the outside world for years to come.

Having a friend from school spend the night at my house was out   12
of the question. Better to be friendless than to have my classmates know my shameful secret. Home visits from teachers or ministers left me in a dither of anticipatory anxiety. As they chattered on and on with Southern small talk about tomato plants and relish recipes, I sat on the edge of my seat, tensed against the dreaded words, "May I use your bathroom, please?" When I began dating in high school, I'd lie in wait behind the front door, ready to dash out as soon as my date pulled in the driveway, never giving him a chance to hear the call of nature while on our property.

With the help of a scholarship I was able to go away to college,   13
where I could choose from dozens of dormitory toilets and take as many hot showers as I wanted, but I could never openly express my joy in using the facilities. My roommates, each a pampered only child from a well-to-do family, whined and complained about having to share a bathroom. I knew that if I expressed delight in simply having a bathroom, I would

immediately be labeled as a hick. The need to conceal my real self by stifling my emotions created a barrier around me and I spent my college years in a vacuum of isolation.

Almost 20 years have passed since I first tried to leave my family's chamber pot behind. For many of those years it followed behind me— the ghost of chamber pots past—clanging and banging and threatening to spill its humiliating contents at any moment. I was convinced that everyone could see it, could smell it even. No college degree or job title seemed capable of banishing it.   14

If finances had permitted, I might have become an Elvis Presley or a Tammy Faye Bakker, easing the pain of remembered poverty with gold-plated bathtub fixtures and leopard-skinned toilet seats. I feel blessed that gradually, ever so gradually, the shame of poverty has begun to fade. The pleasures of the present now take priority over where a long-ago bowel movement did or did not take place. But for many Southerners, chamber pots and outhouses are more than just memories.   15

In North Carolina alone, 200,000 people still live without indoor plumbing. People who haul their drinking water home from a neighbor's house or catch rainwater in barrels. People who can't wash their hands before handling food, the way restaurant employees are required by state law to do. People who sneak into public restrooms every day to wash, shave, and brush their teeth before going to work or to school. People who sacrifice their dignity and self-respect when forced to choose between going homeless and going to an outhouse. People whose children think they deserve the conditions in which they live and hold their heads low to hide the shame. But they're not the ones who should feel ashamed. No, they're not the ones who should feel ashamed.   16

☜ Opening the Dialogue

1. In paragraph 5 Scheller says, "It never occurred to us to demand improvements in the facilities. The ethic of the land said we should take what we could get and be grateful for it." Do you think this attitude is— or was—a practical one? What advantages and disadvantages do you see in not complaining?

2. In paragraph 8 Scheller explains the difference between a life of poverty and a "sojourn in a Third World country." Is this distinction valid? Do you think there is a basic difference in experience and outlook that disqualifies someone who has not grown up in poverty from working to better poor people's lives?

3. In paragraph 16 Scheller sums up the daily humiliations suffered by people who do not have indoor plumbing. Do you think the presence of so many homeless people in America's cities today adds a different dimension to the problem? In what ways do you think rural poverty differs from urban poverty?

✪ Keeping a Notebook

Do you think that it would be difficult for a formerly poor person to adjust to *not* being poor? Has reading Scheller's essay, especially paragraphs 14 and 15, affected your opinion in any way?

✪ Working Together

One of Scheller's problems was what she describes as "the need to conceal my real self"—that is, to conceal her family's secret—which meant sealing herself in a "vacuum of isolation" (paragraph 13). Working in groups, list various "little secrets" families might wish to keep from outsiders. In class discussion, consider the problems created by keeping such secrets. Do you see any advantages?

✪ Writing an Essay

In paragraph 2 Scheller confesses that "toilets, or the lack thereof, have shaped my identity in ways that are painful to admit." Write an essay in which you explain how the lack of something (material, spiritual, or relational) has shaped your life.

MARITA GOLDEN

A Day in April

In "A Day in April"—excerpted from her autobiography, *Migrations of the Heart* (1983)—Marita Golden writes movingly of the bone-deep grief and anger she felt as a fourteen-year-old high school student when Martin Luther King, Jr., was assassinated. She effectively uses the techniques of narration to describe the important effects King's death had on her own life and the lives of her friends.

Golden has said that she "stumbled into" writing her autobiography when she was not yet thirty years old because "I wanted to meditate on what it meant to grow up in the 1960s, what it meant to go to Africa for the first time, what it meant to be a modern black woman living in that milieu. I had to bring order to the chaos of memory. . . . What I wanted to do was write a book that would take my life and shape it into an artifact that could inform and possibly inspire."

Born in 1950 in Washington, D.C., Golden met her Nigerian husband in New York and in the late 1970s, moved to Africa, where she taught at the University of Lagos. Her life in Nigeria, she recalls, "was the most important period in my adult life because I came to terms with my identity, the duality of my heritage."

After her marriage ended and she returned to the United States, Golden continued to teach and write. She comments, "I was trained to be a journalist at Columbia's graduate school of journalism, but I was born, I feel, to simply write, using whatever medium best expresses my obsession at a particular time. I have written poetry and have been included in several anthologies and want in the future to write more. I use and need journalism to explore the external world, to make sense of it. I use and need fiction to give significance to and come to terms with the internal

world of my own particular fears, fantasies, and dreams. . . . I
write essentially to complete myself and to give my vision a significance that the world generally seeks to deny."

Golden lives with her son in Boston. Her novel, *Long Distance Life,*
was published in 1989.

T HE APRIL EVENING WAS MUGGY, our apartment listless beneath the   1
darkness. "The Wild Wild West" filled the television screen as my
mother sat on the sofa beside me, her arthritic knee propped on the coffee table. I watched the television set indifferently, my mind rummaging
through a forest of more immediate concerns—the money for my senior
class ring due next week, ordering a copy of the yearbook, where I should
buy my prom dress. The heat was a blanket tucked under my chin. My
skin was prickly with sweat. Kicking off my sandals, I started unbuttoning
my blouse when the voice of an announcer interrupted the program to
say that Martin Luther King had been shot in Memphis, Tennessee. My
mother struggled upright and grabbed my arm, the wedding band she
still wore cutting into my flesh. The flutter of her heart echoed in the
palm of her hand and beat in spasms against my skin. Then fear crawled
into the room with us. As she huddled me to her breast, I heard her small,
whimpering cry. It sounded like hymns and eulogies dripping from the
air inside a tiny, parched black church. In mourning already, she released
me and wept softly, dabbing her eyes with a handkerchief.

The screen once again filled with scenes of the Old West. Listen-   2
ing to my mother's sobs, my body was set on edge by a raw, hard-edged
anger that nothing in my life up to then had prepared me for. In that
flashing, endless moment that had come on like a seizure, the blood of
my belief in America seeped through my flesh and formed a puddle at my
feet.

Dazed, disbelieving, I reached for the phone and began calling   3
friends. They had all heard the news. Grief, sudden and deep, stripped us
of speech. We clung mutely to the phone as though it were a life raft
bobbing in a sea of cold, lapping madness. If we could just hear another's
voice, even stilled and hurt like our own, then life might go on.

But Washington's ghetto, long voiceless and ignored, scrawled an   4
angry cry along its streets, using bricks, bottles and torches for its song of

sorrow. We knew no one man had killed the prophet. Rather, the combined weight of racism and an absence of moral courage had crushed him. A constitution ignored, laws denied, these were the weapons. America pulled the trigger. For three days and nights a fury of looting and burning cleansed and destroyed the inner core of the city. National Guard troops cordoned off the affected areas. President Johnson appealed on television for an end to the violence, a convulsion spreading across the country. Pacing the apartment, unable to go out because of the curfew, I sympathized with the rioters. A sense of impotence hounded me. I was still numb, catharsis beyond my grasp. I envied their freedom, rooted in the fact that nobody cared about their will or collective rage unless it spilled over the bounds of the ghetto. So the rage continued, taking shape in a death wish–like spiral that devoured only the ghetto, until it was spent and whimpers of regret replaced the shouts.

I walked the streets demolished by the riots a few days after the   5
troops had left and the fires had died. Block after block was filled with only huge hulking store frames turned black from the flames, a damp smell of ashes hanging over each one. Pictures of Robert Kennedy still hung precariously in many store windows. Mountains of rubbish filled the streets. The "Soul Brother" signs that had been pasted on the store windows too late lay burned around the edges among piles of trash. The streets were choked with cars from the Maryland and Virginia suburbs, whites popping their heads out of car windows, snapping pictures.

The days after King's death saw an invisible barricade of tensions   6
rise between the white and black students at Western High School. The black students did not know then that in a few months many of us would repudiate our white friends, no longer finding them "relevant." Finding instead their mere presence inconsistent with a "commitment to the struggle," which is what our lives became overnight. We did not know it, but some of us sensed it, caught tortured, shadowy glimpses of it in the changes festering like mines in the open, dangerous field we would enter upon graduating in June.

Andrea McKinley, small-boned as a deer, with a finely honed sharp   7
wisdom, declared while we were leaving a civics class together that perhaps King's death was a blessing. Shrugging her thin shoulders, removing her glasses and rubbing her eyes, still red from tears, she said, "Let's face it. The movement has changed. He was from another era. He couldn't deal with the ghetto and I think he knew it."

"But how can you say that?" I screamed. "That's the most callous 8
thing I ever heard." We stood in a corner of the crowded hallway, each
hugging books to her chest as for support.

"Do you think that's an easy conclusion for me to come to?" Andrea 9
asked, her look unmasked and pained. "What I'm talking about is a struggle with different rules. Rules that talk about what's really important—
power, community control and identity. How can you talk about love to
people who aren't even listening?" I had never imagined Andrea, so cool
and intellectual, capable of such unflinching anger. At eighteen she had
the demeanor of the Rhodes scholar she would later become. But at that
moment her words sprang from the same place within her where my belief in America had snapped. Her tirade frightened me because she so
precisely articulated my own doubts. It also inspired me because in the
midst of a vacuum it offered hope.

"I'm going to spend the summer with my sister working with 10
SNCC before I go to Oberlin," she said.

"That means you'll be going south?" 11

"Yes. Probably Mississippi." 12

"It's a battleground down there," I whispered, ashamed of the fear 13
evident in my trembling voice.

"Marita, the front lines are everywhere." 14

"I feel like the world's turned upside down. I felt safe before. Now I 15
don't know," I moaned.

"You don't feel safe because now you see the truth. You see how 16
they lied. Integration. Civil Rights." She spat out the words harshly, her
voice a train rushing out of control.

"Just yesterday we cloaked our anger in folk songs and fingers 17
pointed at society," I said.

"Yesterday we had faith," she countered. "Yesterday we were will- 18
ing to wait. I've got a class and I'm already late," she said hurriedly, glancing at her watch.

"We'll talk some more. We *have* to." Unexpectedly, she squeezed 19
my shoulder, as awkwardly as I'd imagined it would be, and strode
quickly down the hall.

In the deserted hallway the silence struck me like a gong. I stood 20
there feeling very old. Unwise. And afraid to look over my shoulder. I
wanted to cut the rest of the day, walk through Georgetown and look in
the opulently decorated store windows, which were like wrapped pack-

ages of silver and gold waiting to be opened. I wished desperately to be frozen in time at that moment, with only this image in my brain. So I ran down the stairs and out the main entrance into a sun so radiant it stabbed my eyes. But even a sun that pure did not destroy the emotional turbulence that whispered in my ear the rest of that day.

⚜ Opening the Dialogue

1. King's death has a tremendous impact on Golden and her friends. What do you see as the most significant change they experienced?

2. In paragraph 6 Golden observes, "The black students did not know then that in a few months many of us would repudiate our white friends, no longer finding them 'relevant.' " Can you explain such a reaction in logical terms? On an emotional level, can you understand why black students would react this way?

3. When Golden's friend Andrea says, " 'Marita, the front lines are everywhere' " (paragraph 14), what do you think she means? Do you believe this statement is accurate today? Does it apply only to race relations, or does it apply to other aspects of life in the United States as well?

⚜ Keeping a Notebook

In paragraph 2 Golden describes her immediate reaction to the news of King's death: "In that flashing, endless moment that had come on like a seizure, the blood of my belief in America seeped through my flesh and formed a puddle at my feet." Do you believe her feeling of being betrayed by her country is justified? Under what circumstances can you imagine yourself reacting in the same way?

⚜ Working Together

In paragraphs 4 and 5 Golden describes the violent aftermath of King's death in scenes familiar to those who watched television coverage of the civil unrest in Los Angeles following the 1992 acquittal of four police officers accused of beating motorist Rodney King. Working in groups, list some *specific* scenes you would choose to film if you were directing television coverage of the 1968 disturbances. In class discussion, consider the pros and cons of showing *any* coverage of such disturbances on national television.

⚙ Writing an Essay

As Golden is well aware, King's assassination will radically change her life. Write an essay about a single political or historical event that you believe has dramatically changed (or will change) the course of your life.

GENE OISHI

In Search of Hiroshi

Gene Oishi was born in 1933 in Guadalupe, California. His first language was Japanese, and he has written that as a young child his life "was a random mixture of East and West. . . . I felt no conflict within myself between American and Japanese things."

His idyllic childhood ended on December 8, 1941, the day after the Japanese attacked Pearl Harbor, when FBI agents came in the middle of the night and arrested his father. Years of anguish and imprisonment in relocation camps followed, and after the war "it was as though the Japanese part of me died," Oishi has said. "Really, the war made me an anti-Japanese bigot. It made me a racist. It made me cut myself off from that child. And to be a racist against yourself is a crippling disability. I tried to overcome it by being a very successful white person."

In large part he succeeded, but at a terrible psychological cost. A reporter for the *Baltimore Sun* and bureau chief in Bonn, Oishi went on to become press secretary for the governor of Maryland in 1979. But, he says, "All my accomplishments felt phony . . . because it wasn't me doing them. . . . It was this Gene Oishi, the white man, who was doing all these things."

Oishi was finally able to reconnect with his past by writing *In Search of Hiroshi* (1988), a memoir of growing up Japanese in America. "Hiroshi is sort of a metaphor for what I was before the trauma," he writes.

Oishi lives in Baltimore, where he works as a public relations specialist and continues to write: "My writing, both fiction and nonfiction, has been part of my attempt to understand the effect [incarceration in an internment camp] had on how I view myself and the world around me. In a broader sense, my writing is a personal exploration of what is involved in living as a [member of a] racial, ethnic minority in the United States, or in any country."

As you read the following, notice that Oishi explores both the causes and the effects of his fear, shame, and guilt in relation to his ethnic heritage.

W HEN I FIRST WENT TO THE *BALTIMORE SUN*, I wrote a piece com-   1 memorating the twentieth anniversary of the ending of World War II, which described the internment of Japanese Americans. The main character in the piece was a boy named Hiroshi, a quasi-fictional character who later became the protagonist in my attempt at writing a novel. Two years later, in 1967, I was asked by West Magazine of the *Los Angeles Times* to write an article on the internment and I insisted that the experience be seen through the eyes of this Hiroshi. The editor at West Magazine was puzzled by that, but he accepted my condition and the magazine published the article with the title, "Remember Pearl Harbor, and then. . . . "

Hiroshi let me write in the third person and sustain the illusion that   2 I was not writing about my own experiences, my own feelings, but those of this imaginary and therefore invulnerable child. I had to set Hiroshi aside, however, when I was asked in 1981 to deliver a briefing paper to the Commission on the Wartime Relocation and Internment of Civilians. The commission wanted a personal account of what the internment was like, so for the first time I wrote in the first person. It was more traumatic than I could have imagined it would be. It took all my strength to keep myself from breaking down as I stood before the commission reading my paper whose principal point was that I was Japanese.

I am an American, but an American of the Japanese race. That sen-   3 tence would have struck me at one time as a contradiction in terms. I had become so used to accommodating the racist attitudes of my fellow Americans that I had become an anti-Japanese racist myself. World War II and the internment offered only a partial explanation and if left unexamined they provided no explanation at all. I needed to look at them not as history, but as events that affected my life and my thoughts. I needed to try to relive my childhood and to rekindle old feelings to see what it was in the past that made the present seem so dark and threatening. What was it that made me so afraid, so ashamed, and feel so guilty?

Because of the stories my mother read to me as a child and those   4
my father told, it was my impression that Japanese history was extraordi-
narily violent and bloody. It appeared to have been a common practice
for warriors to chop off the heads of those they defeated, especially if the
vanquished were of high rank, and carry them back as proof of their
valor. In my imagination I saw fields strewn with headless bodies trampled by fierce samurai with bleeding heads swinging from their belts. It
was a relief to me to read Winston Churchill's *History of the English-Speaking
Peoples,* in which he described the mass slaughter that took place in the
battles on the British Isles. The English, the Scots, and the Irish were
every bit as cruel as the Japanese. When I read Japanese history, it struck
me that compared to Europe and the United States it was remarkably
peaceful. Medieval Japan was racked by civil strife with warring clans
vying for supremacy, but there were also periods of stability and relative
calm. After Tokugawa Ieyasu unified the country in the early seventeenth
century, Japan enjoyed peace and stability that lasted for two-and-a-half
centuries. My mother was right. He was a great man. Compared to U.S.
history, in which hardly thirty years go by without a major war,
Tokugawa Japan was an island of tranquility.

It was more difficult for me to deal with modern Japanese history.   5
Japanese aggression against China troubled me. Japan was behaving just
as badly as the European powers; sometimes worse. There was no justification for the atrocities committed by Japanese troops. I read about the
mass murders, the rapes and pillaging in Nanking, and the "death march
of Bataan," desperately looking for extenuating circumstances, or at least
some explanation for the barbaric behavior and savagery of the Japanese
troops. I could not find any that satisfied me.

When I was writing about ethnic affairs at the *Sun* I did a story on   6
the foreign Islamic community in Baltimore. While researching the piece
I met a Pakistani who asked me whether I was Buddhist. I replied I was at
most a nominal Buddhist. My parents were Buddhist so that might make
me one, but I had never practiced the religion as an adult. He then asked
me whether Buddhists revered life in all forms. I replied that is what I had
read, but I didn't know much about it. Then the man, who seemed to be
getting angrier and angrier, said Buddhists in Burma a few years earlier
had massacred hundreds of Moslems and he asked how that squared with
a reverence for life. He railed at me saying that Buddhists were hypocrites
and glared as if he expected me to defend the actions of the Burmese

Buddhists or perhaps apologize for them. I, of course, could do neither, but the man made me feel guilty. I pondered this feeling of guilt, which seemed to defy all reason, and it ultimately helped me. I began to realize that I did not need to defend or apologize for the evil deeds committed even by Japanese. The Japanese were capable of evil because they were human, and human beings of every race have committed unspeakably cruel and violent acts throughout history. If there were within me the seeds of evil, they were there because I was human. And being human, there was also within me the capacity for goodness. I was as free to choose between good and evil as anybody else and my race was no cause for shame or despair.

I saw, at last, not just the injustice of our being interned during   7 World War II, but the absurdity of it. Just as the Pakistani needed to upbraid me for the actions of the Burmese Buddhists, the American public and the American government needed to take some action against Japanese living in the United States after the attack on Pearl Harbor. When they heard reports of the atrocities committed by Japanese troops against American soldiers in the Philippines there was an even stronger urge to act. If national security were the issue, there was more reason to intern the Japanese in Hawaii, which had been shown to be vulnerable to attack by Japanese naval forces. But there was no mass internment of Japanese there because they constituted a third of the population and a third of the work force. The Japanese on the mainland were expendable and therefore we became the objects against whom the government could take action. The American people and government faced a national crisis and there was an overpowering need to lash out, to do something—anything. And so on the grounds that "a jap is a jap," the government incarcerated Japanese Americans.

The knowledge that my internment had been based on racism and   8 wartime hysteria was not enough to dispel my feelings of shame and guilt. During the war I began to share the anti-Japanese feelings. But I was not angry like other Americans about Pearl Harbor; I felt guilty instead. And when I heard about the atrocities committed by Japanese troops I was ashamed and felt guilty about that, too. We ought to have been interned. I, too, wanted action, vengeance. But can one wreak vengeance against oneself?

I tried to kill the Japanese in me, to submerge myself deeper and   9 deeper into the white world. For many years, it worked; I could succeed and be accepted in a white society. So complete was my psychic submersion at times that when I looked in the mirror I would be surprised to see a Japanese staring back at me. At other times, I felt like an actor on a stage. None of my accomplishments had much meaning for me because they were not my accomplishments, they were those of the characters I had played or was currently playing. I could be equally detached from my failures. Even the thought of suicide and death did not hold the usual terror for me. I could not kill somebody who was not really there, who had not been there for a very long time.

It is often said that time heals all wounds. But some wounds fester   10
subcutaneously even after all outward signs are gone. The Greek tragedians knew that, for what else is a curse that follows a family for generations but a metaphor for the festering effects of an offense that cannot be forgiven or a hurt that will not be soothed. There are times when a wound must be opened and cleansed no matter how painful the process.

While in the Army I read an essay by Alfred North Whitehead, in   11
which he said, "The present contains all that there is. It is holy ground; for it is the past and it is the future." The thought intrigued me and it has stayed with me. What it has come to mean to me is that we carry with us our own reality which shifts and grows and at times retreats, but which at any given moment defines who we are. It is not necessarily true that we are the sum of all our experiences, for we are capable of shrinking our minds and hearts to become less than what we are or are capable of being. That is what I had done and a great many other Japanese in America have done. The bombs that fell on Pearl Harbor on December 7, 1941, set off a chain of events that set me adrift from my past—my parents, my family, and my childhood. I was cut off from that child within me that is the core of my being. I have named that child Hiroshi and in an attempt to find him I have tried writing about him in fiction and nonfiction, but he has remained elusive.

When I first began writing about Hiroshi, around 1965, I did so   12
because I felt I had been cut in half by the war. It seemed to me that my American half survived, but my Japanese half shriveled up and died. Hiroshi was the last image I had of the whole child. He was the child who ate *misoshiru* and shouted *"banzai!"* to the Emperor on his birthday, listened to the Lone Ranger on radio, and followed the adventures of Batman in the comic books. He was neither American nor Japanese, but simply me. I thought I had found him when I visited Japan as a young

man of 27, but concluded before I left that Yoshitaka-*san** was a carica-
ture, a distorted, one-dimensional view of Hiroshi. I saw Hiroshi's
shadow when I visited Guadalupe in 1983, but nothing more. I got a
glimpse of him in the desert wilderness of Arizona when I visited Gila the
following year. Sometimes I see him vaguely, very vaguely, in my children. Where I need to see him is within myself. This book was intended
to clear away the fear and confusion that have attended my search for
Hiroshi. Like a good detective, I needed to determine first when and
where I had lost him. I have done that now, and the search for Hiroshi
can continue.

☺ Opening the Dialogue

1. Why do you think Oishi feels a need to create the fictional persona he
calls Hiroshi? What, if anything, do you believe he loses—as a writer and
as a person—by not writing about his experiences in his own voice?

2. In paragraph 12 Oishi describes Hiroshi as "neither American nor Japanese, but simply me." Do you believe it is possible in a diverse society
such as the United States to be simply a person, with no particular ethnic
or national identity? Do you think such a thing is possible in a nation
with a largely homogeneous population, such as Japan or Norway?

3. Many years after World War II ended, Oishi still felt guilt and shame
both for the U.S. government's internment of Japanese Americans and for
atrocities committed by Japanese soldiers during the war. Why do you
think he felt this way when he was completely innocent of blame?

☺ Keeping a Notebook

In paragraph 6 Oishi explains how he resolved his feelings of irrational
guilt about "the evil deeds committed . . . by Japanese" and accepted the
fact that "the Japanese were capable of evil because they were human,
and human beings of every race have committed unspeakably cruel and
violent acts throughout history." What deeds done by those of your own

*This is Oishi's Japanese name.

ethnic or racial group bother or upset you? How do you manage to feel pride in your heritage despite your knowledge of such acts?

🕲 Working Together

Like other writers, Oishi uses writing for a variety of purposes. Working in groups, identify the various reasons he might have had for writing "In Search of Hiroshi." In class discussion, consider which of these reasons seems to be his primary purpose for writing the essay.

🕲 Writing an Essay

In paragraph 9 Oishi says, "I tried to kill the Japanese in me, to submerge myself deeper and deeper into the white world." Can you imagine yourself rejecting your cultural heritage in this manner? Write an essay in which you consider the emotional, professional, and social effects—both positive and negative—of a "psychic submersion" in another culture.

GARY SOTO

The Savings Book

"As a kid I imagined a dark fate. To marry Mexican poor, work Mexican hours, and in the end die a Mexican death." By the time Gary Soto wrote those words in his memoir *Living Up the Street* (1985), he had escaped that "dark fate." Happily married, considered one of the most talented Chicano poets, an associate professor at the University of California at Berkeley, Soto is a prolific and respected writer. But, as the following selection from his memoir vividly conveys, the fear of poverty can so color reality as to obscure one's ability to recognize opportunity.

Born in 1952 into a working class Mexican-American family in Fresno, California, Soto labored as a migrant worker along with his family during his youth. "I don't think I had any literary aspirations when I was a kid. In fact we were pretty much an illiterate family. We didn't have books and no one encouraged us to read." He enrolled in Fresno Community College in 1970, partly, he recalls, to avoid the draft and partly because "I didn't want to be poor—I'd had enough of that." There he studied with the poet Philip Levine. Soto's first book of poems, *The Elements of San Joaquin* (1977), was strongly autobiographical, but Soto rejects with irritation attempts to stereotype his work, and he has repeatedly emphasized his resistance to ethnic labels: "One of the things I would like to do is make that leap from being a Chicano writer to being a writer. I think the label can be very damaging to the individual. . . . Some critics want to keep Mexicans in the barrio and, once they get out of there, they point the finger and say, 'Shame, shame.' . . . I like to do different things and each book is slightly different from the others."

Soto lives with his family in California. Among his works are poetry, *The Tale of Sunlight* and *Black Hair;* essays, *Lesser Evils: Ten Quartets;* and a second volume of memoirs, *Small Faces.*

In this essay notice how he explores the causal connection between his family's early financial instability and his own obsession with money and savings.

M Y WIFE, CAROLYN, MARRIED ME for my savings: Not the double   1
digit figures but the strange three or four dollar withdrawals and deposits.
The first time she saw my passbook she laughed until her eyes became
moist and then hugged me as she called "Poor baby." And there was truth
to what she was saying: Poor.

I remember opening my savings account at Guarantee Savings May   2
27, 1969, which was a Monday. The previous Saturday my brother and I
had taken a labor bus to chop cotton in the fields west of Fresno. We
returned home in the back of a pickup with fourteen dollars each and a
Mexican national who kept showing us watches and rings for us to buy.
That day my brother and I wouldn't spring for Cokes or sandwiches, as
most everyone else on our crew did when a vending truck drove up at
lunch time, tooting a loud horn. The driver opened the aluminum doors
to display his goods, and the workers, who knew better but couldn't resist, hovered over the iced Cokes, the cellophaned sandwiches, and the
Hostess cupcakes. We look on from the shade of the bus, sullen and most
certainly sensible. Why pay forty cents when you could get a Coke in
town for half the price. Why buy a sandwich for sixty-five cents when
you could have slapped together your own sandwich. That was what our
mother had done for us. She had made us tuna sandwiches which by
noon had grown suspiciously sour when we peeled back the top slice to
peek in. Still, we ate them, chewing slowly and watching each other to
see if he were beginning to double over. Finished, we searched the paper
bag and found a broken stack of saltine crackers wrapped in wax paper.
What a cruel mother, we thought. Dry crackers on a dry day when it was
sure to rise into the nineties as we chopped cotton or, as the saying went,
"played Mexican golf."

We had each earned fourteen dollars for eight hours of work, the   3
most money I had ever made in one day. Two days later, on May 27,
1969, I deposited those dollars; on June 9th I made my first withdrawal—
four dollars to buy a belt to match a pair of pants. I had just been hired to
sell encyclopedias, and the belt was intended to dazzle my prospective

clients when they opened the door to receive me. But in reality few welcomed my presence on their doorsteps and the only encyclopedias I sold that summer were to families on welfare who so desperately wanted to rise from their soiled lives. Buy a set, I told them, and your problems will disappear. Knowledge is power. Education is the key to the future, and so on. The contracts, however, were rescinded and my commissions with them.

On June 20 I withdrew three dollars and twenty-five cents to buy a 4 plain white shirt because my boss had suggested that I should look more "professional." Still, I sold encyclopedias to the poor and again the contracts were thrown out. Finally I was fired, my briefcase taken away, and the company tie undone from my neck. I walked home in the summer heat despairing at the consequence: No new clothes for the fall.

On July 13 I took out five dollars and eighty cents which, including 5 the five cents interest earned, left me with a balance of one dollar. I used the money for bus fare to Los Angeles to look for work. I found it in a tire factory. At summer's end I returned home and walked proudly to Guarantee Savings with my pockets stuffed with ten dollar bills. That was September 5, and my new balance jumped to one hundred and forty-one dollars. I was a senior in high school and any withdrawals from my account went exclusively to buy clothes, never for food, record albums, or concerts. On September 15, for instance, I withdrew fifteen dollars for a shirt and jeans. On September 24 I again stood before the teller to ask for six dollars. I bought a sweater at the Varsity Shop at Coffee's.

Slowly my savings dwindled that fall semester, although I did beef 6 it up with small deposits: Twenty dollars on October 1, ten dollars on November 19, fifteen dollars on December 31, and so on. But by February my savings account balance read three dollars and twelve cents. On March 2 I returned to the bank to withdraw one crisp dollar to do God knows what. Perhaps it was to buy my mother a birthday gift. Seven days later, on March 10, I made one last attempt to bolster my savings by adding eight dollars. By March 23, however, I was again down to one dollar.

By the time I finally closed my account, it had fluctuated for five 7 years, rising and falling as a barometer to my financial quandry. What is curious to me about this personal history are the kinds of transactions that took place—one day I would withdraw three dollars while on another day I would ask for six. How did it vanish? What did it buy? I'm almost certain I bought clothes but for what occasion? For whom? I didn't have a girlfriend in my senior year, so where did the money go?

To withdraw those minor amounts was no easy task. I had to walk   8 or bicycle nearly four miles, my good friend Scott tagging along, and afterward we'd walk up and down the Fresno Mall in search of the elusive girlfriend or, if worse came to worst, to look for trouble.

My savings book is a testimony to my fear of poverty—that by   9 saving a dollar here, another there, it would be kept at bay.

I admit that as a kid I worried about starving, although there was   10 probably no reason. There was always something to eat; the cupboards were weighed down with boxes of this and that. But when I was older the remembrance of difficult times stayed with me: The time Mother was picking grapes and my brother ate our entire lunch while my sister and I played under the vines. For us there was nothing to eat that day. The time I opened the refrigerator at my father's (who was separated from our mother at the time) to stare at one puckered apple that sat in the conspicuous glare of the refrigerator's light. I recalled my uncle lying on a couch dying of cancer. I recalled my father who died from an accident a year later and left us in even more roughed up shoes. I had not been born to be scared out of my wits, but that is what happened. Through a set of experiences early in my life, I grew up fearful that some financial tragedy would strike at any moment, as when I was certain that the recession of 1973 would lead to chaos—burned cars and street fighting. During the recession I roomed with my brother and I suggested that we try to become vegetarians. My brother looked up from his drawing board and replied: "Aren't we already?" I thought about it for a while, and it was true. I was getting most of my hearty meals from my girlfriend, Carolyn, who would later become my wife. She had a job with great pay, and when she opened her refrigerator I almost wept for the bologna, sliced ham, and drumsticks. I spied the cheeses and imported olives, tomatoes, and the artichoke hearts. I opened the freezer—chocolate ice cream!

At the time Carolyn put up with my antics, so when I suggested   11 that we buy fifty dollars worth of peanut butter and pinto beans to store under her bed, she happily wrote out a check because she was in love and didn't know any better. I was certain that in 1974 the country would slide into a depression and those who were not prepared would be lost. We hid the rations in the house and sat at the front window to wait for something to happen.

What happened was that we married and I loosened up. I still fear   12
the worst, but the worst is not what it once was. Today I bought a pair of shoes; tomorrow I may splurge to see a movie, with a box of popcorn and a large soda that will wash it all down. It's time to live, I tell myself, and if a five dollar bill flutters from my hands, no harm will result. I laugh at the funny scenes that aren't funny, and I can't think of any better life.

⊛ Opening the Dialogue

1. In paragraphs 3 and 4 Soto remembers selling encyclopedias to "families on welfare who so desperately wanted to rise from their soiled lives." What parallels do you see between this kind of spending and the kind of spending Soto does?

2. Over and above being poor, how do you think being Mexican American affects Soto's attitude toward money?

3. Soto's reaction to the impending recession is to economize, and even to hoard food because he fears "the country would slide into a depression and those who were not prepared would be lost" (paragraph 11). How would you react to an imminent depression? Would you spend or save, act or hesitate? How do you account for your reactions?

⊛ Keeping a Notebook

In paragraph 9 Soto says, "My savings book is a testimony to my fear of poverty—that by saving a dollar here, another there, it would be kept at bay." What story does your saving and spending pattern tell about you?

⊛ Working Together

List the kinds of expenses you have, and calculate the proportion of your income spent on each category. Then, working in groups, try to create a pie chart representing a typical budget for a student with no dependents. In class discussion, compare such a budget with one for someone who is relatively wealthy and one for someone who is relatively poor. How would the distribution of money within the various categories change in each case? What categories would be included in one type of budget that would not be included in another?

☜ Writing an Essay

How have your culture, your upbringing, and your family's economic status affected your attitude toward earning, spending, and saving money? What other factors have shaped your outlook?

MARY CROW DOG
AND RICHARD ERDOES

Civilize Them with a Stick

"I am Mary Brave Bird," writes Mary Crow Dog, using her given name. "After I had my baby during the siege of Wounded Knee [in 1973] they gave me a special name—*Ohitika Win*, Brave Woman, and fastened an eagle plume in my hair, singing brave heart songs for me. I am a woman of the Red nation, a Sioux woman. That is not easy." In fact, Mary Crow Dog's life has been far more than simply "not easy." The following excerpt from her autobiography (written with Richard Erdoes) *Lakota Woman* (1990) shows the degradation and racism Crow Dog suffered as a young student at a boarding school run by the Bureau of Indian Affairs.

Crow Dog was born on the Rosebud reservation in South Dakota in 1955. Her early life was one of poverty and brutality, marked by fighting, drug abuse, shoplifting, and heavy drinking. Her involvement with the American Indian Movement in 1973 channeled her rage and despair away from self-destructive behavior and into the fight for civil rights. She has explained the different struggles of Native and black Americans: "The blacks want what the whites have, which is understandable. They want *in*. We Indians want *out*." She writes, "I do not consider myself a radical or a revolutionary. It is white people who have put such labels on us. All we ever wanted was to be left alone, to live our lives as we see fit. . . . I could have accepted our flimsy shack, our smelly outhouse, and our poverty—but only on my terms. Yes, I would have accepted poverty, dignified, uninterfered-with poverty, but not the drunken, degrading, and humiliating poverty we had to endure."

Married to Leonard Crow Dog, son of a family of chiefs and medicine men, Mary Crow Dog lives and works on the Rosebud reservation. Richard Erdoes is an artist, civil rights activist, and author
of several books, including *Lame Deer Seeker of Visions, The Sun Dance
People*, and *The Sound of Flutes*.

In the following selection, Crow Dog vividly recalls her experiences in the government-run boarding school. Notice how the
use of many specific incidents from her life in such a school helps
achieve the "almost impossible" task of explaining how these
schools "affected the Indian child suddenly dumped into" them.

> . . . *Gathered from the cabin, the wickiup, and the tepee,*
> *partly by cajolery and partly by threats;*
> *partly by bribery and partly by force,*
> *they are induced to leave their kindred*
> *to enter these schools and take upon themselves*
> *the outward appearance of civilized life.*
> —*Annual report of the Department of Interior, 1901*

I T IS ALMOST IMPOSSIBLE to explain to a sympathetic white person what   1
a typical old Indian boarding school was like; how it affected the Indian
child suddenly dumped into it like a small creature from another world,
helpless, defenseless, bewildered, trying desperately and instinctively to
survive and sometimes not surviving at all. I think such children were like
the victims of Nazi concentration camps trying to tell average, middle-
class Americans what their experience had been like. Even now, when
these schools are much improved, when the buildings are new, all gleaming steel and glass, the food tolerable, the teachers well trained and well
intentioned, even trained in child psychology—unfortunately the psychology of white children, which is different from ours—the shock to the
child upon arrival is still tremendous. Some just seem to shrivel up, don't
speak for days on end, and have an empty look in their eyes. I know of an
eleven-year-old on another reservation who hanged herself, and in our
school, while I was there, a girl jumped out of the window, trying to
kill herself to escape an unbearable situation. That first shock is always
there. . . .

The mission school at St. Francis was a curse for our family for gen-   2 erations. My grandmother went there, then my mother, then my sisters and I. At one time or other every one of us tried to run away. Grandma told me once about the bad times she had experienced at St. Francis. In those days they let students go home only for one week every year. Two days were used up for transportation, which meant spending just five days out of three hundred and sixty-five with her family. And that was an improvement. Before grandma's time, on many reservations they did not let the students go home at all until they had finished school. Anybody who disobeyed the nuns was severely punished. The building in which my grandmother stayed had three floors, for girls only. Way up in the attic were little cells, about five by five by ten feet. One time she was in church and instead of praying she was playing jacks. As punishment they took her to one of those little cubicles where she stayed in darkness because the windows had been boarded up. They left her there for a whole week with only bread and water for nourishment. After she came out she promptly ran away, together with three other girls. They were found and brought back. The nuns stripped them naked and whipped them. They used a horse buggy whip on my grandmother. Then she was put back into the attic—for two weeks.

My mother had much the same experiences but never wanted to   3
talk about them, and then there I was, in the same place. The school is now run by the BIA—the Bureau of Indian Affairs—but only since about fifteen years ago. When I was there, during the 1960s, it was still run by the Church. The Jesuit fathers ran the boys' wing and the Sisters of the Sacred Heart ran us—with the help of the strap. Nothing had changed since my grandmother's days. I have been told recently that even in the '70s they were still beating children at that school. All I got out of school was being taught how to pray. I learned quickly that I would be beaten if I failed in my devotions or, God forbid, prayed the wrong way, especially prayed in Indian to Wakan Tanka, the Indian Creator.

The girls' wing was built like an F and was run like a penal institu-   4
tion. Every morning at five o'clock the sisters would come into our large dormitory to wake us up, and immediately we had to kneel down at the sides of our beds and recite the prayers. At six o'clock we were herded into the church for more of the same. I did not take kindly to the discipline and to marching by the clock, left-right, left-right. I was never one to like being forced to do something. I do something because I feel like doing it. I felt this way always, as far as I can remember, and my sister

Barbara felt the same way. An old medicine man once told me: "Us Lakotas are not like dogs who can be trained, who can be beaten and keep on wagging their tails, licking the hand that whipped them. We are like cats, little cats, big cats, wildcats, bobcats, mountain lions. It doesn't matter what kind, but cats who can't be tamed, who scratch if you step on their tails." But I was only a kitten and my claws were still small.

Barbara was still in the school when I arrived and during my first   5 year or two she could still protect me a little bit. When Barb was a seventh-grader she ran away together with five other girls, early in the morning before sunrise. They brought them back in the evening. The girls had to wait for two hours in front of the mother superior's office. They were hungry and cold, frozen through. It was wintertime and they had been running the whole day without food, trying to make good their escape. The mother superior asked each girl, "Would you do this again?" She told them that as punishment they would not be allowed to visit home for a month and that she'd keep them busy on work details until the skin on their knees and elbows had worn off. At the end of her speech she told each girl, "Get up from this chair and lean over it." She then lifted the girls' skirts and pulled down their underpants. Not little girls either, but teenagers. She had a leather strap about a foot long and four inches wide fastened to a stick, and beat the girls, one after another, until they cried. Barb did not give her that satisfaction but just clenched her teeth. There was one girl, Barb told me, the nun kept on beating and beating until her arm got tired.

I did not escape my share of the strap. Once, when I was thirteen   6 years old, I refused to go to Mass. I did not want to go to church because I did not feel well. A nun grabbed me by the hair, dragged me upstairs, made me stoop over, pulled my dress up (we were not allowed at the time to wear jeans), pulled my panties down, and gave me what they called "swats"—twenty-five swats with a board around which Scotch tape had been wound. She hurt me badly.

My classroom was right next to the principal's office and almost   7 every day I could hear him swatting the boys. Beating was the common punishment for not doing one's homework, or for being late to school. It had such a bad effect upon me that I hated and mistrusted every white person on sight, because I met only one kind. It was not until much later that I met sincere white people I could relate to and be friends with. Racism breeds racism in reverse.

The routine at St. Francis was dreary. Six A.M., kneeling in church   8
for an hour or so; seven o'clock, breakfast; eight o'clock, scrub the floor,
peel spuds, make classes. We had to mop the dining room twice every
day and scrub the tables. If you were caught taking a rest, doodling on
the bench with a fingernail or knife, or just rapping, the nun would come
up with a dish towel and just slap it across your face, saying, "You're not
supposed to be talking, you're supposed to be working!" Monday mornings we had cornmeal mush, Tuesday oatmeal, Wednesday rice and rai-
sins, Thursday cornflakes, and Friday all the leftovers mixed together or
sometimes fish. Frequently the food had bugs or rocks in it. We were
eating hot dogs that were weeks old, while the nuns were dining on ham,
whipped potatoes, sweet peas, and cranberry sauce. In winter our dorm
was icy cold while the nuns' rooms were always warm.

I have seen little girls arrive at the school, first-graders, just fresh   9
from home and totally unprepared for what awaited them, little girls with
pretty braids, and the first thing the nuns did was chop their hair off and
tie up what was left behind their ears. Next they would dump the children into tubs of alcohol, a sort of rubbing alcohol, "to get the germs off."
Many of the nuns were German immigrants, some from Bavaria, so that
we sometimes speculated whether Bavaria was some sort of Dracula
country inhabited by monsters. For the sake of objectivity I ought to
mention that two of the German fathers were great linguists and that the
only Lakota-English dictionaries and grammars which are worth anything were put together by them.

At night some of the girls would huddle in bed together for com-   10
fort and reassurance. Then the nun in charge of the dorm would come in
and say, "What are the two of you doing in bed together? I smell evil in
this room. You girls are evil incarnate. You are sinning. You are going to
hell and burn forever. You can act that way in the devil's frying pan." She
would get them out of bed in the middle of the night, making them kneel
and pray until morning. We had not the slightest idea what it was all
about. At home we slept two and three in a bed for animal warmth and a
feeling of security.

The nuns and the girls in the two top grades were constantly bat-   11
tling it out physically with fists, nails, and hair-pulling. I myself was
growing from a kitten into an undersized cat. My claws were getting bigger and were itching for action. About 1969 or 1970 a strange young
white girl appeared on the reservation. She looked about eighteen or

twenty years old. She was pretty and had long, blond hair down to her waist, patched jeans, boots, and a backpack. She was different from any other white person we had met before. I think her name was Wise. I do not know how she managed to overcome our reluctance and distrust, getting us into a corner, making us listen to her, asking us how we were treated. She told us that she was from New York. She was the first real hippie or Yippie we had come across. She told us of people called the Black Panthers, Young Lords, and Weathermen. She said, "Black people are getting it on. Indians are getting it on in St. Paul and California. How about you?" She also said, "Why don't you put out an underground paper, mimeograph it. It's easy. Tell it like it is. Let it all hang out." She spoke a strange lingo but we caught on fast.

Charlene Left Hand Bull and Gina One Star were two full-blood   12
girls I used to hang out with. We did everything together. They were willing to join me in a Sioux uprising. We put together a newspaper which we called the *Red Panther*. In it we wrote how bad the school was, what kind of slop we had to eat—slimy, rotten, blackened potatoes for two weeks—the way we were beaten. I think I was the one who wrote the worst article about our principal of the moment, Father Keeler. I put all my anger and venom into it. I called him a goddam wasičun son of a bitch. I wrote that he knew nothing about Indians and should go back to where he came from, teaching white children whom he could relate to. I wrote that we knew which priests slept with which nuns and that all they ever could think about was filling their bellies and buying a new car. It was the kind of writing which foamed at the mouth, but which also lifted a great deal of weight from one's soul.

On Saint Patrick's Day, when everybody was at the big powwow,   13
we distributed our newspapers. We put them on windshields and bulletin boards, in desks and pews, in dorms and toilets. But someone saw us and snitched on us. The shit hit the fan. The three of us were taken before a board meeting. Our parents, in my case my mother, had to come. They were told that ours was a most serious matter, the worst thing that had ever happened in the school's long history. One of the nuns told my mother, "Your daughter really needs to be talked to." "What's wrong with my daughter?" my mother asked. She was given one of our *Red Panther* newspapers. The nun pointed out its name to her and then my piece, waiting for mom's reaction. After a while she asked, "Well, what have you got to say to this? What do you think?"

My mother said, "Well, when I went to school here, some years   14
back, I was treated a lot worse then these kids are. I really can't see how
they can have any complaints, because we was treated a lot stricter. We
could not even wear skirts halfway up our knees. These girls have it
made. But you should forgive them because they are young. And it's supposed to be a free country, free speech and all that. I don't believe what
they done is wrong." So all I got out of it was scrubbing six flights of stairs
on my hands and knees, every day. And no boy-side privileges.

The boys and girls were still pretty much separated. The only time   15
one could meet a member of the opposite sex was during free time, between four and five-thirty, in the study hall or on benches or the volley-
ball court outside, and that was strictly supervised. One day Charlene
and I went over to the boys' side. We were on the ball team and they had
to let us practice. We played three extra minutes, only three minutes
more than we were supposed to. Here was the nuns' opportunity for re-
venge. We got twenty-five swats. I told Charlene, "We are getting too
old to have our bare asses whipped that way. We are old enough to have
babies. Enough of this shit. Next time we fight back." Charlene only said,
"Hoka-hay!"

We had to take showers every evening. One little girl did not want   16
to take her panties off and one of the nuns told her, "You take those underpants off—or else!" But the child was ashamed to do it. The nun was
getting her swat to threaten the girl. I went up to the sister, pushed her
veil off, and knocked her down. I told her that if she wanted to hit a little
girl she should pick on me, pick one her own size. She got herself transferred out of the dorm a week later.

In a school like this there is always a lot of favoritism. At St. Francis   17
it was strongly tinged with racism. Girls who were near-white, who came
from what the nuns called "nice families," got preferential treatment.
They waited on the faculty and got to eat ham or eggs and bacon in the
morning. They got the easy jobs while the skins, who did not have the
right kind of background—myself among them—always wound up in the
laundry room sorting out ten bushel baskets of dirty boys' socks every
day. Or we wound up scrubbing the floors and doing all the dishes. The
school therefore fostered fights and antagonism between whites and
breeds, and between breeds and skins. At one time Charlene and I had to
iron all the robes and vestments the priests wore when saying Mass. We
had to fold them up and put them into a chest in the back of the church.

In a corner, looking over our shoulders, was a statue of the crucified Savior, all bloody and beaten up. Charlene looked up and said, "Look at that poor Indian. The pigs sure worked him over." That was the closest I ever came to seeing Jesus.

I was held up as a bad example and didn't mind. I was old enough   18
to have a boyfriend and promptly got one. At the school we had an hour and a half for ourselves. Between the boys' and the girls' wings were some benches where one could sit. My boyfriend and I used to go there just to hold hands and talk. The nuns were very uptight about any boy-girl stuff. They had an exaggerated fear of anything having even the faintest connection with sex. One day in religion class, an all-girl class, Sister Bernard singled me out for some remarks, pointing me out as a bad example, an example that should be shown. She said that I was too free with my body. That I was holding hands which meant that I was not a good example to follow. She also said that I wore unchaste dresses, skirts which were too short, too suggestive, shorter than regulations permitted, and for that I would be punished. She dressed me down before the whole class, carrying on and on about my unchastity.

I stood up and told her, "You shouldn't say any of those things,   19
miss. You people are a lot worse than us Indians. I know all about you, because my grandmother and my aunt told me about you. Maybe twelve, thirteen years ago you had a water stoppage here in St. Francis. No water could get through the pipes. There are water lines right under the mission, underground tunnels and passages where in my grandmother's time only the nuns and priests could go, which were off-limits to everybody else. When the water backed up they had to go through all the water lines and clean them out. And in those huge pipes they found the bodies of newborn babies. And they were white babies. They weren't Indian babies. At least when our girls have babies, they don't do away with them that way, like flushing them down the toilet, almost.

"And that priest they sent here from Holy Rosary in Pine Ridge   20
because he molested a little girl. You couldn't think of anything better than dump him on us. All he does is watch young women and girls with that funny smile on his face. Why don't you point him out for an example?"

Charlene and I worked on the school newspaper. After all we had   21
some practice. Every day we went down to Publications. One of the priests acted as the photographer, doing the enlarging and developing.

He smelled of chemicals which had stained his hands yellow. One day he invited Charlene into the darkroom. He was going to teach her developing. She was developed already. She was a big girl compared to him, taller too. Charlene was nicely built, not fat, just rounded. No sharp edges anywhere. All of a sudden she rushed out of the darkroom, yelling to me, "Let's get out of here! He's trying to feel me up. That priest is nasty." So there was this too to contend with—sexual harassment. We complained to the student body. The nuns said we just had a dirty mind.

We got a new priest in English. During one of his first classes he asked one of the boys a certain question. The boy was shy. He spoke poor English, but he had the right answer. The priest told him, "You did not say it right. Correct yourself. Say it over again." The boy got flustered and stammered. He could hardly get out a word. But the priest kept after him: "Didn't you hear? I told you to do the whole thing over. Get it right this time." He kept on and on.   22

I stood up and said, "Father, don't be doing that. If you go into an Indian's home and try to talk Indian, they might laugh at you and say, 'Do it over correctly. Get it right this time!' "   23

He shouted at me, "Mary, you stay after class. Sit down right now!"   24

I stayed after class, until after the bell. He told me, "Get over here!"   25

He grabbed me by the arm, pushing me against the blackboard, shouting, "Why are you always mocking us? You have no reason to do this."   26

I said, "Sure I do. You were making fun of him. You embarrassed him. He needs strengthening, not weakening. You hurt him. I did not hurt you."   27

He twisted my arm and pushed real hard. I turned around and hit him in the face, giving him a bloody nose. After that I ran out of the room, slamming the door behind me. He and I went to Sister Bernard's office. I told her, "Today I quit school. I'm not taking any more of this, none of this shit anymore. None of this treatment. Better give me my diploma. I can't waste any more time on you people."   28

Sister Bernard looked at me for a long, long time. She said, "All right, Mary Ellen, go home today. Come back in a few days and get your diploma." And that was that. Oddly enough, that priest turned out okay. He taught a class in grammar, orthography, composition, things like that. I think he wanted more respect in class. He was still young and unsure of himself. But I was in there too long. I didn't feel like hearing it. Later he   29 became a good friend of the Indians, a personal friend of myself and my husband. He stood up for us during Wounded Knee and after. He stood up to his superiors, stuck his neck way out, became a real people's priest. He even learned our language. He died prematurely of cancer. It is not only the good Indians who die young, but the good whites, too. It is the timid ones who know how to take care of themselves who grow old. I am still grateful to that priest for what he did for us later and for the quarrel he picked with me—or did I pick it with him?—because it ended a situation which had become unendurable for me. The day of my fight with him was my last day in school.

⏳ Opening the Dialogue

1. Do you see this essay as primarily about education, racism, or something else?

2. Whom do you see as the "villains" in this essay? Individual nuns or priests? White people in general? The Bureau of Indian Affairs? The U.S. government? The Catholic Church? Are there any heroes?

3. Do you think one of the goals of educators should be to actively work to make culturally diverse students more "American"? What dangers, if any, do you see in giving educators such a mission?

⏳ Keeping a Notebook

In the essay's last paragraph Mary Crow Dog says, "It is not only the good Indians who die young, but the good whites, too. It is the timid ones who know how to take care of themselves who grow old." What is your reaction to this observation?

⏳ Working Together

Working in groups, list the times in elementary school when you were misunderstood, or even mistreated, because of your age, your culture, or your position of powerlessness. In class discussion, consider ways in which educational institutions could be changed to be more responsive to the needs of all students.

🔊 Writing an Essay

In paragraph 1 the typical Indian child is likened to "a small creature from another world, helpless, defenseless, bewildered, trying desperately and instinctively to survive and sometimes not surviving at all." Write about a time when you experienced this type of culture shock. How did you react? How were you able to survive?

Writing about Society and Culture

1. The essays in this chapter examine the ways in which global forces—such as war, poverty, and racism—affect individuals and groups. Write an essay in which you consider the effect on your life of a specific political, economic, or social situation or event. You may examine positive or negative effects.

2. Focus on a group of individuals whom you consider different from yourself in terms of age, race, gender, class, or ability. How have your attitudes about this group changed in the last several years? What experiences or observations have contributed to those changes?

3. How do you think you would have to change if you moved from a rural to an urban area, or vice versa? Why do you think change would be necessary? Would such change be positive?

4. How have your parents' attitudes and experiences helped to shape your ideas about the value of work or education?

5. The rate of intermarriage between people of different races and religions has been growing steadily over the years. Why do you think this is so? What do you think has been (or will be) the result of more and more such unions?

CHAPTER 7

ACROSS
CULTURES
COMPARING AND
CONTRASTING

LEYLA TORRES, "MORNING WOMEN" (1991)

Hester Allen, born in 1854, was my maternal great-great-grandmother. A respected member of her rural North Carolina community, she owned a farm and—although she had little formal education—practiced midwifery for more than fifty years. She and her husband had seven children, all of whom finished high school. The five daughters went on to the state normal school and became teachers, and both sons became mail carriers. These were important occupations at the time, especially for people of color in the South. Although I live in an urban area and am the child of two professionals, I see many parallels between Hester Allen's life and my own. Like her, I am proud of my diverse cultural heritage (her mother was Irish, and her father was part Cherokee and part African American). Like her, I value education for myself and for my children. And, like her, I have a desire for success—the desire Hester Allen instilled in her children, who passed it on to my grandmother and my mother.

Jordana Robinson, student

Across Cultures

Comparison and contrast—considering similarities and differences—is central to academic writing, in which you may be asked to do tasks ranging from comparing two characters in a play or a novel to contrasting two theories of human behavior to examining two different methods of generating electricity. When writers examine the diverse cultures that interact in the United States, they find comparison and contrast a natural way to organize their ideas. By comparing and contrasting people, rituals, religions, institutions, or symbols, writers can discover common ground between cultures and thereby understand their own cultures and others' more fully.

Writers can use this pattern of arrangement simply to inform readers about the similarities and differences between two subjects. A writer could, for example, compare the culinary traditions of two ethnic groups or contrast the ability of two groups to gain access to employment. Writers can also use comparison and contrast to explain complicated concepts. They could, for example, show how their own view of some aspect of American culture is similar to or different from that of their parents. Another option writers have is to use comparison and contrast to critique an idea or a position (for example, to criticize the discriminatory treatment of some refugees) or to support one position over another (the desirability of a traditional curriculum over a multicultural curriculum, for instance).

The writers whose works are collected in this chapter use comparison and contrast either to examine two cultures or to measure one view of American culture against another. In "A Change of Worlds" (p. 286), for example, Chief Seattle defines the cultural differences that exist between his people and what he perceives to be the dominant culture of America. Comparison and contrast enables him not only to express basic points of contrast but also to make some pessimistic predictions about the future. More effective than direct statements, Seattle's comparisons lead readers to the conclusion that the white European men who conquered Chief Seattle and his people may have lost more than they gained.

Other writers take a less global, more personal view. In "On Being White, Female, and Born in Bensonhurst" (p. 317), Marianna De Marco Torgovnick uses comparison and contrast to explain how her view of her neighborhood differs from that of her parents; in the process, she shows readers what she has gained and lost by moving out of the safe, but closed, environment of Bensonhurst. Similarly, in "A Farmer's Daughter" (p. 290), Kim Ode compares her life to her mother's and demonstrates how far she has moved from the farm on which she was raised. As she does so, she considers what her life would have been like had she married a farmer and wonders if, in some ways, it might have been more fulfilling than the life she has now.

Elsewhere in the chapter, writers use comparison and contrast to explore different kinds of family issues. In "A Brother's Murder" (p. 301), Brent Staples tries to understand how he and his brother, raised in similar circumstances, turned out so differently. In "Hold the Mayonnaise" (p. 296), Julia Alvarez contrasts Anglo and Latino cultures as she examines a curious parallel: as a child, she feared having an "American" stepmother; now, ironically, she finds herself a Latina stepmother to her husband's blond, mayonnaise-eating daughters.

In your own writing, comparison and contrast can help you communicate your thoughts about the various cultures you encounter. You can use comparison and contrast to show how your ideas are like or unlike someone else's—for instance, how your parents' attitudes toward education, marriage, or religion are like or unlike yours. In addition, you can use comparison and contrast to show how your ideas have changed or remained the same over the years—for example, how your opinions about members of a particular minority group have changed since you came to college. You can also use comparison and contrast to show why one point of view is preferable to another. For example, by demonstrating that immigrants who learn English fare better than those who do not, you can argue in favor of instituting adult English instruction at local high schools.

In the following student essay, notice how the writer uses comparison and contrast to examine the differences between two cultures.

STUDENT VOICE: TIFFANY NGUYEN

Before and After: Two Snapshots

Most people remember their childhoods as happy. Even though happy moments exist in my childhood, I remember the sad moments more clearly. When I look back at my life, I see it as two snapshots—before and after.

In Vietnam, where I was born, my mother had a very successful business. Life was very comfortable. We had everything we needed: nice clothing, a three-story house, and many luxuries. Although we were well off, however, my parents constantly worried about our future because of the political turmoil between North and South Vietnam. If the North were to defeat the South, then our future would be dim. I knew nothing about politics or war at this time, of course. I was a child, and I was happy.

Each morning I put on my uniform—a navy blue skirt with   3
straps that criss-crossed in the back, a white shirt, white socks, and black shoes—and headed for St. Paul, a Catholic school for girls. Noon was the best time of the day because noon meant lunch, and lunch meant home. I went home every day for lunch, which was great because I got to see my mother and to nap a little.

Summer was the second best time of the year because I got to   4
visit my grandparents for three whole months. There was always plenty of fresh fruit growing on the trees on my grandfather's farm. One of my favorites was mangoes. I would eat mangoes three times a day: one in the morning after breakfast, one in the afternoon after my required nap, and one in the evening after dinner.

The best time of the year, not to mention the liveliest, was Tet,   5
the lunar New Year. On New Year's Eve the streets were flooded with people rushing to do their last-minute shopping. When the clock struck midnight, firecrackers exploded everywhere. I then would get a thick red envelope containing the money that symbolized good luck and health for the upcoming year. People would perform the dragon dance in the morning, winding their way through the narrow streets to sounds of exploding firecrackers and beating drums. Standing on the balcony in my new clothes, I could see everything. Later in the afternoon the streets were still crowded as people paid visits to their neighbors, friends, and relatives.

This pleasant life ended, however, on April 30th, 1975, when   6
the city of Saigon fell to the Communists. After the takeover, life
was difficult for everyone, regardless of how rich or poor they
were. When the Viet Cong came into the South, they identified
the well-to-do families, confiscated most of their valuables, and
painted the entrances to their houses blue so they could watch
them. They shut down my mother's business, took most of our belongings, and confiscated all our savings. Then they stationed people in front of our house to make sure that we had not hidden anything. They even looked in during our meals to see what we were
eating.

Without a business, my mother got a job at a mill just to put   7
food on the table. My father was forced to go to a reeducation
camp because he had once been a captain in South Vietnam's army.
My sister and oldest brother were also sent to a camp and forced to
work in the fields. They were fed only yams and water. In school
my two older brothers and I were taught to think that Ho Chi
Minh was the great savior of the Vietnamese people. We were
given red scarves to wear around our necks and taught to sing songs
praising Uncle Ho. All of us, however, wanted to be free. Out in
the streets we pretended to be loyal citizens of the new Vietnam,
but in our hearts we missed our old life.

Realizing that their family could not prosper, my parents de-   8
cided that we should flee. On April 14th, 1979, we left Vietnam on
a small fishing boat and drifted aimlessly for four days and five
nights until we landed on the coast of Indonesia. Four months later
we finally arrived in the United States.

Being on our own in America was a struggle. Communication   9
was very difficult because none of us spoke English well. In addition, we had no money to get food and clothing, so we had to go
on welfare. Aside from going to school, my mother worked by day
at a Vietnamese restaurant that paid minimum wage and sewed by
night. Meanwhile, my father went back to school to get his pharmacy license. My brothers also contributed to our family income
by picking blueberries in the summer. Since money was always in
short supply, we spent with great care. I dared not dream of anything new, even clothes or shoes. I did not play with dolls. Everything I owned was either donated by the churches or bought
second-hand.

In every sense our lives have changed. In Vietnam we pros-   10
pered; now we struggle. When Tet comes no one gets excited, and
no one distributes red envelopes. At times we even experience discrimination. Once my mother and I were hit by glass from a bottle
that someone who called us "chink" had thrown at us. Still, as we
look back and compare what we once had with what we have now,
we all believe that the hardships we are experiencing are worth-
while. We may not have the economic and social status that we
had in Vietnam, but we do have the freedom to go to the schools
we want to and the ability to vote for whomever we please. And as
difficult as it is for some Americans to understand, these privileges
are more precious to us than money or material possessions.

Comparing and Contrasting

People frequently use the term *comparison* when they actually mean **comparison and contrast**. Strictly speaking, **comparison** refers to the similarities between two things, and **contrast** refers to the differences. In many cases, however, these two strategies are used together. Because comparing and contrasting are central to our way of looking at the world, both appear quite frequently in essays.

HAVING A BASIS OF COMPARISON

Before you write a comparison-and-contrast essay, be sure you *have a basis of comparison*—that is, that the items you compare belong to the same general class or group and that the items have enough in common so that a comparison is possible. For example, you could easily compare two individuals who decided to emigrate to the United States. Both individuals are immigrants, so they belong to the same general class. In addition to this general basis of comparison, the individuals have several points in common: they both thought they could better themselves financially; they both wanted freedom; they both wanted to get an education. Certainly differences could exist between the two. For example, one individual might have fled political oppression while the other did not. Even so, the two immigrants share a common characteristic—their desire to come to the United States—and for this reason a definite basis of comparison exists.

A special form of comparison, called *analogy*, compares two essentially different things. Analogy uses a subject that is familiar to explain or to shed light on another that is not. By drawing a brief analogy between trees and immigrants, for example, you could make the point that people, like trees, often have difficulty thriving when uprooted from their native soil. Using this analogy as a starting point, you could then go on to discuss the problems immigrants often face when they are cut off from their cultural and social roots. In this case a concept with which readers are familiar can help to introduce or to explain a problem that they may have difficulty understanding. Keep in mind, though, that analogy and comparison are not the exactly the same. Analogy treats subjects that are very different, using one to explain the other; comparison treats subjects that are similar. In addition, analogy concentrates on similarities, while comparison deals with both similarities *and* differences.

DISCUSSING SIMILAR POINTS

One way to check whether you have a valid comparison is to be sure you *discuss the same or similar points* for both subjects. If you discuss different points for each subject, you are not actually comparing anything. If, for example, you wanted to compare the way in which two nineteenth-century novels characterize women, you could not logically focus on gender stereotyping and class prejudice in one novel, and imagery and literary conventions in the other. To make a valid comparison, you would have to discuss the same topics—gender stereotyping and literary conventions—for both. In "Before and After: Two Snapshots" (p. 278) Tiffany Nguyen compares her life in Vietnam with her life in the United States. In both parts of the essay she covers similar topics: how the family lived and what they had materially, what her parents did for a living, the role of Tet, and how she felt about her life. Although the specific points she discusses are not exactly the same in the "before" and "after" parts of her essay, Tiffany's treatments of her life in the two countries are parallel; therefore, her contrast is effective.

CONVEYING YOUR PURPOSE

Be sure to *convey your purpose* in your comparison-and-contrast essay—that is, give readers a clear idea whether you are emphasizing similarities, differences, or both. If, for example, you wanted to emphasize similarities, you could acknowledge differences in a short paragraph, but you would focus on similarities throughout the rest of the essay. If you wanted to emphasize differences, you would do the opposite. Finally, if you wanted to give equal weight to similarities and differences, you would treat both in the same way. For example, in "Puritans from the Orient: A Chinese Evolution" (p. 306), Jade Snow Wong compares her mother's attachment to traditional Chinese culture with her own. Because she wants readers to draw their own conclusions, she treats both subjects equally—giving the same weight to similarities and differences. If Wong wanted to make the point that her view of Chinese culture was more enlightened than her mother's, she would emphasize differences over similarities.

DECIDING ON AN
ORGANIZATIONAL PATTERN

Decide on an organizational pattern that suits the material you are presenting. Comparison-and-contrast essays generally follow one of two patterns: *Subject-by-subject* comparisons discuss all points having to do with the first subject before discussing the second subject, and *point-by-point* comparisons alternate discussions of the two subjects, considering one point at a time.

Subject-by-Subject	*Point-by-Point*
Vietnamese-American culture	Attitudes toward education
—Attitudes toward education	—Vietnamese-American culture
—Religious affiliation	—Chicano culture
—Ethnic neighborhoods	
	Religious affiliation
Chicano culture	—Vietnamese-American culture
—Atttitudes toward education	—Chicano culture
—Religious affiliation	
—Ethnic neighborhoods	Ethnic neighborhoods
	—Vietnamese-American culture
	—Chicano culture

A subject-by-subject comparison presents each subject as a complete unit. In a sense, then, a subject-by-subject comparison consists of two complete essays linked by the points they discuss in common. This kind of comparison is often preferable for brief essays that discuss only a few points in general terms. For example, because Tiffany Nguyen's essay contrasts general impressions, she finds this type of arrangement useful. Had she wanted to discuss a number of specific points in detail, she might have used a point-by-point arrangement. Chief Seattle uses a point-by-point arrangement in "A Change of Worlds." Although his speech is brief, his ideas are complex. Therefore, his presenting the comparison in two separate units might make it more difficult for readers to understand his point.

PROVIDING CLEAR TRANSITIONS

Be sure that you *provide clear transitions* to signal readers that you are changing subjects or points. When they read an essay with a subject-by-subject arrangement, readers may not realize that you are shifting from one subject to another unless you introduce the shift with clear transitional words, phrases, or sentences. Notice, for example, how Jade Snow Wong uses a transitional sentence to indicate that she is shifting her focus from one subject (her parents' attitude toward her) to another (her attitude toward her children) and how she uses *but* to indicate contrast:

> *Thirty-five years later, I have four children, two sons and two daughters.* In principle we remain true to my father's and mother's tradition, I believe. Our children respect my husband and me, *but* it is not a blind obedience. . . .

Similarly, readers of a point-by-point comparison might be confused when you move from one point to another. To avoid such confusion, Brent Staples in "A Brother's Murder" uses a transitional sentence—"As I fled the past, so Blake embraced it"—to indicate the shift from his view of the past to his brother's. This sentence not only announces that Staples is shifting his focus but also reminds readers what point he has been discussing.

REVIEW CHECKLIST: COMPARING AND CONTRASTING

✓ Have a basis of comparison.
✓ Discuss the same or similar points.
✓ Convey your purpose.
✓ Decide on an organizational pattern.
✓ Provide clear transitions.

CHIEF SEATTLE

A Change of Worlds

The following speech is one of the most famous works of prose ever attributed to a Native American. See-ahth (in the Lushootseed language, which whites found impossible to pronounce and translated as "Seattle") was born in 1786, a member of the Suquamish tribe of the Puget Sound region of what is now western Washington state.

Although little is known of Chief Seattle's early life, he claimed to have witnessed the arrival of the British explorer Vancouver's ships in 1792. Contemporary accounts agree that Seattle was an accomplished speaker and a skilled diplomat, as well as a warrior of some renown. Chief Seattle assumed leadership of his tribe around 1810, and when the first white settlers began arriving in 1851, he counseled cooperation and friendship. Although leaders of his tribe had no authority to compel obedience, Chief Seattle's powers of persuasion were such that he was able to dissuade the Suquamish from participating in the Indian Wars of 1855–1856. Catherine Maynard, one of the first white settlers, proclaimed Chief Seattle to be "the greatest friend of the whites on this side of the continent"; when residents were searching for a name for their settlement, her husband suggested they honor their friend and name it "Seattle."

In 1854, more than a thousand of Chief Seattle's people gathered to greet the government's Indian Superintendent, Isaac Stevens. Seattle spoke on this occasion. The following is a translation of that speech created from notes and recollection by Dr. Henry Smith thirty years after it was delivered. There are no verbatim contemporary transcripts of Chief Seattle's talk, and several versions exist. Poets and scriptwriters have taken creative license

with Chief Seattle's words, and over time his speech has become
a powerful symbol for environmentalists.

Although we cannot know exactly what Chief Seattle said in
1854, or even in what language he spoke, the document provides
a powerful contrast between two ways of viewing the natural and
spiritual worlds.

Y ONDER SKY THAT HAS WEPT TEARS OF COMPASSION upon my people   1
for centuries untold, and which to us appears changeless and eternal, may
change. Today is fair. Tomorrow it may be overcast with clouds. My
words are like the stars that never change. Whatever Seattle says the
great chief at Washington can rely upon with as much certainty as he can
upon the return of the sun or the seasons. The White Chief says that Big
Chief at Washington sends us greetings of friendship and goodwill. That
is kind of him for we know he has little need of our friendship in return.
His people are many. They are like the grass that covers vast prairies. My
people are few. They resemble the scattering trees of a storm-swept
plain. . . . I will not dwell on, nor mourn over, our untimely decay, nor
reproach our paleface brothers with hastening it, as we too may have
been somewhat to blame. . . .

Your God is not our God. Your God loves your people and hates   2
mine. He folds his strong and protecting arms lovingly about the paleface
and leads him by the hand as a father leads his infant son—but He has
forsaken His red children—if they really are His. Our God, the Great
Spirit, seems also to have forsaken us. Your God makes your people
strong every day. Soon they will fill the land. Our people are ebbing
away like a rapidly receding tide that will never return. The white man's
God cannot love our people or He would protect them. They seem to be
orphans who can look nowhere for help. How then can we be brothers? . . . We are two distinct races with separate origins and separate destinies. There is little in common between us.

To us the ashes of our ancestors are sacred and their resting place   3
is hallowed ground. You wander far from the graves of your ancestors and
seemingly without regret. Your religion was written upon tables of stone
by the iron finger of your God so that you could not forget. The Red

Man could never comprehend nor remember it. Our religion is the traditions of our ancestors—the dreams of our old men, given them in solemn hours of night by the Great Spirit; and the visions of our sachems; and it is written in the hearts of our people.

Your dead cease to love you and the land of their nativity as soon   4
as they pass the portals of the tomb and wander way beyond the stars. They are soon forgotten and never return. Our dead never forget the beautiful world that gave them being.

Day and night cannot dwell together. The Red Man has ever fled   5
the approach of the White Man, as the morning mist flees before the morning sun. However, your proposition seems fair and I think that my people will accept it and will retire to the reservation you offer them. Then we will dwell apart in peace. . . . It matters little where we pass the remnant of our days. They will not be many. A few more moons; a few more winters—and not one of the descendants of the mighty hosts that once moved over this broad land or lived in happy homes, protected by the Great Spirit, will remain to mourn over the graves of a people once more powerful and hopeful than yours. But why should I mourn at the untimely fate of my people? Tribe follows tribe, and nation follows nation, like the waves of the sea. It is the order of nature, and regret is useless. Your time of decay may be distant, but it will surely come, for even the White Man whose God walked and talked with him as friend with friend cannot be exempt from the common destiny. We may be brothers after all. We will see. . . .

Every part of this soil is sacred in the estimation of my people.   6
Every hillside, every valley, every plain and grove, has been hallowed by some sad or happy event in days long vanished. The very dust upon which you now stand responds more lovingly to their footsteps than to yours, because it is rich with the blood of our ancestors and our bare feet are conscious of the sympathetic touch. Even the little children who lived here and rejoiced here for a brief season will love these somber solitudes and at eventide they greet shadowy returning spirits. And when the last Red Man shall have perished, and the memory of my tribe shall have become a myth among the White Men, these shores will swarm with the invisible dead of my tribe, and when your children's children think themselves alone in the field, the store, the shop, upon the highway, or in the silence of the pathless woods, they will not be alone. At night when the streets of your cities and villages are silent and you think them deserted,

they will throng with the returning hosts that once filled and still love this beautiful land. The White Man will never be alone.

Let him be just and deal kindly with my people, for the dead are   7 not powerless. Dead, did I say? There is no death, only a change of worlds.

⚓ Opening the Dialogue

1. Do you agree with Chief Seattle's statement in paragraph 2 that whites and Native Americans are two distinct races with separate destinies?

2. Chief Seattle expresses little hope for the future of Native Americans. Do you think present-day Native Americans have the same feelings? Would they be as willing to concede defeat as he seems to be?

3. In paragraph 6 Chief Seattle says, "The White Man will never be alone." What do you think he means?

⚓ Keeping a Notebook

If Chief Seattle were alive today, do you think he would be more or less optimistic than he was in 1854 about the future of the United States? Of Native Americans?

⚓ Working Together

Working in groups, identify Chief Seattle's attitudes toward the land, religion, and racial pride. In class discussion, decide in what respects your values are similar to and different from those of Chief Seattle.

⚓ Writing an Essay

Write an essay in which you compare your attitudes about other cultures, about nature, and about religion with those expressed by Chief Seattle.

Kim Ode

A Farmer's Daughter

In the following essay, Kim Ode considers how economics and technology have changed life on a family farm. As both choice and economic reality lead more "farm wives" to employment in cities and towns, the arduous, exhausting, and—for her mother—ultimately fulfilling life of the farmer is disappearing quickly.

Ode's essay evokes the childhood she recently described as "wonderful," on a small farm outside of Sioux Falls, South Dakota, where she was born in 1955. After earning a degree in English and journalism, she began her career as a newspaper reporter, married, and moved to upstate New York. However, she "grew homesick for the Great Plains" and now lives with her family in Minneapolis, where she is a feature writer for the *Star Tribune* newspaper.

"I am a general assignment writer, preferring the vagaries of the day to delving into a specific topic," Ode explains. "My goal in writing is not necessarily to win someone over to my point of view (although that's a nice result). I aim to write in such a way that the narrative carries readers effortlessly through the piece until they see, to their surprise, the end coming into view and realize that they haven't formed a judgment. Then, when they finish, they can ponder what they've read. I've found this grasp on the reader is best tightened through the use of compelling, relevant detail."

Notice how Ode uses a point-by-point arrangement to contrast farm life today with what she remembers from childhood, to compare and contrast her mother's generation with her own, and to reflect on the similarities in her attitudes now and then.

I AM A FARMER'S DAUGHTER, but I live in the city now, harvesting pay-　1
checks from the acres of asphalt around me. Still I think I'd make a
heckuva farm wife. On rare occasions, I say that out loud to friends. Usually, there's a gentle but firm reminder that it's not possible and a firm but
gentle rebuke about romantic notions. But sometimes I say it to a close
friend who is another farmer's daughter and the skein of conversation
unravels a bit further before it is again, inevitably, tied off. She knows
what I mean about yearning for horizons, about eating sweet corn 20
minutes off the stalk, about dishing up casserole in the shade of the combine, about playing in the hayloft. We both had the same role models,
women who spent a lot of time over the stove, in front of the sewing
machine, and behind the wheel—and who always seemed happy. Yet we
both ended up seeking other role models, encouraged more often than
not by our mothers, who after all were the best judges of their happiness.

　　Every generation, another group of farmers' daughters faces the　2
question of moving on or staying put. Yet theirs today is a different world
from the one I encountered 18 years ago in the Brandon, South Dakota,
high school gymnasium as I shifted my graduation tassel from left to
right. The farm crisis of the past decade is responsible for much of the
change, but there also has been a shift toward acknowledging a broader
range of career options for women.

　　I once asked Mom if she'd ever thought she'd end up where she　3
was. She'd grown up on a small farm near my dad's family farm. Well, she
said, she never thought she'd end up anywhere else, and her reply was in
a tone that hid no regret, no undertone of missed opportunity.

　　Oh, there had been a chance, shortly after they married and were　4
living near San Diego, where Dad was stationed as a Marine during the
Korean conflict. He'd toyed with the notion of being an architect, and
they'd even gone so far as to investigate some schools he could attend
after his tour of duty was up. But Grandpa said he'd always counted on
Dad coming back to the farm, and then Mom got pregnant (with me) and
the future fell into place.

　　After answering my question, Mom turned the tables on me, asking　5
if I ever felt—she groped for a term—if I had ever felt second-class growing up on a farm. I could truthfully answer that I never had, but what
bothers me is the reaction I sometimes get, like from the woman in Roch-

ester, New York, where my husband and I lived in the early 1980s. She confided in words clearly meant to comfort and compliment, "You don't look like a farm girl."

I knew what she was thinking: I didn't scrape my shoes out of habit   6
when walking into a restaurant. I didn't wear bright blue eye shadow or order polyester suits from the Sears catalog. There wasn't a telltale crease on my lower lip from years of chewing wheatstraws. In short, I seemed to be someone like her. I decided not to declare that I once was runner-up for state dairy princess.

Mom said she also felt herself being measured against a stereotype   7
at times, on infrequent occasions when she was with wives of doctors or professors or lawyers and the subject turned to what their husbands did. "I never felt bad about being married to a farmer," she said. "But I felt strange that they thought it was something I might feel bad about."

The farm woman I hark back to doesn't exist anymore. Although   8
the worst of the farm crisis has passed, it's not unusual for farm women to have at least a part-time job in town. And there are many who enjoy this new life.

Mom has a job in the nearby city of Sioux Falls now, partly because   9
all of us kids are grown, partly because the extra income doesn't hurt. She takes orders over the phone for cable television programs and talks to people from all over the country, which she likes, although she frets at times that the house doesn't get the care it used to, nor the community the time she once volunteered.

She still considers herself very much a farm wife, but life is nothing   10
like it used to be, and thank goodness, she says. When I ask her about what her life as a young farm wife was like, Mom leans against the doorpost and gets that sort of tired look in her eyes that meets halfway down her face with a smile she's trying to raise. I realize it's a look I've seen many times before. "It was so busy," she says quietly. She tells of coming home from the hospital with my brother, their third child, on the same sweltering August day that work began on a new milkhouse. That meant fixing food for midmorning break, dinner, and midafternoon break for a crew of workmen until the first of the year. Then the silo builders arrived. All this in addition to caring for two preschoolers and a baby with a stomach ailment who required frequent feedings and didn't sleep through the night for months. Nowadays, such a crew wouldn't expect to be fed by the farm family; they'd bring lunches or drive into town.

I never saw that side of her life, and even had I married a farmer, I   11
couldn't have drawn on that experience. Technology has changed so
many things: The days of cooking for baling crews—mostly ravenous
high school boys who smelled of sweat and alfalfa and Lava soap—are
rare now with machines that shape the hay into loaves and cylinders.
Air-conditioned tractor cabs eliminate the need for bringing an afternoon
cold drink to the fields, and farmers can stow brownies without worrying
that the frosting will melt.

But more to the point, had I married a farmer, there's no guarantee   12
we'd still be farming.

My parents tried to dissuade my brother, now 31, from going into   13
farming, even while they were proud that he wanted to. They saw the
farm crisis looming on the horizon and suggested that he could remain
close to agriculture as an extension agent or implement salesman or who
knows what. But he was determined, and though he's often tired and
strapped for extra money and has a wife who works in town, he doesn't
regret his decision. He and my husband canoed in the Boundary Waters
of northern Minnesota last summer, one of his few breaks from the farm,
and they came back a day early. My husband still shakes his head: "He
just said he missed his animals."

I'll never live on a farm again. I know that. Still, that doesn't stop   14
me and a girlhood friend from regularly mourning the fact that we aren't
living our mothers' lives—that we're rushing off to jobs instead of can-
ning peaches, or making after-school treats, or sharing a second cup of
coffee with our husbands on weekday mornings.

She went to college, too, getting a degree as a dental hygienist.   15
When we got together, it was as two career girls. Yet eventually there
was that afternoon, maybe a half-dozen years ago, when we were sitting
around her kitchen table. I don't remember which of us made the first
admission, but we agreed that we never foresaw this life we were now
living and that we had this great yearning to live our mothers' lives. We
both regarded farm life as a high calling, regarded our mothers as happy
women.

Our mothers, of course, laugh. They say they envy us. Where we   16
see complications, they see diversity. Where we see a simpler life, they
see less security. Where we see job stress, they see skills that offer independence.

The ironic thing is that my girlfriend is a farmer's wife. But she, like   17 many farmers' partners, will never have the life her mother led because times are so different. These days, her income is consequential to their farm, so she adds doing her job in town to what her mother always did: running the oldest daughter to ball games and swimming lessons, the youngest to day-care, doing the housework and cooking the meals. And I realize that had I married a farmer, or remained on the farm in any other capacity, I'd likely still be sitting before some computer screen.

Yet I still dream of living in the country even while I'm tethered by 18 my job to downtown Minneapolis. I wonder how spending perhaps two hours in the car every day, time that could be spent at home with my family, would balance against being able to hear rain approach across a cornfield. I wonder how much of my ruralness I'm suppressing when I talk to people, while at the same time wondering how many stereotypes I can dash. I wonder if I would have felt betrayed by the times had I remained on the farm, or if the times are conspiring to keep me away.

ⓔ Opening the Dialogue

1. What ideas about living on a farm did you have before you read Ode's essay? In what specific ways did her essay reinforce or challenge these beliefs?

2. In paragraph 7 Ode implies that people who live in cities unfairly stereotype women—and, by implication, men—from rural backgrounds. Do you agree?

3. Do you think women have an especially difficult life on a farm? Or do you think that men and women share the burden equally?

ⓔ Keeping a Notebook

Acknowledging that broader career options have enabled farmers' wives to work off the farm, Ode wonders whether her life would have been better had she stayed there. In what ways do you think her life would have been different had she remained?

☜ Working Together

Many of our images of farms and rural life come from television. Working in groups, identify programs that focus on rural culture. In class discussion, determine how rural life is portrayed by these shows, and decide what stereotypes of rural culture these portrayals create.

☜ Writing an Essay

Write an essay in which you compare the career you have decided to pursue with the one your parents (or someone else) might have wanted you to follow. In what ways would your life be different had you done what you were encouraged to do?

Julia Alvarez

Hold the Mayonnaise

Julia Alvarez's family emigrated from the Dominican Republic to Queens, New York, in the late 1960s when she was ten years old. In her novel *How the Garcia Girls Lost Their Accents* (1992), the struggles of the fictionalized Garcia family reflect Alvarez's own struggle to reconcile the privileged life left behind in the Dominican Republic with that of Spanish-speaking immigrants in Queens. "Here they were trying to fit into America as Americans," she writes, "They needed help figuring out who they were, why the Irish kids whose grandparents had been micks were calling them spics. Why had they come to this country in the first place?"

The gulf between alienation and assimilation may never be completely and comfortably bridged. In the following essay Alvarez uses a point-by-point arrangement to explore the uneasiness she sometimes feels in adjusting to her role as daughter in her large and exuberant Dominican family and as stepmother to her husband's American daughters. But, as Alvarez says, as an immigrant she enjoys a special vantage point: "We travel on that border between two worlds and we can see both points of view."

Alvarez lives with her family in Vermont, where she teaches at Middlebury College. She is also the author of *Homecoming* (1986), a volume of poetry.

"IF I DIE FIRST AND PAPI EVER GETS REMARRIED," Mami used to tease   1
when we were kids, "don't you accept a new woman in my house. Make her life impossible, you hear?" My sisters and I nodded obediently, and a filial shudder would go through us. We were Catholics, so of course, the only kind of remarriage we could imagine had to involve our mother's death.

We were also Dominicans, recently arrived in Jamaica, Queens, in   2
the early 60's, before waves of other Latin Americans began arriving. So,
when we imagined who exactly my father might possibly ever think of
remarrying, only American women came to mind. It would be bad
enough having a *madrastra*, but a "stepmother.". . .

All I could think of was that she would make me eat mayonnaise, a   3
food I identified with the United States and which I detested. Mami understood, of course, that I wasn't used to that kind of food. Even a
madrastra, accustomed to our rice and beans and tostones and pollo frito,
would understand. But an American stepmother would think it was normal to put mayonnaise on food, and if she were at all strict and a little
mean, which all stepmothers, of course, were, she would make me eat
potato salad and such. I had plenty of my own reasons to make a potential
stepmother's life impossible. When I nodded obediently with my sisters,
I was imagining not just something foreign in our house, but in our refrigerator.

So it's strange now, almost 35 years later, to find myself a Latina   4
stepmother of my husband's two tall, strapping, blond, mayonnaise-
eating daughters. To be honest, neither of them is a real aficionado of the
condiment, but it's a fair thing to add to a bowl of tuna fish or diced
potatoes. Their American food, I think of it, and when they head to their
mother's or off to school, I push the jar back in the refrigerator behind
their chocolate pudding and several open cans of Diet Coke.

What I can't push as successfully out of sight are my own immi-   5
grant childhood fears of having a *gringa* stepmother with foreign tastes in
our house. Except now, I am the foreign stepmother in a gringa household. I've wondered what my husband's two daughters think of this
stranger in their family. It must be doubly strange for them that I am from
another culture.

Of course, there are mitigating circumstances—my husband's two   6
daughters were teen-agers when we married, older, more mature, able to
understand differences. They had also traveled when they were children
with their father, an eye doctor, who worked on short-term international
projects with various eye foundations. But still, it's one thing to visit a
foreign country, another altogether to find it brought home—a real bear
plopped down in a Goldilocks house.

Sometimes, a whole extended family of bears. My warm, loud   7
Latino family came up for the wedding: my *tia* from Santo Domingo;

three dramatic, enthusiastic sisters and their families; my papi, with a thick accent I could tell the girls found it hard to understand; and my mami, who had her eye trained on my soon-to-be stepdaughters for any sign that they were about to make my life impossible. "How are they behaving themselves?" she asked me, as if they were 7 and 3, not 19 and 16. "They're wonderful girls," I replied, already feeling protective of them.

I looked around for the girls in the meadow in front of the house   8 we were building, where we were holding the outdoor wedding ceremony and party. The oldest hung out with a group of her own friends. The younger one whizzed in briefly for the ceremony, then left again before the congratulations started up. There was not much mixing with me and mine. What was there for them to celebrate on a day so full of confusion and effort?

On my side, being the newcomer in someone else's territory is a   9 role I'm used to. I can tap into that struggling English speaker, that skinny, dark-haired, olive-skinned girl in a sixth grade of mostly blond and blue-eyed giants. Those tall, freckled boys would push me around in the playground. "Go back to where you came from!" *"No comprendo!"* I'd reply, though of course there was no misunderstanding the fierce looks on their faces.

Even now, my first response to a scowl is that old pulling away.   10 (My husband calls it "checking out.") I remember times early on in the marriage when the girls would be with us, and I'd get out of school and drive around doing errands, killing time, until my husband, their father, would be leaving work. I am not proud of my fears, but I understand—as the lingo goes—where they come from.

And I understand, more than I'd like to sometimes, my   11 stepdaughters' pain. But with me, they need never fear that I'll usurp a mother's place. No one has ever come up and held their faces and then addressed me, "They look just like you." If anything, strangers to the remarriage are probably playing Mr. Potato Head in their minds, trying to figure out how my foreign features and my husband's fair Nebraskan features got put together into these two tall, blond girls. "My husband's daughters," I kept introducing them.

Once, when one of them visited my class and I introduced her as   12 such, two students asked me why. "I'd be so hurt if my stepmom introduced me that way," the young man said. That night I told my stepdaughter what my students had said. She scowled at me and agreed. "It's so weird how you call me Papa's daughter. Like you don't want to be related to me or something."

"I didn't want to presume," I explained. "So it's O.K. if I call you my   13
stepdaughter?"

"That's what I am," she said. Relieved, I took it for a teensy inch of   14
acceptance. The takings are small in this stepworld, I've discovered. Sort of like being a minority. It feels as if all the goodies have gone somewhere else.

Day to day, I guess I follow my papi's advice. When we first came,   15
he would talk to his children about how to make it in our new country. "Just do your work and put in your heart, and they will accept you!" In this age of remaining true to your roots, of keeping your Spanish, of fighting from inside your culture, that assimilationist approach is highly suspect. My Latino students—who don't want to be called Hispanics anymore—would ditch me as faculty adviser if I came up with that play-nice message.

But in a stepfamily where everyone is starting a new life together, it   16
isn't bad advice. Like a potluck supper, an American concept my mami never took to. ("Why invite people to your house and then ask them to bring the food?") You put what you've got together with what everyone else brought and see what comes out of the pot. The luck part is if every-one brings something you like. No potato salad, no deviled eggs, no little party sandwiches with you know what in them.

🜲 Opening the Dialogue

1. What foods do you identify with your culture? Are there some that many Americans eat but that represent something foreign to you? How do you account for this foreignness?

2. Do you think Alvarez accurately identifies the causes of the problems she discusses in her essay? For example, could Alvarez's own insecurities about her "foreign" features and her Nebraskan husband's tall, blond chil-dren be causing problems in her family?

3. In paragraph 15 Alvarez says that her Latino students who want to emphasize their cultural identities would "ditch" her if she delivered the

"play-nice" advice her father gave her. But in a way she follows his advice when dealing with her stepfamily. To what extent do you believe people should "play nice," and to what extent do you think they should assert their cultural independence?

✏ Keeping a Notebook

What assumptions does Alvarez make about what an American should look like? Do you think her assumptions are valid?

✏ Working Together

Identify a specific ethnic group—Vietnamese, African American, Jewish, Puerto Rican, Italian American or Native American, for example—that is not represented by anyone in your group. Then list the problems you would face if you were trying to raise a child from that background. In class discussion, decide what common problems are faced by people raising children from cultures different from their own.

✏ Writing an Essay

Write an essay about a time you confronted another culture. You can focus on a visit with a friend's family or on a time you visited a foreign country or an ethnic neighborhood in the United States. Comparing this culture to your own, write an essay in which you consider similarities as well as differences.

BRENT STAPLES

A Brother's Murder

In 1986, Brent Staples's brother Blake was violently murdered by his former best friend. The following, from the anthology of African-American writing entitled *Bearing Witness*, is a wrenching account of Blake's seduction by violence and crime—the sirens that have lured so many young men to destruction.

Brent Staples managed to elude that fate (as the headnote on page 199 explains), but he so feared for his brother that, as he has said, "I began to envision my brother's death, to see him lying at the end of some tenement hallway, at least two years before he was murdered. At first it came to me by accident. But as the years went by I began to summon it up voluntarily to prepare for what was inevitable."

Staples was moved to write *Parallel Time: A Memoir* in part to examine the gulf between his own life and the one that ultimately claimed his brother. He did not attend his brother's funeral: "I didn't think I could survive it. I tried to talk to my brother, but he had to want to change."

Note how Staples uses a subject-by-subject arrangement to highlight the tragic contrast between his own life and that of other young men he grew up with, particularly the brother he could not save.

IT HAS BEEN MORE THAN TWO YEARS since my telephone rang with the   1
news that my younger brother Blake—just 22 years old—had been murdered. The young man who killed him was only 24. Wearing a ski mask, he emerged from a car, fired six times at close range with a massive .44 Magnum, then fled. The two had once been inseparable friends. A senseless rivalry—beginning, I think, with an argument over a girlfriend—

escalated from posturing, to threats, to violence, to murder. The way the two were living, death could have come to either of them from anywhere. In fact, the assailant had already survived multiple gunshot wounds from an incident much like the one in which my brother lost his life.

As I wept for Blake I felt wrenched backward into events and cir-   2
cumstances that had seemed light-years gone. Though a decade apart, we both were raised in Chester, Pennsylvania, an angry, heavily black, heavily poor, industrial city southwest of Philadelphia. There, in the 1960's, I was introduced to mortality, not by the old and failing, but by beautiful young men who lay wrecked after sudden explosions of violence. The first, I remember from my 14th year—Johnny, brash lover of fast cars, stabbed to death two doors from my house in a fight over a pool game. The next year, my teen-age cousin, Wesley, whom I loved very much, was shot dead. The summers blur. Milton, an angry young neighbor, shot a crosstown rival, wounding him badly. William, another teen-age neighbor, took a shotgun blast to the shoulder in some urban drama and displayed his bandages proudly. His brother, Leonard, severely beaten, lost an eye and donned a black patch. It went on.

I recall not long before I left for college, two local Vietnam veter-   3
ans—one from the Marines, one from the Army—arguing fiercely, nearly at blows about which outfit had done the most in the war. The most killing, they meant. Not much later, I read a magazine article that set that dispute in a context. In the story, a noncommissioned officer—a sergeant, I believe—said he would pass up any number of affluent, suburban-born recruits to get hard-core soldiers from the inner city. They jumped into the rice paddies with "their manhood on their sleeves," I believe he said. These two items—the veterans arguing and the sergeant's words—still characterize for me the circumstances under which black men in their teens and 20's kill one another with such frequency. With a touchy paranoia born of living battered lives, they are desperate to be *real* men. Killing is only *machismo* taken to the extreme. Incursions to be punished by death were many and minor, and they remain so: they include stepping on the wrong toe, literally; cheating in a drug deal; simply saying "I dare you" to someone holding a gun; crossing territorial lines in a gang dispute. My brother grew up to wear his manhood on his sleeve. And when he died, he was in that group—black, male and in its teens and early 20's—that is far and away the most likely to murder or be murdered.

I left the East Coast after college, spent the mid- and late-1970's in   4
Chicago as a graduate student, taught for a time, then became a journalist. Within 10 years of leaving my hometown, I was overeducated and
"upwardly mobile," ensconced on a quiet, tree-lined street where voices
raised in anger were scarcely ever heard. The telephone, like some grim
umbilical, kept me connected to the old world with news of deaths, im-
prisonings, and misfortune. I felt emotionally beaten up. Perhaps to protect myself, I added a psychological dimension to the physical distance I
had already achieved. I rarely visited my hometown. I shut it out.

As I fled the past, so Blake embraced it. On Christmas of 1983, I   5
traveled from Chicago to a black section of Roanoke, Virginia, where he
then lived. The desolate public housing projects, the hopeless, idle
young men crashing against one another—these reminded me of the
embittered town we'd grown up in. It was a place where once I would
have been comfortable, or at least sure of myself. Now, hearing of my
brother's forays into crime, his scrapes with police and street thugs, I was
scared, unsteady on foreign terrain.

I saw that Blake's romance with the street life and the hustler image   6
had flowered dangerously. One evening that late December, standing in
some Roanoke dive among drug dealers and grim, hair-trigger losers, I
told him I feared for his life. He had affected the image of the tough he
wanted to be. But behind the dark glasses and the swagger, I glimpsed the
baby-faced toddler I'd once watched over. I nearly wept. I wanted desperately for him to live. The young think themselves immortal, and a
dangerous light shone in his eyes as he spoke laughingly of making fools
of the policemen who had raided his apartment looking for drugs. He
cried out as I took his right hand. A line of stitches lay between the
thumb and index finger. Kickback from a shotgun, he explained, nothing
serious. Gunplay had become part of his life.

I lacked the language simply to say: Thousands have lived this for   7
you and died. I fought the urge to lift him bodily and shake him. This
place and the way you are living smells of death to me, I said. Take some
time away, I said. Let's go downtown tomorrow and buy a plane ticket
anywhere, take a bus trip, anything to get away and cool things off. He
took my alarm casually. We arranged to meet the following night—an
appointment he would not keep. We embraced as though through glass.
I drove away.

As I stood in my apartment in Chicago holding the receiver that   8 evening in February 1984, I felt as though part of my soul had been cut away. I questioned myself then, and I still do. Did I not reach back soon or earnestly enough for him? For weeks I awoke crying from a recurrent dream in which I chased him, urgently trying to get him to read a document I had, as though reading it would protect him from what had happened in waking life. His eyes shining like black diamonds, he smiled and danced just beyond my grasp. When I reached for him, I caught only the space where he had been.

❦ Opening the Dialogue

1. In paragraph 3 Staples talks about young African-American men "wearing their manhood on their sleeves." What do you think this phrase means? Do you agree with Staples when he says in paragraph 3, "Killing is only *machismo* taken to the extreme"?

2. Implicitly and explicitly, "A Brother's Murder" communicates what Brent Staples would like to tell his brother. What do you think his brother would have liked to tell him?

3. How do you account for the differences between Staples and his brother? Why do you think one brother became a successful writer and the other became a street hustler?

❦ Keeping a Notebook

Staples feels a great deal of guilt about his brother's death. Do you think his feelings are justified? What, if anything, could Staples have done to help his brother?

❦ Working Together

Working in groups, try to determine what encouraged Staples's brother to act the way he did. In class discussion, examine what steps could be taken to break the cycle of violence that seems to operate in communities such as the one in which the brothers lived.

✒ Writing an Essay

Assume you are a friend of Staples's family. Write a letter of condolence to Brent Staples in which you compare him to his brother. In your letter, suggest what American society can do to make more young men turn out like Brent Staples and fewer like his brother Blake.

JADE SNOW WONG

Puritans from the Orient: A Chinese Evolution

When Jade Snow Wong (b. 1922) published her autobiography *Fifth Chinese Daughter* in 1950, she was one of the first Chinese-American women ever to be published in the United States. She said at the time, "My story was written during many hours when I unhappily asked myself why I ever chose to write it. Of course, I knew that the English-reading public had rarely had a clear picture of Chinese-American family life as a Chinese saw it. . . . Nevertheless, it is not easy to be first in anything, and I had grave doubts about breaking traditional silence as I wrote."

That ambivalence in trying to reconcile the weight of Chinese tradition with the freedom of American ways is echoed in "Puritans from the Orient," a selection from the anthology *The Immigrant Experience* (1971). She has been quoted as saying she eventually learned that "my background as a Chinese was my particular asset, a point of distinction not to be rejected."

Although she has contributed to periodicals, written a newspaper column, and published a second autobiography (*No Chinese Stranger*, 1975), Wong's primary occupation has been as a potter. The mother of four, she raised her family with traditional Chinese values and has emphasized that her focus is on her role as wife and mother: "My writing is nonfiction based on personal experiences. So few Chinese Americans have published that I think it is my responsibility to try to create understanding between Chinese and Americans. . . . Though I don't think being a woman has been any problem, I give priority to women's responsibility for a good home life; hence, I put my husband and four children before my writing or ceramics. I also believe in serving my community, and this work has taken more time than writing a book."

As you read, consider why Wong devotes so much more attention to her early family life than she does to her family life as an
adult.

F ROM INFANCY TO MY SIXTEENTH YEAR, I was reared according to nine-   1
teenth century ideals of Chinese womanhood. I was never left alone,
though it was not unusual for me to feel lonely, while surrounded by a
family of seven others, and often by ten (including bachelor cousins) at
meals.

My father (who enjoyed our calling him Daddy in English) was the   2
vital, temperamental, dominating, and unquestioned head of our household. He was not talkative, being preoccupied with his business affairs
and with reading constantly otherwise. My mother was mistress of domestic affairs. Seldom did these two converse before their children, but
we knew them to be a united front, and suspected that privately she both
informed and influenced him about each child. . . .

My earliest memories of companionship with my father were as his   3
passenger in his red wheelbarrow, sharing space with the piles of blue-
jean materials he was delivering to a worker's home. He must have been
forty. He was lean, tall, inevitably wearing blue overalls, rolled shirt
sleeves, and high black kid shoes. In his pockets were numerous keys,
tools, and pens. On such deliveries, I noticed that he always managed
time to show a mother how to sew a difficult seam, or to help her repair
a machine, or just to chat.

I observed from birth that living and working were inseparable. My   4
mother was short, sturdy, young looking, and took pride in her appearance. She was at her machine the minute housework was done, and she
was the hardest working seamstress, seldom pausing, working after I went
to bed. The hum of sewing machines continued day and night, seven
days a week. She knew that to have more than the four necessities, she
must work and save. We knew that to overcome poverty, there were only
two methods: working and education. It was our personal responsibility.
Being poor did not entitle us to benefits. When welfare programs were
created in the depression years of the thirties, my family would not make
application.

Having provided the setup for family industry, my father turned his   5
attention to our education. Ninety-five per cent of the population in

China had been illiterate. He knew that American public schools would take care of our English, but he had to be the watchdog to nurture our Chinese knowledge. Only the Cantonese tongue was ever spoken by him or my mother. When the two oldest girls arrived from China, the schools of Chinatown received only boys. My father tutored his daughters each morning before breakfast. In the midst of a foreign environment, he clung to a combination of the familiar old standards and what was permissible in the newly learned Christian ideals.

My eldest brother was born in America, the only boy for fourteen 6 years, and after him three daughters—another older sister, myself, and my younger sister. Then my younger brother, Paul, was born. That older brother, Lincoln, was cherished in the best Chinese tradition. He had his own room; he kept a German Shepherd as his pet; he was tutored by a Chinese scholar; he was sent to private school for American classes. As a male Wong, he would be responsible some day for the preservation of and pilgrimages to ancestral graves—his privileges were his birthright. We girls were content with the unusual opportunities of working and attending two schools.

For by the time I was six, times in Chinatown were changing. The 7 Hip Wo Chinese Christian Academy (in the same building as the Methodist Mission) had been founded on a coeducational basis, with nominal tuition. Financial support came from three Protestant church boards: the Congregational, Presbyterian, and Methodist churches contributed equal shares. My father was on the Hip Wo School Board for many years. By day, I attended American public school near our home. From 5:00 P.M. to 8:00 P.M. on five weekdays and from 9:00 A.M. to 12 noon Saturdays, I attended the Chinese school. Classes numbered twenty to thirty students, and were taught by educated Chinese from China. We studied poetry, calligraphy, philosophy, literature, history, correspondence, religion, all by exacting memorization. The Saturday morning chapel services carried out the purposes of the supporting churches.

Daddy emphasized memory development; he could still recite flu- 8 ently many lengthy lessons of his youth. Every evening after both schools, I'd sit by my father, often as he worked at his sewing machine, sing-songing my lessons above its hum. Sometimes I would stop to hold a light for him as he threaded the difficult holes of a specialty machine, such as one for bias bindings. After my Chinese lessons passed his approval, I was allowed to attend to American homework. I was made to feel luckier than other Chinese girls who didn't study Chinese, and also luckier than Western girls without a dual heritage.

We lived on both levels of our factory, which had moved out of the   9 basement to street level. The kitchen, bathroom, and sitting-dining room were at the rear of the street floor. Kitchen privileges were granted employee seamstresses, who might wish to heat lunch or wash hands; our family practically never had privacy. Floorboards ran the length of the factory; we were never permitted to play on them because of the danger of splinters. My mother carried each child on her back with a traditional Chinese support until he was able to walk firmly, to eliminate the necessity of crawling and the danger of injury by machine pulleys and motor belts. Only the living quarters were laid with what was known as "battleship linoleum," which was an uninspired brown, but unquestionably durable.

Bedrooms were upstairs, both in the front and the rear of the fac-   10 tory, to be where there were windows. Between front and rear bedrooms were more machines and the long cutting tables, which were partially lit by the skylights. I shared a room with my younger sister, and later with my baby brother, too. Windows were fitted with opaque glass to eliminate the necessity for curtains, and iron bars were installed by Daddy across the entire length of those upstairs windows to keep out intruders and keep in peeping children.

Both my older sisters married when I was a child, and my third   11 older sister went to live with the oldest of them, for which my father paid room and board. Thus, congestion at our factory-home was relieved. There was little time for play and toys were unknown to me. In any spare time, I was supplied with embroidery and sewing for my mother.

The Chinese New Year, which by the old lunar calendar would fall   12 sometime in late January or early February of the Western Christian calendar, was the most special time of the year, for then the machines stopped for three days. Mother would clean our living quarters very thoroughly, decorate the sitting room with flowering branches, fresh oranges, and arrange candied fruits or salty melon seeds for callers. All of us would be dressed in bright new clothes, and relatives or close friends, who came to call, would give each of us a red paper packet containing a good luck coin—usually a quarter. I remember how my classmates would gleefully talk of *their* receipts. But my mother made us give our money to her, for she said that she needed it to reciprocate to others.

Yet there was little reason for unhappiness. I was never hungry.   13
Though we had no milk, there was all the rice we wanted. We had hot
and cold running water—a rarity in Chinatown, as well as our own bathtub. Others in the community used the YWCA or YMCA facilities,
where for twenty-five cents, a family could draw six baths. Our sheets
were pieced from dishtowels, but we had sheets. I was never neglected,
for my mother and father were always at home. During school vacation
periods, I was taught to operate many types of machines—tacking (for
pockets), overlocking (for the raw edges of seams), buttonhole, double
seaming; and I learned all the stages in producing a pair of jeans to its
final inspection, folding, and tying in bundles of a dozen pairs by size,
ready for pickup. Denim jeans are heavy—my shoulders ached often. My
father set up a modest nickel-and-dime piecework reward for me, which
he recorded in my own notebook, and he paid me regularly.

On Sundays, we never failed to attend the Methodist Church, as   14
my father's belief in the providence of God strengthened with the years,
and his wife and family shared that faith. My father's faith in God was
unwavering and unshakable. (Some day, we were to hear his will, which
he wrote in Chinese, and which began, "I believe in God, Jehovah. . . . ")
I have no statistics on the percentage of Christians in Chinatown at that
time, but I am sure they were a minority. Our Methodist branch could
not have had more than a hundred adult members, with less than fifty
regular Sunday attendants. Many of Daddy's contemporaries scoffed at
or ridiculed Christians as "do-gooders" who never gambled, when Mah-
Jongg games were Chinatown's favorite pastime. Father used to chase lot-
tery peddlers away from his factory; cards were never allowed in our
home. I suppose that for him, the Christian faith at first comforted him
far from his loved ones. Secondly, it promised him individual worth and
salvation, when all his life in China had been devoted only to his family's
continuity and glorification. Third, to this practical man who was virtually self-taught in all his occupations, Christianity suggested action on
behalf of others in the community, while Confucianism was more concerned with regulating personal relationships. Daddy seldom hesitated to
stick his neck out if he thought social action or justice were involved. For
instance, he was on the founding board of the Chinese YMCA and
fought for its present location, though he was criticized for its being on a
hill, for being near the YWCA, for including a swimming pool.

Group singing and community worship in a church must have been   15

dramatically different from the lonely worship of Chinese ancestral tablets at home. He listened to weekly sermons, expounding new ideas or
reiterating old ones, and sometimes they were translated from the English spoken by visiting pastors. His daughters learned to sing in the
choir and were permitted to join escorted church visits to Western
churches—their only contact with a "safe" organization outside of Chinatown.

    If my father had one addiction, it was to reading. He eagerly   16
awaited the delivery of each evening's Chinese newspaper—for there
had been none where he came from. His black leather-bound Testa-
ments, translated into Chinese, were worn from constant reference. Before our Sunday morning departure for Sunday School, he conducted his
own lessons at our dining table. No meal was tasted before we heard his
thankful grace.

    In a conservative, reactionary community, most members either   17
peacefully avoided criticism, or if involved in controversial occupations
(such as gambling, smuggling), joined the strength of the tongs for self-
defense. My father was neither type. He was genial, well known to the
man on the street, liked to talk in public, but he had few intimate friends.
Cousins and uncles sought his counsel; he never sought theirs. He contributed to causes or to individuals when he could scarcely provide for his
own family, but he never asked another for help. During China's long
years of conflict, first for the sake of the Revolution, and later against the
Japanese, he worked tirelessly in the name of our church, to raise funds
here for China war relief.

    My mother dutifully followed my father's leadership. Because of his   18
devotion to Christian principles, she was on the path to economic security. She was extremely thrifty, but the thrifty need pennies to manage,
and the old world of Fragrant Mountains had denied her those. Upon
arrival in the new world of San Francisco, she accepted the elements her
mate had selected to shape her new life: domestic duties, seamstress work
in the factory-home, mothering each child in turn, church once a week,
and occasional movies. Daddy frowned upon the community Chinese
operas because of their very late hours (they did not finish till past midnight) and their mixed audiences.

    Very early in my life, the manners of a Chinese lady were taught to   19
me. How to hold a pair of chopsticks (palm up, not down); how to hold
a bowl of rice (one thumb on top, not resting in an open palm); how to

pass something to elders (with both hands, never one); how to pour tea into the tiny, handleless porcelain cups (seven-eighths full so that the top edge would be cool enough to hold); how to eat from a center serving dish (only the piece in front of your place; never pick around); not to talk at table; not to show up outside of one's room without being fully dressed; not to be late, ever; not to be too playful—in a hundred and one ways, we were molded to be trouble-free, unobstrusive, quiescent, cooperative.

We were disciplined by first being told, and then by punishment if   20
we didn't remember. Punishment was instant and unceremonious. At the table, it came as a sudden whack from Daddy's chopsticks. Away from the table, punishment could be the elimination of a privilege or the blow on our legs from a bundle of cane switches. My father used the switch, but mother favored a wooden clotheshanger. Now that I have four children myself, I can see that my parents' methods insured "domestic tranquility." Once, when I screamed from the sting of his switch, my father reminded me of my good fortune. In China, he had been hung by his thumbs before being whipped by an uncle or other older family member, called to do the job dispassionately.

Only Daddy and Oldest Brother were allowed individual idiosyn-   21
crasies. Daughters were all expected to be of one standard. To allow each one of many daughters to be different would have posed enormous problems of cost, energy, and attention. No one was shown physical affection. Such familiarity would have weakened my parents and endangered the one-answer authoritative system. One standard from past to present, whether in China or in San Francisco, was simpler to enforce. Still, am I not lucky that I am alive to tell this story? Mother used to point out to me one of the old women seamstresses, tiny of build, with bound feet. She came from another village which practiced the killing of unwanted newborn females, and admitted that she had done so herself in China. But a daughter was born here to her, and I remember her. She was constantly cowed by her mother's merciless tongue-lashings, the sounds of a bitter woman who had not been blessed by any son.

Thirty-five years later, I have four children, two sons and two   22
daughters. In principle we remain true to my father's and mother's tradition, I believe. Our children respect my husband and me, but it is not a blind obedience enforced by punishment. It is a respect won from observing us and rounded by friendship. My parents never said "please" or

"thank you" for any service or gift. In Chinese, both "please" and "thank you" can be literally translated as "I am not worthy" and naturally, no parent is going to say that about a service which should be their just due. There is no literal translation for "sorry" in Chinese. If someone dies, we can say, "It is truly regrettable." But if we regret an act, we say again, "I am not worthy." Now I say "thank you," "please," and "sorry" to my children, in English, and I do not think it lessens my dignity. The ultimate praise I ever remember from my parents was a single word, "good."

We do not abhor a show of affection. Each child looks forward to   23
his goodnight kiss and tuck-in. Sometimes one or more of them will throw his arms around one of us and cry out, "I love you so."

My son, Mark, has completed more than eight years of night Chi-   24
nese school, the same one I attended. I have also served on that school board, as my father before me. Unlike my well-attended Chinese classes—nearly every Chinese child in the community of my childhood was sent to night school for some years—Mark's last Chinese grade included only a handful of students. When I enrolled my youngest boy, Lance, in first grade this fall, the principal was distressed that the entering students were half the number entering in previous years. I saw parents and grandparents proudly shepherding the little ones who were to be his classmates—obviously, these were the parents who cared. The movement of second-generation Chinese Americans has been to the suburbs or to other parts of San Francisco, and it is no longer practical to send their children, the third generation, to Chinese school in Chinatown. My husband and I cherish our Chinese ties and knowledge, and waited many years to purchase a home which would be within walking distance of Chinatown. If a child has difficulty with homework, Chinese or American, he or she can come to see us at our office-studio, and we drop everything to help.

As in my own dual education, the children are learning Chinese   25
history, culture, or what being a member of the Chinese race means. The six-year-old learns one new ideograph a day. After a week, he knew that one writes Chinese from top to bottom, from left to right. They do not lack time for playing, drawing, reading, or TV viewing. Sometimes they do complain, because Chinese is not taught as pleasurably as subjects at American school. When they ask why they must attend Chinese school, I say firmly, "This is our standard. If you lived in another home, you could do as they do." Our children chatter among themselves in English, but

they can understand and speak Chinese when desired. It is a necessity when with their grandmothers. Even this simple ability contrasts with some children of Chinese ancestry. As my mother exclaimed in dismay when such a grandchild visited her, "We were as a duck and a chicken regarding each other without understanding."

As a wife and mother, I have naturally followed my Chinese train-   26
ing to wait on my husband and serve my children. While ceramics is my career, the members of my family know they come first, and they do not pay any penalty for my work. Chinese men expect to be family heads, and to receive loving service from wife and children, but they are also marvelously helpful as fathers, and nearly all Chinese men I know enjoy being creative cooks on occasion. If you visit the parks of Chinatown, you are likely to see more men than women overseeing the laughing children. If you shop in Chinatown, you find as many men as women choosing the groceries. My husband has given our children from birth more baths and shampoos than I have. He has also been their manicurist and ear cleaner, for once a week, when they were smaller, there were eight ears to swab clean and eighty nails to trim.

Selective self-expression, which was discouraged in my father's   27
household, has been encouraged in our family. About two years ago, my husband established this tradition: every Sunday evening each child presents an original verbal or verbal-visual project, based on a news article, a school project, a drawing (since the youngest can't read yet), a film. We correct diction, posture, presentation, in the hope that each will be able to think aloud on his feet someday. Each of the three older children has one or more special friends. I have met these friends at our home, preferring that they be invited here rather than have our children leave home. Seldom do we plan children's parties, but when we entertain our adult friends, our children are included. How else would they learn correct etiquette and expect to fit into an adult world some day? At their age, I used to be uncertain to the point of being terrified of "foreigners." Thanks to the hospitality of our Western friends, we and our children have been guests at their homes, their pools, their country retreats. And when they come to our home, the whole family delights in helping to prepare Chinese treats to serve them.

Traditional Chinese parents pit their children against a standard of   28
perfection without regard to personality, individual ambitions, tolerance for human error, or exposure to the changing social scene. It never oc-

curred to that kind of parent to be friends with their children on common ground. Unlike our parents, we think we tolerate human error and human change. Our children are being encouraged to develop their individual abilities. They all draw and can use their hands in crafts, are all familiar with our office and love to experiment with the potter's wheel or enameling supplies at our studio. Sometimes I have been asked, "What would you like your children to be?" Let each choose his or her career. The education of our girls will be provided by us as well as that of our boys. My father used to say, "If no one educated girls, how can we have educated mothers for our sons?" I hope each one will be a civilized, constructive, creative, conservative nonconformist.

☜ Opening the Dialogue

1. In paragraph 22 Wong says that although her child-rearing practices are different from those of her parents, she remains true to their traditions. Do you agree, or do you think that Wong's child-rearing methods depart from the traditions of her parents?

2. Do you think Wong's children will raise their own children as they are being raised? What factors might lead them to depart from their parents' approach?

3. In what way do you think a person committed to expanding the rights of women would react to Wong's description of her relationship with her husband and children?

☜ Keeping a Notebook

Wong's essay discusses the education of her children. In what respects is her concept of education consistent and inconsistent with yours?

☜ Working Together

Compile a list of your family's child-rearing practices. Then, compare your list with those compiled by others in your group. In class discussion, try to decide on the advantages and disadvantages of various approaches to bringing up children.

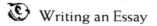 Writing an Essay

Would you raise a child differently from the way in which your parents have raised you? Compare and contrast your approach to child rearing with theirs, being sure to comment on the relative merits of each method.

MARIANNA DE MARCO TORGOVNICK

On Being White, Female, and Born in Bensonhurst

In the summer of 1989, a young African-American man was shot and killed in the Italian-American Brooklyn neighborhood where Marianna Torgovnick was born (1949) and grew up. This tragic shooting set off weeks of racially charged violence and confrontation. Almost immediately, she writes, "I began to plan [the following] essay, to tell the world what I knew, even though I was aware that I could publish the piece only someplace my parents or their neighbors would never see or hear about it."

A professor of English at Duke University in North Carolina and a respected literary critic, Torgovnick was determined from childhood to establish herself in a professional and intellectual milieu far removed from her working class background. However, somewhat reluctantly, she acknowledges the influence of her Italian-American heritage: "When I wrote in 1986 about Mario Puzo's *The Godfather*, it seemed necessary for the first time in my career to talk about my history as an Italian-American woman and to use my full name: Marianna De Marco Torgovnick. My Italian origins had been a peculiar taboo in my life as a critic, since I associated Italian-Americans with a certain anti-intellectualism. My essay on Puzo and the essay on Bensonhurst that follow depend for their authority on my personal experience of what, for better and worse, it means to be an Italian-American female: rivalry with brothers, low professional expectations, intellectual scrappiness, politeness and euphemism, concern for the neighbors and what people will think, and above all a sense of family."

In the essay that follows, Torgovnick sets up a variety of comparisons and contrasts—Bensonhurst today versus Bensonhurst thirty years ago, her childhood versus her adult life, her values versus those of her parents and their neighbors. As you read, identify these various subjects and notice how she weaves them together into a coherent whole.

THE MAFIA PROTECTS THE NEIGHBORHOOD, our fathers say, with   1
that peculiar satisfied pride with which law-abiding Italian Americans refer to the Mafia: the Mafia protects the neighborhood from "the coloreds." In the fifties and sixties, I heard that information repeated, in whispers, in neighborhood parks and in the yard at school in Bensonhurst. The same information probably passes today in the parks (the word now "blacks," not "coloreds") but perhaps no longer in the schoolyards. From buses each morning, from neighborhoods outside Bensonhurst, spill children of all colors and backgrounds—American black, West Indian black, Hispanic, and Asian. But the blacks are the only ones especially marked for notice. Bensonhurst is no longer entirely protected from "the coloreds." But in a deeper sense, at least for Italian Americans, Bensonhurst never changes.

Italian-American life continues pretty much as I remember it. Fam-   2
ilies with young children live side by side with older couples whose children are long gone to the suburbs. Many of those families live "down the block" from the last generation or, sometimes still, live together with parents or grandparents. When a young family leaves, as sometimes happens, for Long Island or New Jersey or (very common now) for Staten Island, another arrives, without any special effort being required, from Italy or a poorer neighborhood in New York. They fill the neat but anonymous houses that make up the mostly tree-lined streets: two-, three-, or four-family houses for the most part (this is a working, lower to middle-middle class area, and people need rents to pay mortgages), with a few single family or small apartment houses tossed in at random. Tomato plants, fig trees, and plaster madonnas often decorate small but well-tended yards which face out onto the street; the grassy front lawn, like the grassy back yard, is relatively uncommon.

Crisscrossing the neighborhood and marking out ethnic zones—   3
Italian, Irish, and Jewish, for the most part, though there are some Asian Americans and some people (usually Protestants) called simply Americans—are the great shopping streets: Eighty-sixth Street, Kings High-

way, Bay Parkway, Eighteenth Avenue, each with its own distinctive character. On Eighty-sixth Street, crowds bustle along sidewalks lined with ample, packed fruit stands. Women wheeling shopping carts or baby strollers check the fruit carefully, piece by piece, and often bargain with the dealer, cajoling for a better price or letting him know that the vegetables, this time, aren't up to snuff. A few blocks down, the fruit stands are gone and the streets are lined with clothing and record shops, mobbed by teenagers. Occasionally, the el rumbles overhead, a few stops out of Coney Island on its way to the city, a trip of around one hour.

On summer nights, neighbors congregate on stoops which during   4
the day serve as play yards for children. Air conditioning exists everywhere in Bensonhurst, but people still sit outside in the summer—to supervise children, to gossip, to stare at strangers. *"Buona sera,"* I say, or *"Buona notte,"* as I am ritually presented to Sal and Lily and Louie, the neighbors sitting on the stoop. *"Grazie,"* I say when they praise my children or my appearance. It's the only time I use Italian, which I learned at high school, although my parents (both second-generation Italian Americans, my father Sicilian, my mother Calabrian) speak it at home to each other but never to me or my brother. My accent is the Tuscan accent taught at school, not the southern Italian accents of my parents and the neighbors.

It's important to greet and please the neighbors; any break in this   5
decorum would seriously offend and aggrieve my parents. For the neighbors are the stern arbiters of conduct in Bensonhurst. Does Mary keep a clean house? Did Gina wear black long enough after her mother's death? Was the food good at Tony's wedding? The neighbors know and pass judgment. Any news of family scandal (my brother's divorce, for example) provokes from my mother the agonized words: "But what will I *tell* people?" I sometimes collaborate in devising a plausible script.

A large sign on the church I attended as a child sums up for me the   6
ethos of Bensonhurst. The sign urges contributions to the church building fund with the message, in huge letters: "EACH YEAR ST. SIMON AND JUDE SAVES THIS NEIGHBORHOOD ONE MILLION DOLLARS IN TAXES." Passing the church on the way from largely Jewish and middle-class Sheepshead Bay (where my in-laws live) to Bensonhurst, year after year, my husband and I look for the sign and laugh at the crass level of its pitch, its utter lack of attention to things spiritual. But we also understand exactly the values it represents.

In the summer of 1989, my parents were visiting me at my house in   7
Durham, North Carolina, from the apartment in Bensonhurst where they
have lived since 1942: three small rooms, rent-controlled, floor clean
enough to eat off, every corner and crevice known and organized. My
parents' longevity in a single apartment is unusual even for Bensonhurst,
but not that unusual; many people live for decades in the same place or
move within a ten-block radius. When I lived in this apartment, there
were four rooms; one has since been ceded to a demanding landlord, one
of the various landlords who have haunted my parents' life and must always be appeased lest the ultimate threat—removal from the rent-
controlled apartment—be brought into play. That summer, during their
visit, on August 23 (my younger daughter's birthday) a shocking, disturbing, news report issued from the neighborhood: it had become another
Howard Beach.

Three black men, walking casually through the streets at night,   8
were attacked by a group of whites. One was shot dead, mistaken, as it
turned out, for another black youth who was dating a white, although
part-Hispanic, girl in the neighborhood. It all made sense: the crudely
protective men, expecting to see a black arriving at the girl's house and
overreacting; the rebellious girl dating the outsider boy; the black dead as
a sacrifice to the feelings of the neighborhood.

I might have felt outrage, I might have felt guilt or shame, I might   9
have despised the people among whom I grew up. In a way I felt all four
emotions when I heard the news. I expect that there were many people in
Bensonhurst who felt the same rush of emotions. But mostly I felt that,
given the set-up, this was the only way things could have happened. I
detested the racial killing, but I also understood it. Those streets, which
should be public property available to all, belong to the neighborhood.
All the people sitting on the stoops on August 23 knew that as well as
they knew their own names. The black men walking through probably
knew it too—though their casual walk sought to deny the fact that, for
the neighbors, even the simple act of blacks walking through the neighborhood would be seen as invasion.

Italian Americans in Bensonhurst are notable for their cohesiveness   10
and provinciality; the slightest pressure turns those qualities into prejudice and racism. Their cohesiveness is based on the stable economic and
ethical level that links generation to generation, keeping Italian Americans in Bensonhurst and the Italian-American community alive as the

Jewish-American community of my youth is no longer alive. (Its young people routinely moved to the suburbs or beyond and were never replaced, so that Jews in Bensonhurst today are almost all very old people.) Their provinciality results from the Italian Americans' devotion to jealous distinctions and discriminations. Jews are suspect, but (the old Italian women admit) "they make good husbands." The Irish are okay, fellow Catholics, but not really "like us"; they make bad husbands because they drink and gamble. Even Italians come in varieties, by region (Sicilian, Calabrian, Neapolitan, very rarely any region further north) and by history in this country (the newly arrived and ridiculed "gaffoon" versus the second or third generation).

Bensonhurst is a neighborhood dedicated to believing that its values are the only values; it tends toward certain forms of inertia. When my parents visit me in Durham, they routinely take chairs from the kitchen and sit out on the lawn in front of the house, not on the chairs on the back deck; then they complain that the streets are too quiet. When they walk around my neighborhood (these De Marcos who have friends named Travaglianti and Occhipinti), they look at the mailboxes and report that my neighbors have strange names. Prices at my local supermarket are compared, in unbelievable detail, with prices on Eighty-sixth Street. Any rearrangement of my kitchen since their last visit is registered and criticized. Difference is not only unwelcome, it is unacceptable. One of the most characteristic things my mother ever said was in response to my plans for renovating my house in Durham. When she heard my plans, she looked around, crossed her arms, and said, "If it was me, I wouldn't change nothing." My father once asked me to level with him about a Jewish boyfriend who lived in a different part of the neighborhood, reacting to his Jewishness, but even more to the fact that he often wore Bermuda shorts: "Tell me something, Marianna. Is he a Communist?" Such are the standards of normality and political thinking in Bensonhurst.

I often think that one important difference between Italian Americans in New York neighborhoods like Bensonhurst and Italian Americans elsewhere is that the others moved on—to upstate New York, to Pennsylvania, to the Midwest. Though they frequently settled in communities of fellow Italians, they did move on. Bensonhurst Italian Americans seem to have felt that one large move, over the ocean, was enough. Future moves could be only local: from the Lower East Side, for example, to

11

12

Brooklyn, or from one part of Brooklyn to another. Bensonhurst was for many of these people the summa of expectations. If their America were to be drawn as a *New Yorker* cover, Manhattan itself would be tiny in proportion to Bensonhurst and to its satellites, Staten Island, New Jersey, and Long Island.

"Oh, no," my father says when he hears the news about the shoot-   13
ing. Though he still refers to blacks as "coloreds," he's not really a racist and is upset that this innocent youth was shot in his neighborhood. He has no trouble acknowledging the wrongness of the death. But then, like all the news accounts, he turns to the fact, repeated over and over, that the blacks had been on their way to look at a used car when they encountered the hostile mob of whites. The explanation is right before him but, "Yeah," he says, still shaking his head, "yeah, but what were they *doing* there? They didn't belong."

Over the next few days, the television news is even more disturb-   14
ing. Rows of screaming Italians lining the streets, most of them looking like my relatives. I focus especially on one woman who resembles almost completely my mother: stocky but not fat, mid-seventies but well preserved, full face showing only minimal wrinkles, ample steel-gray hair neatly if rigidly coiffed in a modified beehive hairdo left over from the sixties. She shakes her fist at the camera, protesting the arrest of the Italian-American youths in the neighborhood and the incursion of more blacks into the neighborhood, protesting the shooting. I look a little nervously at my mother (the parent I resemble), but she has not even noticed the woman and stares impassively at the television.

What has Bensonhurst to do with what I teach today and write?   1:
Why did I need to write about this killing in Bensonhurst, but not in the manner of a news account or a statistical sociological analysis? Within days of hearing the news, I began to plan this essay, to tell the world what I knew, even though I was aware that I could publish the piece only someplace my parents or their neighbors would never see or hear about it. I sometimes think that I looked around from my baby carriage and decided that someday, the sooner the better, I would get out of Bensonhurst. Now, much to my surprise, Bensonhurst—the antipode of the intellectual life I sought, the least interesting of places—had become a respectable intellectual topic. People would be willing to hear about Bensonhurst—and all by the dubious virtue of a racial killing in the streets.

The story as I would have to tell it would be to some extent a class   16
narrative: about the difference between working class and upper middle
class, dependence and a profession, Bensonhurst and a posh suburb. But I
need to make it clear that I do not imagine myself as writing from a position of enormous self-satisfaction, or even enormous distance. You can
take the girl out of Bensonhurst (that much is clear), but you may not be
able to take Bensonhurst out of the girl. And upward mobility is not the
essence of the story, though it is an important marker and symbol.

In Durham today, I live in a twelve-room house surrounded by an   17
acre of trees. When I sit on my back deck on summer evenings, no houses
are visible through the trees. I have a guaranteed income, teaching English at an excellent university, removed by my years of education from
the fundamental economic and social conditions of Bensonhurst. The
one time my mother ever expressed pleasure at my work was when I got
tenure, what my father still calls, with no irony intended, "ten years."
"What does that mean?" my mother asked when she heard the news.
Then she reached back into her experience as a garment worker, subject
to periodic layoffs. "Does it mean they can't fire you just for nothing and
can't lay you off?" When I said that was exactly what it means, she said,
"Very good. Congratulations. That's *wonderful.*" I was free from the *padro-
nes*, from the network of petty anxieties that had formed, in large part, her
very existence. Of course, I wasn't really free of petty anxieties: would my
salary increase keep pace with my colleagues', how would my office compare, would this essay be accepted for publication, am I happy? The line
between these worries and my mother's is the line between the working
class and the upper middle class.

But getting out of Bensonhurst never meant to me a big house, or   18
nice clothes, or a large income. And it never meant feeling good about
looking down on what I left behind or hiding my background. Getting
out of Bensonhurst meant freedom—to experiment, to grow, to change.
It also meant knowledge in some grand, abstract way. All the material
possessions I have acquired, I acquired simply along the way—and for
the first twelve years after I left Bensonhurst, I chose to acquire almost
nothing at all. Now, as I write about the neighborhood, I recognize that
although I've come far in physical and material distance, the emotional
distance is harder to gauge. Bensonhurst has everything to do with who I
am and even with what I write. Occasionally I get reminded of my roots,
of their simultaneously choking and nutritive power.

Scene one: It's after a lecture at Duke, given by a visiting professor   19
from Princeton. The lecture was long and a little dull and—bad luck—I
had agreed to be one of the people having dinner with the lecturer afterward. We settle into our table at the restaurant: this man, me, the head of
the comparative literature program (also a professor of German), and a
couple I like who teach French, the husband at my university, the wife at
one nearby. The conversation is sluggish, as it often is when a stranger,
like the visiting professor, has to be assimilated into a group, so I ask the
visitor from Princeton a question to personalize things a bit. "How did
you get interested in what you do? What made you become a professor
of German?" The man gets going and begins talking about how it was
really unlikely that he, a nice Jewish boy from Bensonhurst, would have
chosen, in the mid-fifties, to study German. Unlikely indeed.

I remember seeing *Judgment at Nuremberg* in a local movie theater and   20
having a woman in the row in back of me get hysterical when some clips
of a concentration camp were shown. "My God," she screamed in a European accent, "look at what they did. Murderers, MURDERERS!"—and she
had to be supported out by her family. I couldn't see, in the dark, whether
her arm bore the neatly tattooed numbers that the arms of some of my
classmates' parents did—and that always affected me with a thrill of horror. Ten years older than me, this man had lived more directly through
those feelings, lived with and *among* those feelings. The first chance he
got, he raced to study in Germany. I myself have twice chosen not to visit
Germany, but I understand his impulse to identify with the Other as a
way of getting out of the neighborhood.

At the dinner, the memory about the movie pops into my mind but   21
I pick up instead on the Bensonhurst—I'm also from there, but Italian
American. Like a flash, he asks something I haven't been asked in years:
Where did I go to high school and (a more common question) what was
my maiden name? I went to Lafayette High School, I say, and my name
was De Marco. Everything changes: his facial expression, his posture, his
accent, his voice. "Soo, Dee Maw-ko," he says, "dun anything wrong at
school today—got enny pink slips? Wanna meet me later at the park or
maybe bye the Baye?" When I laugh, recognizing the stereotype that Italians get pink slips for misconduct at school and the notorious chemistry
between Italian women and Jewish men, he says, back in his Princetonian
voice: "My God, for a minute I felt like I was turning into a werewolf."

It's odd that although I can remember almost nothing else about   22
this man—his face, his body type, even his name—I remember this lapse
into his "real self" with enormous vividness. I am especially struck by how
easily he was able to slip into the old, generic Brooklyn accent. I myself
have no memory of ever speaking in that accent, though I also have no
memory of trying not to speak it, except for teaching myself, carefully, to
say "oil" rather than "earl."

But the surprises aren't over. The female French professor, whom I   23
have known for at least five years, reveals for the first time that she is also
from the neighborhood, though she lived across the other side of Kings
Highway, went to a different, more elite high school, and was Irish
American. Three of six professors, sitting at an eclectic vegetarian restaurant in Durham, all from Bensonhurst—a neighborhood where (I swear)
you couldn't get the *New York Times* at any of the local stores.

Scene two: I still live in Bensonhurst. I'm waiting for my parents to   24
return from a conference at my school, where they've been summoned to
discuss my transition from elementary to junior high school. I am already
a full year younger than any of my classmates, having skipped a grade, a
not uncommon occurrence for "gifted" youngsters. Now the school is
worried about putting me in an accelerated track through junior high,
since that would make me two years younger. A compromise was
reached: I would be put in a special program for gifted children, but one
that took three, not two, years. It sounds okay.

Three years later, another wait. My parents have gone to school   25
this time to make another decision. Lafayette High School has three
tracks: academic, for potentially college-bound kids; secretarial, mostly
for Italian-American girls or girls with low aptitude-test scores (the high
school is de facto segregated, so none of the tracks is as yet racially
coded, though they are coded by ethnic group and gender); and voca-
tional, mostly for boys with the same attributes, ethnic or intellectual.
Although my scores are superb, the guidance counselor has recom-
mended the secretarial track; when I protested, the conference with my
parents was arranged. My mother's preference is clear: the secretarial
track—college is for boys; I will need to make a "good living" until I
marry and have children. My father also prefers the secretarial track, but
he wavers, half proud of my aberrantly high scores, half worried. I press
the attack, saying that if I were Jewish I would have been placed, without

question, in the academic track. I tell him I have sneaked a peek at my files and know that my IQ is at genius level. I am allowed to insist on the change into the academic track.

What I did, and I was ashamed of it even then, was to play upon my   26
father's competitive feelings with Jews: his daughter could and should be as good as theirs. In the bank where he was a messenger, and at the insurance company where he worked in the mailroom, my father worked with Jews, who were almost always his immediate supervisors. Several times, my father was offered the supervisory job but turned it down after long conversations with my mother about the dangers of making a change, the difficulty of giving orders to friends. After her work in a local garment shop, after cooking dinner and washing the floor each night, my mother often did piecework making bows; sometimes I would help her for fun, but it *wasn't* fun, and I was free to stop while she continued for long, tedious hours to increase the family income. Once a week, her part-time boss, Dave, would come by to pick up the boxes of bows. Short, round, with his shirttails sloppily tucked into his pants and a cigar almost always dangling from his lips, Dave was a stereotyped Jew but also, my parents always said, a nice guy, a decent man.

Years after, similar choices come up, and I show the same assertive-   27
ness I showed with my father, the same ability to deal for survival, but tinged with Bensonhurst caution. Where will I go to college? Not to Brooklyn College, the flagship of the city system—I know that, but don't press the invitations I have received to apply to prestigious schools outside of New York. The choice comes down to two: Barnard, which gives me a full scholarship, minus five hundred dollars a year that all scholarship students are expected to contribute from summer earnings, or New York University, which offers me one thousand dollars above tuition as a bribe. I waver. My parents stand firm: they are already losing money by letting me go to college; I owe it to the family to contribute the extra thousand dollars plus my summer earnings. Besides, my mother adds, harping on a favorite theme, there are no boys at Barnard; at NYU I'm more likely to meet someone to marry. I go to NYU and do marry in my senior year, but he is someone I didn't meet at college. I was secretly relieved, I now think (though at the time I thought I was just placating my parents' conventionality), to be out of the marriage sweepstakes.

The first boy who ever asked me for a date was Robert Lubitz, in   28
eighth grade: tall and skinny to my average height and teenage chubbi-

ness. I turned him down, thinking we would make a ridiculous couple. Day after day, I cast my eyes at stylish Juliano, the class cutup; day after day, I captivated Robert Lubitz. Occasionally, one of my brother's Italian-American friends would ask me out, and I would go, often to ROTC dances. My specialty was making political remarks so shocking that the guys rarely asked me again. After a while I recognized destiny: the Jewish man was a passport out of Bensonhurst. I of course did marry a Jewish man, who gave me my freedom and, very important, helped remove me from the expectations of Bensonhurst. Though raised in a largely Jewish section of Brooklyn, he had gone to college in Ohio and knew how important it was, as he put it, "to get past the Brooklyn Bridge." We met on neutral ground, in Central Park, at a performance of Shakespeare. The Jewish-Italian marriage is a common enough catastrophe in Bensonhurst for my parents to have accepted, even welcomed, mine— though my parents continued to treat my husband like an outsider for the first twenty years ("Now Marianna. Here's what's going on with you brother. But don't tell-a you husband").

Along the way I make other choices, more fully marked by Bensonhurst cautiousness. I am attracted to journalism or the arts as careers, but the prospects for income seem iffy. I choose instead to imagine myself as a teacher. Only the availability of NDEA fellowships when I graduate, with their generous terms, propels me from high school teaching (a thought I never much relished) to college teaching (which seems like a brave new world). Within the college teaching profession, I choose offbeat specializations: the novel, interdisciplinary approaches (not something clear and clubby like Milton or the eighteenth century). Eventually I write the book I like best about primitive others as they figure within Western obsessions: my identification with "the Other," my sense of being "Other," surfaces at last. I avoid all mentoring structures for a long time but accept aid when it comes to me on the basis of what I perceive to be merit. I'm still, deep down, Italian-American Bensonhurst, though by this time I'm a lot of other things as well.   29

Scene three: In the summer of 1988, a little more than a year before the shooting in Bensonhurst, my father woke up trembling and in what appeared to be a fit. Hospitalization revealed that he had a pocket of blood on his brain, a frequent consequence of falls for older people. About a year earlier, I had stayed home, using my children as an excuse, when my aunt, my father's much loved sister, died, missing her funeral;   30

only now does my mother tell me how much my father resented my taking his suggestion that I stay home. Now, confronted with what is described as brain surgery but turns out to be less dramatic than it sounds, I
fly home immediately.

My brother drives three hours back and forth from New Jersey   31
every day to chauffeur me and my mother to the hospital: he is being a
fine Italian-American son. For the first time in years, we have long conversations alone. He is two years older than I am, a chemical engineer
who has also left the neighborhood but has remained closer to its values,
with a suburban, Republican inflection. He talks a lot about New York,
saying that (except for neighborhoods like Bensonhurst) it's a "third-
world city now." It's the summer of the Tawana Brawley incident, when
Brawley accused white men of abducting her and smearing racial slurs on
her body with her own excrement. My brother is filled with dislike for Al
Sharpton and Brawley's other vocal supporters in the black community—
not because they're black, he says, but because they're troublemakers,
stirring things up. The city is drenched in racial hatred that makes itself
felt in the halls of the hospital: Italians and Jews in the beds and as doctors; blacks as nurses and orderlies.

This is the first time since I left New York in 1975 that I have vis-   32
ited Brooklyn without once getting into Manhattan. It's the first time I
have spent several days alone with my mother, living in her apartment in
Bensonhurst. My every move is scrutinized and commented on. I feel like
I am going to go crazy.

Finally, it's clear that my father is going to be fine, and I can go   33
home. She insists on accompanying me to the travel agent to get my
ticket for home, even though I really want to be alone. The agency (a
Mafia front?) has no one who knows how to ticket me for the exotic
destination of North Carolina and no computer for doing so. The one
person who can perform this feat by hand is out. I have to kill time for an
hour and suggest to my mother that she go home, to be there for my
brother when he arrives from Jersey. We stop in a Pork Store, where I
buy a stash of cheeses, sausages, and other delicacies unavailable in Durham. My mother walks home with the shopping bags, and I'm on my
own.

More than anything I want a kind of *sorbetto* or ice I remember from   34
my childhood, a *cremolata*, almond-vanilla-flavored with large chunks of
nuts. I pop into the local bakery (at the unlikely hour of 11 A.M.) and ask

for a *cremolata*, usually eaten after dinner. The woman—a younger version of my mother—refuses: they haven't made a fresh ice yet, and what's left from the day before is too icy, no good. I explain that I'm about to get on a plane for North Carolina and want that ice, good or not. But she has her standards and holds her ground, even though North Carolina has about the same status in her mind as Timbuktoo and she knows I will be banished, perhaps forever, from the land of *cremolata*.

Then, while I'm taking a walk, enjoying my solitude, I have another 35 idea. On the block behind my parents' house, there's a club for men, for men from a particular town or region in Italy: six or seven tables, some on the sidewalk beneath a garish red, green, and white sign; no women allowed or welcome unless they're with men, and no women at all during the day when the real business of the club—a game of cards for old men—is in progress. Still, I know that inside the club would be coffee and a *cremolata* ice. I'm thirty-eight, well-dressed, very respectable looking; I know what I want. I also know I'm not supposed to enter that club. I enter anyway, asking the teenage boy behind the counter firmly, in my most professional tones, for a *cremolata* ice. Dazzled, he complies immediately. The old men at the card table have been staring at this scene, unable to place me exactly, though my facial type is familiar. Finally, a few old men's hisses pierce the air. *"Strega,"* I hear as I leave, *"mala strega"*— "witch," or "brazen whore." I have been in Bensonhurst less than a week, but I have managed to reproduce, on my final day there for this visit, the conditions of my youth. Knowing the rules, I have broken them. I shake hands with my discreetly rebellious past, still an outsider walking through the neighborhood, marked and insulted—though unlikely to be shot.

⟨Ͼ⟩ Opening the Dialogue

1. Torgovnick clearly considers herself an outsider in Bensonhurst. Do you agree?

2. How do you suppose Torgovnick's father would react to this essay? Specifically, how might he react to her comments about Italian Americans? About Jews and African Americans?

3. The racial killing that took place in Bensonhurst is a thread that runs

throughTorgovnick's essay. What significance do you think this killing has in the essay?

⟨℮⟩ Keeping a Notebook

Is there anything about the neighborhood in which you grew up that would lead you not to raise your own children there?

⟨℮⟩ Working Together

Working in groups, list the advantages and disadvantages of growing up female in Bensonhurst. In class discussion, debate whether Torgovnick succeeded because of or in spite of Bensonhurst.

⟨℮⟩ Writing an Essay

Write an essay about a time when you, like Torgovnick, knowingly broke the rules. Make sure you compare your sense of what you were supposed to do with what you eventually decided to do.

Writing: Across Cultures

1. Write a letter to a real or an imagined relative who did not emigrate to the United States. In your letter discuss how you imagine your life to be different from his or hers. Before writing this essay, you may want to get some background information from an older family member.

2. Write an essay in which you—like Kim Ode—compare yourself to one of your parents. In what ways are you the same? In what ways are you different? How do you account for the differences?

3. In "A Change of Worlds" Chief Seattle gives his view of his culture and what it means to him. Compare his view with those of other Native Americans—Mary Crow Dog or N. Scott Momaday, for example.

4. Write an essay in which you—like Jade Snow Wong—compare the difficulties of being a parent twenty years ago with the difficulties that exist now. Interview your parents as well as some of your friends' parents for information.

5. Many of the writers in this chapter try to understand family members who hold values that are different from theirs. Choose two writers in this chapter and compare their attitudes toward their relatives.

CHAPTER 8

CATEGORIZING
CULTURES
CLASSIFYING AND
DIVIDING

GRANT WOOD, "TREE PLANTING GROUP" (1937)

More than by ethnicity or race, the students in my high school were divided by economic class. There were basically three groups. First, there were the rich kids. Most of them lived in big houses on the ridge, and we assumed their fathers were all lawyers or executives. By junior year, most had their own cars—new cars—and they were talking about going to private out-of-state colleges. Next there was my group, the kids in the middle. Our fathers were small businessmen or blue-collar workers, and our mothers worked too, usually as secretaries or sales clerks. We lived in smaller houses, and if we had our own cars they'd be second-hand, and we'd have to work to earn the money to buy them. Finally, there were the kids who lived (literally, as it happened) on the other side of the railroad tracks. These kids were poor, and we didn't know them well enough to know what their houses looked like or what their parents did for a living; we assumed in our ignorance that their fathers were unemployed bikers and their mothers just had babies. These kids had cars too—beat-up pick-ups and vans that never seemed to have mufflers. Through all four years of high school, the three groups kept their distance, and this separateness fed our stereotypes.

Michael Jennings, student

Categorizing Cultures

Classification and division—dividing a whole and categorizing its parts—is a useful organizing principle in a variety of academic subjects, where it helps writers make sense of complex information. For example, writers can classify literary or artistic works according to genres or periods and social problems according to causes. Similarly, writers can divide a discussion of the human body into sections based on its systems (circulatory, digestive, and so on) or divide a discussion of government into sections based on its branches (executive, legislative, judicial). As writers explore various aspects of the American experience, classification and division can be a helpful strategy for understanding large, abstract concepts such as race or ethnicity. Breaking down a whole into parts can make the whole manageable and the parts identifiable. For example, writers can divide a city into neighborhoods or classify a region's (or a culture's) food, music, films, heroes, political beliefs, languages, rituals, customs, attitudes, or styles of dress, speech, or interpersonal communication.

The writers whose essays are collected in this chapter use classification and division to gain an understanding of their own cultural experiences. Mary Mebane tells how, as a student at North Carolina College at Durham in the 1950s, she learned that "social class and color were the primary criteria used in determining status on the campus" (p. 342); she introduces this system of classification in order to explore the wider implications of stereotypes based on skin color. Alan M. Dershowitz also relates classification to stereotyping as he explains a hierarchy within the legal profession based not on merit but on ethnic identity. Unlike Mebane and Dershowitz, who focus on classification systems outside their control, both Amy Tan and Scott Russell Sanders devise their own systems—more flexible than those imposed from outside—to help them understand their own backgrounds.

As these writers focus on specific, personal experiences, they use classification and division to explore the larger issues many Americans confront: they think about the complex relationship between education (or work) and self-esteem; they consider the harmful effects of stereotyping and prejudice; they examine the limitations imposed upon them by social class; they express concern over the ways in which their desire to move up the socioeconomic ladder may be limited by factors they cannot control; and they consider the problems of assimilation and upward mobility faced by previous generations as well as by their own.

In much the same way, classification and division can work well as an organizational strategy in your essays, helping you to categorize—and thereby better understand—various cultures and cultural perspectives.

The student essay that follows uses classification and division to explore the dangers inherent in seeing people as stereotypes.

STUDENT VOICE: ALEX NOLAN

Stereotypes

None of us likes to be deprived of our individuality, but that is 1
exactly what we do when we stereotype others. Although some kinds of stereotypes may seem fairly harmless, all stereotypes make it harder for us to see the people around us as individuals. And the worst stereotypes are the ones we do not even recognize as stereotypes but accept as fact. We assume, for example, that all people in wheelchairs are helpless and that all elderly people are so hard of hearing we have to shout when we speak to them; obviously, generalizations such as these affect our behavior toward others. Some stereotypes are dangerous; all of them prevent us from understanding and respecting the differences in people around us.

Probably the most common stereotypes are based on physical 2
characteristics. Blond-haired people are often stereotyped as "dumb" or "shallow," but for every "dumb" blond there is a Sandra Day O'Connor or a Ted Koppel who breaks the stereotype. People are also stereotyped by their height; their weight; the way they walk, talk, and dress; and even the way they wear their hair. I remember a letter to Dear Abby in which the writer described her new neighbor: "She always wears jeans and a workshirt, her hair is very short, and she talks in a deep voice. Abby, do you think she could be Lebanese?" Stereotypes such as these, based on physical characteristics, can and often do hurt, especially when they keep the person being stereotyped from being taken seriously.

The next most common kind of stereotype is based on lifestyle,   3
including personal interests and career. If you are a jock, you cannot be a good student. If you are a brain, you cannot be much fun.
If you are a lawyer, you are not to be trusted. If you are a factory
worker, you move your lips when you read. If you are gay, you are
a bad influence on children. If you live in the inner city, you are on
welfare. If you live in the suburbs, you are bland and Republican. At
their worst, stereotypes like these result in prejudice and discrimination. Even at their best, they keep people apart, suspicious and
separate, and prevent them from trying to understand each other.

The worst prejudice results from a third kind of stereotype, the   4
kind based on a person's race or ethnic background. Whole tribes
were eradicated when the Europeans first came to the New World
just because they were perceived as "barbarians." Africans were enslaved because they were "uncivilized." Hitler used age-old stereotypes of Jews to justify their extermination. Unfortunately, such
stereotypes and prejudice are still with us today, passed on from
generation to generation to generation. Because of their skin color
or their language or their country of origin, some people are perceived as being not as good as "we" are. This kind of thinking has
done serious psychological harm to individuals of all backgrounds
and has weakened our society as a whole.

Stereotypes are the result of limited knowledge. We see people   5
as stereotypes instead of as individuals because we do not really
know much about them or the groups they belong to. No one who
has blond friends would automatically assume that a blond person is dumb. No one who has worked in the inner city would as-

sume that people who live there are all on welfare. No one who really knew many individuals of a particular racial or ethnic group would accept the stereotypes of that group that more ignorant people believe. A country founded on respect and tolerance for differences should celebrate, not fear, diversity among its citizens.

Classifying and Dividing

Classification and division enables a writer to break a single entity or class into smaller parts and arrange those parts into categories. The related processes of classifying and dividing make it possible for both writer and reader to understand the whole and to see the relationships of the parts to one another.

Writers of classification-and-division essays can classify and divide people, experiences, families, climates, behavior, illnesses, habits, transportation systems, scientific phenomena, social movements, organizations, social or political institutions, educational systems—in short, any entity whose parts can be identified and arranged into categories on the basis of one or more shared characteristics. Thus residents of a particular neighborhood can be *divided* into categories based on age (preschool children, school-age children, young adults, middle-aged adults, the elderly), race or ethnicity, occupation, social class, sexual orientation, or any of a great number of other factors. Then—theoretically at least—each resident of the community could be *classified* in an appropriate category.

Keep in mind that the goal of classification and division is not to oversimplify or trivialize the whole but to understand it better: to identify similarities and differences among groups and subgroups and see their relationships to one another and to the whole. When dealing with people, it is important to remember that each group is made up of individuals. Take great care to avoid unfair, reductive stereotyping; do not assume, for example, that people or cultures can be divided into neat, mutually exclusive categories, or that all people in a given group are alike.

Establishing a Logical System of Classification

When you plan a classification-and-division essay, you should *establish a logical system of classification*, assigning items to categories on the basis of a single principle of classification. Naturally, most items can be classified according to more than one principle; the one you select should be the one that best serves your purpose. For example, law firms can be classified according to location, size, specialization, philosophy, or any number of other characteristics. Because Alan M. Dershowitz seeks to expose the bias that was inherent in hiring practices among certain law firms, however, the classification system he presents is based on how likely a given firm was to hire lawyers who were not white Anglo-Saxon Protestants. Similarly, Mary Mebane emphasizes the unfairness of one system of classification by explaining how college students were classified not by major, extracurricular interests, or any other reasonable system, but solely on the basis of skin color and social class.

As you develop your system of classification, be sure you are not forcing items into a system with which they are incompatible. If you see that an item does not easily conform to a system of classification that otherwise seems logical, consider narrowing or broadening the scope of the categories—or, if an important item cannot readily be classified, even creating a new system of classification.

Keeping Categories Distinct

As you write and revise, do your best to *establish distinct yet flexible categories.* Strictly speaking, the categories in a classification-and-division essay should not overlap. That is, each item should logically fit into only one category. Ideally, you should be able to identify each category by a title that clearly defines its boundaries. When you are writing about issues that are subjectively viewed or emotionally charged, however, such precision is not always possible, or even desirable. What you should aim for, then, is a classification-and-division system that is logical but not inflexible.

In "Learning about Anti-Semitism in the Real World" (p. 356) Alan M. Dershowitz wishes to make a point about the rigidity of the hierarchy he describes. Therefore, he identifies four categories of law firms—

"white shoe firms," "quota firms," "balanced firms," and "Jewish firms"—and defines them in terms that make clear that the categories do not overlap. In "The Men We Carry in Our Minds" (p. 362) Scott Russell Sanders makes the point that the men he knew when he was growing up are not like the professionals with whom others assume he identifies. To underscore this difference, he first identifies two discrete categories, which he calls "warriors" and "toilers," and then goes on to establish a third, unnamed category—distinct from the other two—composed of successful professionals. Here, too, the categories do not overlap.

In "Mother Tongue," however, Amy Tan deals with a more amorphous, dynamic entity—her "Englishes"—so her categories, while still distinct, are somewhat less clearly defined. For example, she refers to a single category by more than one name as she struggles to define it, wrestling with terms like *broken, fractured,* and *limited* English. What she winds up with are four subjectively determined categories representing, she tells us, "all the Englishes I grew up with: the English I spoke to my mother, which for lack of a better term might be described as 'simple'; the English she used with me, which for lack of a better term might be described as 'broken'; my translation of her Chinese, which could certainly be described as 'watered down'; and what I imagined to be her translation of her Chinese if she could speak in perfect English" (p. 354).

TREATING CATEGORIES IN PARALLEL TERMS

In general, you should try to *treat categories in parallel terms.* Whenever possible, you should make your treatment of categories comparable. If you give examples for one category, do so for all, and if you provide an extended definition or lengthy background for one category, do so in all cases.

In "Stereotypes" (p. 335) Alex Nolan is careful to treat his three categories of stereotypes—those based on physical characteristics, lifestyle, and race or ethnic background—in parallel terms. He defines each category of stereotype, lists common misconceptions associated with it, and explains why such misconceptions are harmful. Such parallel treatment ensures that readers see his discussion as balanced and complete, with no one category dominant.

CONSIDERING ENOUGH CATEGORIES

As you write and revise, be sure that you *consider all relevant categories*. If, for example, you are making a point about patterns of immigration from Europe to the United States during the late nineteenth century, you cannot logically limit your focus to immigrants from Germany and Italy. To do so would distract or irritate your readers, who could surely name other European countries from which immigrants came at that time. Your omissions would thus undermine your credibility. Naturally, you cannot consider *every* category, but you should consider every *significant* one.

REVIEW CHECKLIST: CLASSIFYING AND DIVIDING

✓ Establish a logical system of classification.
✓ Establish distinct yet flexible categories.
✓ Treat categories in parallel terms.
✓ Consider all relevant categories.

MARY MEBANE

Shades of Black

"It is my belief," Mary Mebane once told a researcher, "that the black folk are the most creative, viable people that America can produce. They just don't know it." Through essays, a play, and autobiographical volumes, Mebane has expressed her own creativity and chronicled the viability of a life that began in 1933 on an impoverished farm in North Carolina.

"Historically, my lifetime is important," she wrote in 1983, "because I was part of the last generation born into a world of total legal segregation in the southern United States." The following excerpt from *Mary: An Autobiography* (1981) is chilling in its depiction of skin color as a measure of caste and intellectual ability. Mebane realized that the impoverished and segregated world in which she grew up was a "world without options," and she was determined to escape the fate imposed on her: "At first I thought people all over the world washed clothes in the back yard, cooked supper out of the garden, churned milk, and picked blackberries. . . . I began to perceive that I was being prepared for my life's work. Black women like me have scrubbed a hundred million miles of tiled corridors and washed an equal number of dishes. I wasn't going to do that."

Mebane's determination earned her an education and a career as a teacher and college instructor. She received a Ph.D. from the University of North Carolina at Chapel Hill and has written of her exposure to integration there: "For the first time in my life my work was recognized and I was given some support—this in an environment I had been taught to suspect as totally and unrelentingly hostile and threatening."

Mebane is the author of a second volume of autobiography, *Mary, Wayfarer,* as well as the play *Take a Sad Song.* Her work has been anthologized in *A Galaxy of Black Writers* and *The Eloquence of Protest: Voices of the Seventies.*

In the following, Mebane describes a world in which people are rigidly classified by "social class and color."

D URING MY FIRST WEEK OF CLASSES AS A FRESHMAN, I was stopped   1
one day in the hall by the chairman's wife, who was indistinguishable in color from a white woman. She wanted to see me, she said.

This woman had no official position on the faculty, except that she   2
was an instructor in English; nevertheless, her summons had to be obeyed. In the segregated world there were (and remain) gross abuses of authority because those at the pinnacle, and even their spouses, felt that the people "under" them had no recourse except to submit—and they were right except that sometimes a black who got sick and tired of it would go to the whites and complain. This course of action was severely condemned by the blacks, but an interesting thing happened—such action always got positive results. Power was thought of in negative terms: I can deny someone something, I can strike at someone who can't strike back, I can ride someone down; that proves I am powerful. The concept of power as a force for good, for affirmative response to people or situations, was not in evidence.

When I went to her office, she greeted me with a big smile. "You   3
know," she said, "you made the highest mark on the verbal part of the examination." She was referring to the examination that the entire freshman class took upon entering the college. I looked at her but I didn't feel warmth, for in spite of her smile her eyes and tone of voice were saying, "How could this black-skinned girl score higher on the verbal than some of the students who've had more advantages than she? It must be some sort of fluke. Let me talk to her." I felt it, but I managed to smile my thanks and back off. For here at North Carolina College at Durham, as it had been since the beginning, social class and color were the primary criteria used in determining status on the campus.

First came the children of doctors, lawyers, and college teachers.   4
Next came the children of public-school teachers, businessmen, and anybody else who had access to more money than the poor black working class. After that came the bulk of the student population, the children of

the working class, most of whom were the first in their families to go beyond high school. The attitude toward them was: You're here because we need the numbers, but in all other things defer to your betters.

The faculty assumed that light-skinned students were more intelli-   5
gent, and they were always a bit nonplussed when a dark-skinned student did well, especially if she was a girl. They had reason to be appalled when they discovered that I planned to do not only well but better than my light-skinned peers.

I don't know whether African men recently transported to the New   6
World considered themselves handsome or more important, whether they considered African women beautiful in comparison with Native American Indian women or immigrant European women. It is a question that I have never heard raised or seen research on. If African men consid-ered African women beautiful, just when their shift in interest away from black black women occurred might prove to be an interesting topic for researchers. But one thing I know for sure: by the twentieth century, really black skin on a woman was considered ugly in this country. This was particularly true among those who were exposed to college.

Hazel, who was light brown, used to say to me, "You are *dark*, but   7
not *too* dark." This saved commiserating with the damned. I had the feel-ing that if nature had painted one more brushstroke on me, I'd have had to kill myself.

Black skin was to be disguised at all costs. Since a black face is   8
rather hard to disguise, many women took refuge in ludicrous makeup. Mrs. Burry, one of my teachers in elementary school, used white face powder. But she neglected to powder her neck and arms, and even the black on her face gleamed through the white, giving her an eerie appear-ance. But she did the best she could.

I observed all through elementary and high school that for various   9
entertainments the girls were placed on the stage in order of color. And very black ones didn't get into the front row. If they were past caramel-brown, to the back row they would go. And nobody questioned the jus-tice of these decisions—neither the students nor the teachers.

One of the teachers at Wildwood School, who was from the Deep   10
South and was just as black as she could be, had been a strict enforcer of these standards. That was another irony—that someone who had been judged outside the realm of beauty herself because of her skin tones

should have adopted them so wholeheartedly and applied them herself without question.

One girl stymied that teacher, though. Ruby, a black cherry of a girl, not only got off the back row but off the front row as well, to stand alone at stage center. She could outsing, outdance, and outdeclaim everyone else, and talent proved triumphant over pigmentation. But the May Queen and her Court (and in high school, Miss Wildwood) were always chosen from among the lighter ones.   11

When I was a freshman in high school, it became clear that a light-skinned sophomore girl named Rose was going to get the "best girl scholar" prize for the next three years, and there was nothing I could do about it, even though I knew I was the better. Rose was caramel-colored and had shoulder-length hair. She was highly favored by the science and math teacher, who figured the averages. I wasn't. There was only one prize. Therefore, Rose would get it until she graduated. I was one year behind her, and I would not get it until after she graduated.   12

To be held in such low esteem was painful. It was difficult not to feel that I had been cheated out of the medal, which I felt that, in a fair competition, I perhaps would have won. Being unable to protest or do anything about it was a traumatic experience for me. From then on I instinctively tended to avoid the college-exposed dark-skinned male, knowing that when he looked at me he saw himself and, most of the time, his mother and sister as well, and since he had rejected his blackness, he had rejected theirs and mine.   13

Oddly enough, the lighter-skinned black male did not seem to feel so much prejudice toward the black black woman. It was no accident, I felt, that Mr. Harrison, the eighth-grade teacher, who was reddish-yellow himself, once protested to the science and math teacher about the fact that he always assigned sweeping duties to Doris and Ruby Lee, two black black girls. Mr. Harrison said to them one day, right in the other teacher's presence, "You must be some bad girls. Every day I come down here ya'll are sweeping." The science and math teacher got the point and didn't ask them to sweep anymore.   14

Uneducated black males, too, sometimes related very well to the black black woman. They had been less firmly indoctrinated by the white society around them and were more securely rooted in their own culture.   15

Because of the stigma attached to having dark skin, a black black woman had to do many things to find a place for herself. One possibility   16 was to attach herself to a light-skinned woman, hoping that some of the magic would rub off on her. A second was to make herself sexually available, hoping to attract a mate. Third, she could resign herself to a more chaste life-style—either (for the professional woman) teaching and work in established churches or (for the uneducated woman) domestic work and zealous service in the Holy and Sanctified churches.

Even as a young girl, Lucy had chosen the first route. Lucy was   17 short, skinny, short-haired, and black black, and thus unacceptable. So she made her choice. She selected Patricia, the lightest-skinned girl in the school, as her friend, and followed her around. Patricia and her friends barely tolerated Lucy, but Lucy smiled and doggedly hung on, hoping that someone who noticed Patricia might notice her, too. Though I felt shame for her behavior, even then I understood.

As is often the case of the victim agreeing with and adopting the   18 attitudes of oppressor, so I have seen it with black black women. I have seen them adopt the oppressor's attitude that they are nothing but "sex machines," and their supposedly superior sexual performance becomes their sole reason for being and for esteeming themselves. Such women learn early that in order to make themselves attractive to men they have somehow to shift the emphasis from physical beauty to some other area—usually sexual performance. Their constant talk is of their desirability and their ability to gratify a man sexually.

I knew two such women well—both of them black black. To hear   19 their endless talk of sexual conquests was very sad. I have never seen the category that these women fall into described anywhere. It is not that of promiscuity or nymphomania. It is the category of total self-rejection: "Since I am black, I am ugly, I am nobody. I will perform on the level that they have assigned to me." Such women are the pitiful results of what not only white America but also, and more important, black America has done to them.

Some, not taking the sexuality route but still accepting black   20 society's view of their worthlessness, swing all the way across to intense religiosity. Some are staunch, fervent workers in the more traditional Southern churches—Baptist and Methodist—and others are leaders and ministers in the lower status, more evangelical Holiness sects.

Another avenue open to the black black woman is excellence in a   21 career. Since in the South the field most accessible to such women is education, a great many of them prepared to become teachers. But here, too, the black black woman had problems. Grades weren't given to her lightly in school, nor were promotions on the job. Consequently, she had to prepare especially well. She had to pass examinations with flying colors or be left behind; she knew that she would receive no special consideration. She had to be overqualified for a job because otherwise she didn't stand a chance of getting it—and she was competing only with other blacks. She had to have something to back her up: not charm, not personality—but training.

The black black woman's training would pay off in the 1970s. With   22 the arrival of integration the black black woman would find, paradoxically enough, that her skin color in an integrated situation was not the handicap it had been in an all-black situation. But it wasn't until the middle and late 1960s, when the post-1945 generation of black males arrived on college campuses, that I noticed any change in the situation at all. *He* wore an afro and *she* wore an afro, and sometimes the only way you could tell them apart was when his afro was taller than hers. Black had become beautiful, and the really black girl was often selected as queen of various campus activities. It was then that the dread I felt at dealing with the college-educated black male began to ease. Even now, though, when I have occasion to engage in any type of transaction with a college-educated black man, I gauge his age. If I guess he was born after 1945, I feel confident that the transaction will turn out all right. If he probably was born before 1945, my stomach tightens, I find myself taking shallow breaths, and I try to state my business and escape as soon as possible.

☜ Opening the Dialogue

1. Why do you think people at Mebane's high school and college associated light skin color with high status and intelligence? Do you think people were aware of why they reacted the way they did?

2. Mebane asserts that "by the twentieth century, really black skin on a woman was considered ugly in this country" (paragraph 6). Why do you suppose black skin was a greater handicap for women than for men?

3. Beginning in paragraph 16, Mebane presents three possible avenues open to a "black black woman." Which of these alternatives do you think would enable such a woman to gain the most power and status? Which

option do you think was likely to be most—and least—damaging to her self-esteem?

✪ Keeping a Notebook

In paragraph 2 Mebane comments, "Power was thought of in negative terms: I can deny someone something, I can strike at someone who can't strike back, I can ride someone down; that proves I am powerful. The concept of power as a force for good, for affirmative response to people or situations, was not in evidence." In your experience, is power more often used as a positive or a negative force?

✪ Working Together

Is there a hierarchy among students on your college campus? What factors determine how it is set up? Working in groups, list the categories that make up this hierarchy, and rank the categories according to the amount of power and prestige each has. In class discussion, try to determine what specific attributes give a group its status.

✪ Writing an Essay

What kinds of individuals and institutions are responsible for creating and perpetuating stratified social systems such as the one Mebane describes? Write an essay in which you examine a hierarchy in your school, family, or neighborhood, explaining how and why various people and institutions contribute to maintaining the system.

Amy Tan

Mother Tongue

Amy Tan began writing short stories as do-it-yourself therapy in 1987 after the psychiatrist she was consulting for workaholism kept falling asleep during their sessions. Three years later, her first novel, *The Joy Luck Club,* was published to critical acclaim. The theme of the novel is the impact of past generations on the present, told through the stories of four immigrant Chinese women and their American-born daughters.

Herself the daughter of Chinese parents, Tan was born in Oakland, California, in 1952. After both her brother and father died tragically of brain tumors when she was fifteen years old, Tan reflected on the "terrible irony" that her parents had always wanted her to be a brain surgeon. Tan spent much of her adolescence in Europe, studied linguistics in the United States, and worked with disabled children before turning to writing. A visit to China with her mother in 1987 focused her work on the sometimes uneasy clash of culture and expectation that is embodied in her own Chinese-American heritage.

Tan explores her relationship with her mother and considers the symbolism of their different uses of language in the following essay, "Mother Tongue." She expanded on those differences in a recent interview: "[My mother] speaks English as if it's a direct translation from Chinese. But it's more than that: Her language also has more imagery than English. [For example,] somebody might say to me, 'Don't work so hard. You'll kill yourself.' My mother will say to me, 'Why do you squeeze all your brains out on this page for someone else?' So it's very vivid, and visceral. That's the way that she talks. It's almost as if the language makes you see things and feel things differently."

Tan's essays have appeared in national publications; her second novel, *The Kitchen God's Wife*, was published in 1991.

In "Mother Tongue" notice that Tan not only describes the various categories of English she speaks in her life, but also draws from these categories a larger point about the value of her various voices.

I AM NOT A SCHOLAR of English or literature. I cannot give you much   1
more than personal opinions on the English language and its variations in this country or others.

I am a writer. And by that definition, I am someone who has always   2
loved language. I am fascinated by language in daily life. I spend a great deal of my time thinking about the power of language—the way it can evoke an emotion, a visual image, a complex idea, or a simple truth. Language is the tool of my trade. And I use them all—all the Englishes I grew up with.

Recently, I was made keenly aware of the different Englishes I do   3
use. I was giving a talk to a large group of people, the same talk I had already given to half a dozen other groups. The nature of the talk was about my writing, my life, and my book, *The Joy Luck Club*. The talk was going along well enough, until I remembered one major difference that made the whole talk sound wrong. My mother was in the room. And it was perhaps the first time she had heard me give a lengthy speech, using the kind of English I have never used with her. I was saying things like, "The intersection of memory upon imagination" and "There is an aspect of my fiction that relates to thus-and-thus"—a speech filled with carefully wrought grammatical phrases, burdened, it suddenly seemed to me, with nominalized forms, past perfect tenses, conditional phrases, all the forms of standard English that I had learned in school and through books, the forms of English I did not use at home with my mother.

Just last week, I was walking down the street with my mother, and   4
I again found myself conscious of the English I was using, and the English I do use with her. We were talking about the price of new and used furniture and I heard myself saying this: "Not waste money that way." My husband was with us as well, and he didn't notice any switch in my English. And then I realized why. It's because over the twenty years we've been together I've often used that same kind of English with him, and

sometimes he even uses it with me. It has become our language of intimacy, a different sort of English that relates to family talk, the language I grew up with.

So you'll have some idea of what this family talk I heard sounds like, I'll quote what my mother said during a recent conversation which I videotaped and then transcribed. During this conversation, my mother was talking about a political gangster in Shanghai who had the same last name as her family's, Du, and how the gangster in his early years wanted to be adopted by her family, which was rich by comparison. Later, the gangster became more powerful, far richer than my mother's family, and one day showed up at my mother's wedding to pay his respects. Here's what she said in part:

"Du Yusong having business like fruit stand. Like off the street kind. He is Du like Du Zong—but not Tsung-ming Island people. The local people call putong, the river east side, he belong to that side local people. That man want to ask Du Zong father take him in like become own family. Du Zong father wasn't look down on him, but didn't take seriously, until that man big like become a mafia. Now important person, very hard to inviting him. Chinese way, came only to show respect, don't stay for dinner. Respect for making big celebration, he shows up. Mean gives lots of respect. Chinese custom. Chinese social life that way. If too important won't have to stay too long. He come to my wedding. I didn't see, I heard it. I gone to boy's side, they have YMCA dinner. Chinese age I was nineteen."

You should know that my mother's expressive command of English belies how much she actually understands. She reads the *Forbes* report, listens to *Wall Street Week*, converses daily with her stockbroker, reads all of Shirley MacLaine's books with ease—all kinds of things I can't begin to understand. Yet some of my friends tell me they understand 50 percent of what my mother says. Some say they understand 80 to 90 percent. Some say they understand none of it, as if she were speaking pure Chinese. But to me, my mother's English is perfectly clear, perfectly natural. It's my mother tongue. Her language, as I hear it, is vivid, direct, full of observation and imagery. That was the language that helped shape the way I saw things, expressed things, made sense of the world.

Lately, I've been giving more thought to the kind of English my mother speaks. Like others, I have described it to people as "broken" or "fractured" English. But I wince when I say that. It has always bothered me that I can think of no way to describe it other than "broken," as if it were damaged and needed to be fixed, as if it lacked a certain wholeness and soundness. I've heard other terms used, "limited English," for example. But they seem just as bad, as if everything is limited, including people's perceptions of the limited English speaker.

I know this for a fact, because when I was growing up, my mother's 9 "limited" English limited *my* perception of her. I was ashamed of her English. I believed that her English reflected the quality of what she had to say. That is, because she expressed them imperfectly her thoughts were imperfect. And I had plenty of empirical evidence to support me: the fact that people in department stores, at banks, and at restaurants did not take her seriously, did not give her good service, pretended not to understand her, or even acted as if they did not hear her.

My mother has long realized the limitations of her English as well. 10 When I was fifteen, she used to have me call people on the phone to pretend I was she. In this guise, I was forced to ask for information or even to complain and yell at people who had been rude to her. One time it was a call to her stockbroker in New York. She had cashed out her small portfolio and it just so happened we were going to go to New York the next week, our very first trip outside California. I had to get on the phone and say in an adolescent voice that was not very convincing, "This is Mrs. Tan."

And my mother was standing in the back whispering loudly, "Why 11 he don't send me check, already two weeks late. So mad he lie to me, losing me money."

And then I said in perfect English, "Yes, I'm getting rather con- 12 cerned. You had agreed to send the check two weeks ago, but it hasn't arrived."

Then she began to talk more loudly. "What he want, I come to 13 New York tell him front of his boss, you cheating me?" And I was trying to calm her down, make her be quiet, while telling the stockbroker, "I can't tolerate any more excuses. If I don't receive the check immediately, I am going to have to speak to your manager when I'm in New York next week." And sure enough, the following week there we were in front of this astonished stockbroker, and I was sitting there red-faced and quiet, and my mother, the real Mrs. Tan, was shouting at his boss in her impeccable broken English.

We used a similar routine just five days ago, for a situation that was   14
far less humorous. My mother had gone to the hospital for an appointment, to find out about a benign brain tumor a CAT scan had revealed a
month ago. She said she had spoken very good English, her best English,
no mistakes. Still, she said, the hospital did not apologize when they said
they had lost the CAT scan and she had come for nothing. She said they
did not seem to have any sympathy when she told them she was anxious
to know the exact diagnosis, since her husband and son had both died of
brain tumors. She said they would not give her any more information
until the next time and she would have to make another appointment for
that. So she said she would not leave until the doctor called her daughter.
She wouldn't budge. And when the doctor finally called her daughter,
me, who spoke in perfect English—lo and behold—we had assurances
the CAT scan would be found, promises that a conference call on Monday would be held, and apologies for any suffering my mother had gone
through for a most regrettable mistake.

I think my mother's English almost had an effect on limiting my   15
possibilities in life as well. Sociologists and linguists probably will tell
you that a person's developing language skills are more influenced by
peers. But I do think that the language spoken in the family, especially in
immigrant families which are more insular, plays a large role in shaping
the language of the child. And I believe that it affected my results on
achievement tests, IQ tests, and the SAT. While my English skills were
never judged as poor, compared to math, English could not be considered my strong suit. In grade school I did moderately well, getting perhaps B's, sometimes B-pluses, in English and scoring perhaps in the sixti-
eth or seventieth percentile on achievement tests. But those scores were
not good enough to override the opinion that my true abilities lay in
math and science, because in those areas I achieved A's and scored in the
ninetieth percentile or higher.

This was understandable. Math is precise; there is only one correct   16
answer. Whereas, for me at least, the answers on English tests were always a judgment call, a matter of opinion and personal experience. Those
tests were constructed around items like fill-in-the-blank sentence
completion, such as, "Even though Tom was _____ , Mary thought he
was _____ ." And the correct answer always seemed to be the most bland
combinations of thoughts, for example, "Even though Tom was shy,
Mary thought he was charming," with the grammatical structure "even

though" limiting the correct answer to some sort of semantic opposites, so you wouldn't get answers like, "Even though Tom was foolish, Mary thought he was ridiculous." Well, according to my mother, there were very few limitations as to what Tom could have been and what Mary might have thought of him. So I never did well on tests like that.

The same was true with word analogies, pairs of words in which   17
you were supposed to find some sort of logical, semantic relationship—for example, "*Sunset* is to *nightfall* as _____ is to _____." And here you would be presented with a list of four possible pairs, one of which showed the same kind of relationship: *red* is to *stoplight*, *bus* is to *arrival*, *chills* is to *fever*, *yawn* is to *boring*. Well, I could never think that way. I knew what the tests were asking, but I could not block out of my mind the images already created by the first pair, "*sunset* is to *nightfall*"—and I would see a burst of colors against a darkening sky, the moon rising, the lowering of a curtain of stars. And all the other pairs of words—red, bus, stoplight, boring—just threw up a mass of confusing images, making it impossible for me to sort out something as logical as saying: "A sunset precedes nightfall" is the same as "a chill precedes a fever." The only way I would have gotten that answer right would have been to imagine an associative situation, for example, my being disobedient and staying out past sunset, catching a chill at night, which turns into feverish pneumonia as punishment, which indeed did happen to me.

I have been thinking about all this lately, about my mother's English,   18
about achievement tests. Because lately I've been asked, as a writer, why there are not more Asian Americans represented in American literature. Why are there few Asian Americans enrolled in creative writing programs? Why do so many Chinese students go into engineering? Well, these are broad sociological questions I can't begin to answer. But I have noticed in surveys—in fact, just last week—that Asian students, as a whole, always do significantly better on math achievement tests than in English. And this makes me think that there are other Asian-American students whose English spoken in the home might also be described as "broken" or "limited." And perhaps they also have teachers who are steering them away from writing and into math and science, which is what happened to me.

Fortunately, I happen to be rebellious in nature and enjoy the chal-   19
lenge of disproving assumptions made about me. I became an English

major my first year in college, after being enrolled as pre-med. I started writing nonfiction as a freelancer the week after I was told by my former boss that writing was my worst skill and I should hone my talents toward account management.

But it wasn't until 1985 that I finally began to write fiction. And at first I wrote using what I thought to be wittily crafted sentences, sentences that would finally prove I had mastery over the English language. Here's an example from the first draft of a story that later made its way into *The Joy Luck Club*, but without this line: "That was my mental quandary in its nascent state." A terrible line, which I can barely pronounce.

Fortunately, for reasons I won't get into today, I later decided I should envision a reader for the stories I would write. And the reader I decided upon was my mother, because these were stories about mothers. So with this reader in mind—and in fact she did read my early drafts—I began to write stories using all the Englishes I grew up with: the English I spoke to my mother, which for lack of a better term might be described as "simple"; the English she used with me, which for lack of a better term might be described as "broken"; my translation of her Chinese, which could certainly be described as "watered down"; and what I imagined to be her translation of her Chinese if she could speak in perfect English, her internal language, and for that I sought to preserve the essence, but neither an English nor a Chinese structure. I wanted to capture what language ability tests can never reveal: her intent, her passion, her imagery, the rhythms of her speech and the nature of her thoughts.

Apart from what any critic had to say about my writing, I knew I had succeeded where it counted when my mother finished reading my book and gave me her verdict: "So easy to read."

⟨ε⟩ Opening the Dialogue

1. Given parents' key role in helping to shape their children's language, and the burden placed on children whose parents do not speak English, could you argue that immigrant parents such as Tan's have a responsibility to learn English as soon as possible and to speak English, rather than their native language, at home? Or do you believe that the value of maintaining one's own language and passing it on to one's children outweighs such a responsibility?

2. What efforts, if any, should a multicultural society such as ours make to accommodate the use of different languages among its citizens? For example, should street signs, voting instructions, and product labels be printed in languages other than English? Should public schools offer bilingual education programs, with classes conducted in the native languages of children who do not speak English? Or do you believe such accommodations ultimately fragment society and make it harder for immigrants to assimilate?

3. Do you think people in the United States are judged on the basis of their command of the English language? To what extent do you believe it is fair to judge someone on this basis?

Keeping a Notebook

Can you think of ways to make standardized college entrance examinations fairer for non-native speakers? Do you believe this is a desirable goal? Do standardized tests have any place in a nation as linguistically diverse as ours?

Working Together

Tan mentions some specific situations—communicating with the doctor in the hospital, for example—in which her mother's "limited English" was a handicap. Working in groups, list as many additional examples of such situations as you can. In class discussion, consider possible ways of making life easier for people like Mrs. Tan.

Writing an Essay

Write an essay in which you define and illustrate each of the different "Englishes" (or other languages) you use in your daily life as a student, family member, and citizen. In what situations, and with whom, do you use each kind of language?

ALAN M. DERSHOWITZ

Learning about Anti-Semitism in the Real World

A self-described "Jewish Jew," the youngest tenured professor in the history of Harvard Law School, and a renowned civil rights activist, Alan Dershowitz was born in 1938 to an Orthodox family in Brooklyn, New York. Although he was a poor student in high school, he excelled at Yale Law School and began to build a reputation as, according to the *Los Angeles Times*, "the attorney of last resort for the desperate and despised, counselor for lost causes and forlorn hopes."

Dershowitz's fierce dedication to the cause of civil rights has led him to defend clients as diverse as black activist Angela Davis and millionaire Claus Von Bulow (the subject of his book *Reversal of Fortune*). He has appeared frequently on *Nightline* and the *Mac-Neil/Lehrer Newshour* as well as with Phil Donahue and Oprah Winfrey because, he says, "I don't believe the Supreme Court should have the last word on civil liberties. I want to convince every American that civil liberties matter to them, and [these shows] give me a wonderful opportunity to talk to an audience that never before cared about civil liberties."

Dershowitz is the author of several nonfiction works, including *The Best Defense* (1982); a weekly syndicated column; and a best-selling autobiography, *Chutzpah* (1991), from which the following selection is excerpted. A Yiddish word, *chutzpah* has been humorously defined as the quality of being able to murder one's parents and then plead for mercy because one is an orphan, but Dershowitz explains its serious significance for Jewish Americans: "The byword of past generations of Jewish Americans has been *shanda*—fear of embarrassment in front of our hosts. The byword of the next generation should be *chutzpah*—assertive insistence on first-class status among our peers." He believes that Jews should no longer accept "that American presidents must all be Christians, that anchorpersons on the network news may not 'look Jewish,' or that there will always be ceilings on the proportions of Jews in our great universities, on our courts, and in our corporations."

In the following, Dershowitz recalls a lesson about prejudice he learned early in his law career to show how Jews and other minorities were systematically excluded from certain categories of New York legal firms.

Y ALE LAW SCHOOL IN THE EARLY 1960S was regarded as a true meritoc-   1
racy. Though my fellow classmates numbered among them children of presidents, Supreme Court justices, and multimillionaire industrialists, the only hierarchy I ever saw at Yale Law School was based on grades, *Law Journal* writing, moot court competition, and classroom performance. I later learned that there existed a number of "exclusive" clubs among the students from which Jews—certainly Eastern European Jews from New York City colleges—were excluded. But these clubs were so secret that I didn't learn of their existence until after I had graduated. I had experienced no overt anti-Semitism among my fellow students and absolutely no hint of it among the faculty. A large percentage of the professors were Jewish, some overtly and proudly so. The dean was Jewish, as was his predecessor. I felt like a first-class citizen as a Jew at Yale Law School.

Class rank and position on the *Law Journal* determined status. I was   2
fortunate in both regards, ranking at the top of the class and having been elected editor in chief of the *Yale Law Journal*. That made me something of a celebrity in the small world in which we lived. Professors called me Chief, directed the hardest questions at me in class, and asked me to work as their research assistant. I had also published two well-received *Law Journal* articles and had excellent faculty references. In fact, Harvard Law School had already expressed interest in recruiting me for its faculty. Stu-

dents regarded me as something between a student and a junior faculty member. I mention this privileged status in the Yale hierarchy only to make a point about the rude awakening that came with my first quest for a job.

It was an absolute shock to me when I learned that there was an   3
entirely different hierarchy that operated within the legal profession, especially—though not exclusively—in the Wall Street firms to which most Yale law students aspired.

The summer between the second and third years in law school is   4
job time. In the spring, the students don their "lawyer suits" and line up for interviews with the big firms. I had my heart set on the Washington firm of Covington and Burling or the New York firms of Cravath, Swaine, and Moore, or Paul, Weiss, Rifkind, Wharton, and Garrison. I was interviewed by these and a few dozen other "white shoe" firms. The interviewers were polite and the interviews seemed to go well. I was surprised at the questions about high school and college, however, since I was applying for a law job and thought my law school record was what counted. To my chagrin, I began to get a few rejection notices. At first I thought the competition for the few jobs was just too keen. Then I began to learn who had been offered the jobs for which I had been turned down. Some were students at the middle or bottom of the class, the ones who generally got the answers wrong and came to me and my *Law Journal* colleagues after class for the right answers.

Soon a pattern began to emerge. The students who got the best   5
jobs were the white Anglo-Saxon Protestants. Of course, the Wasps with higher grades got better jobs than the Wasps with lower grades, but the lowest-ranking Wasps got better job offers than the higher-ranking Jews. Some Jewish students—a very few—near the top of the class did receive job offers from the elite firms, and I simply didn't understand this apparent break in the pattern.

I began to ask around and finally was "initiated" into the "facts of   6
life" by a third-year student, in much the same whispered way that an elementary school kid learns about sex from an upperclassman in the schoolyard. My initiator, a Jewish *Law Journal* editor, told me about the different types of firms and the kinds of students they were looking for.

"First there are the 'white shoe' firms. All the partners and associates   7
are Wasps, except for maybe one real estate or tax partner. They don't

have any Jews, unless their names are Lehman or Morgenthau. Don't even bother to apply.

"Then there are the 'quota firms.' They'll take a Jew or two every   8
year, but you have to have gone through the 'Waspification' process of attending Yale, Princeton, or Harvard, and preferably a prep school like Exeter or Groton. Even then, they probably will skip over the Jew when it comes to partnership decisions, but they'll help him get a partnership with a good Jewish firm.

"After the quota firms come the 'balanced firms.' These are firms   9
with a balance between Jewish and Wasp partners, and they want to keep it that way. Since these firms are very popular with Jewish applicants and not so popular with Wasp applicants, it's much more difficult for a Jew than for a Wasp to get an offer. In fact, the only Wasps who apply to mixed firms are those who can't make it to the Wasp firms. You've got a real shot at one of these firms.

"Finally, there are the Jewish firms. Even they prefer Wasps when   10
they can get them—these firms are always trying to become elevated to the status of balanced firms, but hardly any Wasps apply. They also prefer Wasp-looking and Wasp-sounding Jews, but they'll grab a smart Yid like you." As an afterthought, my coach told me that none of the firms that came to recruit at Yale hired blacks or women, except for an occasional token, and that ethnic Catholics—Irish and Italian American—had problems of their own, as well as firms of their own.

That, in a nutshell, was my introduction to the world of bigotry,   11
discrimination, racism, and anti-Semitism called the American bar. Its distinguished leaders—who are still honored by law school scholarships, in paintings in law libraries, and in the mastheads of the great firms— were operating an apartheid-like system of law practice, nearly a decade after *Brown v. Board of Education* and nearly two decades after the Nuremberg trials.[1]

---

[1]*Brown v. Board of Education* (1954) resulted in the Supreme Court ruling that led to the end of public school segregation. Nazi leaders responsible for the Holocaust were tried at Nuremberg after World War II.

☉ Opening the Dialogue

1. In his essay's opening paragraphs, Dershowitz characterizes Yale Law School in the 1960s as "a true meritocracy," with status determined by "class rank and position on the *Law Journal.*" Do you see the schools you have attended as "true meritocracies," or do you believe that factors other than merit determine students' status?

2. In paragraph 11 Dershowitz describes the legal field as "an apartheid-like system" and implies analogies with *Brown v. Board of Education* and the Nuremberg trials. Is he justified in drawing such parallels, or is he exaggerating the problem just to make his point?

3. Should Dershowitz have tried to gain acceptance into a "white shoe" or "quota" firm, or should he have settled for a "balanced" or "Jewish" firm? What do you see as the advantages and disadvantages of each option?

☉ Keeping a Notebook

Dershowitz writes about anti-Semitism in the early 1960s. Do you believe that Jewish "quotas"—or other quotas based on race, gender, or similar criteria—still exist in any professions? Do you believe it is possible to justify quotas that limit the number of representatives of certain groups in an institution? Is it possible to justify quotas that *increase* the representation of members of certain groups?

☉ Working Together

The Supreme Court has ruled that a private business, club, or school is free to accept—or reject—whomever it wishes. Would you consider joining such a resticted group or voting for someone who belonged to one? Do you believe that membership in such groups, regardless of their legality, should be rejected on principle? Working in groups, generate reasons for and against each position. In class discussion, debate the issue.

✪ Writing an Essay

Dershowitz's essay uses classification to expose a system that pigeon-holes and demeans individuals. Write an essay in which you show how arbitrary categories are used to justify a system or tradition—for example, pledging a fraternity or sorority, drafting professional athletes, or choosing beauty queens.

SCOTT RUSSELL SANDERS

The Men We Carry in Our Minds

Born in 1945 in Memphis, Tennessee, to a family of cotton farmers, Scott Russell Sanders spent his school years in Ohio and studied physics and English at Brown University, where he graduated
first in his class in 1967. "I have long been divided, in my life and
in my work," Sanders once explained, "between science and the
arts. . . . When I began writing fiction in my late twenties, I
wanted to ask, through literature, many of the fundamental questions that scientists ask. In particular, I wanted to understand our
place in nature, trace the sources of our violence, and speculate
about the future evolution of our species."

Sanders has written fourteen books, including the fictional works
Wilderness Plots (1983), *Fetching the Dead* (1984), and *The Engineer of
Beasts* (1988); and a collection of essays, *The Paradise of Bombs*
(1987), for which he won the Associated Writing Programs
Award for Creative Nonfiction. Of his varied media Sanders says,
"My writing might seem diverse in form—realistic fiction, folk-
tales, stories for children, personal essays, historical novels—yet
it is bound together by this web of questions. In all of my work,
regardless of period or style, I am concerned with the ways in
which human beings come to terms with the practical problems
of living on a small planet, in nature and in communities. I am
concerned with the life people make together, in marriages and
families and towns, more than with the life of isolated individuals."

In the following essay, excerpted from *The Paradise of Bombs*, Sanders explores how our beliefs are formed: "We all carry images of
what it means to be a man, what it means to be a woman. We acquire those images from our families, our neighbors, and our culture, but above all from the people we knew in childhood. My

own background was rural and working class, a place and people not often represented in our literature. I have tried in my writing to understand how my notions of manhood and womanhood have been shaped, and where those notions are flawed or limited, I have tried to imagine my way beyond them."

Here, as a way of exploring his own concept of manhood, Sanders divides into particular categories the various men who have played a part in his life.

THE FIRST MEN, BESIDES MY FATHER, I remember seeing were black 1 convicts and white guards, in the cottonfield across the road from our farm on the outskirts of Memphis. I must have been three or four. The prisoners wore dingy gray-and-black zebra suits, heavy as canvas, sodden with sweat. Hatless, stooped, they chopped weeds in the fierce heat, row after row, breathing the acrid dust of boll-weevil poison. The overseers wore dazzling white shirts and broad shadowy hats. The oiled barrels of their shotguns flashed in the sunlight. Their faces in memory are utterly blank. Of course those men, white and black, have become for me an emblem of racial hatred. But they have also come to stand for the twin poles of my early vision of manhood—the brute toiling animal and the boss.

When I was a boy, the men I knew labored with their bodies. They 2 were marginal farmers, just scraping by, or welders, steelworkers, carpenters; they swept floors, dug ditches, mined coal, or drove trucks, their forearms ropy with muscle; they trained horses, stoked furnaces, built tires, stood on assembly lines wrestling parts onto cars and refrigerators. They got up before light, worked all day long whatever the weather, and when they came home at night they looked as though somebody had been whipping them. In the evenings and on weekends they worked on their own places, tilling gardens that were lumpy with clay, fixing broken-down cars, hammering on houses that were always too drafty, too leaky, too small.

The bodies of the men I knew were twisted and maimed in ways 3 visible and invisible. The nails of their hands were black and split, the hands tattooed with scars. Some had lost fingers. Heavy lifting had given many of them finicky backs and guts weak from hernias. Racing against conveyor belts had given them ulcers. Their ankles and knees ached from years of standing on concrete. Anyone who had worked for long around machines was hard of hearing. They squinted, and the skin of their faces was creased like the leather of old work gloves. There were times, studying them, when I dreaded growing up. Most of them coughed, from dust or cigarettes, and most of them drank cheap wine or whiskey, so their eyes looked bloodshot and bruised. The fathers of my friends always seemed older than the mothers. Men wore out sooner. Only women lived into old age.

As a boy I also knew another sort of men, who did not sweat and   4 break down like mules. They were soldiers, and so far as I could tell they scarcely worked at all. During my early school years we lived on a military base, an arsenal in Ohio, and every day I saw GIs in the guardshacks, on the stoops of barracks, at the wheels of olive drab Chevrolets. The chief fact of their lives was boredom. Long after I left the Arsenal I came to recognize the sour smell the soldiers gave off as that of souls in limbo. They were all waiting—for wars, for transfers, for leaves, for promotions, for the end of their hitch—like so many braves waiting for the hunt to begin. Unlike the warriors of older tribes, however, they would have no say about when the battle would start or how it would be waged. Their waiting was broken only when they practiced for war. They fired guns at targets, drove tanks across the churned-up fields of the military reservation, set off bombs in the wrecks of old fighter planes. I knew this was all play. But I also felt certain that when the hour for killing arrived, they would kill. When the real shooting started, many of them would die. This was what soldiers were *for*, just as a hammer was for driving nails.

Warriors and toilers: those seemed, in my boyhood vision, to be   5 the chief destinies for men. They weren't the only destinies, as I learned from having a few male teachers, from reading books, and from watching television. But the men on television—the politicians, the astronauts, the generals, the savvy lawyers, the philosophical doctors, the bosses who gave orders to both soldiers and laborers—seemed as removed and unreal to me as the figures in tapestries. I could no more imagine growing up to become one of these cool, potent creatures than I could imagine becoming a prince.

A nearer and more hopeful example was that of my father, who had   6 escaped from a red-dirt farm to a tire factory, and from the assembly line to the front office. Eventually he dressed in a white shirt and tie. He carried himself as if he had been born to work with his mind. But his body, remembering the earlier years of slogging work, began to give out on him in his fifties, and it quit on him entirely before he turned sixty-five. Even such a partial escape from man's fate as he had accomplished did not seem possible for most of the boys I knew. They joined the Army, stood in line for jobs in the smoky plants, helped build highways. They were bound to work as their fathers had worked, killing themselves or preparing to kill others.

A scholarship enabled me not only to attend college, a rare enough   7 feat in my circle, but even to study in a university meant for the children of the rich. Here I met for the first time young men who had assumed from birth that they would lead lives of comfort and power. And for the first time I met women who told me that men were guilty of having kept all the joys and privileges of the earth for themselves. I was baffled. What privileges? What joys? I thought about the maimed, dismal lives of most of the men back home. What had they stolen from their wives and daughters? The right to go five days a week, twelve months a year, for thirty or forty years to a steel mill or a coal mine? The right to drop bombs and die in war? The right to feel every leak in the roof, every gap in the fence, every cough in the engine, as a wound they must mend? The right to feel, when the lay-off comes or the plant shuts down, not only afraid but ashamed?

I was slow to understand the deep grievances of women. This was   8 because, as a boy, I had envied them. Before college, the only people I had ever known who were interested in art or music or literature, the only ones who read books, the only ones who ever seemed to enjoy a sense of ease and grace were the mothers and daughters. Like the menfolk, they fretted about money, they scrimped and made-do. But, when the pay stopped coming in, they were not the ones who had failed. Nor did they have to go to war, and that seemed to me a blessed fact. By comparison with the narrow, ironclad days of fathers, there was an expansiveness, I thought, in the days of mothers. They went to see neighbors, to shop in town, to run errands at school, at the library, at church. No doubt, had I looked harder at their lives, I would have envied them less. It was not my fate to become a woman, so it was easier for me to see the graces. Few of them held jobs outside the home, and those who did filled thankless roles as clerks and waitresses. I didn't see, then, what a prison a house could be, since houses seemed to me brighter, handsomer places than any factory.

I did not realize—because such things were never spoken of—how often women suffered from men's bullying. I did learn about the wretchedness of abandoned wives, single mothers, widows; but I also learned about the wretchedness of lone men. Even then I could see how exhausting it was for a mother to cater all day to the needs of young children. But if I had been asked, as a boy, to choose between tending a baby and tending a machine, I think I would have chosen the baby. (Having now tended both, I know I would choose the baby.)

So I was baffled when the women at college accused me and my sex   9
of having cornered the world's pleasures. I think something like my baf-
flement has been felt by other boys (and by girls as well) who grew up in
dirt-poor farm country, in mining country, in black ghettos, in Hispanic
barrios, in the shadows of factories, in Third World nations—any place
where the fate of men is as grim and bleak as the fate of women. Toilers
and warriors. I realize now how ancient these identities are, how deep the
tug they exert on men, the undertow of a thousand generations. The mis-
eries I saw, as a boy, in the lives of nearly all men I continue to see in the
lives of many—the body-breaking toil, the tedium, the call to be tough,
the humiliating powerlessness, the battle for a living and for territory.

When the women I met at college thought about the joys and priv-   10
ileges of men, they did not carry in their minds the sort of men I had
known in my childhood. They thought of their fathers, who were bankers, physicians, architects, stockbrokers, the big wheels of the big cities.
These fathers rode the train to work or drove cars that cost more than any
of my childhood houses. They were attended from morning to night by
female helpers, wives and nurses and secretaries. They were never laid
off, never short of cash at month's end, never lined up for welfare. These
fathers made decisions that mattered. They ran the world.

The daughters of such men wanted to share in this power, this   11
glory. So did I. They yearned for a say over their future, for jobs worthy
of their abilities, for the right to live at peace, unmolested, whole. Yes, I
thought, yes yes. The difference between me and these daughters was
that they saw me, because of my sex, as destined from birth to become
like their fathers, and therefore as an enemy to their desires. But I knew
better. I wasn't an enemy, in fact or in feeling. I was an ally. If I had
known, then, how to tell them so, would they have believed me? Would
they now?

☯ Opening the Dialogue

1. What difficulties would you expect a person to encounter in trying to raise his or her status from one category of worker to another—for example, from "warrior" or "toiler" to teacher or lawyer? How do people generally accomplish such a change in status?

2. In paragraph 8 Sanders enumerates the "grievances" of women and concludes that if asked to "choose between tending a baby and tending a machine" he would choose the baby. Do you agree that so-called "women's work" is generally less enslaving and more fulfilling than "men's work"?

3. In paragraph 11 Sanders presents himself as an ally of women. He sees himself, like them, as an outsider who lacks—and longs for—the professional status, comfort, financial security, and power of men like their fathers. Do you think the women who see him as "destined from birth to become like their fathers, and therefore as an enemy to their desires" are justified in feeling this way?

☯ Keeping a Notebook

How do you feel about the kind of work your parents do? Are you proud of their accomplishments? Can you see yourself in the same line of work?

☯ Working Together

Which occupations have the most status in our society? Is status determined by how much money is earned? How much education is required? How selective the field is? Whether the occupation is identified with men or with women? Working in groups, decide on the five occupations that you believe are associated with the highest level of power and prestige. In class discussion, identify the specific criteria that determine the status of these occupations.

🌐 Writing an Essay

Classify the members of your family according to their occupational roles, explaining how they came to fill those roles rather than others. In which category can you see yourself, and why?

Writing: Categorizing Cultures

1. Identify three or four categories of worker on your college campus, and write an essay in which you name, define, and give several examples of each and discuss their shared characteristics. Try to draw some conclusions about the hierarchy you observe.

2. What kinds of role models are important to children who are members of your ethnic group or residents of your community? Establish several different categories of role models, and explain and illustrate each. In each case, consider why a particular type of role model is important.

3. Classify the different ways in which various friends of yours see their future lives. Try to account for the differences in their expectations and aspirations.

4. Write an essay in which you classify kinds of discrimination. Your principle of classification can be based on the source, degree, intent, or target of the discrimination.

5. Differences in gender, age, class, race, or ability can sometimes make people feel like outsiders in a community. Write an essay in which you identify several categories of outsider within a community with which you are familiar, and explain what specific characteristics set each group apart. Is their isolation necessarily a loss for the outsiders? For the community?

CHAPTER 9

CULTURE
AND IDENTITY
DEFINING
TERMS

ROMARE BEARDEN, "THE PREVALENCE OF RITUAL BAPTISM" (1964)

A *quinceañera* is a ceremony that commemorates the fifteenth birthday of a young Latina, marking her initiation into womanhood, her acceptance of the Catholic faith, and her entrance into society. Such ceremonies, increasingly popular in the United States among girls of Mexican, Cuban, and Puerto Rican descent, traditionally begin with a Catholic Mass, which is followed by an elaborate dinner dance. Here several girls—dressed in formal, floor-length gowns and attended by *damas*—are presented to society, often at a hotel or community center on a Saturday night. Although some dioceses expect girls to prepare for the *quinceañera* by taking classes in religion, values, or Hispanic history, the focus is usually on the party, which can include such "extras" as limos, bands, and a tiered cake. Even at the most elaborate party, though, the traditional waltz by the *damas* and their escorts (meant to suggest the girl's passage from childhood into womanhood) reminds guests that the *quinceañera* is a traditional religious and cultural rite of passage as well as a social event.

Ramon Battista, student

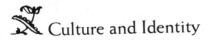

Culture and Identity

Definition—explaining what something means—is an essential academic skill. In nearly every college course, students are asked to define terms—schools of painting, historical movements, political parties, scientific phenomena, psychological syndromes, and so on. Definition is also central to writing about the American experience. Writers may try to explore the meanings of terms that are important to them and communicate those meanings to others of similar (or different) backgrounds. Writers may, for example, define what they mean by *culture, ethnic pride, patriotism, prejudice, ambition,* or *upward mobility;* what it means to be a person

of color, an individual with a physical disability, or a member of a particular community, religion, or political party; what it means to be an "in-
sider" or an "outsider"; or what it means to be educated, successful, or
assimilated. They may also define terms specific to their ethnic or national identity—*potlatch* or *Tet, mestizo* or *nisei, kente cloth* or *sari, Ramadan* or
Kwanzaa—or terms they find offensive, ambiguous, or misleading. Writers may use definition to help explain the difference between similar or
overlapping terms—for example, *black* and *African American, Chicano* and
Latino, Indian and *Native American, handicapped* and *disabled.* In each of these
cases and numerous others, definition can help writers to probe their
unique personal experiences as Americans.

In this chapter, writers use definition to clarify their thinking about
key terms and concepts and to communicate their interpretations of
these terms to others. In doing so, they begin to understand and accept
their own cultures. Richard Rodriguez struggles to answer the question
"What is culture?"—specifically, Hispanic-American culture—and Gloria
Naylor explores the ways in which different connotations of the word
nigger affected her perception of herself and her race. Roberto Santiago,
Kesaya Noda, and Bar..ara Ehrenreich all try to define their own cultural
identities. For Santiago, defining cultural identity means explaining his
position within a "duo-culture," where he is *both* black and Puerto Rican;
for Noda, it means reconciling competing images of herself as Japanese,
Japanese American, and a Japanese-American woman; for Ehrenreich, it
means learning to see herself as someone with no particular ethnic or
religious identity.

In addition to these specific issues, the writers deal with broad
themes, such as the search for racial, national, and cultural identity; the
conflict between a desire to assimilate and the need to retain ties to an
older culture; the difficulty of moving from one world to another; and the
misunderstandings that arise when cultures clash.

As you write about your experiences as an American and explore
your attitudes about others, you can use definition to help you understand important issues and concepts, both those relating to personal
values and those touching on broader themes.

In the essay that follows, a student uses definition to explore her
identity as a Palestinian American.

STUDENT VOICE: HANAN ABDELHADY

My Palestinian-American Identity

A Palestinian is a person whose ancestors were born in Palestine. 1
Today, this area is more commonly known as Israel, but the more
than five million Palestinians either born there or in other places
after their dispersion still call this country Palestine.

The present situation of the Palestinian people is a result of the 2
partition of Palestine by the United Nations in 1947 and the creation of the state of Israel in May 1948. After partition, which was
followed by war, many Palestinians fled or were expelled from the
areas that came under Israel's control. Palestinians who were present for the 1949 Israeli census and their descendants are citizens of
Israel. Those living in the part of Palestine that came under Jordan's
control (now known as the West Bank) were granted Jordanian citizenship. Because my parents were born on the West Bank of Palestine, their passports list their birthplace as Jordan; they are not
Jordanian, however, but Palestinian. I am a first-generation Palestinian American.

As a result of their history of fragmentation and dispersion, the 3
Palestinian people no longer have any real authority to guide, direct, or sustain a national life in their homeland. Although the Palestinians have all the elements of a nation—a common history,
flag, language (Arabic), and culture, as well as shared national institutions and representatives at the Mideast peace talks—they do not
have a nation of their own. In most places the very word *Palestinian*
is either denied or in some way used as a term of discrimination, as
when the words *Palestinian* and *terrorist* are equated. Today, more

Palestinians than ever are born in exile and face the prospect of continued exile until an independent Palestinian state is returned to them.

As one of these Palestinians born in exile, I have grown up with parents very determined to preserve their culture and raise their children as they were raised in their homeland. This means that I have had different rules from most Americans my age. Palestinian girls do not date; they do not go out with friends every night; they do not sleep over at friends' houses. Palestinian children have a great deal of respect for their parents and will not disobey their wishes. Now, my college friends tell me I should live my own life and do what I want. They can't understand why I won't challenge my parents' control over me.

My college friends see me in shorts or a miniskirt or whatever I want to wear. They hear me express my ideas freely and often agree with things I know would be totally unacceptable in my culture. But with my Palestinian relatives I am always properly attired in dress slacks and a matching blouse or a skirt or dress that is at least shin length. When I talk, I make sure what I say is in sync with my relatives' ideas and what they would like to hear from me.

Living the "double life" is very difficult because I am often torn between two sets of ideas and values. On the one hand, I have grown up in American society and don't feel I should have to settle for less freedom than my American friends have. On the other hand, I don't want to abandon the culture my family has struggled so hard to maintain. This conflict has led me to decide that if I wish to raise my own children with the values of Palestinian culture, I will not raise them in this country. My cousins who were born and raised in Palestine have not experienced the conflicts I have because they don't know any lifestyle other than their own. They cannot long for something they know nothing about. I hope that in the future I, unlike my parents, will have the option of raising my children in a Palestinian homeland if I so choose.

Being Palestinian American has not been easy, but in many ways 7 I like being different from my American friends. Take my name, Hanan. As my friends and I often say, if someone calls "Hanan" down the hall, only one person will turn around. Like my culture, my name gives me an identity that is uniquely mine.

Defining Terms

Defining terms enables a writer to begin a dialogue with readers by establishing some common ground about the possible meanings of a word or phrase. In the worlds of business, science, politics, the arts, and elsewhere, writers are constantly defining terms. Because new terms are always being introduced into languages, because meanings change as societies evolve, and because a single term may have different meanings to different people, there is a continuing need for definition and redefinition.

A **definition** essay states, explains, and illustrates what something— a term, a concept, a belief—means. In the simplest form, a *formal definition* names the term to be defined, the general class to which that term belongs, and the features that distinguish it from other terms in its class:

A *quinceañera* is a ceremony that commemorates the fifteenth birthday of a young Latina, marking her initiation into womanhood, her acceptance of the Catholic faith, and her entrance into society.

Although it is certainly possible, and often desirable, to define a term in a single sentence, more complex terms may require several paragraphs—or several pages—of definition. In the case of *quinceañera*, defined briefly here and in the student paragraph on page 371, an *extended definition* might include an English translation of the Spanish word, historical background explaining the origins of the celebration and its significance in different countries, and an enumeration and description of the celebration's distinctive features. If readers are unfamiliar with the term, they may require additional explanation. Analogies with secular or religious coming-of-age rituals in other cultures—Sweet Sixteen or Bat Mitzvah celebrations, for example—might be helpful.

FOCUSING ON THE TERM TO BE DEFINED

As you begin your definition essay, *focus clearly on the term you want to define.* Remember to consider not just the term's *denotation* (its literal or "dictionary" definition), but also its *connotations* (the other, more subtle, meanings the term suggests).

Try to include a concise one-sentence definition somewhere in your essay. If this brief definition appears early in the essay, it will give your readers a context for your expanded discussion; if it appears toward the end, it can provide a useful summary. Often, however, you will not be able to define a term in a single sentence—particularly if the term is one that may be defined in several different ways (such as Naylor's *nigger*) or one you yourself are having a hard time defining (such as Rodriguez's *culture*). If your definition continues for several paragraphs, be careful to maintain your focus on the word or phrase you are defining. Using clear transitional signals, repeating the term being defined at regular intervals, and avoiding tangential discussions can all help to keep you (and your readers) on track.

USING VARIOUS PATTERNS OF DEVELOPMENT

As you write your definition essay, you should *use various patterns of development*—classification and division, cause and effect, comparison and contrast, and so on—to expand your definition. You may choose to focus on a single pattern of development, or you may combine several different ones in a single essay, as many of the writers of this chapter's essays do.

- In "My Palestinian-American Identity" (p. 373) Hanan Abdel-hady uses *narrative* to trace the history of the Palestinian people, *exemplification* to illustrate the rules imposed on her by her parents, and *comparison and contrast* to show how her behavior is different in each of the two worlds in which she lives.
- In "The Fear of Losing a Culture" (p. 399) Richard Rodriguez relies primarily on *exemplification* to expand his definition, citing examples of entertainers, foods, and films that he associates with Hispanic-American culture.
- In "Mommy, What Does 'Nigger' Mean?" (p. 379) Gloria Naylor uses several strategies to develop her definition. She uses a series of *examples* to illustrate different uses of the word; she uses *narrative* to relate brief anecdotes about her experiences; and she uses *cause and effect* when she discusses the impact the word had on her the first time she heard it.
- In "Black *and* Latino" (p. 385) Roberto Santiago uses *narrative* to recount a particularly upsetting childhood incident; elsewhere he briefly *compares and contrasts* reactions and expectations of his African-American and Puerto Rican friends.
- Kesaya Noda, in "Asian in America" (p. 389), uses *classification and division* to establish three distinct categories that define who she is. Within these categories, she uses *description* to create vivid pictures of the people and places that help her to understand the three parts of her identity.
- Finally, in "Cultural Baggage" (p. 405) Barbara Ehrenreich relies primarily on *narrative* (to recount incidents from her childhood and family life) and *cause and effect* (to explain the impact of various events on the development of her philosophy).

USING OTHER STRATEGIES

As you write and revise, you can also *use other strategies* to develop your extended definitions. You can, for example, define by the process of elimination—that is, by reviewing what the term is *not*. You can also define by providing synonyms or near-synonyms, by enumerating a term's characteristics, or by examining the origin of the term or its changing usage. None of these strategies alone can generate enough material for a full-length definition essay, but each of them can enrich your definitions.

REVIEW CHECKLIST: DEFINING TERMS

✓ Focus clearly on the term you want to define.

✓ Use various patterns of development.

✓ Use other strategies.

GLORIA NAYLOR

Mommy, What Does "Nigger" Mean?

Gloria Naylor was twenty-seven years old before she read Toni
Morrison's novel *The Bluest Eye* and realized that a story about
black women written by a black woman might have a place in
American literature: "It sounds strange now, but it was my second
year of college before I realized black women wrote books. I had
been writing all my life because I had no choice, just to make
sense of the world and my feelings, but I had never read a book
about me."

Born in New York in 1950 shortly after her parents moved from
Mississippi, Naylor says of her upbringing, "Technically, I'm a
New Yorker who grew up in a southern home. That meant that I
heard stories all my life about the South. And being a quiet kid, I
was the one who sat still long enough to listen to them." Those
stories resonate throughout her work.

Naylor sold her first short story to *Essence* magazine in 1977 and
continued to write while earning a master's degree in Afro-
American studies from Yale University. Her first novel, *The
Women of Brewster Place* (1982), won the American Book Award for
First Fiction and served as the basis for an acclaimed television
production. Her exploration of the black female experience has
continued in two subsequent novels, *Linden Hills* (1985) and *Mama
Day* (1988), which draw heavily on her own experience with her
extended family of strong black women.

In the following essay Naylor ponders the nuances of the word
nigger and discusses how the racist pejorative can be transmuted
to a term of admiration and even affection. The need to escape
the strictures of stereotype is profoundly important to Naylor: "I
believe literature goes hand in hand with reality. I'm accepted as
a writer to the same extent that I'm accepted as a human being in

379

society. . . . All human beings love and hate and have aspirations. You begin there and start to build. If you are willing to work at understanding other human beings, you're not going to create a stereotype."

In the following essay, Naylor provides a variety of definitions to show how "a word whites used to signify worthlessness or degradation" was transformed by her family "to signify the varied and complex human beings they knew themselves to be."

L ANGUAGE IS THE SUBJECT. It is the written form with which I've   1
managed to keep the wolf away from the door and, in diaries, to keep my sanity. In spite of this, I consider the written word inferior to the spoken, and much of the frustration experienced by novelists is the awareness that whatever we manage to capture in even the most transcendent passages falls far short of the richness of life. Dialogue achieves its power in the dynamics of a fleeting moment of sight, sound, smell and touch.

I'm not going to enter the debate here about whether it is language   2
that shapes reality or vice versa. That battle is doomed to be waged whenever we seek intermittent reprieve from the chicken and egg dispute. I will simply take the position that the spoken word, like the written word, amounts to a nonsensical arrangement of sounds or letters without a consensus that assigns "meaning." And building from the meanings of what we hear, we order reality. Words themselves are innocuous; it is the consensus that gives them true power.

I remember the first time I heard the word nigger. In my third-   3
grade class, our math tests were being passed down the rows, and as I handed the papers to a little boy in back of me, I remarked that once again he had received a much lower mark than I did. He snatched his test from me and spit out that word. Had he called me a nymphomaniac or a necrophiliac, I couldn't have been more puzzled. I didn't know what a nigger was, but I knew that whatever it meant, it was something he shouldn't have called me. This was verified when I raised my hand, and in a loud voice repeated what he had said and watched the teacher scold him for using a "bad" word. I was later to go home and ask the inevitable question that every black parent must face—"Mommy, what does 'nigger' mean?"

And what exactly did it mean? Thinking back, I realize that this   4
could not have been the first time the word was used in my presence. I
was part of a large extended family that had migrated from the rural
South after World War II and formed a close-knit network that gravitated
around my maternal grandparents. Their ground-floor apartment in one
of the buildings they owned in Harlem was a weekend mecca for my
immediate family, along with countless aunts, uncles and cousins who
brought along assorted friends. It was a bustling and open house with
assorted neighbors and tenants popping in and out to exchange bits of
gossip, pick up an old quarrel or referee the ongoing checkers game in
which my grandmother cheated shamelessly. They were all there to let
down their hair and put up their feet after a week of labor in the factories,
laundries and shipyards of New York.

Amid the clamor, which could reach deafening proportions—two   5
or three conversations going on simultaneously, punctuated by the sound
of a baby's crying somewhere in the back rooms or out on the street—
there was still a rigid set of rules about what was said and how. Older
children were sent out of the living room when it was time to get into the
juicy details about "you-know-who" up on the third floor who had gone
and gotten herself "p-r-e-g-n-a-n-t-!" But my parents, knowing that I
could spell well beyond my years, always demanded that I follow the
others out to play. Beyond sexual misconduct and death, everything else
was considered harmless for our young ears. And so among the anecdotes
of the triumphs and disappointments in the various workings of their
lives, the word nigger was used in my presence, but it was set within
contexts and inflections that caused it to register in my mind as something else.

In the singular, the word was always applied to a man who had   6
distinguished himself in some situation that brought their approval for
his strength, intelligence or drive:

"Did Johnny really do that?"   7

"I'm telling you, that nigger pulled in $6,000 of overtime last year.   8
Said he got enough for a down payment on a house."

When used with a possessive adjective by a woman—"my nig-   9
ger"—it became a term of endearment for husband or boyfriend. But it
could be more than just a term applied to a man. In their mouths it became the pure essence of manhood—a disembodied force that channeled
their past history of struggle and present survival against the odds into a

victorious statement of being: "Yeah, that old foreman found out quick enough—you don't mess with a nigger."

In the plural, it became a description of some group within the   10 community that had overstepped the bounds of decency as my family defined it: Parents who neglected their children, a drunken couple who fought in public, people who simply refused to look for work, those with excessively dirty mouths or unkempt households were all "trifling niggers." This particular circle could forgive hard times, unemployment, the occasional bout of depression—they had gone through all of that themselves—but the unforgivable sin was lack of self-respect.

A woman could never be a "nigger" in the singular, with its conno-   11 tation of confirming worth. The noun girl was its closest equivalent in that sense, but only when used in direct address and regardless of the gender doing the addressing. "Girl" was a token of respect for a woman. The one-syllable word was drawn out to sound like three in recognition of the extra ounce of wit, nerve or daring that the woman had shown in the situation under discussion.

"G-i-r-l, stop. You mean you said that to his face?"   12

But if the word was used in a third-person reference or shortened so   13 that it almost snapped out of the mouth, it always involved some element of communal disapproval. And age became an important factor in these exchanges. It was only between individuals of the same generation, or from an older person to a younger (but never the other way around), that "girl" would be considered a compliment.

I don't agree with the argument that use of the word nigger at this   14 social stratum of the black community was an internalization of racism. The dynamics were the exact opposite: the people in my grandmother's living room took a word that whites used to signify worthlessness or degradation and rendered it impotent. Gathering there together, they transformed "nigger" to signify the varied and complex human beings they knew themselves to be. If the word was to disappear totally from the mouths of even the most liberal of white society, no one in that room was naïve enough to believe it would disappear from white minds. Meeting the word head-on, they proved it had absolutely nothing to do with the way they were determined to live their lives.

So there must have been dozens of times that the word "nigger" was   15 spoken in front of me before I reached the third grade. But I didn't "hear" it until it was said by a small pair of lips that had already learned it could be a way to humiliate me. That was the word I went home and asked my mother about. And since she knew that I had to grow up in America, she took me in her lap and explained.

✿ Opening the Dialogue

1. Naylor recounts in paragraph 3 how she went home to ask her mother "the inevitable question that every black parent must face." What other "inevitable questions" do you imagine black parents face? Do you think these questions are different from the ones confronting other minority parents?

2. Do you think Naylor is being intellectually honest when she says that by repeating the word *nigger* blacks "rendered it impotent" (paragraph 14)? Does she convince you that the black community's use of the word is *not* an "internalization of racism"?

3. Naylor explains that the word *nigger* has different connotations depending on whether it is used among African Americans or by outsiders. Can you think of other expressions that operate in this way? Do you see any danger in preserving such expressions within a minority culture?

✿ Keeping a Notebook

In paragraph 2 Naylor comments, "Words themselves are innocuous; it is the consensus that gives them true power." What does she mean by this statement? Do you think she is correct?

✿ Working Together

Working in groups, list all the negative terms you can think of that are commonly applied to women, people with disabilities, the elderly, and people from rural areas. In class discussion, consider how these words seek to demean and offend. Is this kind of name-calling as dangerous as the use of racial epithets?

☯ Writing an Essay

Write an essay defining a term that has been used to label you. What negative connotations was the word meant to have? Under what circumstances was this term used, and what effect did its use have on you?

Roberto Santiago

Black *and* Latino

"When we write essays that expose out greatest fears, those fears cease to have power over us," says Roberto Santiago. "A personal essay must speak from the soul. It's the source of the most powerful writing."

In the following personal essay, reprinted from *Essence* magazine, Santiago writes of the resentment and confusion he experienced as a child as he tried to reconcile peculiarly American attitudes toward race and skin color with his own self-definition.

Santiago was born in New York in 1963 to Puerto Rican parents. Inheriting a blend of his mother's dark skin and his father's white complexion, Santiago refused to be arbitrarily defined as "black" or "Latino," because, as the title of his essay points out, he is both. His essay also suggests some important distinctions between Latino and American definitions of race.

Santiago is a newspaper columnist for *The Plain Dealer* in Cleveland, Ohio. His work has appeared in *Omni* and *Rolling Stone*, among other publications, and includes journalism, fiction, drama, and screenplays.

"THERE IS NO WAY THAT YOU can be black and Puerto Rican at the 1
same time." What? Despite the many times I've heard this over the years, that statement still perplexes me. I *am* both and always have been. My color is a blend of my mother's rich, dark skin tone and my father's white complexion. As they were both Puerto Rican, I spoke Spanish before English, but I am totally bilingual. My life has been shaped by my black and Latino heritages, and despite other people's confusion, I don't feel I have to choose one or the other. To do so would be to deny a part of myself.

There has not been a moment in my life when I did not know that 2

I looked black—and I never thought that others did not see it, too. But growing up in East Harlem, I was also aware that I did not "act black," according to the African-American boys on the block.

My lighter-skinned Puerto Rican friends were less of a help in this   3 department. "You're not black," they would whine, shaking their heads. "You're a *boriqua* [slang for Puerto Rican], you ain't no *moreno* [black]." If that was true, why did my mirror defy the rules of logic? And most of all, why did I feel that there was some serious unknown force trying to make me choose sides?

Acting black. Looking black. Being a real black. This debate among us is   4 almost a parody. The fact is that I am black, so why do I need to prove it?

The island of Puerto Rico is only a stone's throw away from Haiti,   5 and, no fooling, if you climb a palm tree, you can see Jamaica bobbing on the Atlantic. The slave trade ran through the Caribbean basin, and virtually all Puerto Rican citizens have some African blood in their veins. My grandparents on my mother's side were the classic *negro como carbón* (black as carbon) people, but despite the fact that they were as dark as can be, they are officially not considered black.

There is an explanation for this, but not one that makes much   6 sense, or difference, to a working-class kid from Harlem. Puerto Ricans identify themselves as Hispanics—part of a worldwide race that originated from eons of white Spanish conquests—a mixture of white, African, and *Indio* blood, which, categorically, is apart from black. In other words, the culture is the predominant and determinant factor. But there are frustrations in being caught in a duo-culture, where your skin color does not necessarily dictate what you are. When I read Piri Thomas's searing autobiography, *Down These Mean Streets,* in my early teens, I saw that he couldn't figure out other people's attitudes toward his blackness, either.

My first encounter with this attitude about the race thing rode on   7 horseback. I had just turned six years old and ran toward the bridle path in Central Park as I saw two horses about to trot past. "Yea! Horsie! Yea!" I yelled. Then I noticed one figure on horseback. She was white, and she shouted, "Shut up, you f—g nigger! Shut up!" She pulled back on the reins and twisted the horse in my direction. I can still feel the spray of gravel that the horse kicked at my chest. And suddenly she was gone. I looked back, and, in the distance, saw my parents playing Whiffle Ball with my sister. They seemed miles away.

They still don't know about this incident. But I told my Aunt Aure-   8
lia almost immediately. She explained what the words meant and why
they were said. Ever since then I have been able to express my anger
appropriately through words or action in similar situations. Self-preservation, ego, and pride forbid men from ever ignoring, much less forgetting,
a slur.

Aunt Aurelia became, unintentionally, my source for answers I   9
needed about color and race. I never sought her out. She just seemed to
appear at my home during the points in my childhood when I most
needed her for solace. "Puerto Ricans are different from American
blacks," she told me once. "There is no racism between what you call
white and black. Nobody even considers the marriages interracial." She
then pointed out the difference in color between my father and mother.
"You never noticed that," she said, "because you were not raised with that
hang-up."

Aunt Aurelia passed away before I could follow up on her observa-   10
tion. But she had made an important point. It's why I never liked the
attitude that says I should be exclusive to one race.

My behavior toward this race thing pegged me as an iconoclast of   11
sorts. Children from mixed marriages, from my experience, also share
this attitude. If I have to beat the label of iconoclast because the world
wants people to be in set categories and I don't want to, then I will.

A month before Aunt Aurelia died, she saw I was a little down   12
about the whole race thing, and she said, "Roberto, don't worry. Even
if—no matter what you do—black people in this country don't, you can
always depend on white people to treat you like a black."

⟪ Opening the Dialogue

1. In Puerto Rico, according to Santiago, culture—not race—is central
to a person's identity. Why, then, do you think it is so difficult for Santiago to consider his *culture*, rather than his race, the "predominant and determinant factor" (paragraph 6) in defining his ethnic identity?

2. In paragraph 8 Santiago says, "Self-preservation, ego, and pride forbid
men from ever ignoring, much less forgetting, a slur." Instead, he believes, one should "express . . . anger appropriately through words or ac-

tions. . . . " Do you agree? What might constitute an "appropriate" expression of anger in response to a slur that expresses racist, sexist, or homophobic attitudes?

3. What advantages might be associated with defining oneself as black rather than Latino? As Latino rather than black?

⟨€⟩ Keeping a Notebook

Do you believe that someone who has roots in more than one cultural heritage or ethnic group has to "choose one or the other"? Or can one be, for example, both black and Latino?

⟨€⟩ Working Together

Do you believe that people's ethnic identity is determined by how they look, where their ancestors come from, what language they or their parents speak, or what they consider themselves to be? Working in groups, list reasons to support each position. In class discussion, try to answer the question. Are there different answers for different ethnic groups?

⟨€⟩ Writing an Essay

With what community or group do you identify most strongly? Write an essay in which you define yourself in terms of race, ethnicity, or geography. If you believe that two or more groups compete for your loyalty, write about how you attempt to reconcile their demands as you define your cultural identity.

KESAYA E. NODA

Asian in America

Kesaya Noda was born in California but was raised in rural New Hampshire. She and her family were the only Asian Americans in their small community, and Noda grew up, she says, in "almost total isolation from other Japanese Americans."

After high school Noda moved to Japan, where she immersed herself in an intensive eighteen-month study of Japanese language and culture, finding it a shock to be both "mute and illiterate." Later, at Stanford University, she began to research and write about the Japanese community in California where her grandparents had settled and her parents had been raised. As she studied archival records and interviewed the elderly original settlers for her book *The Yamato Colony*, she realized just how disconnected her own generation had become from its past: "I felt a real sense of mourning because of that disconnection. Racism toward Asian Americans on the West Coast was formidable. It has a long history—beginning with the Chinese and spreading to the Filipinos and the Japanese and now the Southeast Asians. Our parents suffered during the war from the terrible lie that there is no such thing as a Japanese American. You were either American or Japanese and therefore the enemy." Noda regrets that so many *sansei*, or third-generation Japanese Americans, had at first lost their sense of history. "I grew up unable to speak to my own grandmother [who spoke only Japanese]," she recalls.

Noda spent another year in Japan, where she made a spiritual pilgrimage around the island of Shikoku, walking nine hundred miles from temple to temple. Upon her return to the United States, she entered divinity school and became interested in Shinto, the native Japanese religion.

Deeply committed to the elimination of racism, sexism, and classism, Noda believes that "it is possible for us to value the differences between people and also have space for the reality of our oneness . . . I write about the things I feel deeply but don't understand; somehow understanding comes from images and stories. I treasure particularity very much and want to affirm that. Racism is built on stereotypes and lies; particularity is truth."

Notice how Noda goes beyond a one-dimensional definition of "Asian in America" to explore the multiple realities the term ultimately contains.

SOMETIMES WHEN I WAS GROWING UP, my identity seemed to hurtle   1
toward me and paste itself right to my face. I felt that way, encountering the stereotypes of my race perpetuated by non-Japanese people (primarily white) who may or may not have had contact with other Japanese in America. "You don't like cheese, do you?" someone would ask. "I know your people don't like cheese." Sometimes questions came making allusions to history. That was another aspect of the identity. Events that had happened quite apart from the me who stood silent in that moment connected my face with an incomprehensible past. "Your parents were in California? Were they in those camps during the war?" And sometimes there were phrases or nicknames: "Lotus Blossom." I was sometimes addressed or referred to as racially Japanese, sometimes as Japanese-American, and sometimes as an Asian woman. Confusions and distortions abounded.

How is one to know and define oneself? From the inside—within a   2
context that is self-defined, from a grounding in community and a connection with culture and history that are comfortably accepted? Or from the outside—in terms of messages received from the media and people who are often ignorant? Even as an adult I can still see two sides of my face and past. I can see from the inside out, in freedom. And I can see from the outside in, driven by the old voices of childhood and lost in anger and fear.

I AM RACIALLY JAPANESE

A voice from my childhood says: "You are other. You are less than.   3
You are unalterably alien." This voice has its own history. We have indeed been seen as other and alien since the early years of our arrival in
the United States. The very first immigrants were welcomed and sought
as laborers to replace the dwindling numbers of Chinese, whose influx
had been cut off by the Chinese Exclusion Act of 1882. The Japanese fell
natural heir to the same anti-Asian prejudice that had arisen against the
Chinese. As soon as they began striking for better wages, they were no
longer welcomed.

I can see myself today as a person historically defined by law and   4
custom as being forever alien. Being neither "free white" nor "African,"
our people in California were deemed "aliens, ineligible for citizenship,"
no matter how long they intended to stay here. Aliens ineligible for citizenship were prohibited from owning, buying, or leasing land. They did
not and could not belong here. The voice in me remembers that I am
always a *Japanese*-American in the eyes of many. A third-generation
German-American is an American. A third-generation Japanese-American
is a Japanese-American. Being Japanese means being a danger to the
country during the war and knowing how to use chopsticks. I wear this
history on my face.

I move to the other side. I see a different light and claim a different   5
context. My race is a line that stretches across ocean and time to link me
to the shrine where my grandmother was raised. Two high, white ban-
ners lift in the wind at the top of the stone steps leading to the shrine. It
is time for the summer festival. Black characters are written against the
sky as boldly as the clouds, as lightly as kites, as sharply as the big black
crows I used to see above the fields in New Hampshire. At festival time
there is liquor and food, ritual, discipline, and abandonment. There is
music and drunkenness and invocation. There is hope. Another season
has come. Another season has gone.

I am racially Japanese. I have a certain claim to this crazy place   6
where the prayers intoned by a neighboring Shinto priest (standing in for
my grandmother's nephew who is sick) are drowned out by the rehearsals
for the pop singing contest in which most of the villagers will compete
later that night. The village elders, the priest, and I stand respectfully
upon the immaculate, shining wooden floor of the outer shrine, bowing

our heads before the hidden powers. During the patchy intervals when I can hear him, I notice the priest has a stutter. His voice flutters up to my ears only occasionally because two men and a woman are singing gustily into a microphone in the compound, testing the sound system. A prerecorded tape of guitars, samisens, and drums accompanies them. Rock music and Shinto prayers. That night, to loud applause and cheers, a young man is given the award for the most *netsuretsu*—passionate, burning—rendition of a song. We roar our approval of the reward. Never mind that his voice had wandered and slid, now slightly above, now slightly below the given line of the melody. Netsuretsu. Netsuretsu.

In the morning, my grandmother's sister kneels at the foot of the   7
stone stairs to offer her morning prayers. She is too crippled to climb the stairs, so each morning she kneels here upon the path. She shuts her eyes for a few seconds, her motions as matter of fact as when she washes rice. I linger longer than she does, so reluctant to leave, savoring the connection I feel with my grandmother in America, the past, and the power that lives and shines in the morning sun.

Our family has served this shrine for generations. The family's need   8
to protect this claim to identity and place outweighs any individual claim to any individual hope. I am Japanese.

I AM A JAPANESE-AMERICAN

"Weak." I hear the voice from my childhood years. "Passive," I hear.   9
Our parents and grandparents were the ones who were put into those camps. They went without resistance; they offered cooperation as proof of loyalty to America. "Victim," I hear. And, "Silent."

Our parents are painted as hard workers who were socially uncom-   10
fortable and had difficulty expressing even the smallest opinion. Clean, quiet, motivated, and determined to match the American way; that is us, and that is the story of our time here.

"Why did you go into those camps?" I raged at my parents, fright-   11
ened by my own inner silence and timidity. "Why didn't you do anything to resist? Why didn't you name it the injustice it was?" Couldn't our parents even think? Couldn't they? Why were we so passive?

I shift my vision and my stance. I am in California. My uncle is in   12
the midst of the sweet potato harvest. He is pressed, trying to get the harvesting crews onto the field as quickly as possible, worried about the

flow of equipment and people. His big pickup is pulled off to the side, motor running, door ajar. I see two tractors in the yard in front of an old shed; the flatbed harvesting platform on which the workers will stand has already been brought over from the other field. It's early morning. The workers stand loosely grouped and at ease, but my uncle looks as harried and tense as a police officer trying to unsnarl a New York City traffic jam. Driving toward the shed, I pull my car off the road to make way for an approaching tractor. The front wheels of the car sink luxuriously into the soft, white sand by the roadside and the car slides to a dreamy halt, tail still on the road. I try to move forward. I try to move back. The front bites contentedly into the sand, the back lifts itself at a jaunty angle. My uncle sees me and storms down the road, running. He is shouting before he is even near me.

"What's the matter with you?" he screams. "What the hell are you   13
doing?" In his frenzy, he grabs his hat off his head and slashes it through the air across his knee. He is beside himself. "Don't you know how to drive in sand? What's the matter with you? You've blocked the whole roadway. How am I supposed to get my tractors out of here? Can't you use your head? You've cut off the whole roadway, and we've got to get out of here."

I stand on the road before him helplessly thinking, "No, I don't   14
know how to drive in sand. I've never driven in sand."

"I'm sorry, uncle," I say, burying a smile beneath a look of sincere   15
apology. I notice my deep amusement and my affection for him with great curiosity. I am usually devastated by anger. Not this time.

During the several years that follow I learn about the people and   16
the place, and much more about what has happened in this California village where my parents grew up. The *issei*, our grandparents, made this settlement in the desert. Their first crops were eaten by rabbits and ravaged by insects. The land was so barren that men walking from house to house sometimes got lost. Women came here too. They bore children in 114-degree heat, then carried the babies with them into the fields to nurse when they reached the end of each row of grapes or other truck-farm crops.

I had had no idea what it meant to buy this kind of land and make   17
it grow green. Or how, when the war came, there was no space at all for the subtlety of being who we were—Japanese-Americans. Either/or was the way. I hadn't understood that people were literally afraid for their

lives then, that their money had been frozen in banks; that there was a
five-mile travel limit; that when the early evening curfew came and they
were inside their houses, some of them watched helplessly as people they
knew went into their barns to steal their belongings. The police were
patrolling the road, interested only in violators of curfew. There was no
help for them in the face of thievery. I had not been able to imagine
before what it must have felt like to be an American—to know absolutely
that one is an American—and yet to have almost everyone else deny it.
Not only deny it, but challenge that identity with machine guns and
troops of white American soldiers. In those circumstances it was difficult
to say, "I'm a Japanese-American." "American" had to do.

But now I can say that I am a Japanese-American. It means I have a   18
place here in this country, too. I have a place here on the East Coast,
where our neighbor is so much a part of our family that my mother never
passes her house at night without glancing at the lights to see if she is
home and safe; where my parents have hauled hundreds of pounds of
rocks from fields and arduously planted Christmas trees and blueberries,
lilacs, asparagus, and crab apples; where my father still dreams of angling
a stream to a new bed so that he can dig a pond in the field and fill it with
water and fish. "The neighbors already came for their Christmas tree?" he
asks in December. "Did they like it? Did they like it?"

I have a place on the West Coast where my relatives still farm,   19
where I heard the stories of feuds and backbiting, and where I saw that
people survived and flourished because fundamentally they trusted and
relied upon one another. A death in the family is not just a death in a
family; it is a death in the community. I saw people help each other with
money, materials, labor, attention, and time. I saw men gather once a
year, without fail, to clean the grounds of a ninety-year-old woman who
had helped the community before, during, and after the war. I saw her
remembering them with birthday cards sent to each of their children.

I come from a people with a long memory and a distinctive grace.   20
We live our thanks. And we are Americans. Japanese-Americans.

I AM A JAPANESE-AMERICAN WOMAN

Woman. The last piece of my identity. It has been easier by far for   21
me to know myself in Japan and to see my place in America than it has
been to accept my line of connection with my own mother. She was my

dark self, a figure in whom I thought I saw all that I feared most in myself. Growing into womanhood and looking for some model of strength, I turned away from her. Of course, I could not find what I sought. I was looking for a black feminist or a white feminist. My mother is neither white nor black.

My mother is a woman who speaks with her life as much as with   22
her tongue. I think of her with her own mother. Grandmother had Parkinson's disease and it had frozen her gait and set her fingers, tongue, and feet jerking and trembling in a terrible dance. My aunts and uncles wanted her to be able to live in her own home. They fed her, bathed her, dressed her, awoke at midnight to take her for one last trip to the bathroom. My aunts (her daughters-in-law) did most of the care, but my mother went from New Hampshire to California each summer to spend a month living with Grandmother, because she wanted to and because she wanted to give my aunts at least a small rest. During those hot summer days, mother lay on the couch watching the television or reading, cooking foods that Grandmother liked, and speaking little. Grandmother thrived under her care.

The time finally came when it was too dangerous for Grandmother   23
to live alone. My relatives kept finding her on the floor beside her bed when they went to wake her in the mornings. My mother flew to California to help clean the house and make arrangements for Grandmother to enter a local nursing home. On her last day at home, while Grandmother was sitting in her big, overstuffed armchair, hair combed and wearing a green summer dress, my mother went to her and knelt at her feet. "Here, Mamma," she said. "I've polished your shoes." She lifted Grandmother's legs and helped her into the shiny black shoes. My Grandmother looked down and smiled slightly. She left her house walking, supported by her children, carrying her pocket book, and wearing her polished black shoes. "Look, Mamma," my mom had said, kneeling. "I've polished your shoes."

Just the other day, my mother came to Boston to visit. She had   24
recently lost a lot of weight and was pleased with her new shape and her feeling of good health. "Look at me, Kes," she exclaimed, turning toward me, front and back, as naked as the day she was born. I saw her small breasts and the wide, brown scar, belly button to pubic hair, that marked her because my brother and I were both born by Caesarean section. Her hips were small. I was not a large baby, but there was so little room for me

in her that when she was carrying me she could not even begin to bend over toward the floor. She hated it, she said.

"Don't I look good? Don't you think I look good?"   25

I looked at my mother, smiling and as happy as she, thinking of all   26
the times I have seen her naked. I have seen both my parents naked throughout my life, as they have seen me. From childhood through adulthood we've had our naked moments, sharing baths, idle conversations picked up as we moved between showers and closets, hurried moments at the beginning of days, quiet moments at the end of days.

I know this to be Japanese, this ease with the physical, and it makes   27
me think of an old Japanese folk song. A young nursemaid, a fifteen-year-old girl, is singing a lullaby to a baby who is strapped to her back. The nursemaid has been sent as a servant to a place far from her own home. "We're the beggars," she says, "and they are the nice people. Nice people wear fine sashes. Nice clothes."

If I should drop dead,   28
bury me by the roadside!
I'll give a flower
to everyone who passes.

What kind of flower?
The cam-cam-camellia [*tsun-tsun-tsubaki*]
watered by Heaven:
alms water.

The nursemaid is the intersection of heaven and earth, the intersec-   29
tion of the human, the natural world, the body, and the soul. In this song, with clear eyes, she looks steadily at life, which is sometimes so very terrible and sad. I think of her while looking at my mother, who is standing on the red and purple carpet before me, laughing, without any clothes.

I am my mother's daughter. And I am myself.   30
I am a Japanese-American woman.   31

Epilogue

I recently heard a man from West Africa share some memories of   32
his childhood. He was raised Muslim, but when he was a young man, he

found himself deeply drawn to Christianity. He struggled against his inner impulse for years, trying to avoid the church yet feeling pushed to return to it again and again. "I would have done *anything* to avoid the change," he said. At last he became Christian. Afterwards he was afraid to go home, fearing that he would not be accepted. The fear was groundless, he discovered, when at last he returned—he had separated himself, but his family and friends (all Muslim) had not separated themselves from him.

The man, who is now a professor of religion, said that in the Africa   33
he knew as a child and a young man, pluralism was embraced rather than feared. There was "a kind of tolerance that did not deny your particularity," he said. He alluded to zestful, spontaneous debates that would sometimes loudly erupt between Muslims and Christians in the village's public spaces. His memories of an atheist who harangued the villagers when he came to visit them once a week moved me deeply. Perhaps the man was an agricultural advisor or inspector. He harrassed the women. He would say: "Don't go to the fields! Don't even bother to go to the fields. Let God take care of you. He'll send you the food. If you believe in God, why do you need to work? You don't need to work! Let God put the seeds in the ground. Stay home."

The professor said, "The women laughed, you know? They just   34
laughed. Their attitude was, 'Here is a child of God. When will he come home?' "

The storyteller, the professor of religion, smiled a most fantastic   35
tender smile as he told this story. "In my country, there is a deep affirmation of the oneness of God," he said. "The atheist and the women were having quite different experiences in their encounter, though the atheist did not know this. He saw himself as quite separate from the women. But the women did not see themselves as being separate from him. 'Here is a child of God,' they said. 'When will he come home?' "

⟨℮⟩ Opening the Dialogue

1. In paragraph 4 Noda says, "A third-generation German-American is an American. A third-generation Japanese-American is a Japanese-American." Do you think she is correct? If so, how do you account for the

differences in the way German Americans and Japanese Americans are perceived?

2. Noda is able to get in touch with her identities as "racially Japanese" and "Japanese-American" by examining her historical and geographical roots. What aspects of history and geography would you have to explore before understanding your culture?

3. In paragraph 30 Noda says, "I am my mother's daughter. And I am myself." In what respects do you see yourself as your mother's daughter (or your father's son)? In what respects are you simply yourself?

✪ Keeping a Notebook

On the basis of the distinction Noda makes in paragraph 2, would you say you define yourself "from the inside" out or "from the outside" in? Why?

✪ Working Together

In paragraph 3 Noda says that early immigrants from Japan "fell natural heir to the same anti-Asian prejudice that had arisen against the Chinese." Working in groups, list examples of the kinds of biases against Asian Americans that you believe exist in the United States today. In class discussion, consider how prejudice directed at Japanese Americans differs from prejudice directed at other Asian Americans. How do you account for the differences you observe?

✪ Writing an Essay

To what extent is your gender part of your cultural identity? Write an essay in which you define yourself on the basis of your gender, as Noda does in the section of her essay called "I Am a Japanese-American Woman." Do you think you have more in common with those of your gender or those of your ethnic group?

RICHARD RODRIGUEZ

The Fear of Losing a Culture

"As a boy," says Richard Rodriguez, "I grew up thinking that real writers lived in big cities—like New York and Paris—and lived lives very different from my own in Sacramento, California. It took me many years to realize that 'literature' is not about exotic experiences in faraway places, but books are about lives all of us can recognize. I became a writer the day I realized that I could write about my own life; I ended up a man, able to write about my boyhood in Sacramento."

Rodriguez's autobiography, *Hunger of Memory* (1982), was one of the first works by a Hispanic-American author to be published by a major New York publisher and receive extensive attention and acclaim from the mainstream press. At the same time, the book was angrily attacked by other critics, including many Hispanic-Americans, for its uncompromising condemnation of affirmative action programs. Rodriguez's life, like this work, seems to embrace enigma and paradox. A Roman Catholic homosexual whose life contrasts starkly with the teachings of the Church, a political conservative who contributes frequently to bastions of the liberal media such as *Harpers* and *The MacNeil/Lehrer Newshour* on PBS, Rodriguez received assistance through ten years of graduate and postgraduate study in part because of his minority status. However, he declined several prestigious teaching positions because of his opposition to affirmative action: "By being called a 'minority student' at the point at which I was no longer in any real sense disadvantaged, I became the beneficiary of truly disadvantaged Mexican Americans. Their absence in the university made my presence valuable; their lack of visibility made me numerically significant. So in every real way, I benefitted on their backs. . . .

When people tell me I should be a 'leader of my people,' some-how that relieves *them* of the responsibility of helping the educa-tion of all people."

Born in 1944 to immigrant parents, Rodriguez was so successful in achieving their goals that he learn English and become edu-cated that by the time he completed his education in 1973, he felt he had lost his ethnicity. His acutely felt sense of duality and ambivalence can be perceived in his explanation for why he writes: "I think it has something to do with the fact that I was a brooder as a child. Writing, the craft, can be acquired; all you have to do is sit there long enough and you'll learn it. But the pre-occupation, the inclination to be alone, the inclination to remem-ber what your mother said thirty years ago and to make some-thing of it, is a gift or a curse."

In the following essay, Rodriguez "broods" on a particularly perti-nent issue: how to define Hispanic-American culture at a time when melding the two cultures represents both an inevitable goal and a potential threat.

WHAT IS CULTURE? 1

The immigrant shrugs. Latin American immigrants come to the 2 United States with only the things they need in mind—not abstractions like culture. Money. They need dollars. They need food. Maybe they need to get out of the way of bullets.

Most of us who concern ourselves with Hispanic-American culture, 3 as painters, musicians, writers—or as sons and daughters—are the chil-dren of immigrants. We have grown up on this side of the border, in the land of Elvis Presley and Thomas Edison; our lives are prescribed by the mall, by the DMV and the Chinese restaurant. Our imaginations yet vas-cillate between an Edenic Latin America (the blue door)—which never-theless betrayed our parents—and the repellent plate glass of a real American city—which has been good to us.

Hispanic-American culture is where the past meets the future. 4 Hispanic-American culture is not a Hispanic milestone only, not simply a celebration at the crossroads. America transforms into pleasure what

America cannot avoid. Is it any coincidence that at a time when Americans are troubled by the encroachment of the Mexican desert, Americans discover a chic in cactus, in the decorator colors of the Southwest? In sand?

Hispanic-American culture of the sort that is now showing (the teen movie, the rock songs) may exist in an hourglass; may in fact be irrelevant to the epic. The U.S. Border Patrol works through the night to arrest the flow of illegal immigrants over the border, even as Americans wait in line to get into "La Bamba." Even as Americans vote to declare, once and for all, that English shall be the official language of the United States, Madonna starts recording in Spanish.

But then so is Bill Cosby's show irrelevant to the 10 o'clock news, where families huddle together in fear on porches, pointing at the body of the slain boy bagged in tarpaulin. Which is not to say that Bill Cosby or Michael Jackson are irrelevant to the future or without neo-Platonic influence. Like players within the play, they prefigure, they resolve. They make black and white audiences aware of a bond that may not yet exist.

Before a national TV audience, Rita Moreno tells Geraldo Rivera that her dream as an actress is to play a character rather like herself: "I speak English perfectly well . . . I'm not dying from poverty . . . I want to play *that* kind of Hispanic woman, which is to say, an American citizen." This is an actress talking, these are show-biz pieties. But Moreno expresses as well the general Hispanic-American predicament. Hispanics want to belong to America without betraying the past.

Hispanics fear losing ground in any negotiation with the American city. We come from an expansive, an intimate culture that has been judged second-rate by the United States of America. For reasons of pride, therefore, as much as of affection, we are reluctant to give up our past. Hispanics often express a fear of "losing" culture. Our fame in the United States has been our resistance to assimilation.

The symbol of Hispanic culture has been the tongue of flame—Spanish. But the remarkable legacy Hispanics carry from Latin America is not language—an inflatable skin—but breath itself, capacity of soul, an inclination to live. The genius of Latin America is the habit of synthesis.

We assimilate. Just over the border there is the example of Mexico, the country from which the majority of U.S. Hispanics come. Mexico is *mestizo*—Indian and Spanish. Within a single family, Mexicans are light-skinned and dark. It is impossible for the Mexican to say, in the scheme of things, where the Indian begins and the Spaniard surrenders.

In culture as in blood, Latin America was formed by a rape that   11
became a marriage. Due to the absorbing generosity of the Indian, European culture took on new soil. What Latin America knows is that people create one another as they marry. In the music of Latin America you will hear the litany of bloodlines—the African drum, the German accordion, the cry from the minaret.

The United States stands as the opposing New World experiment.   12
In North America the Indian and the European stood apace. Whereas Latin America was formed by a medieval Catholic dream of one world—of meltdown conversion—the United States was built up from Protestant individualism. The American melting pot washes away only embarrassment; it is the necessary initiation into public life. The American faith is that our national strength derives from separateness, from "diversity." The glamour of the United States is a carnival promise: You can lose weight, get rich as Rockefeller, tough up your roots, get a divorce.

Immigrants still come for the promise. But the United States wavers   13
in its faith. As long as there was space enough, sky enough, as long as economic success validated individualism, loneliness was not too high a price to pay. (The cabin on the prairie or the Sony Walkman.)

As we near the end of the American century, two alternative cul-   14
tures beckon the American imagination—both highly communal cultures—the Asian and the Latin American. The United States is a literal culture. Americans devour what we might otherwise fear to become. Sushi will make us corporate warriors. Combination Plate #3, smothered in *mestizo* gravy, will burn a hole in our hearts.

Latin America offers passion. Latin America has a life—I mean   15
life—big clouds, unambiguous themes, death, birth, faith, that the United States, for all its quality of life, seems without now. Latin America offers communal riches: an undistressed leisure, a kitchen table, even a full sorrow. Such is the solitude of America, such is the urgency of American need, Americans reach right past a fledgling, homegrown Hispanic-American culture for the real thing—the darker bottle of Mexican beer; the denser novel of a Latin American master.

For a long time, Hispanics in the United States withheld from the   16
United States our Latin American gift. We denied the value of assimila-

tion. But as our presence is judged less foreign in America, we will produce a more generous art, less timid, less parochial. Carlos Santana, Luis
Valdez, Linda Ronstadt—Hispanic Americans do not have a "pure" Latin
American art to offer. Expect bastard themes, expect ironies, comic conclusions. For we live on this side of the border, where Kraft manufactures
bricks of "Mexican style" Velveeta, and where Jack in the Box serves
"Fajita Pita."

The flame-red Chevy floats a song down the Pan American Highway: From a   17
rolled-down window, the grizzled voice of Willie Nelson rises in disembodied harmony
with the voice of Julio Iglesias. Gabby Hayes and Cisco are thus resolved.

Expect marriage. We will change America even as we will be   18
changed. We will disappear with you into a new miscegenation.

Along the border, real conflicts remain. But the ancient tear sepa-   19
rating Europe from itself—the Catholic Mediterranean from the Protestant north—may yet heal itself in the New World. For generations, Latin
America has been the place—the bed—of a confluence of so many races
and cultures that Protestant North America shuddered to imagine it.

Imagine it.   20

⟨☉⟩ Opening the Dialogue

1. Do you think Rodriguez sees himself as American or Hispanic American? In what sense do you think his characterization of himself is accurate? In what sense do you see it as unrealistic?

2. In paragraph 15 Rodriguez explains in abstract terms what Latin
America has to offer the United States. Do you agree that Latin American
culture possesses certain positive attributes that U.S. culture lacks? Or do
you think Rodriguez underestimates, misunderstands, or misrepresents
U.S. culture?

3. "Expect marriage," Rodriguez says in paragraph 18. "We will change
America even as we will be changed. We will disappear with you into a
new miscegenation." Do you think this "new miscegenation" is an inevitable outcome of two cultures' living together? In what ways do you think
the character of the United States will be changed by such marriages? Do
you see these changes as positive or negative?

✪ Keeping a Notebook

People of Hispanic descent constitute the most rapidly growing minority group in the United States. Do you see this growth as a gift or as a threat to your idea of American culture?

✪ Working Together

Working in groups, list all the public figures, foods, expressions, films, music, and so on that you identify with Hispanic-American culture. In class discussion, consider what the prevalence and the nature of these items reveal about the influence of Hispanic culture on the United States. Where do items like "'Mexican style' Velveeta" fit into the scheme?

✪ Writing an Essay

How do you define your culture in strictly ethnic terms? Write an essay in which you answer the question Rodriguez poses in paragraph 1, paying particular attention to the influence your culture has had on life in the United States.

BARBARA EHRENREICH

Cultural Baggage

Feminist, atheist, populist, and socialist, Barbara Ehrenreich is
one of our most widely read and controversial social critics. A columnist for *Time* magazine, she has contributed to numerous other
publications and is the author of seven books, including *The Hearts
of Men: American Dreams and the Flight from Commitment* (1983) and *The
Worst Years of Our Lives: Irreverent Notes on a Decade of Greed* (1991).

In the following essay, which was originally published in 1992,
Ehrenreich explores her lack of identification with a cultural and
religious heritage. Ironically, Ehrenreich's lack of "tradition" is in
itself a family tradition. She was born in 1941 in the mining town
of Butte, Montana, to a family who was proud that they had been
"free thinkers" for many years: "I am a fourth- or fifth-generation
atheist. This has been a tradition in my family since the late nineteenth century. . . . I grew up with stories . . . of great defiance."
Further, she says, "a lot of the miners were atheists because it was
part of the general class resentment. They equated the clergy
with lawyers and doctors and bosses—guys who sat around and
didn't do anything while other men broke their backs and risked
their lives."

Ehrenreich is a cultural critic whose work focuses on issues of
class, race, and dissent. In response to a question about the role
of secular humanism in American political thought, Ehrenreich recently explained, "There's a wonderful anecdote . . . about a rabbi
who advises anybody who has been in trouble, anybody who's
really hurting, to go see an atheist, because an atheist will not expect God to take care of you; an atheist knows he or she has to
take that responsibility. And to me, that's the core of it. We can

engage in all kinds of speculation about whether or not there is some conscious force outside of us at work in the universe. But if we are secular humanists, we accept the responsibility to do everything we can in our lives to ease human suffering."

As you read, notice how Ehrenreich uses a variety of examples to present her own very distinctive definition of an "ideal cultural heritage."

AN ACQUAINTANCE WAS TELLING ME about the joys of rediscovering 1 her ethnic and religious heritage. "I know exactly what my ancestors were doing 2,000 years ago," she said, eyes gleaming with enthusiasm, "and *I can do the same things now.*" Then she leaned forward and inquired politely, "And what is your ethnic background, if I may ask?"

"None," I said, that being the first word in line to get out of my 2 mouth. Well, not "none," I backtracked. Scottish, English, Irish—that was something, I supposed. Too much Irish to qualify as a WASP; too much of the hated English to warrant a "Kiss Me, I'm Irish" button; plus there are a number of dead ends in the family tree due to adoptions, missing records, failing memories and the like. I was blushing by this time. Did "none" mean I was rejecting my heritage out of Anglo-Celtic self-hate? Or was I revealing a hidden ethnic chauvinism in which the Britannically derived served as a kind of neutral standard compared with the ethnic "others"?

Throughout the 60's and 70's, I watched one group after another— 3 African-Americans, Latinos, Native Americans—stand up and proudly reclaim their roots while I just sank back ever deeper into my seat. All this excitement over ethnicity stemmed, I uneasily sensed, from a past in which *their* ancestors had been trampled upon by *my* ancestors, or at least by people who looked very much like them. In addition, it had begun to seem almost un-American not to have some sort of hyphen at hand, linking one to more venerable times and locales.

But the truth is, I was raised with none. We'd eaten ethnic foods in 4 my childhood home, but these were all borrowed, like the pasties, or Cornish meat pies, my father had picked up from his fellow miners in Butte, Montana. If my mother had one rule, it was militant ecumenism in all matters of food and experience. "Try new things," she would say, meaning anything from sweetbreads to clams, with an emphasis on the "new."

As a child, I briefly nourished a craving for tradition and roots. I   5
immersed myself in the works of Sir Walter Scott. I pretended to believe that the bagpipe was a musical instrument. I was fascinated to learn from a grandmother that we were descended from certain Highland clans and longed for a pleated skirt in one of their distinctive tartans.

But in "Ivanhoe," it was the dark-eyed "Jewess" Rebecca I identified   6
with, not the flaxen-haired bimbo Rowena. As for clans: Why not call them "tribes," those bands of half-clad peasants and warriors whose idea of cuisine was stuffed sheep gut washed down with whisky? And then there was the sting of Disraeli's remark—which I came across in my early teens—to the effect that his ancestors had been leading orderly, literate lives when my ancestors were still rampaging through the Highlands daubing themselves with blue paint.

Motherhood put the screws on me, ethnicity-wise. I had hoped   7
that by marrying a man of Eastern European–Jewish ancestry I would acquire for my descendants the ethnic genes that my own forebears so sadly lacked. At one point, I even subjected the children to a seder of my own design, including a little talk about the flight from Egypt and its relevance to modern social issues. But the kids insisted on buttering their matzohs and snickering through my talk. "Give me a break, Mom," the older one said. "You don't even believe in God."

After the tiny pagans had been put to bed, I sat down to brood over   8
Elijah's wine. What had I been thinking? The kids knew that their Jewish grandparents were secular folks who didn't hold seders themselves. And if ethnicity eluded me, how could I expect it to take root in my children, who are not only Scottish-English-Irish, but Hungarian-Polish-Russian to boot?

But, then, on the fumes of Manischewitz, a great insight took form   9
in my mind. It was true, as the kids said, that I didn't "believe in God." But this could be taken as something very different from an accusation—a reminder of a genuine heritage. My parents had not believed in God either, nor had my grandparents or any other progenitors going back to the great-great level. They had become disillusioned with Christianity generations ago—just as, on the in-law side, my children's other ancestors

had shaken off their Orthodox Judaism. This insight did not exactly furnish me with an "identity," but it was at least something to work with: we are the kind of people, I realized—whatever our distant ancestors' religions—who do *not* believe, who do not carry on traditions, who do not do things just because someone has done them before.

The epiphany went on: I recalled that my mother never introduced   10
a procedure for cooking or cleaning by telling me, "Grandma did it this way." What did Grandma know, living in the days before vacuum cleaners and disposable toilet mops? In my parents' general view, new things were better than old, and the very fact that some rituals had been performed in the past was a good reason for abandoning it now. Because what was the past, as our forebears knew it? Nothing but poverty, superstition and grief. "Think for yourself," Dad used to say. "Always ask why."

In fact, this may have been the ideal cultural heritage for my partic-   11
ular ethnic strain—bounced as it was from the Highlands of Scotland across the sea, out to the Rockies, down into the mines and finally spewed out into high-tech, suburban America. What better philosophy, for a race of migrants, than "Think for yourself"? What better maxim, for people whose whole world was rudely inverted every 30 years or so, than "Try new things"?

The more tradition-minded, the newly enthusiastic celebrants of   12
Purim and Kwanzaa and Solstice, may see little point to survival if the survivors carry no cultural freight—religion, for example, or ethnic tradition. To which I would say that skepticism, curiosity and wide-eyed ecumenical tolerance are also worthy elements of the human tradition and are at least as old as such notions as "Serbian" or "Croatian," "Scottish" or "Jewish." I make no claims for my personal line of progenitors except that they remained loyal to the values that may have induced all of our ancestors, long, long ago, to climb down from the trees and make their way into the open plains.

A few weeks ago, I cleared my throat and asked the children, now   13
mostly grown and fearsomely smart, whether they felt any stirrings of ethnic or religious identity, etc., which might have been, ahem, insufficiently nourished at home. "None," they said, adding firmly, "and the world would be a better place if nobody else did, either." My chest swelled with pride, as would my mother's, to know that the race of "none" marches on.

ⓒ Opening the Dialogue

1. Do you believe it is possible for Ehrenreich to shed her "cultural baggage"? Is she doing her children a favor by freeing them of this baggage, or is she depriving them, and herself, of something valuable?

2. In a letter commenting on this essay, a reader says that Ehrenreich is able to have the luxury of calling herself "none of the above" only because she is white. People of color, the writer argues, have their cultural baggage forced upon them by others. Do you think this is true? Do you believe *all* whites have this "luxury"?

3. In paragraph 2 Ehrenreich wonders whether claiming to have no ethnic background really means she is "rejecting [her] heritage out of Anglo-Celtic self-hate." Do you think she actually has such feelings of hatred or shame, or does she imply a basic respect and affection for her heritage? Do you think she feels the same way about her husband's heritage? Her children's?

ⓒ Keeping a Notebook

What connotations does the word *baggage* have for you? What other terms could Ehrenreich have used to convey her point?

ⓒ Working Together

Working in groups, list the advantages individuals gain from carrying "cultural baggage." In class discussion, explore the idea of cultural baggage on a more global level. At what point does the so-called cultural baggage carried by individuals or groups within a nation (for example, the Serbs and Croats Ehrenreich mentions) weaken or even threaten that nation?

⚙ Writing an Essay

Should various groups blend together to find a common cultural identity, or should each group continue to proclaim and celebrate its own cultural identity? Would the world really be, as Ehrenreich suggests, a better place if people had no ethnic or religious identity? Write an essay in which you define a society that achieves an ideal balance between these two extremes.

Writing: Culture and Identity

1. What does *success* mean to you? Do you define it, for example, in terms of education, professional status, economic level, or personal fulfillment? In defining success, you may include information about how your definition has evolved over the years, an explanation of how your definition differs from you parents' or friends' definitions, or examples of achievements that constitute success for you.

2. Define a word used among members of your culture or community that you believe would be unfamiliar to others from different backgrounds. Expand your definition with examples that illustrate how the word is used in various situations.

3. Define the term *educated* by considering the various components required for a thorough, balanced education (either formal or informal).

4. How do you interpret the term *melting pot*? Write a definition of a community or society that you believe qualifies as a true melting pot. You may take a positive or negative view of this community.

5. How do you define yourself? Do you see your identity in terms of your age, gender, race, sexual orientation, economic class, religion, ethnicity, talents, family role, marital status, intended profession, abilities, appearance—or in terms of several of these criteria?

CHAPTER 10

CULTURE AND
DIVERSITY
TAKING A STAND

GARRETT KELLEY, "SOUNDS OF THE SUBWAY" (1992)

We Puerto Ricans who have been raised in the United States must fight not only against a society that insists we should be American, but also against ourselves. We must struggle to find a place for ourselves within the two cultures: Puerto Rican and American. Some Puerto Ricans choose to assimilate, to become part of the "melting pot," preferring to ignore their culture rather than confronting the problems that arise because of it. They may change their names, refuse to speak Spanish, deny their heritage, or simply refuse to have anything to do with the Puerto Rican community. Although such assimilation can be successful, it can also be harmful. These people may identify themselves as American rather than Puerto Rican, but their action does not ensure that others will accept them. As a result, they may find themselves ostracized by both groups. And, by denying their heritage, they also deny themselves and future generations the opportunity to be part of a rich and diverse ethnic culture.

Ivelys Figueroa, student

Culture and Diversity

Much of the writing you do requires you to take a stand. **Persuasion**—the use of various strategies to influence the opinions of readers—enables you to convey your ideas at school, on the job, and in your social and political lives. Because the interaction of various cultures can inspire divergent points of view, persuasion is a natural strategy for writers seeking to discuss America's cultures. When writers in this chapter examine various aspects of the American experience, they use persuasion to gain an audience's confidence, agreement, or acceptance. Unlike the writers whose essays appear in the other chapters, they do not simply state their ideas and support them with examples. They assume controversy; they expect that their ideas must be defended and that opposing arguments must be taken into consideration and refuted.

Writers can use persuasion to convince readers that a problem exists and that something should be done to correct it. They can, for example, try to persuade readers that current laws regulating immigration to the United States unfairly exclude those fleeing economic oppression. They can argue for or against the idea that people with disabilities should have access to jobs, education, and medical care. Writers can also use persuasion to address points of view with which they disagree. For example, they can refute the argument that racial, ethnic, and gender stereotyping in current films has little or no effect on viewers' attitudes.

The writers in this chapter use persuasion to convince readers that their ideas about culture and diversity are worth accepting. In "The Cult of Ethnicity, Good and Bad" (p. 445) Arthur Schlesinger, Jr., uses logic as his primary method of persuading readers that their excessive celebration of ethnic values could undermine the unity of the United States. To develop a convincing case, he uses facts and expert testimony. Schlesinger hopes that even readers who disagree with his ideas will acknowledge the strength of his evidence and the soundness of his argument. In addition, he relies on his reputation as a historian and well-known author to help him make his case. The many examples he uses and his references to historical figures also enhance his credibility with readers.

In "A Haitian Father" (p. 451) A. M. Rosenthal relies on emotion to convince readers that Haitians, like other immigrants fleeing economic hardships and oppression, should be allowed to enter this country freely. Unlike the other writers in this chapter, Rosenthal relies almost totally on anecdotal evidence to establish his case. Drawing an analogy between his father—who illegally crossed the Canadian border into the United States—and present-day Haitian immigrants, Rosenthal calls upon the United States to change its immigration policy. Although anecdotal evidence is open to the charge that it is limited and almost totally subjective, it can have a very powerful emotional appeal—as "A Haitian Father" illustrates.

Other writers in this chapter use both emotion and logic to support their points about culture and diversity. In "Let's Tell the Story of All America's Cultures" (p. 434) Ji-Yeon Mary Yuhfill addresses the objections some people have to a multicultural curriculum. In addition to presenting a solidly reasoned argument, she tells of the discrimination she faced every day as she went through school. By appealing to her readers' sense of fair play, she encourages them to accept her ideas. Yuhfill's emotional appeal is especially convincing because it is supported with facts.

Martin Luther King, Jr., also uses a combination of emotional and logical appeals to accomplish his purpose. In "I Have a Dream" (p. 427), historical analysis is combined with passionate oratory to present a powerful message to readers. King's use of analogy ("America has defaulted on this promissory note. . . . "), repetition ("I have a dream today. I have a dream that one day. . . . "), quotation ("Free at last! Thank God almighty. . . ."), and allusion ("Five score years ago. . . . ") aims directly at readers' hearts as well as their intellects.

In your own writing, persuasion can help you communicate your ideas about cultural diversity to your readers. For example, you could argue that immigration restrictions should be eased, or even eliminated, because new immigrants are good for the United States. Or, you could argue that immigration should be severely limited because the United States needs to provide for its own citizens first. More specifically, you could use persuasion to propose solutions to problems. You could write an essay proposing changes in a history course to reflect the cultural diversity of your school, or you could argue for the support of ethnically diverse neighborhoods in your hometown. You could also use persuasion to refute arguments with which you disagree. You could, for example, refute the argument made by one of the writers in this chapter.

The following student essay uses persuasion to convince readers that the differences among cultures need not divide people.

STUDENT VOICE: LEONA THOMAS

Black and White

Who am I? In a society that is so defined by black or white, 1 where do I belong? I am both black and white, yet in many people's eyes, I am neither. *Half and half, interracial, mixed, mulatto, oreo,* and *zebra* are but a few of the names that are used to describe me, but when the form says "choose one," none of these terms is listed. Do

I choose *white, black,* or *other?* And why should I always have to choose, not only on forms but everywhere, and then fight to be accepted? As far as I am concerned, I should not have to.

Looking at me, most people assume I am white. My skin color is   2
usually fair although I tan very easily. My hair, although dark and curly, is "white" hair. It is very easy for me to blend into the white community. My presence rarely causes the uneasy reactions that often occur when someone black enters a predominantly white social setting. I am accepted as one of the group and treated as such unless I identify myself otherwise.

"Why not just pass? Why tell anyone?" I've been asked on sev-   3
eral occasions—as if I should be ashamed of being black. I am embarrassed to admit there were times in my life when I did pass because I couldn't handle the sudden rejection. I have had "friends" never speak to me again, parents forbid their children to play with me, job offers suddenly evaporate; I have been forced to leave places where I was previously welcome and even physically assaulted when people found out that my father is black. Although I will no longer deny who I am, people still assume I am white, and there are still conflicts when I am identified.

When I try to enter the black community, there is a very differ-   4
ent reaction. Here too I am assumed to be white and immediately identified as an outsider. Often, instead of being welcomed into the black community, I have to defend my right to be there. To some, I will never be black enough. To many others, my acceptance is conditional: I'm all right as long as I don't listen to white music, "dress white," or associate with too many white people.

When I was growing up, the line between the two cultures was   5
very distinct. Because my parents were divorced when I was young,
I lived at the extremes: poor black neighborhoods in the city and
comfortable white suburbs. I encountered constant conflicts as I
went from one neighborhood to another, but I always thought that
things would change when I left the neighborhoods to go to college. I believed that once I achieved a certain level of education,
people would begin to accept me as I am. I received a rude awakening on my first day at school.

My roommate and I had exchanged phone calls, letters, and pic-   6
tures over the summer. She came from a white southern family, but
we appeared to be compatible, with enough interests in common
to get along. When I finally met her and her parents on move-in
day, everything seemed fine at first. Later, though, when they met
my father, their attitude suddenly changed. My roommate's cool-
ness continued throughout the year.

My problem was not limited to the white community. Having   7
identified myself as a black student, I received invitations to become a member of two black sororities, the Society of Black Engi-
neers, and the Black Student Union. When I went to join these
organizations, I received very mixed reactions. At one of the black
sororities, I was asked to leave. At the other, after my invitation had
been checked three times, I was allowed to stay at the meeting but
ignored. I was welcomed as a member of the Society of Black Engi-
neers, but the true surprise was the Black Student Union. Since the
Black Student Union was at the time controlled by a militant separatist president, my presence at the meeting caused a considerable

stir. I was asked to leave, and when I and a few others protested, we were threatened and forced out. Anonymous threats against me and some of my friends continued for almost a month. I decided I really did not want to be part of a group with those values.

Being the child of a white mother and a black father is no longer   8
a daily conflict in my life. I have surrounded myself with friends who are supportive, and I have accepted myself as I am. Now, when a situation occurs that throws me back to that freshman at college defending myself and questioning my right to be somewhere, I no longer accept the problems as being my fault. I will no longer compromise myself to let someone, white or black, force me to accept or condone racism.

Where do I belong? The answer should be wherever I decide.   9
Unfortunately, that sometimes means fighting for that right and not always winning. Who am I? I am black and white, both races, both cultures, and both heritages. It is not possible for me to separate one from the other, nor do I want to. It is time for people to start accepting me and other people who are combinations of any races for who we are. Yes, there are differences among the cultures in this society, but it is time to realize that these differences do not need to define opposing poles. Racism and hatred only divide people; it is time to start building bridges and to stop destroying one another.

Taking a Stand

Persuasion is the means by which a writer secures the confidence of readers and either moves them to action or convinces them to accept an idea. Persuasive essays appeal to readers in three ways. A persuasive essay can appeal to the *emotions*—relying on language calculated to stir the passions of a particular audience. A persuasive essay can also appeal to the *intellect*—finding arguments that logically persuade readers. Finally, a persuasive essay can focus on the *character of the writer*—emphasizing his or her knowledge or fairness to gain the trust of a reader. Even though some essays use just one of these strategies, many of the most effective persuasive essays rely on all three—appealing to a reader's emotions, logic, and impression of the writer.

The following paragraph, excerpted from "Letter from Birmingham Jail" by Martin Luther King, Jr., illustrates a number of techniques that are characteristic of persuasive writing. Written in 1963, at a time when African Americans were struggling for basic civil rights, this essay asserts that individuals have the obligation to disobey unjust laws.

We have waited for more than 340 years for our constitutional and Godgiven rights. The nations of Asia and Africa are moving with jetlike speed toward gaining political independence, but we still creep at horse-and-buggy pace toward gaining a cup of coffee at a lunch counter. Perhaps it is easy for those who have never felt the stinging darts of segregation to say, "Wait." But when you have seen vicious mobs lynch your mothers and fathers at will and drown your sisters and brothers at whim; when you have seen hate-filled policemen curse, kick, and even kill your black brothers and sisters; when you see the vast majority of your twenty million Negro brothers smothering in an airtight cage of poverty in the midst of an affluent society; when you suddenly find your tongue twisted and your speech stammering as you seek to explain to your six-year-old daughter why she can't go to the public amusement park that has just been advertised on television, and see the tears welling up her eyes when she is told that Funtown is closed to colored children, and see the ominous clouds of inferiority beginning to form in her little mental sky, and see her beginning to destroy her personality by developing an unconscious bitterness toward white people; when you have to concoct an answer for a five-year-old son who is asking, "Daddy, why do white people treat colored people so mean?"; when you take a cross-country drive and find it necessary to sleep night after night in uncomfortable corners of your automobile because no motel will accept you; when you are humiliated day in and day out by nagging signs reading "white" and "colored"; when your first name becomes "nigger," your middle name becomes "boy" (however old you are), and your last name becomes "John," and your wife and mother are never given the respected title "Mrs."; when you are harried by day and haunted by night by the fact that you are a Negro, living constantly at tiptoe stance, never quite knowing what to expect next, and are plagued with inner fears and outer resentments; when you are forever fighting a degenerating sense of "nobodiness"—then you will understand why we find it difficult to wait. There comes a time when the cup of endurance runs over, and men are no longer willing to be plunged into the abyss of despair. I hope, sirs, you can understand our legitimate and unavoidable impatience.

In this passage King appeals to his readers' emotions by discussing the pain and anguish he feels when he must explain to his children why they are victims of discrimination. King purposely chooses examples with which his readers will identify—a child excluded from an amusement park, a man forced to sleep in his car, humiliating signs and modes of address. As King presents these examples, he acknowledges his readers' possible objections and assures them of his good will ("I hope, sirs, you can understand. . . . "). Overstating his case or presenting it in an overly passionate way would most likely cause readers to doubt his accuracy or question his motives.

Notice also how King uses logic in this passage. He begins by saying that some people think African Americans should stop protesting and give conditions more time to improve. After thoroughly supporting the point that segregation is widespread and damaging, King states his conclusion—which by this time seems self-evident—that all people should understand why African Americans can no longer wait. Not only does King make his case, but he also refutes a major objection that some readers may have to his actions.

Finally, notice how King establishes himself as a trustworthy and knowledgeable person. Throughout the passage King shows that he has personally suffered as a result of racial discrimination and segregation. As he does so, he displays a remarkable capacity to maintain a balanced view of the situation and to treat those who disagree with him fairly. His sincerity and his composure reassure readers that he is an honorable person who deserves a hearing.

USING INDUCTIVE OR DEDUCTIVE REASONING

When you write a persuasive essay, you *use inductive or deductive reasoning, or a combination of the two.* **Inductive reasoning** moves from particular to general, beginning with a series of specific examples and proceeding to a general conclusion. For example, if you observe that there are a disproportionately large number of Korean produce merchants in a particular neighborhood, you could conclude that Korean merchants dominate the produce trade in this area. If you repeatedly buy high-quality produce from one of these stores, you could conclude that the store carries high-quality fruits and vegetables.

A conclusion reached through inductive reasoning is never certain, only probable: you must make an *inductive leap* every time you use specific observations to draw a general conclusion. The more evidence you supply, the smaller the gap between your observations and your generalizations, and the more likely your readers will be to accept your conclusion. If you reach a conclusion based on too little evidence, you will be accused of jumping to a conclusion or making a premature inductive leap. As you revise, be sure that your inductive arguments are supported by sufficient evidence—examples, statistics, or expert opinion, for example.

Unlike inductive reasoning, **deductive reasoning** moves from general to particular, beginning with the conclusion and moving to specific situations. Deductive arguments follow a three-step form of reasoning called a *syllogism*. The syllogism begins with a general statement, the *major premise*. It is followed by a specific statement, the *minor premise*, about a member of the group defined by the major premise. The syllogism ends with a *conclusion* about the member of the group defined in the minor premise. The following syllogism illustrates this structure:

MAJOR PREMISE: In 1900, garment workers on the Lower East Side were not union members.

MINOR PREMISE: My grandfather was a garment worker on the Lower East Side in 1900.

CONCLUSION: Therefore, my grandfather was not a union member.

The strength of deductive reasoning is its certainty. Unlike inductive conclusions, deductive conclusions require no leap in reasoning. If you grant a syllogism's major and minor premises, you must also grant its conclusion.

To be sound, a syllogism must be *valid*—logically consistent—and *true*. If a syllogism contains faulty logic or is based on false assumptions, it is both invalid and untrue and therefore unsound. Be sure that you do not begin your argument with a *sweeping generalization*—a conclusion that is usually sound applied to a situation for which it is not justified—or a *hasty generalization*—a conclusion based on too little evidence. You should also be certain that your deductive argument is based on premises that are factually accurate. The following syllogism contains a *false premise* and is therefore untrue:

MAJOR PREMISE: All minorities are entitled to affirmative action consideration for college admission.
MINOR PREMISE: Italian students are members of a minority group.
CONCLUSION: Therefore, Italian students are entitled to affirmative action consideration for college admission.

The major premise of the syllogism is false: not all minorities are entitled to affirmative action consideration. Because large numbers of Italian students attend college, they are not granted minority status for the purpose of college admissions. Even though the conclusion follows from the premises, the syllogism is unsound.

The deductive arguments you will make in your essays will not be as simple as the ones contained in syllogisms. Often they will be in the form of *enthymemes*—arguments that have missing or implied premises that readers are supposed to accept. For example, the slogan "Buy American" is actually an enthymeme. Once you supply the missing premises, you can easily see that slogans such as these can oversimplify very complicated problems.

MAJOR PREMISE: All Americans should buy goods manufactured in the United States.
MINOR PREMISE: You are an American.
CONCLUSION: Therefore, you should buy goods manufactured in the United States.

Although you may use enthymemes in your persuasive essays, be certain that the implied premises are not illogical, misleading, or untrue. Careful readers will realize what premises are implied and will question the accuracy of your thinking.

Citing Authorities

As you plan and write persuasive essays, one way to strengthen your case is to *cite the opinions of authorities*. Many professional writers support their claims by citing experts. As you revise, however, keep in mind that readers must be able to identify the source of an opinion to judge its usefulness and its accuracy. Unidentified spokespersons or so-called reliable sources may pass for evidence in the popular press, but they have no place in academic writing. As you revise, then, make certain that you have identified all your sources and that you have acknowledged any disagreements that may exist between them. Selective use of expert opinion—presenting only those who agree with you and ignoring those who disagree—is unfair and unethical. If you encounter two experts who disagree, present both sides of the issue and give your evaluation of their positions. Finally, make certain that the expert you are citing actually has credibility in the area you are discussing. The opinion of a person who won a Nobel Prize in physics, for example, has little value in a paper about IQ testing and racial stereotypes.

Refuting Opposing Arguments

When you plan your essay, prepare to *refute opposing arguments*. As you write and revise, make certain that you have addressed all the major arguments against your position. Identifying these arguments in advance and demonstrating that they are illogical or untrue will help you construct a compelling case. For example, if you were arguing for bilingual education in the public schools, you would have to deal with at least some of the following objections advanced by those who oppose your position:

- Bilingual students take too long to master English.
- Students' traditional culture is reinforced by bilingual education; therefore, students have difficulty assimilating.
- Bilingual education helps create a permanent underclass.

- Bilingual education fragments our culture into a series of subcultures.

Remember, an effective argument does not ignore opposing views; it defines opposing points of view and addresses them. If you find that a particular argument is strong, concede its strength. This technique will demonstrate to readers that you are a reasonable person. In "Black and White" (p. 415) Leona Thomas concedes the strength of an opposing argument. Realizing that many white readers will not understand why she does not just "pass," she acknowledges that there were times in her life when she did. She goes on, however, to say that she no longer denies who she is, despite the price she sometimes has to pay. By dealing with the issue in this way, Leona shows that she is fallible like everyone else and encourages readers to identify with her dilemma.

RECOGNIZING FALLACIES

Logical fallacies are gaps in logic that can seriously undermine your essay. As you revise, *watch for logical fallacies* that commonly occur in arguments.

POST HOC THINKING The *post hoc* fallacy (from the Latin *post hoc, ergo propter hoc,* meaning "after this, therefore because of this") occurs when you say that because one event preceded the other, the first event caused the second (see Chapter 6). For example, immediately after Vietnamese immigrant fishermen settled along the Gulf Coast of Texas, the shrimp population of the area declined. Some people linked the two events and blamed the Vietnamese fishermen for the problem. The causes of the decline of the shrimp-fishing industry were actually quite complex. For one thing, the shrimpers had been overfishing the Gulf for years, well before the Vietnamese arrived. In addition, pollution that ran into the Gulf after spring flooding had killed large numbers of shrimp. Certainly the Vietnamese fishermen put additional strain on the Texas shrimp-fishing industry, but they were not solely responsible for its decline. In fact, if the other factors were not present, the problem could have been easily corrected. As you revise, make sure you have not concluded that a cause-and-effect relationship exists where one does not. Make certain that you have considered all the major factors that have contributed to the situation you are discussing.

AD HOMINEM ARGUMENT The *ad hominem* fallacy (from the Latin, meaning "to the man") occurs when you attack the person making an argument rather than the argument itself. This can occur inadvertently—especially when you try to appeal to readers' emotions—or it can be a purposeful strategy calculated to distract readers from the real issues. At their worst, *ad hominem* arguments can be racial slurs or personal attacks. A politician may call women who have abortions murderers; an editorial writer may portray Arab-American activists as terrorists; the writer of a letter to a newspaper may characterize Haitian immigrants as opportunists: All are committing ad hominem fallacies. As you revise, remember that a personal attack is no substitute for a well-reasoned argument.

NON SEQUITUR REASONING A *non sequitur* (from the Latin, meaning "it does not follow") occurs when you draw a conclusion that is not supported by the evidence. Consider the following statement:

> Urban ethnic neighborhoods are disappearing; therefore, ethnic ties are weakening.

Certainly some ethnic neighborhoods are disappearing, but this fact does not prove that ethnic ties are weakening. Indeed, the fact that ethnic neighborhoods are gradually disappearing may be irrelevant to the conclusion. In order to establish the validity of the claim, the writer must provide evidence to support it.

BEGGING THE QUESTION Begging the question occurs when you present a debatable point as if it were true. In a recent speech, a presidential candidate said that no good American would deny the idea that welfare saps a person's desire to work. This statement begs the question because it assumes that the term *good American* already has been defined. In addition, the speaker does not prove that so-called good Americans would agree with his conclusion about welfare. In its extreme form such reasoning is circular: Aliens should be barred from the United States because they are alien to its culture.

BANDWAGON FALLACY This fallacy occurs when you lead readers to believe that just because a belief is widely held, it must be true. In effect, you ask readers to climb aboard the bandwagon and follow the crowd. Statements like "everyone knows . . . " and "hundreds of people believe . . . " attempt to present consensus as proof. Careful readers will realize, however, that a position's popularity does not make it true.

UNFAIR APPEALS TO THE EMOTIONS

Appeals to the emotions are most effective when they are supported by evidence. Leona Thomas's essay illustrates this point. Although she appeals to her readers' emotions—through the list of racial epithets in the introduction, for example—she also supports her argument with examples. By describing specific instances of the prejudice she faces daily because she is a mixed-race child, she introduces readers to a situation that is unfamiliar to them. These examples bolster her case and, along with her emotional appeal, lead readers to the conclusion that differences between cultures need not divide individuals.

Emotional appeals can be destructive, however, when they are used to appeal to readers' baser instincts. Demagogues frequently exhort listeners to preserve the purity of their country, their race, or their religion. Quite often such writers address the fears of readers and attempt to exploit them for their own ends. As you write and revise, be sure to *avoid unfair appeals to the emotions*. Remember, many readers know that an emotional response is not the best basis for a decision. They will see beyond attempts to gain their sympathy and look for the evidence that supports your case. Unsupported appeals to fear or pity often backfire and cause readers to think you are trying to divert their attention from the real issues.

REVIEW CHECKLIST: TAKING A STAND
✓ Use inductive or deductive reasoning, or a combination of the two.
✓ Cite the opinions of authorities.
✓ Refute opposing arguments.
✓ Watch for logical fallacies.
✓ Avoid unfair appeals to the emotions.

Martin Luther King, Jr.

I Have a Dream

"Rarely has one individual, espousing so difficult a philosophy, served as a catalyst for so much significant social change. . . . There are few men of whom it can be said that their lives changed the world." The judgment of two of Martin Luther King's biographers, Flip Schulke and Penelope O. McPhee, is echoed in the national remembrance of a man who may be the most influential and revered African American in our history.

Born on January 15, 1929, in Atlanta, Georgia, King attended Morehouse College and was ordained a Baptist minister in 1948. After being introduced to the philosophy of Mahatma Gandhi, King embraced nonviolence as a method of social reform. The first test of King's commitment to nonviolent reform came in 1955 during a boycott of the segregated bus system in Montgomery, Alabama. Protesters were often met with violent retaliation, but despite threats, arrest, and the bombing of his home, King (and the boycott) prevailed. By 1957 King had become an international spokesman for civil rights. A *Time* magazine cover story called him "a scholarly Baptist minister . . . who in little more than a year has risen from nowhere to become one of the nation's remarkable leaders of men."

As the leader of the burgeoning civil rights movement, King continued to espouse nonviolence. On August 28, 1963, over 250,000 Americans marched on Washington to demand equal rights for blacks, other minorities, and the poor. There, on the steps of the Capitol, King delivered the following speech, said by his biographers to be the "most eloquent of his career." "I Have a Dream" has become for millions a stirring symbol of the fight for human rights. "The orderly conduct of the massive march was an active tribute to [King's] philosophy of nonviolence," write his biographers. "Equally significant, his speech made his voice familiar to the world and lives today as one of the most moving orations of our time."

In 1964 King was named "Man of the Year" by *Time*, the first African-American man to be so honored; in December of that year he became the youngest person ever to receive the Nobel Peace Prize. In succeeding years, his commitment to the cause never wavered. On April 3, 1968, the day before his tragic assassination in Memphis, Tennessee, King gave a speech that was both a prophesy of his death and a challenge to those he left behind: "We've got some difficult days ahead, but it doesn't really matter now, because I've been to the mountaintop. . . . And I've seen the promised land. I may not go there with you. But I want you to know tonight that we as a people will get to the promised land."

If you can, listen to the following speech on audio or videotape. (Many libraries include such holdings.) Notice how King's repetition of phrases and sentence patterns contributes to his persuasive effect.

F IVE SCORE YEARS AGO, a great American, in whose symbolic shadow   1
we stand, signed the Emancipation Proclamation. This momentous decree came as a great beacon light of hope to millions of Negro slaves who had been seared in the flames of withering injustice. It came as a joyous daybreak to end the long night of captivity.

But one hundred years later, we must face the tragic fact that the   2
Negro is still not free. One hundred years later, the life of the Negro is still sadly crippled by the manacles of segregation and the chains of discrimination. One hundred years later, the Negro lives on a lonely island of poverty in the midst of a vast ocean of material prosperity. One hundred years later, the Negro is still languishing in the corners of American society and finds himself an exile in his own land. So we have come here today to dramatize an appalling condition.

In a sense we have come to our nation's capital to cash a check.   3
When the architects of our republic wrote the magnificent words of the Constitution and the Declaration of Independence, they were signing a promissory note to which every American was to fall heir. This note was

a promise that all men—yes, black men as well as white men—would be guaranteed the unalienable rights of life, liberty, and the pursuit of happiness.

It is obvious today that America has defaulted on this promissory   4
note insofar as her citizens of color are concerned. Instead of honoring this sacred obligation, America has given the Negro people a bad check, a check which has come back marked "insufficient funds." But we refuse to believe that there are insufficient funds in the great vaults of opportunity of this nation. So we have come to cash this check—a check that will give us upon demand the riches of freedom and the security of justice. We have also come to this hallowed spot to remind America of the fierce urgency of *now*. This is no time to engage in the luxury of cooling off or to take the tranquilizing drugs of gradualism. *Now* is the time to make real the promises of Democracy. *Now* is the time to rise from the dark and desolate valley of segregation to the sunlit path of racial justice. *Now* is the time to open the doors of opportunity to all of God's children. *Now* is the time to lift our nation from the quicksands of racial injustice to the solid rock of brotherhood.

It would be fatal for the nation to overlook the urgency of the mo-   5
ment and to underestimate the determination of the Negro. This sweltering summer of the Negro's legitimate discontent will not pass until there is an invigorating autumn of freedom and equality; 1963 is not an end, but a beginning. Those who hope that the Negro needed to blow off steam and will now be content will have a rude awakening if the nation returns to business as usual. There will be neither rest nor tranquility in America until the Negro is granted his citizenship rights. The whirlwinds of revolt will continue to shake the foundations of our nation until the bright day of justice emerges.

But there is something that I must say to my people who stand on   6
the warm threshold which leads into the palace of justice. In the process of gaining our rightful place we must not be guilty of wrongful deeds. Let us not seek to satisfy our thirst for freedom by drinking from the cup of bitterness and hatred. We must forever conduct our struggle on the high plane of dignity and discipline. We must not allow our creative protest to degenerate into physical violence. Again and again we must rise to the majestic heights of meeting physical force with soul force. The marvelous new militancy which has engulfed the Negro community must not lead us to a distrust of all white people, for many of our white brothers, as

evidenced by their presence here today, have come to realize that their destiny is tied up with our destiny and their freedom is inextricably bound to our freedom. We cannot walk alone.

And as we walk, we must make the pledge that we shall march   7
ahead. We cannot turn back. There are those who are asking the devotees of civil rights, "When will you be satisfied?" We can never be satisfied as long as the Negro is the victim of the unspeakable horrors of police brutality. We can never be satisfied as long as our bodies, heavy with the fatigue of travel, cannot gain lodging in the motels of the highways and the hotels of the cities. We cannot be satisfied as long as the Negro's basic mobility is from a smaller ghetto to a larger one. We can never be satisfied as long as a Negro in Mississippi cannot vote and a Negro in New York believes he has nothing for which to vote. No, no, we are not satisfied, and we will not be satisfied until justice rolls down like waters and righteousness like a mighty stream.

I am not unmindful that some of you have come here out of great   8
trials and tribulations. Some of you have come fresh from narrow jail cells. Some of you have come from areas where your quest for freedom left you battered by the storms of persecution and staggered by the winds of police brutality. You have been the veterans of creative suffering. Continue to work with the faith that unearned suffering is redemptive.

Go back to Mississippi, go back to Alabama, go back to South Car-   9
olina, go back to Georgia, go back to Louisiana, go back to the slums and ghettos of our northern cities, knowing that somehow this situation can and will be changed. Let us not wallow in the valley of despair.

I say to you today, my friends, that in spite of the difficulties and   10
frustrations of the moment I still have a dream. It is a dream deeply rooted in the American dream.

I have a dream that one day this nation will rise up and live out the   11
true meaning of its creed: "We hold these truths to be self-evident, that all men are created equal."

I have a dream that one day on the red hills of Georgia the sons of   12
former slaves and the sons of former slaveowners will be able to sit down together at the table of brotherhood.

I have a dream that one day even the state of Mississippi, a desert   13
state sweltering with the heat of injustice and oppression, will be transformed into an oasis of freedom and justice.

I have a dream that my four little children will one day live in a   14 nation where they will not be judged by the color of their skin but by the content of their character.

    I have a dream today.   15

    I have a dream that one day the state of Alabama, whose governor's 16 lips are presently dripping with the words of interposition and nullification, will be transformed into a situation where little black boys and black girls will be able to join hands with little white boys and white girls and walk together as sisters and brothers.

    I have a dream today.   17

    I have a dream that one day every valley shall be exalted, every hill 18 and mountain shall be made low, the rough places will be made plain, and the crooked places will be made straight, and the glory of the Lord shall be revealed, and all flesh shall see it together.

    This is our hope. This is the faith with which I return to the South. 19 With this faith we will be able to hew out of the mountain of despair a stone of hope. With this faith we will be able to transform the jangling discords of our nation into a beautiful symphony of brotherhood. With this faith we will be able to work together, to pray together, to struggle together, to go to jail together, to stand up for freedom together, knowing that we will be free one day.

    This will be the day when all of God's children will be able to sing 20 with new meaning

> My country, 'tis of thee,
> Sweet land of liberty,
>   Of thee I sing:
> Land where my fathers died,
> Land of the pilgrims' pride,
> From every mountainside,
>   Let freedom ring.

    So let freedom ring from the prodigious hilltops of New Hamp- 21 shire. Let freedom ring from the mighty mountains of New York. Let freedom ring from the heightening Alleghenies of Pennsylvania. Let freedom ring from the snowcapped Rockies of Colorado. Let freedom ring from the curvaceous peaks of California.

    But not only that. Let freedom ring from Stone Mountain of Geor- 22 gia. Let freedom ring from Lookout Mountain of Tennessee. Let freedom ring from every hill and molehill of Mississippi. From every mountain-side, let freedom ring.

When we let freedom ring, when we let it ring from every village   23
and every hamlet, from every state and every city, we will be able to
speed up that day when all of God's children, black men and white men,
Jews and Gentiles, Protestants and Catholics, will be able to join hands
and sing in the words of the old Negro spiritual, "Free at last! Free at last!
Thank God almighty, we are free at last!"

🕯️ Opening the Dialogue

1. Do you consider King's speech optimistic or pessimistic? Do you
think that in spite of his strong criticisms, King has faith in the American
dream?

2. King's speech focuses on the problems faced by African Americans.
What other groups do you think might identify with the sentiments King
expresses?

3. In paragraph 6 King urges his listeners not to resort to violence to
achieve their ends. Under what circumstances, if any, do you believe violence (or the threat of violence) can be justified?

🕯️ Keeping a Notebook

Do any remarks in King's speech seem dated? What changes have occurred since King delivered his speech in 1963 that make some points
seem no longer relevant?

🕯️ Working Together

Working in groups, develop a definition of the American dream. In class
discussion, determine which group's definition best expresses the goals
and aspirations of the diverse people who live in this country.

Writing an Essay

In "A Day in April" (p. 245) Marita Golden quotes a friend who says of King, "He was from another era. He couldn't deal with the ghetto and I think he knew it" (paragraph 7). "How can you talk about love," she continues, "to people who aren't even listening" (paragraph 9)? Write an essay in which you agree or disagree with this criticism, considering how King might modify his speech if he gave it today.

JI-YEON MARY YUHFILL

Let's Tell the Story
of All America's Cultures

"I write," says Ji-Yeon Mary Yuhfill, "because it's high time for us as Asian Americans to assert our place in the American pantheon and help bring about a truly equal and multicultural country. But the truth is that I write because otherwise I would just explode. Explode from the pain of rejection and degradation that is racism, from the heartache of unrequited love because you love America but just can't help feeling it doesn't love you and 'your kind,' from the rebellion that boils up after years of being looked down on for nothing more than the face you were born with. So I write: from my gut about the America I experienced, and from my dreams about the America I envision."

Born Yuh Ji-Yeon in 1965 in Seoul, Korea, Yuhfill immigrated with her family to the United States in 1970 and settled in Chicago. In 1987 she graduated from Stanford University with a master's degree in cognitive science, "a love of writing, and a renewed interest in America as a multicultural country." That deep interest is reflected in the following editorial essay, which was originally printed in the *Philadelphia Inquirer*.

Yuhfill's career has taken her across the country and, indeed, across the world: from Chicago to California to Nebraska, where she worked as an agricultural reporter for the *Omaha World-Herald*; to Long Island, where she was a general assignment reporter for *Newsday*; to the University of Pennsylvania, where she is pursuing a doctorate in history, focusing on America's immigration history; to Korea, where she is currently living and working. In 1990 Yuh Ji-Yeon married a man named Highfill: "We joined not only our lives but also our family names, both of us becoming Yuhfill."

Yuhfill's argument in "Let's Tell the Story of All America's Cultures" is based at first on her own early experiences as a student.
As you read, notice where she broadens the scope of her argument to call for a fundamental change in the curricula America
provides all its students.

I GREW UP HEARING, seeing and almost believing that America was   1
white—albeit with a little black tinged here and there—and that white
was best.

The white people were everywhere in my 1970s Chicago child-   2
hood: Founding Fathers, Lewis and Clark, Lincoln, Daniel Boone, Carnegie, presidents, explorers and industrialists galore. The only black people
were slaves. The only Indians were scalpers.

I never heard one word about how Benjamin Franklin was so im-   3
pressed by the Iroquois federation of nations that he adapted that model
into our system of state and federal government. Or that the Indian tribes
were systematically betrayed and massacred by a greedy young nation
that stole their land and called it the United States.

I never heard one word about how Asian immigrants were among   4
the first to turn California's desert into fields of plenty. Or about Chinese
immigrant Ah Bing, who bred the cherry now on sale in groceries across
the nation. Or that plantation owners in Hawaii imported labor from
China, Japan, Korea and the Philippines to work the sugar cane fields. I
never learned that Asian immigrants were the only immigrants denied
U.S. citizenship, even though they served honorably in World War I. All
the immigrants in my textbook were white.

I never learned about Frederick Douglass, the runaway slave who   5
became a leading abolitionist and statesman, or about black scholar
W.E.B. Du Bois. I never learned that black people rose up in arms against
slavery. Nat Turner wasn't one of the heroes in my childhood history
class.

I never learned that the American Southwest and California were   6
already settled by Mexicans when they were annexed after the Mexican-
American War. I never learned that Mexico once had a problem keeping
land-hungry white men on the U.S. side of the border.

So when other children called me a slant-eyed chink and told me   7 to go back where I came from, I was ready to believe that I wasn't really an American because I wasn't white.

America's bittersweet legacy of struggling and failing and getting   8
another step closer to democratic ideals of liberty and equality and justice for all wasn't for the likes of me, an immigrant child from Korea. The
history books said so.

Well, the history books were wrong.   9

Educators around the country are finally realizing what I realized as   10
a teenager in the library, looking up the history I wasn't getting in school.
America is a multicultural nation, composed of many people with varying
histories and varying traditions who have little in common except their
humanity, a belief in democracy and a desire for freedom.

America changed them, but they changed America too.   11

A committee of scholars and teachers gathered by the New York   12
State Department of Education recognizes this in their recent report,
"One Nation, Many Peoples: A Declaration of Cultural Interdepend-
ence."

They recommend that public schools provide a "multicultural edu-   13
cation, anchored to the shared principles of a liberal democracy."

What that means, according to the report, is recognizing that   14
America was shaped and continues to be shaped by people of diverse
backgrounds. It calls for students to be taught that history is an ongoing
process of discovery and interpretation of the past, and that there is more
than one way of viewing the world.

Thus, the westward migration of white Americans is not just a   15
heroic settling of an untamed wild, but also the conquest of indigenous
peoples. Immigrants were not just white, but Asian as well. Blacks were
not merely passive slaves freed by northern whites, but active fighters for
their own liberation.

In particular, according to the report, the curriculum should help   16
children "to assess critically the reasons for the inconsistencies between
the ideals of the U.S. and social realities. It should provide information
and intellectual tools that can permit them to contribute to bringing reality closer to the ideals."

In other words, show children the good with the bad, and give   17
them the skills to help improve their country. What could be more patri-
otic?

Several dissenting members of the New York committee publicly   18
worry that America will splinter into ethnic fragments if this multicultural
curriculum is adopted. They argue that the committee's report puts the
focus on ethnicity at the expense of national unity.

But downplaying ethnicity will not bolster national unity. The his-   19
tory of America is the story of how and why people from all over the
world came to the United States, and how in struggling to make a better
life for themselves, they changed each other, they changed the country,
and they all came to call themselves Americans.

E pluribus unum. Out of many, one.   20

This is why I, with my Korean background, and my childhood tor-   21
mentors, with their lost-in-the-mist-of-time European backgrounds, are
all Americans.

It is the unique beauty of this country. It is high time we let all our   22
children gaze upon it.

Opening the Dialogue

1. Did you, like Yuhfill, grow up believing that the United States was
white? Did you also believe it was Christian and middle class?

2. Do you think that it is advisable (or possible) for the schools to "tell
the story of all America's cultures"? What do you think would be gained
and lost if they tried?

3. In paragraph 18 Yuhfill says that some educators fear that a multicultural curriculum would cause the United States to "splinter into ethnic
fragments." Do you agree? How would you counter this argument?

Keeping a Notebook

What was your secondary school history curriculum like? Did it stress the
contributions of people of diverse cultures, or did it focus mainly on Europeans?

☞ Working Together

Working in groups, list the ways in which different groups—African Americans, Native Americans, and Latinos, for example—might view Columbus's discovery of America. In class discussion, decide whether or not their viewpoints are valid.

☞ Writing an Essay

Write an essay in which you argue for or against the development of a multicultural curriculum for your school. Make certain that you support your ideas with examples from your own experience and that you refute the obvious arguments against your position.

ISHMAEL REED

America's Multinational Heritage

To say that Ishmael Reed is merely outspoken is to downplay the impact of this prolific writer and critic. Like his writing, Reed's opinions are witty, complex, and deeply felt. A self-described ringleader in the defense of the image of black men, Reed has been called misogynist and paranoid for his criticism of feminist black women like Alice Walker (author of *The Color Purple*). Reed's response is characteristically blunt: "There doesn't seem to be any room in the feminist movement for poor women. This is a palace revolt. . . . Alice Walker lives in Marin County. She ought to go on the road and see that benefits are spread around."

Reed himself lives with his wife and daughter in a tough West Oakland neighborhood, which Reed calls "the front lines" (described in his essay on page 105). He is fiercely dedicated to being "a voice in the wilderness" bent on exposing hypocrisy and injustice. "I was born on February 22—George Washington's birthday," he laughs, "so I'm bound to tell the truth!"

The following selection is from Reed's collection of essays and reviews, *Writin' Is Fightin': Thirty-Seven Years of Boxing on Paper* (1983). His writing, he has explained, is part of the African-American tradition of the "trickster." The trickster uses his wits to deflate pomposity and upset the status quo. In Reed's words, "He prods sacred cows, shows the absurdity of positions and theories people cherish. 'The emperor has no clothes' is a typical trickster observation. I'm naturally ornery and skeptical. Maybe that is what has kept me in the writing business for almost forty years. I'm saying things in a way that other people don't. I can be a conservative one minute and on the left wing the next minute. A trickster's hard to define."

In this essay Reed begins by piling up a number of specific examples before asserting the thesis that those examples support.

At the annual Lower East Side Jewish Festival yesterday, a Chinese woman ate a pizza slice in front of Ty Thuan Duc's Vietnamese grocery store. Beside her a Spanish-speaking family patronized a cart with two signs: "Italian Ices" and "Kosher by Rabbi Alper." And after the pastrami ran out, everybody ate knishes.

　　　　　　　　　　　　　　　　　　　　　(New York Times, 23 June 1983)

ON THE DAY BEFORE MEMORIAL DAY, 1983, a poet called me to describe a city he had just visited. He said that one section included mosques, built by the Islamic people who dwelled there. Attending his reading, he said, were large numbers of Hispanic people, forty thousand of whom lived in the same city. He was not talking about a fabled city located in some mysterious region of the world. The city he'd visited was Detroit.

A few months before, as I was leaving Houston, Texas, I heard it announced on the radio that Texas's largest minority was Mexican American, and though a foundation recently issued a report critical of bilingual education, the taped voice used to guide the passengers on the air trams connecting terminals in Dallas Airport is in both Spanish and English. If the trend continues, a day will come when it will be difficult to travel through some sections of the country without hearing commands in both English and Spanish; after all, for some western states, Spanish was the first written language and the Spanish style lives on in the western way of life.

Shortly after my Texas trip, I sat in an auditorium located on the campus of the University of Wisconsin at Milwaukee as a Yale professor—whose original work on the influence of African cultures upon those of the Americas has led to his ostracism from some monocultural intellectual circles—walked up and down the aisle, like an old-time southern evangelist, dancing and drumming the top of the lectern, illustrating his points before some serious Afro-American intellectuals and artists who cheered and applauded his performance and his mastery of information. The professor was "white." After his lecture, he joined a group of

Milwaukeeans in a conversation. All of the participants spoke Yoruban, though only the professor had ever traveled to Africa.

One of the artists told me that his paintings, which included Afri-   4 can and Afro-American mythological symbols and imagery, were hanging in the local McDonald's restaurant. The next day I went to McDonald's and snapped pictures of smiling youngsters eating hamburgers below paintings that could grace the walls of any of the country's leading museums. The manager of the local McDonald's said, "I don't know what you boys are doing, but I like it," as he commissioned the local painters to exhibit in his restaurant.

Such blurring of cultural styles occurs in everyday life in the   5 United States to a greater extent than anyone can imagine and is probably more prevalent than the sensational conflict between people of different backgrounds that is played up and often encouraged by the media. The result is what the Yale professor, Robert Thompson, referred to as a cultural bouillabaisse, yet members of the nation's present educational and cultural Elect still cling to the notion that the United States belongs to some vaguely defined entity they refer to as "Western civilization," by which they mean, presumably, a civilization created by the people of Europe, as if Europe can be viewed in monolithic terms. Is Beethoven's Ninth Symphony, which includes Turkish marches, a part of Western civilization, or the late nineteenth- and twentieth-century French paintings, whose creators were influenced by Japanese art? And what of the cubists, through whom the influence of African art changed modern painting, or the surrealists, who were so impressed with the art of the Pacific Northwest Indians that, in their map of North America, Alaska dwarfs the lower forty-eight in size?

Are the Russians, who are often criticized for their adoption of   6 "Western" ways by Tsarist dissidents in exile, members of Western civilization? And what of the millions of Europeans who have black African and Asian ancestry, black Africans having occupied several countries for hundreds of years? Are these "Europeans" members of Western civilization, or the Hungarians, who originated across the Urals in a place called Greater Hungary, or the Irish, who came from the Iberian Peninsula?

Even the notion that North America is part of Western civilization   7 because our "system of government" is derived from Europe is being challenged by Native American historians who say that the founding fathers,

Benjamin Franklin especially, were actually influenced by the system of government that had been adopted by the Iroquois hundreds of years prior to the arrival of large numbers of Europeans.

Western civilization, then, becomes another confusing category   8
like Third World, or Judeo-Christian culture, as man attempts to impose his small-screen view of political and cultural reality upon a complex world. Our most publicized novelist recently said that Western civilization was the greatest achievement of mankind, an attitude that flourishes on the street level of scribbles in public restrooms: "White Power," "Niggers and Spics Suck," or "Hitler was a prophet," the latter being the most telling, for wasn't Adolf Hitler the archetypal monoculturalist who, in his pigheaded arrogance, believed that one way and one blood was so pure that it had to be protected from alien strains at all costs? Where did such an attitude, which has caused so much misery and depression in our national life, which has tainted even our noblest achievements, begin? An attitude that caused the incarceration of Japanese-American citizens during World War II, the persecution of Chicanos and Chinese Americans, the near-extermination of the Indians, and the murder and lynchings of thousands of Afro-Americans.

Virtuous, hardworking, pious, even though they occasionally   9
would wander off after some fancy clothes, or rendezvous in the woods with the town prostitute, the Puritans are idealized in our schoolbooks as "a hardy band" of no-nonsense patriarchs whose discipline razed the forest and brought order to the New World (a term that annoys Native American historians). Industrious, responsible, it was their "Yankee ingenuity" and practicality that created the work ethic. They were simple folk who produced a number of good poets, and they set the tone for the American writing style, of lean and spare lines, long before Hemingway. They worshiped in churches whose colors blended in with the New England snow, churches with simple structures and ornate lecterns.

The Puritans were a daring lot, but they had a mean streak. They   10
hated the theater and banned Christmas. They punished people in a cruel and inhuman manner. They killed children who disobeyed their parents. When they came in contact with those whom they considered heathens or aliens, they behaved in such a bizarre and irrational manner that this chapter in the American history comes down to us as a late-movie horror film. They exterminated the Indians, who taught them how to survive in a world unknown to them, and their encounter with the calypso culture

of Barbados resulted in what the tourist guide in Salem's Witches' House refers to as the Witchcraft Hysteria.

The Puritan legacy of hard work and meticulous accounting led to   11
the establishment of a great industrial society; it is no wonder that the American industrial revolution began in Lowell, Massachusetts, but there was the other side, the strange and paranoid attitudes toward those different from the Elect.

The cultural attitudes of that early Elect continue to be voiced in   12
everyday life in the United States: the president of a distinguished university, writing a letter to the *Times*, belittling the study of African civilizations; the television network that promoted its show on the Vatican art with the boast that this art represented "the finest achievements of the human spirit." A modern up-tempo state of complex rhythms that depends upon contacts with an international community can no longer behave as if it dwelled in a "Zion Wilderness" surrounded by beasts and pagans.

When I heard a schoolteacher warn the other night about the inva-   13
sion of the American educational system by foreign curriculums, I wanted to yell at the television set, "Lady, they're already here." It has already begun because the world is here. The world has been arriving at these shores for at least ten thousand years from Europe, Africa, and Asia. In the late nineteenth and early twentieth centuries, large numbers of Europeans arrived, adding their cultures to those of the European, African, and Asian settlers who were already here, and recently millions have been entering the country from South America and the Caribbean, making Yale Professor Bob Thompson's bouillabaisse richer and thicker.

One of our most visionary politicians said that he envisioned a time   14
when the United States could become the brain of the world, by which he meant the repository of all of the latest advanced information systems. I thought of that remark when an enterprising poet friend of mine called to say that he had just sold a poem to a computer magazine and that the editors were delighted to get it because they didn't carry fiction or poetry. Is that the kind of world we desire? A humdrum homogenous world of all brains but no heart, no fiction, no poetry; a world of robots with human attendants bereft of imagination, of culture? Or does North America deserve a more exciting destiny? To become a place where the cultures of the world crisscross. This is possible because the United States is unique in the world: The world is here.

☯ Opening the Dialogue

1. In paragraph 5 Reed says that the media play up conflict between people of different backgrounds and ignore the fact that most of the time these groups seem to get along. Do you agree? If so, why do you think the media do this?

2. Do you agree with Reed when he says, in paragraph 5, that America's cultural and educational elite still cling to the idea that the United States is a country created primarily by people of European origins?

3. Do you think Reed accurately assesses the dangers of monoculturalism, or does he overstate his case? For example, does his analysis of the Puritan heritage in paragraph 10 seem reasonable?

☯ Keeping a Notebook

Walk or drive around the city or town in which you live. What things do you see that indicate the presence of other cultures? Do you see the same signs of diversity that Reed discusses in paragraph 1?

☯ Working Together

Working in groups, list the advantages and disadvantages of a multicultural society. In class discussion debate whether Reed gives an accurate picture of what occurs when people from diverse backgrounds attempt to live together.

☯ Writing an Essay

Write an essay in which you present your plan for the future of the United States. Should it be "a place where the cultures of the world crisscross," or should it be a country that follows only the principles of Western civilization?

Arthur Schlesinger, Jr.

The Cult of Ethnicity, Good and Bad

"Since World War II," declares the *Dictionary of Literary Biography*, "Arthur Meier Schlesinger, Jr., has been perhaps the nation's most widely known and controversial historian." His prodigious literary and scholarly output (author of fifteen works of biography and historical analysis and editor of many more) has earned him two Pulitzer Prizes (for *The Age of Jackson* [1946] and *A Thousand Days: John F. Kennedy and the White House* [1966]) and two National Book Awards (for *A Thousand Days* and *Robert Kennedy and His Times* [1979]), as well as many other awards and honors.

Born in Columbus, Ohio, in 1917, Schlesinger seemed destined for a remarkable career from the beginning. The son of an esteemed historian, he majored in history and literature at Harvard University. His senior honors thesis won critical acclaim and brought Schlesinger several awards and a reputation as a "new and distinguished talent in the field of historical portraiture."

Schlesinger has been a strong presence in American politics as well. He joined President John Kennedy's administration as a special assistant in 1960, and his political activism has sometimes been a source of controversy.

Schlesinger's work emphasizes the importance of historical context in interpreting political approaches to society's needs. In a recent interview, he talked about the need for a sense of history and political awareness in young people: "The nineties will be a much more liberal period. It seems there is a discernible rhythm in our politics. . . . It is a thirty-year cycle. . . . Generations tend to be formed politically by the ideals that are dominant when they come of age politically, between the ages of sixteen and twenty-five. Thirty years later, when their turn in power comes, they tend to carry forward the ideals they imbibed when they were young. . . . I think history is to a nation [what] memory is to an individual. Just as an individual deprived of memory becomes disoriented and doesn't know where he's going or what he's doing, so a nation that has forgotten its history may become disoriented."

In "The Cult of Ethnicity, Good and Bad," Schlesinger argues against the current movement to preserve individual cultures, basing his argument on a fundamental definition of the United States as a country that "escaped the divisiveness of a multiethnic society by a brilliant solution: the creation of a brand-new national identity . . . a new, *American* culture," that transcends its citizens' individual origins.

THE HISTORY OF THE WORLD has been in great part the history of the   1
mixing of peoples. Modern communication and transport accelerate mass migrations from one continent to another. Ethnic and racial diversity is more than ever a salient fact of the age.

But what happens when people of different origins, speaking differ-   2
ent languages and professing different religions, inhabit the same locality and live under the same political sovereignty? Ethnic and racial conflict—far more than ideological conflict—is the explosive problem of our times.

On every side today ethnicity is breaking up nations. The Soviet   3
Union, India, Yugoslavia, Ethiopia, are all in crisis. Ethnic tensions disturb and divide Sri Lanka, Burma, Indonesia, Iraq, Cyprus, Nigeria, Angola, Lebanon, Guyana, Trinidad—you name it. Even nations as stable and civilized as Britain and France, Belgium and Spain, face growing ethnic troubles. Is there any large multiethnic state that can be made to work?

The answer to that question has been, until recently, the United   4
States. "No other nation," Margaret Thatcher[1] has said, "has so successfully combined people of different races and nations within a single culture." How have Americans succeeded in pulling off this almost unprecedented trick?

[1]Thatcher is a former British Prime Minister.

We have always been a multiethnic country. Hector St. John de   5
Crèvecoeur,[2] who came from France in the 18th century, marveled at the
astonishing diversity of the settlers—"a mixture of English, Scotch, Irish,
French, Dutch, Germans and Swedes . . . this promiscuous breed." He
propounded a famous question: "What then is the American, this new
man?" And he gave a famous answer: "Here individuals of all nations are
melted into a new race of men." *E pluribus unum.*

The United States escaped the divisiveness of a multiethnic society   6
by a brilliant solution: the creation of a brand-new national identity. The
point of America was not to preserve old cultures but to forge a new,
American culture. "By an intermixture with our people," President George
Washington told Vice President John Adams, immigrants will "get assimilated to our customs, measures, and laws; in a word, soon become one
people." This was the ideal that a century later Israel Zangwill crystal-
lized in the title of his popular 1908 play *The Melting Pot.* And no institution was more potent in molding Crèvecoeur's "promiscuous breed" into
Washington's "one people" than the American public school.

The new American nationality was inescapably English in lan-   7
guage, ideas, and institutions. The pot did not melt everybody, not even
all the white immigrants: deeply bred racism put black Americans, yellow
Americans, red Americans, and brown Americans well outside the pale.
Still, the infusion of other stocks, even of nonwhite stocks, and the experience of the New World reconfigured the British legacy and made the
United States, as we all know, a very different country from Britain.

In the 20th century, new immigration laws altered the composition   8
of the American people, and a cult of ethnicity erupted both among non-
Anglo whites and among nonwhite minorities. This had many healthy
consequences. The American culture at last began to give shamefully
overdue recognition to the achievements of groups subordinated and
spurned during the high noon of Anglo dominance, and it began to acknowledge the great swirling world beyond Europe. Americans acquired
a more complex and invigorating sense of their world—and of themselves.

But, pressed too far, the cult of ethnicity has unhealthy conse-   9
quences. It gives rise, for example, to the conception of the United States
as a nation composed not of individuals making their own choices but of

[2]Crèvecoeur was a writer who wrote extensively about early U.S. culture.

inviolable ethnic and racial groups. It rejects the historic American goals of assimilation and integration. And, in an excess of zeal, well-intentioned people seek to transform our system of education from a means of creating "one people" into a means of promoting, celebrating and perpetuating separate ethnic origins and identities. The balance is shifting from *unum* to *pluribus*.

That is the issue that lies behind the hullabaloo over "multicultural- 10 ism" and "political correctness," the attack on the "Eurocentric" curriculum, and the rise of the notion that history and literature should be taught not as disciplines but as therapies whose function is to raise minority self-esteem. Group separatism crystallizes the differences, magnifies tensions, intensifies hostilities. Europe—the unique source of the liberating ideas of democracy, civil liberties and human rights—is portrayed as the root of all evil, and non-European cultures, their own many crimes deleted, are presented as the means of redemption.

I don't want to sound apocalyptic about these developments. Edu- 11 cation is always in ferment, and a good thing too. The situation in our universities, I am confident, will soon right itself. But the impact of separatist pressures on our public schools is more troubling. If a Kleagle of the Ku Klux Klan wanted to use the schools to disable and handicap black Americans, he could hardly come up with anything more effective than the "Afrocentric" curriculum. And if separatist tendencies go unchecked, the result can only be the fragmentation, resegregation and tribalization of American life.

I remain optimistic. My impression is that the historic forces driv- 12 ing toward "one people" have not lost their power. The eruption of ethnicity is, I believe, a rather superficial enthusiasm stirred by romantic ideologues on the one hand and by unscrupulous con men on the other: self-appointed spokesmen whose claim to represent their minority groups is carelessly accepted by the media. Most American-born members of minority groups, white or nonwhite, see themselves primarily as Americans rather than primarily as members of one or another ethnic group. A notable indicator today is the rate of intermarriage across ethnic lines, across religious lines, even (increasingly) across racial lines. "We Americans," said Theodore Roosevelt, "are children of the crucible."

The growing diversity of the American population makes the quest 13 for unifying ideals and a common culture all the more urgent. In a world savagely rent by ethnic and racial antagonisms, the United States must continue as an example of how a highly differentiated society holds itself together.

☜ Opening the Dialogue

1. What do you think Schlesinger means by "the cult of ethnicity"? Do you agree with him when he says, "pressed too far, the cult of ethnicity has unhealthy consequences" (paragraph 9)? How far do you think is "too far"?

2. In paragraph 12 Schlesinger says that he thinks the cult of ethnicity will be a short-lived phenomenon because most members of minority groups think of themselves as Americans. Does Schlesinger's observation hold true for you and your friends?

3. In paragraph 8 Schlesinger says that the cult of ethnicity originated among non-Anglo whites and nonwhite minorities. Do you think that only these two groups can celebrate their separate ethnic origins?

☜ Keeping a Notebook

What does the word *cult* mean to you? At what point does ethnic pride become a *cult* of ethnicity?

☜ Working Together

In paragraph 11 Schlesinger says that "the impact of separatist pressures on our public schools is . . . troubling." The result of various groups pursuing their own educational agendas, he says, can only lead to "the fragmentation, resegregation, and tribalization of American life." Working in groups, list some "worst case" scenarios that could result from this fragmentation—for example, a student knowing all about Hispanics fighting in the American Civil War, but not knowing anything about the economic or political reasons for which the war was fought. In class discussion, decide whether the advantages of stressing multicultural contributions outweigh the disadvantages.

☯ Writing an Essay

Do you think the people of the United States are developing a common culture with a set of unifying ideals, or do you believe they are retreating into cultural and ethnic isolation? Write an essay in which you take one position or the other, supporting your points with your own experiences as well as with information from the media.

A. M. ROSENTHAL

A Haitian Father

Alexander Michael Rosenthal was born in 1922 in Sault Ste. Marie, Ontario, and became a naturalized American citizen in 1951. As he relates in the following essay, his father entered the country illegally in 1926, found work in New York, and brought his wife and six children across the border.

After earning a B.S. degree in 1944 from City College in New York, Rosenthal joined the staff of the *New York Times* and began a long and distinguished career in American journalism. Serving as the paper's United Nations correspondent from 1946 to 1954 and as a foreign correspondent in India, Poland, Switzerland, and Japan from 1954 to 1963, Rosenthal rose steadily through the editorial ranks until he became executive editor in 1977.

The recipient of numerous awards and honors, Rosenthal has won the Overseas Press Club citation (three times), the Pulitzer Prize, and the George Polk Memorial Award (twice). He has authored or edited nine books, including *The New York Times of New York: An Uncommon Guide to the City of Fantasies* (1986).

Rosenthal became an associate editor for the *Times* in 1986 and began writing a regular column for the editorial page, "On My Mind," in which he explores a variety of personal and political topics from a conservative point of view. He has said of "On My Mind," "I loved being a reporter, but I love writing my column more than anything. I didn't enjoy being editor as much as I love being a columnist."

Rosenthal also contributes regularly to *The New York Times Magazine*, *Collier's*, and *Foreign Affairs*.

In the following editorial, Rosenthal uses the story of his own immigrant father as a way of persuading other second- and third-
generation Americans to sympathize with the plight of Haitian
families being denied admittance to the United States.

ALMOST ALWAYS NOW, when I read about Haitians who risk the seas   1
to get to this country but wind up on distant shores behind barbed wire,
I think of an illegal immigrant I happened to know myself, and of his
daughters and his son.

Then a shiver of shame and embarrassment goes through me, for a   2
particular and large group of Americans.

This fellow I am talking about needed work to help support his   3
wife and six children. He was living at the time in Canada, where he had
once found the outdoor work he loved—farming, laying track, traveling
to the far country to trade. But work dried up in Canada, so he took the
night train from Toronto to New York.

There he found employment as a house painter, which he hated.   4
But he was an excellent painter as he had been an excellent farmer and fur
trader. One day he fell off the scaffold; he died.

This man, who was known as Harry, never told his children exactly   5
how he managed to cross the border. After Harry died, immigration authorities could never discover any record of his entry, or of his son's, who
was also on that train from Toronto. They both were declared illegals—
night-train wetbacks.

But in the meantime Harry's daughters and son had grown up in the   6
United States. Always Harry, his wife and his children blessed America.
Many years later, when his children told the story of their father and his
determination to find work in America, to hell with borders, people
smiled in admiration of this man. And always, his children were filled
with pride about him, and gratitude.

So of course when I read about the Haitians I think of my father,   7
Harry, the illegal who came in search of work. Of course, Harry never
went through the hells of the Haitians. He had left Russia for Canada,
sick of the stench of czarism and longing for the clean air of political and
religious liberty. But when he left Canada he was not in fear of being shot

in the streets, as are the Haitians. He was just looking for work, which means not only bread but self-respect.

But I know that if he had been born in Haiti or lived there, he 8 would have broken every law that stood between him and work in the U.S. But where are Harry's children now?

Where are all the American Jews, and Poles, and Irish, and Balts, 9 and Italians who can remember a parent or a grandparent who came to this country looking for work, when visas were bought by steamship agents, or who borrowed a cousin's papers, or who just took a night train from someplace to someplace?

Don't they ever feel like getting on their knees and thanking God 10 that at least their folks never had to crawl into stinking, pitching boats out of fear and hunger?

American Jewish organizations are proud that their money helped 11 Ethiopian Jews get to Israel, and Irish-American groups rally round the thousands of illegal Irish immigrants. The Eastern Europeans of America struggled to get to America's grace, and for their parents' homelands to be free of Communism. Does not one of these organizations understand their causes would be stronger and cleaner if they could manage, in their sympathy for refugees and work-hunters, to cross religious, national and color lines?

Forget about blaming the White House and the bureaucrats. Blame 12 ourselves, children of Harry. Imagine what a quick pickup lobby, or parade, demanding succor for Haitians could do if it were headed by a few Irish-American Cardinals, a batch of rabbis and the presidents of Eastern European, Greek, Italian, Arab and Turkish organizations. American blacks and wasps welcome, too!

We are told, be reasonable, America can't open its doors to eco- 13 nomic refugees. Pull up the gangplank, Jack, I'm aboard. Maybe, but the Pakistanis, who have barely a half-penny to our dollar, give refuge to millions of Afghans and Washington scolds Hong Kong and Britain for not accepting the Vietnamese refugees.

But even reluctantly recognizing some economic limitations, this 14 country should have the moral elegance to accept neighbors who flee countries where life is terror and hunger, and are run by murderous gangs left over from dictatorships we ourselves maintained and cosseted.

If that were a qualification for entry into our golden land, the Hai-   15
tians should be welcomed with song, embrace and memories.

☜ Opening the Dialogue

1. At one time the United States placed no limits on immigration. Why
do you think we no longer allow unrestricted immigration?

2. Shortly after Rosenthal wrote his article, the United States Coast
Guard stopped rescuing Haitian refugees on the high seas. Instead, they
began returning them to Haiti before they could enter the territorial waters of the United States. How do you think Rosenthal could have used
this information in his essay?

3. At present, only immigrants who can demonstrate that they are political refugees or that their lives are in danger can bypass the immigration
quotas of the United States. Immigrants who claim economic hardship—
even extreme economic hardship—do not qualify for admission. Do you
think this policy is fair? What problems would you expect to encounter if
you were trying to enforce this policy?

☜ Keeping a Notebook

How convincing is the analogy Rosenthal draws between Haitian refugees and his Jewish father? Do the fundamental differences between the
two weaken his argument?

☜ Working Together

In groups, list the specific conditions under which immigration to the
United States should be allowed. Also, decide on any exceptions to these
conditions. In class discussion, design a set of immigration laws that
would regulate the number of immigrants allowed into the United States
each year.

🐚 Writing an Essay

Do you believe that the United States should still regard itself as the refuge for the poor and downtrodden of the earth? Write an essay in which you argue for or against the idea that the United States should open its doors to all those who wish to come to this country to make better lives for themselves and their families.

JAKE LAMAR

The Problem with You People

"For a long time I pretended my father was dead." This arresting first line of Jake Lamar's memoir, *Bourgeois Blues* (1991), shocks readers with its anger and ambivalence. A college graduate who struggled from poverty in Georgia to success as a self-made businessman in New York, Lamar's father demanded achievement and financial success from his son as well.

Lamar was born in 1965 at the height of the civil rights movement. He grew up as part of the privileged middle class in a racially integrated neighborhood, attended private schools, and after graduation from Harvard became one of the youngest writers ever hired by *Time* magazine and one of the few African Americans on its staff.

In his anecdotal memoir, Lamar explores the sources of his ambivalence and anger as he reflects on his racial identity and on his tempestuous relationship with a father who sometimes treated his family brutally, flaunted a white mistress, and was obsessed with caste and class. Lamar recalls that playmates disparaged him for sounding "white": "[They said] you're too white for black people and too black for white people. I began to wonder, Am I some sort of freak?" When *Bourgeois Blues* was published, Lamar commented, "I grew up hearing what the black experience was, and there was always the sense that the genuine African American is poor and in the inner city. I wanted to write about a person who didn't grow up in poverty. I wanted to say, 'This is my experience.'"

"There are so many stereotypes: The two main categories are the homeboy and, at the other extreme, the Clarence Thomas type," Lamar said recently. "Most black people I've met don't fit any mold."

In "The Problem with You People," printed in *Esquire* in 1992, Lamar turns the stereotyping of African Americans on its head by ironically lumping all white Americans together as "you people." Notice how, in the course of his argument, he moves away from irony to present specific evidence in support of his concluding point.

I'M CONCERNED ABOUT the state of white America. It's not just the   1
major problems plaguing the white community that worry me—the breakdown of the white family, the growing white underclass, the rampant social pathology—but the more subtle convolutions of white consciousness. In Caucasian-American habitats across the country, from the bowling alleys to the boardrooms, from trailer park to yacht club, a malaise is thickening. I'm writing in an attempt to fathom the white experience.

Pardon me for generalizing about whites and whiteness, but turn-   2
about is fair play. I've grown up hearing whites expound on "the Negro question" and "the race problem." I've encountered many a white pundit who, when not offering me prescriptions for curing one "black dilemma" or another, has expected me to serve as a spokesman for my race, to intuit the views of thirty million African Americans of varying social, economic, educational, and religious backgrounds and boil them down into a single comprehensive and generic "black view." And it's not just me. Any time a black cultural figure comes to the fore—director Spike Lee, playwright August Wilson, actor Eddie Murphy, for example—whites expect him somehow to encompass in his person and work all the hopes and aspirations of "his people."

So these days, I'm inclined to abstract the folks on the other side of   3
the racial equation. At times I might address "you" while implying "you people." Sometimes "you" might mean "some of you people" or "most of you people, but not necessarily you." As in, how come I haven't heard *you* stand up and speak out against Guns N' Roses? You'll probably find this hard to get used to.

You may not want to face the hard truths of the matter, but America   4
is on the brink of a white-identity meltdown. Your people, who are accustomed to defining great masses of other citizens by the fact that we are not you—that is, nonwhite—confront the specter of an America in which the mainstream has been altered beyond recognition.

The notion of the mainstream is crucial to understanding today's   5
white crisis. The desperate yearning to be considered normal, part of
some standard Disneyfied American citizenry, runs deep in white consciousness. I've witnessed the poignant efforts of young whites striving to
conform to the vague tenets of the mainstream, taking crushingly dull
jobs, settling down with the least challenging of spouses, dreaming of the
perfect family, groping for an illusory sense of security. The quest for
conformity can be fraught with doubt, and doubt is anathema to the
mainstream. To reaffirm your conventionality, you must constantly tell
yourself what you are not.

This need for reassurance has led in recent years to an obsession   6
with the people whom you mainstreamers consider most unlike you: the
infamous underclass. The underclass—you needn't even say *black* anymore; it's a code word—is a handy Dumpster for all your problems. You
mainstreamers may live far beyond your means, piling up thousands of
dollars of debt on credit, skimping on your tax returns. But when it comes
time to tally the ills of the country, you bemoan "the pathology of the
underclass." And as your less scrupulous colleagues avoid taking responsibility for the stunning perfidy of your investment bankers and the prof-
ligacy of your S&L operators, you return blithely to the conviction that
all those awful *urban*—another code word—problems persist because of
anonymous blacks who are "afraid of a hard day's work." And then there's
that story you like to tell about the woman on welfare—she *must* be
black—who used her food stamps to buy alcohol. . . .

Today, things are falling apart for the mainstream. The grim statis-   7
tics needn't be rehearsed here: the large number of whites who have lost
their jobs, defaulted on their loans, been forced to seek government
handouts. There has been a disturbing increase in white rage. While
whites grow ever more hysterical about "black crime," criminal acts that
are traditionally Caucasian American—white-on-white violence, if you
will—are on the rise. The spectacle of white males walking into post of-
fices or cafeterias and shooting everyone in sight has become almost
common. And as America's superpower status recedes as rapidly as its
economy, you have become more vociferous in your attacks on nonwhites, not just the underclass but all the others who have threatened
your world order.

The current world situation doesn't look promising, for all the talk   8 of the end of the Cold War and the victory of market capitalism. Your tribes seem unable to keep the peace among yourselves—the Yugoslavians are killing each other like animals, the Soviet republics are reverting to atavistic loyalties, and radical nationalists are popping up all over the place. Given your bloody past, one can't help but wonder: Can you be trusted to run a country in a civilized manner?

You probably think none of this has anything to do with you, so let 9 me narrow my focus a bit. As one of the children of the civil-rights movement assigned with integrating society, I've spent a good deal of time among the sort of white people you know. These are the whites who pride themselves on their fair-mindedness and lack of prejudice, the well-intentioned "color-blind." Like the rest of white America, they are struggling with pesky nonwhites who refuse to stay in their place. The color-blind are just more reluctant to admit it.

Your feelings toward nonwhites in general and black Americans 10 in particular are more tangled than those of some other mainstreamers. You appropriate the clothes, philosophies, and art of other cultures, sometimes out of sincere interest, more often to make a fashion statement.

You think Jonathan Demme is a hip filmmaker because his films are 11 populated on the margins by "authentic" blacks singing the music of our people. Perhaps you enjoy the fact that the Rolling Stones, like countless other rock bands, tours with black backup singers—in your gut, you believe that proximity to blackness confers a soulfulness. There is a subterranean but direct lineage from Norman Mailer in the late Fifties hailing "the Negro hipster" who lives on the edge of danger to today's white rappers contorting their faces and flailing their arms about in absurd attempts at street credibility.

When it comes to art produced *by* African Americans, you laud "the 12 gritty urban drama" of the new black directors, groove to the antiwhite lyrics of NWA and Ice Cube, and dress in the latest inner-city-inspired fashions on sale at your local malls. You like your blacks badass and hostile, as long as we're available in a CD format.

You like reading books and articles about impoverished blacks, 13 preferably those written by white journalists who have braved pilgrimages into the urban wilderness. You respond to the earnest piety of Alex Kotlowitz's best-selling *There Are No Children Here*, his tale of humanity amid grinding poverty and despair, and feel vaguely edified as you peruse this genre of ghetto pastorale. Or you shake your head sadly as you read the tough-love philosophizing of Joe Klein and Pete Hamill, and ask along with them, "What can be done?" before quickly answering your own question: "Not much, really." When solutions are offered, they are along the lines of "We need to get more blacks into the mainstream." In other words, we should become more like you.

I remember well my first righteous white liberal. It was the fall of   14
1970, my first day of fourth grade at a racially mixed, lower-middle-class parochial school in the Bronx. My new teacher—I'll call him Mr. Palomino—fancied himself a rebel. He wanted to create an "open" classroom. He also wanted to be my buddy, but there was something strained and clammy about his overtures. I'd been taught by two nuns and one female lay teacher in the previous three years and had encountered a wide range of Catholic authority figures. But I'd never met one who looked at me with Mr. Palomino's clinical gaze. Did this zealous reformer view me as some sort of anthropological specimen?

Mr. Palomino marveled one day when I put out a one-boy newspa-   15
per with sports, comics, and a national news section. Pulling me aside, he asked, "Where do you get your ideas?" I sensed not admiration but mystification in his voice, and a trace of disbelief that I might actually have created the paper on my own. Mr. Palomino seemed amazed that I might be a reasonably bright kid. I knew he was trying to "get through" to me, but his awkward, patronizing manner made me want to keep him out.

"I don't know where I get my ideas," I replied. I could tell Mr. Palo-   16
mino didn't appreciate my answer. He probed a little further. I shrugged and gave more vague answers. Finally, the teacher gave up and walked away, clearly disappointed.

The weirdness between us increased. Mr. Palomino stopped calling   17
on me in class, even if I was the only student raising my hand. He began grading my homework more harshly and punishing me for minor transgressions like not finishing my milk at lunchtime. Over the years I've often wondered about him, about why he turned hostile toward me when I didn't respond to his unctuous chumminess. Was it that I wasn't grateful enough?

In the sixth grade, I transferred to the sort of reform-minded "secu-   18

lar humanist" private school whose nonregimented atmosphere Mr. Palomino had tried to imitate. I went on to Harvard and a job at *Time* magazine, lived in once-segregated neighborhoods, and along the way met a
lot of you who, despite your studious liberalism, just couldn't keep from
being condescendingly caste-conscious. I saw that you might, for instance, go out of your way to address the black woman who empties your
office wastebaskets in the evenings by her first name. "Well, hello . . .
Janet. How are you tonight . . . *Janet?* Thank you so much . . . *Janet.*" I'm
not suggesting that this was an unkind gesture. What always rankled was
the excessive magnanimity in your voices, a tone, an emphasis that indi-
cated that you were congratulating yourselves for knowing the cleaning
woman's name, and the implication that Janet should be thankful for such
a small courtesy.

Yet dealing with the help is often easier for you than knowing what   19
to make of blacks who inhabit the mainstream. After Clarence Thomas
was nominated to the Supreme Court last summer, but before the start of
his confirmation hearings, a curious argument commenced between your
liberal and conservative pundits. The liberals kept demanding that
Thomas "remember where he came from." The conservative mandarins
responded that Judge Thomas had "never forgotten where he came
from." In this particular debate, political ideology—not to mention actual
judicial achievement—became beside the point. The Left was demanding humility and the Right was saying, "Don't worry, he's humble."

When Thomas finally took the stand in the first, pre–Anita Hill   20
phase of his confirmation hearings, he not only remembered where he
came from, he obsessed on it—his roots, in fact, were all he wanted to
talk about. Instead of discussing judicial philosophy, Thomas couldn't
help becoming choked up about his ascent from poverty. Instead of defending his actions as chairman of the Equal Employment Opportunity
Commission, Thomas spoke, misty-eyed, about staring out the window
of his office at the EEOC, watching busloads of black criminals on their
way to jail. "There but for the grace of God go I," he remembered thinking. Some of you who loathed the judge's politics still gave Thomas
points for this oozy gratitude.

Perhaps there was something innately appealing to a lot of you   21
about Thomas's relationship with John Danforth, the Missouri senator

who was usually described as the judge's "patron." Wasn't there something inspirational about the way Danforth was always hovering, speaking for Thomas, singing his praises, defending him against his critics with
a paternal protectiveness? A political Huck-and-Jim camaraderie.

During the second phase of Thomas's hearings, after the Anita Hill   22
scandal exploded, liberal and conservative whites agreed on one thing:
how wonderful it was to see so many black professionals paraded across
the TV screen. You praised the African Americans who testified for and
against Thomas or Hill for being "dignified." In characterizing the
witnesses, your media commentators consistently used that favorite adjective of whites who are surprised to discover the existence of intelligent
blacks: *articulate*. Across the political spectrum, you spoke in amazed
tones about the brainy buppies, as if you had stumbled upon some new
species of American citizen: the black mainstreamer. What a pleasant surprise it was to you!

Even your most excruciatingly high-minded leaders can be befud-   23
dled by a face-to-face encounter with a mainstream black. One afternoon
in 1988, when I was working at *Time* magazine, I attended a luncheon for
your political icon Mario Cuomo. Several correspondents escorted the
governor into the *Time* corporate dining room, where about twenty staffers awaited him. We stood in a sort of receiving line as Cuomo shook
each journalist's hand and made chitchat. When he got to me, the governor said, "Ah, you must be the softball player."

I had no idea what the governor was talking about. It had been at   24
least ten years since I'd touched a softball. As a kid, I'd been a clumsy
athlete; as far as I was concerned, one of the best things about adulthood
was that it had no gym requirement. "No, that's not me," I told Cuomo.

Uncertainty flashed in the governor's enormous eyes. Evidently,   25
one of the *Time* reporters had mentioned a softball player to him, and
Cuomo had assumed that I, the only African American in the receiving
line, had to be the jock. As a righteous white liberal, Cuomo knew he'd
just made a classic faux pas. He stared at me blankly, seemingly at a most
uncharacteristic loss for words. A white reporter, one who'd spent some
time with Cuomo before, stepped forward. "Actually, Governor, maybe
you were thinking of me. We talked once about basketball."

Cuomo tried to recover. "Yes, of course," he said, acknowledging   26
the reporter, then turning back to me. "I was talking about what a won-

derful sport basketball is, how it creates synergy." Cuomo stopped short, wondering perhaps if now he'd really blundered into cultural-cliché territory, talking to a black journalist about basketball. The governor muttered something else about synergy before quickly turning away and moving on down the receiving line.

Mario knows rhetorical correctness; real people can be harder to handle.   27

I know what you're probably thinking: Why pick on the liberals? We're on your side. Why make everything racial? We're not the racists!   28

Strange the way you often consider "racial" and "racist" synonymous terms. When an African American points out the racial attitudes of well-intentioned bourgeois whites, you get riled up and defensive, taking any observation as an accusation of racism. And since whites like you consider yourselves so thoroughly unbiased, utterly free of anything so heinous as a racist thought, nothing in your thinking can have a racial aspect at all. This allows you to make easy calls against the real racists— David Duke, say—while rarely questioning anything racial in your own politically enlightened sphere. You suffer from liberal cognitive dissonance. You consider yourself most astute on race issues, yet you cannot acknowledge presumptions you make solely on the basis of race. You steadfastly refuse to confront the mystery of your own manners.   29

So what can you do? You folks love grand prescriptions, pithy cure-all pronouncements. It seems to be part of your nature to abhor a conundrum. Instead of any sweeping solutions, however, I will submit just one leading question: Aren't you all still feeling just the least bit guilty?   30

Perhaps that's why you embrace every moderate-to-conservative black thinker who comes along—every Shelby Steele, Glenn Loury, or Thomas Sowell. It's comforting to be told, *by a black person,* that racial problems are not really your responsibility anymore. Doesn't guilt lead to modest proposals like the one made not too long ago by columnist Charles Krauthammer?—he suggested that the government pay reparations to us for slavery and be done with it. And doesn't an emphasis on black "moral decay" and "pathology" make it easier for you to justify doing nothing? I wonder whether your "black problem" has less to with solutions and more to do with absolution.   31

🔇 Opening the Dialogue

1. Do you think being African American gives Lamar a unique perspective from which to view white America? Does the same hold true for whites viewing black America?

2. In a letter responding to this essay, a writer says that she is troubled to read that Lamar thinks that no white attitude toward blacks can ever be trusted. She points out that Lamar is not speaking for all blacks and that he is putting up barriers between himself and whites. How valid do you think these criticisms of Lamar's essay are?

3. In his essay Lamar takes aim at white liberals. Do you think this strategy is counterproductive? Does he risk alienating those who support many of his positions while ignoring those who are the real racists?

🔇 Keeping a Notebook

Do you find Lamar's remarks offensive? Do his remarks make you angry, guilty, or uncomfortable? Why do you think you react the way you do?

🔇 Working Together

Working in groups, identify the characteristics of what Lamar refers to as mainstream white culture. Then, list the ways in which you do and do not conform to his view of the mainstream. In class discussion, consider whether American society needs a mainstream culture to which most people conform.

🔇 Writing an Essay

Write an essay in which you respond to Lamar's assertion in paragraph 7 that "Today, things are falling apart for the mainstream." Do you think Lamar has a point, or is he simplifying a very complicated issue just to support his argument? In your essay, address the specific arguments that Lamar makes.

Arturo Madrid

Diversity and Its Discontents

"I have spent most of my adult life explaining who I am not. I am exotic, but . . . not exotic enough . . . not Peruvian, or Pakistani, or whatever. I am, however, very clearly the *other*, if only your everyday, garden-variety . . . *other*."

As Madrid explains in the following essay, despite the fact that his family's presence in what is now the United States predates the Pilgrims and despite the fact that many of his ancestors were American citizens, he does not "fit those mental sets that define America and Americans. . . . My normal experience is to be asked, 'And where are *you* from?' "

A respected and influential scholar, Madrid holds a doctorate in Hispanic languages and literatures from the University of California at Los Angeles and is the founding president of the Tomas Rivera Center, the nation's first institute for policy studies on Latino issues. For the past two decades Madrid has been involved in establishing and directing programs to develop the intellectual resources of the Latino community and to ensure that Latinos are full participants in American universities. More recently he has worked to ensure that Latino needs and concerns are addressed as public policy issues.

Madrid has held academic and administrative positions at Dartmouth College, the University of California at San Diego, and the University of Minnesota. He has served on numerous national panels and is currently a trustee of the National Center for Education and the Economy and of the Latino Museum, as well as a member of the Council for Foreign Relations and a fellow of the National Academy of Public Administration.

Like Martin Luther King's "I Have a Dream," Madrid's essay was originally delivered as a public speech, though not to nearly so immediately sympathetic an audience. Note how Madrid establishes throughout the speech a connection between himself and his audience in order to further his persuasive purpose.

M Y NAME IS ARTURO MADRID. I am a citizen of the United States,   1
as are my parents and as were my grandparents and my great-grandparents. My ancestors' presence in what is now the United States antedates Plymouth Rock, even without taking into account any American Indian heritage I might have.

I do not, however, fit those mental sets that define America and   2
Americans. My physical appearance, my speech patterns, my name, my profession (a professor of Spanish) create a text that confuses the reader. My normal experience is to be asked, "And where are *you* from?" My response depends on my mood. Passive-aggressive, I answer, "From here." Aggressive-passive, I ask, "Do you mean where I am originally from?" But ultimately my answer to those follow-up questions that will ask about origins will be that we have always been from here.

Overcoming my resentment I try to educate, knowing that nine   3
times out of ten my words fall on inattentive ears. I have spent most of my adult life explaining who I am not. I am exotic, but—as Richard Rodriguez of *Hunger of Memory* fame so painfully found out—not exotic enough . . . not Peruvian, or Pakistani, or whatever. I am, however, very clearly the *other*, if only your everyday, garden-variety, domestic *other*. I will share with you another phenomenon that I have been a part of, that of being a missing person, and how I came late to that awareness. But I've always known that I was the *other*, even before I knew the vocabulary or understood the significance of otherness.

I grew up in an isolated and historically marginal part of the United   4
States, a small mountain village in the state of New Mexico, the eldest child of parents native to that region, whose ancestors had always lived there. In those vast and empty spaces people who look like me, speak as I do, and have names like mine predominate. But the *americanos* lived among us: the descendants of those nineteenth-century immigrants who

dispossessed us of our lands; missionaries who came to convert us and stayed to live among us; artists who became enchanted with our land and humanscape and went native; refugees from unhealthy climes, crowded spaces, unpleasant circumstances; and, of course, the inhabitants of Los Alamos, whose sociocultural distance from us was accentuated by the fact that they occupied a space removed from and proscribed to us. More importantly, however, they—*los americanos*—were omnipresent (and almost exclusively so) in newspapers, magazines, books, on radio, in movies, and, ultimately, on television.

Despite the operating myth of the day, school did not erase my   5 otherness. It did try to deny it, and in doing so only accentuated it. To this day what takes place in schools is more socialization than education, but when I was in elementary school—and given where I was—socialization was everything. School was where one became an American, because there was a pervasive and systematic denial by the society that surrounded us that we were Americans. That denial was both explicit and implicit.

Quite beyond saluting the flag and pledging allegiance to it (a very   6 intense and meaningful action, given that the United States was involved in a war and our brothers, cousins, uncles, and fathers were on the frontlines), becoming American was learning English, and its corollary: not speaking Spanish. Until very recently ours was a proscribed language, either *de jure*—by rule, by policy, by law—or *de facto*—by practice, implicitly if not explicitly, through social and political, and economic pressure. I do not argue that learning English was not appropriate. On the contrary. Like it or not, and we had no basis to make any judgments on that matter, we were Americans by virtue of having been born Americans and English was the common language of Americans. And there was a myth, a pervasive myth, to the effect that if only we learned to speak English well—and particularly without an accent—we would be welcomed into the American fellowship.

Sam Hayakawa and the official English movement folks notwith-   7 standing, the true text was not our speech, but rather our names and our appearance, for we would always have an accent, however perfect our pronunciation, however excellent our enunciation, however divine our diction. That accent would be heard in our pigmentation, our physiognomy, our names. We were, in short, the *other*.

Being the *other* involves contradictory phenomena. On the one   8
hand being the *other* frequently means being invisible. Ralph Ellison[1]
wrote eloquently about that experience in his magisterial novel, *Invisible
Man*. On the other hand, being the *other* sometimes involves sticking out
like a sore thumb. What is she/he doing here?

For some of us being the *other* is only annoying; for others it is de-   9
bilitating; for still others it is damning. Many try to flee otherness by
taking on protective colorations that provide invisibility, whether of
dress or speech or manner or name. Only a fortunate few succeed. For the
majority of us otherness is permanently sealed by physical appearance.
For the rest, otherness is betrayed by ways of being, speaking, or doing.

The first half of my life I spent downplaying the significance and   10
consequences of otherness. The second half has seen me wrestling to understand its complex and deeply ingrained realities; striving to fathom
why otherness denies us a voice or visibility or validity in American society and its institutions; struggling to make otherness familiar, reasonable,
even normal to my fellow Americans.

I spoke earlier of another phenomenon that I am a part of: that of   11
being a missing person. Growing up in northern New Mexico I had only
a slight sense of us being missing persons. *Hispanos*, as we called (and call)
ourselves in New Mexico, were very much a part of the fabric of the
society, and there were *hispano* professionals everywhere about me: doctors, lawyers, schoolteachers, and administrators. My people owned businesses, ran organizations, and were both appointed and elected public
officials.

My awareness of our absence from the larger institutional life of   12
the society became sharper when I went off to college, but even then it
was attenuated by the circumstances of history and geography. The demography of Albuquerque still strongly reflected its historical and cultural origins, despite the influx of Midwesterners and Easterners. Moreover, many of my classmates at the University of New Mexico were
hispanos, and even some of my professors. I thought that would obtain at

---

[1]Ellison is an African-American novelist and essayist, born in 1914. *Invisible Man* recounts the
struggles of a nameless black protagonist.

UCLA, where I began graduate studies in 1960. Los Angeles had a very large Mexican population and that population was visible even in and around Westwood and on the campus. Many of the groundskeepers and food-service personnel at UCLA were Mexican. But Mexican-American students were few and mostly invisible, and I do not recall seeing or knowing a single Mexican-American (or, for that matter, African-American, Asian, or American Indian) professional on the staff or faculty of that institution during the five years I was there. Needless to say, people like me were not present in any capacity at Dartmouth College, the site of my first teaching appointment, and of course were not even part of the institutional or individual mind-set. I knew then that we—a we that had come to encompass American Indians, Asian-Americans, African-Americans, Puerto Ricans, and women—were truly missing persons in American institutional life.

Over the past three decades the *de jure* and *de facto* types of segrega-   13
tion that have historically characterized American institutions have been under assault. As a consequence, minorities and women have become part of American institutional life. Although there are still many areas where we are not to be found, the missing persons phenomenon is not as pervasive as it once was. However, the presence of the *other*, particularly minorities, in institutions and in institutional life resembles what we call in Spanish a *flor de tierra* (a surface phenomenon): we are spare plants whose roots do not go deep, vulnerable to inclemencies of an economic, or political, or social nature.

Our entrance into and our status in institutional life are not unlike   14
a scenario set forth by my grandmother's pastor when she informed him that she and her family were leaving their mountain village to relocate to the Rio Grande Valley. When he asked her to promise that she would remain true to the faith and continue to involve herself in it, she asked why he thought she would do otherwise. "Doña Trinidad," he told her, "in the Valley there is no Spanish church. There is only an American church." "But," she protested, "I read and speak English and would be able to worship there." The pastor responded, "It is possible that they will not admit you, and even if they do, they might not accept you. And that is why I want you to promise me that you are going to go to church. Because if they don't let you in through the front door, I want you to go in through the back door. And if you can't get in through the back door, go

in the side door. And if you are unable to enter through the side door I
want you to go in through the window. What is important is that you
enter and stay."

Some of us entered institutional life through the front door; others   15
through the back door; and still others through side doors. Many, if not
most of us, came in through windows, and continue to come in through
windows. Of those who entered through the front door, some never
made it past the lobby; others were ushered into corners and niches.
Those who entered through back and side doors inevitably have remained in back and side rooms. And those who entered through windows
found enclosures built around them. For, despite the lip service given to
the goal of the integration of minorities into institutional life, what has
frequently occurred instead is ghettoization, marginalization, isolation.

Not only have the entry points been limited, but in addition the   16
dynamics have been singularly conflictive. Gaining entry and its corollary, gaining space, have frequently come as a consequence of demands
made on institutions and institutional officers. Rather than entering institutions more or less passively, minorities have of necessity entered them
actively, even aggressively. Rather than waiting to receive, they have demanded. Institutional relations have thus been adversarial, infused with
specific and generalized tensions.

The nature of the entrance and the nature of the space occupied   17
have greatly influenced the view and attitude of the majority population
within those institutions. All of us are put into the same box; that is, no
matter what the individual reality, the assessment of the individual is inevitably conditioned by a perception that is held of the class. Whatever
our history, whatever our record, whatever our validations, whatever our
accomplishments, by and large we are perceived unidimensionally and
dealt with accordingly. I remember an experience I had in this regard,
atypical only in its explicitness. A few years ago I allowed myself to be
persuaded to seek the presidency of a well-known state university. I was
invited for an interview and presented myself before the selection committee, which included members of the board of trustees. The opening
question of that brief but memorable interview was directed at me by a
member of that august body. "Dr. Madrid," he asked, "why does a one-
dimensional person like you think he can be the president of a multidi-
mensional institution like ours?"

Over the past four decades America's demography has undergone   18
significant changes. Since 1965 the principal demographic growth we
have experienced in the United States has been of peoples whose national origins are non-European. This population growth has occurred
both through birth and through immigration. A few years ago discussion
of the national birthrate had a scare dimension: the high—"inordinately
high"—birthrate of the Hispanic population. The popular discourse was
informed by words such as "breeding." Several years later, as a consequence of careful tracking by government agencies, we now know that
what has happened is that the birthrate of the majority population has
decreased. When viewed historically and comparatively, the minority
populations (for the most part) have also had a decline in birthrate, but
not one as great as that of the majority.

There are additional demographic changes that should give us   19
something to think about. African-Americans are now to be found in significant numbers in every major urban center in the nation. Hispanic-
Americans now number over 15 million people, and although they are a
regionally concentrated (and highly urbanized) population, there is a
Hispanic community in almost every major urban center of the United
States. American Indians, heretofore a small and rural population, are increasingly more numerous and urban. The Asian-American population,
which has historically consisted of small and concentrated communities
of Chinese-, Filipino, and Japanese-Americans, has doubled over the past
decade, its complexion changed by the addition of Cambodians, Ko-
reans, Hmongs, Vietnamese, et al.

Prior to the Immigration Act of 1965, 69 percent of immigration   20
was from Europe. By far the largest number of immigrants to the United
States since 1965 have been from the Americas and from Asia: 34 percent
are from Asia, another 34 percent are from Central and South America;
16 percent are from Europe; 10 percent are from the Caribbean; the remaining 6 percent are from other continents and Canada. As was the case
with previous immigration waves, the current one consists principally of
young people: 60 percent are between the ages of 16 and 44. Thus, for
the next few decades, we will continue to see a growth in the percentage
of non-European-origin Americans as compared to European-Americans.

To sum up, we now live in one of the most demographically diverse   21
nations in the world, and one that is increasingly more so.

During the same period social and economic change seems to have   22
accelerated. Who would have imagined at mid-century that the pro-
totypical middle-class family (working husband, wife as homemaker, two
children) would for all intents and purposes disappear? Who could have
anticipated the rise in teenage pregnancies, children in poverty, drug use?
Who among us understood the implications of an aging population?

We live in an age of continuous and intense change, a world in   23
which what held true yesterday does not today, and certainly will not
tomorrow. What change does, moreover, is bring about even more
change. The only constant we have at this point in our national development is change. And change is threatening. The older we get the more
likely we are to be anxious about change, and the greater our desire to
maintain the status quo.

Evident in our public life is a fear of change, whether economic or   24
moral. Some who fear change are responsive to the call of economic protectionism, others to the message of moral protectionism. Parentheti-
cally, I have referred to the movement to require more of students without in turn giving them more as academic protectionism. And the
pronouncements of E.D. Hirsch and Allan Bloom[2] are, I believe, informed by intellectual protectionism. Much more serious, however, is the
dark side of the populism which underlies this evergoing protectionism—the resentment of the *other*. An excellent and fascinating example of
that aspect of populism is the cry for linguistic protectionism—for making English the official language of the United States. And who among us
is unaware of the tensions that underlie immigration reform, of the under-
side of demographic protectionism?

A matter of increasing concern is whether this new protectionism,   25
and the mistrust of the *other* which accompanies it, is not making more
significant inroads than we have supposed in higher education. Specifically, I wish to discuss the question of whether a goal (quality) and a reality (demographic diversity) have been erroneously placed in conflict,
and, if so, what problems this perception of conflict might present.

As part of my scholarship I turn to dictionaries for both origins and   26

---

[2]Both men are critics of American education who have advocated greater emphasis on traditional European culture, less on ethnic and contemporary studies.

meanings of words. Quality, according to the *Oxford English Dictionary*, has multiple meanings. One set defines quality as being an essential character, a distinctive and inherent feature. A second describes it as a degree of excellence, of conformity to standards, as superiority in kind. A third makes reference to social status, particularly to persons of high social status. A fourth talks about quality as being a special or distinguishing attribute, as being a desirable trait. Quality is highly desirable in both principle and practice. We all aspire to it in our own person, in our experiences, in our acquisitions and products, and of course we all want to be associated with people and operations of quality.

But let us move away from the various dictionary meanings of the   27
word and to our own sense of what it represents and of how we feel about it. First of all we consider quality to be finite; that is, it is limited with respect to quantity; it has very few manifestations; it is not widely distributed. I have it and you have it, but they don't. We associate quality with homogeneity, with uniformity, with standardization, with order, regularity, neatness. All too often we equate it with smoothness, glibness, slickness, elegance. Certainly it is always expensive. We tend to identify it with those who lead, with the rich and famous. And, when you come right down to it, it's inherent. Either you've got it or you ain't.

Diversity, from the Latin *divertere*, meaning to turn aside, to go dif-   28
ferent ways, to differ, is the condition of being different or having differences, is an instance of being different. Its companion word, diverse, means differing, unlike, distinct; having or capable of having various forms; composed of unlike or distinct elements. Diversity is lack of standardization, of regularity, of orderliness, homogeneity, conformity, uniformity. Diversity introduces complications, is difficult to organize, is troublesome to manage, is problematical. Diversity is irregular, disorderly, uneven, rough. The way we use the word diversity gives us away. Something is too diverse, is extremely diverse. We want a little diversity.

When we talk about diversity, we are talking about the *other*, what-   29
ever that other might be: someone of a different gender, race, class, national origin; somebody at a greater or lesser distance from the norm; someone outside the set; someone who possesses a different set of characteristics, features, or attributes; someone who does not fall within the taxonomies we use daily and with which we are comfortable; someone who does not fit into the mental configurations that give our lives order and meaning.

In short, diversity is desirable only in principle, not in practice.   30
Long live diversity . . . as long as it conforms to my standards, my mind-
set, my view of life, my sense of order. We desire, we like, we admire
diversity, not unlike the way the French (and others) appreciate women;
that is, *Vive la différence!*—as long as it stays in its place.

What I find paradoxical about and lacking in this debate is that   31
diversity is the natural order of things. Evolution produces diversity.
Margaret Visser, writing about food in her latest book, *Much Depends on
Dinner*, makes an eloquent statement in this regard:

> Machines like, demand, and produce uniformity. But nature loathes
> it: her strength lies in multiplicity and in differences. Sameness in
> biology means fewer possibilities and therefore weakness.

The United States, by its very nature, by its very development, is   32
the essence of diversity. It is diverse in its geography, population, institutions, technology; its social, cultural, and intellectual modes. It is a society that at its best does not consider quality to be monolithic in form or
finite in quantity, or to be inherent in class. Quality in our society pro-
ceeds in large measure out of the stimulus of diverse modes of thinking
and acting; out of the creativity made possible by the different ways in
which we approach things; out of diversion from paths or modes hallowed by tradition.

One of the principal strengths of our society is its ability to ad-   33
dress, on a continuing and substantive basis, the real economic, political,
and social problems that have faced and continue to face us. What makes
the United States so attractive to immigrants is the protections and opportunities it offers; what keeps our society together is tolerance for cultural, religious, social, political, and even linguistic difference; what
makes us a unique, dynamic, and extraordinary nation is the power and
creativity of our diversity.

The true history of the United States is one of struggle against in-   34
tolerance, against oppression, against xenophobia, against those forces
that have prohibited persons from participating in the larger life of the
society on the basis of their race, their gender, their religion, their national origin, their linguistic and cultural background. These phenomena

are not consigned to the past. They remain with us and frequently take on virulent dimensions.

If you believe, as I do, that the well-being of a society is directly   35
related to the degree and extent to which all of its citizens participate in its institutions, then you will have to agree that we have a challenge before us. In view of the extraordinary changes that are taking place in our society we need to take up the struggle again, irritating, grating, troublesome, unfashionable, unpleasant as it is. As educated and educator members of this society we have a special responsibility for ensuring that all American institutions, not just our elementary and secondary schools, our juvenile halls, or our jails, reflect the diversity of our society. Not to do so is to risk greater alienation on the part of a growing segment of our society; is to risk increased social tension in an already conflictive world; and, ultimately, is to risk the survival of a range of institutions that, for all their defects and deficiencies, provide us the opportunity and the freedom to improve our individual and collective lot.

Let me urge you to reflect on these two words—quality and diver-   36
sity—and on the mental sets and behaviors that flow out of them. And let me urge you further to struggle against the notion that quality is finite in quantity, limited in its manifestations, or is restricted by considerations of class, gender, race, or national origin; or that quality manifests itself only in leaders and not in followers, in managers and not in workers, in breeders and not in drones; or that it has to be associated with verbal agility or elegance of personal style; or that it cannot be seeded, nurtured, or developed.

Because diversity—the *other*—is among us, will define and deter-   37
mine our lives in ways that we still do not fully appreciate, whether that other is women (no longer bound by tradition, house, and family); or Asians, African-Americans, Indians, and Hispanics (no longer invisible, regional, or marginal); or our newest immigrants (no longer distant, exotic, alien). Given the changing profile of America, will we come to terms with diversity in our personal and professional lives? Will we begin to recognize the diverse forms that quality can take? If so, we will thus initiate the process of making quality limitless in its manifestations, infinite in quantity, unrestricted with respect to its origins, and more importantly, virulently contagious.

I hope we will. And that we will further join together to expand—   38
not to close—the circle.

✆ Opening the Dialogue

1. Do you agree with Madrid that "what takes place in schools is more socialization than education . . . " (paragraph 5)? Is school, as Madrid asserts, the place where a person is supposed to become an American?

2. Madrid implies that whatever he does, he will always be tainted with the stain of "otherness." Do you think he is correct? Do you think other people of color feel the way he does?

3. Madrid's first teaching appointment was at Dartmouth College. Does the fact that he was able to earn a doctorate as well as secure a position at a highly selective school in any way undercut his point that Hispanics have had limited access to American institutions?

✆ Keeping a Notebook

Were you ever in a situation in which you felt like "the *other*"? What made you feel this way? How did you deal with this feeling?

✆ Working Together

In paragraph 2 Madrid talks about "mental sets" that define a person as an American. Working in groups, list all the characteristics that you associated with being an American. As a class, determine how many of these characteristics actually apply to the various people you know.

✆ Writing an Essay

Do you agree with Madrid when he says that what makes the United States unique is the power and creativity of its diversity? Write an essay in which you support or challenge his assertion.

Writing about Culture and Diversity

1. Write an essay in which you argue for or against the idea that a culturally diverse curriculum would improve education at your college or university.

2. Read either Ishmael Reed's "America's Multinational Heritage" or Arthur Schlesinger, Jr.'s, "The Cult of Ethnicity, Good and Bad." Then write an essay in which you explicitly refute several of the writer's ideas with which you disagree. Be specific, and use your own experience to support your points.

3. Write a persuasive essay in which you support or challenge the legitimacy of the idea of the melting pot (p. 3). Do you think this metaphor accurately describes life in the United States? Do you think another image is more accurate?

4. Do you think the present educational system empowers minority students or holds them back? Use a combination of emotional and logical appeals to make your case.

5. In paragraph 30 of his essay Jake Lamar mentions that columnist Charles Krauthammer suggested—perhaps tongue-in-cheek—that the government of the United States pay reparations to African Americans to make up for the injuries they suffered during slavery. Recently, some people have been taking this idea seriously and asking why the descendants of African-American slaves should be treated any differently from the descendants of Japanese Americans who were incarcerated during World War II. Write an essay in which you support or oppose this proposal. Use information from the essays in this chapter and your own ideas for support.

ACKNOWLEDGMENTS

Alvarez, Julia, "Hold the Mayonnaise." Copyright © by Julia Alvarez 1992. First published in *The New York Times Magazine*, May 1992. Reprinted by permission of Susan Bergholz Literary Services, New York.

Angelou, Maya, "Graduation." From *I Know Why the Caged Bird Sings* ("I Shall Not Be Moved"). Copyright © 1969 by Maya Angelou. Reprinted by permission of Random House, Inc.

Blew, Mary Clearman, "The Unwanted Child." "The Unwanted Child," from *All But the Waltz* by Mary Clearman Blew. Copyright © 1991 Mary Clearman Blew. Used by permission of Viking Penguin, a division of Penguin Books USA, Inc.

Cofer, Judith Ortiz, "The Myth of the Latin Woman: I Just Met a Girl Named Maria." Copyright © 1993 by Judith Ortiz Cofer. From *The Latin Deli*. Published by the University of Georgia Press.

Cofer, Judith Ortiz, "Silent Dancing." "Silent Dancing" by Judith Ortiz Cofer is reprinted with permission of the publisher from *Silent Dancing: A Partial Remembrance of a Puerto Rican Childhood* (Houston: Arte Publico Press, University of Houston, 1991).

Crow Dog, Mary, and Erdoes, Richard, "Civilize Them with a Stick." From *Lakota Woman* by Mary Crow Dog. Copyright © 1990. Reprinted with permission of Grove Press, Inc.

Dershowitz, Alan M., "Learning about Anti-Semitism in the Real World." Excerpt from *Chutzpah*, pp. 50–52, Little, Brown & Co., 1991.

Didion, Joan, "Miami: The Cuban Presence." Copyright © 1987 by Joan Didion. Reprinted by permission of Simon & Schuster, Inc.

Ehrenreich, Barbara, "Cultural Baggage." Copyright © 1992 by The New York Times Company. Reprinted by permission.

Gates, Henry Louis, Jr., "A Giant Step." Copyright © 1989 by The New York Times Company. Reprinted by permission.

Golden, Marita, "A Day in April." Copyright © 1983 by Marita Golden.

Gomez, Rogelio R., "Foul Shots." Copyright © 1991 by The New York Times Company. Reprinted by permission.

Graham, Lawrence Otis, "The 'Black Table' Is Still There." Copyright © 1986 by The New York Times Company. Reprinted by permission.

Houston, Jeanne Wakatsuki, "Manzanar, U.S.A." From *Farewell to Manzanar* by James D. and Jeanne Wakatsuki Houston. Copyright © 1973 by James D. Houston. Reprinted by permission of Houghton Mifflin Co. All rights reserved.

King, Martin Luther, Jr., "I Have a Dream." Copyright © 1963 by Martin Luther King, Jr., copyright © renewed 1991 by Coretta Scott King. Reprinted by arrangement with the heirs of the estate of Martin Luther King, Jr. Care of the Joan Daves Agency as agents of proprietor.

Lamar, Jake, "The Problem with You People." First appeared in *Esquire* magazine, February 1992. Reprinted by permission of International Creative Management and the author. Copyright © 1992.

Lorde, Audre, "The Fourth of July." Excerpt from *Zami: A New Spelling of My Name*, 1982. Copyright © Audre Lorde. The Crossing Press, Freedom, CA.

Madrid, Arturo, "Diversity and Its Discontents." Copyright © Arturo Madrid. Arturo Madrid is the founding president of the Tomas Rivera Center, Claremont, CA.

Mebane, Mary, "Shades of Black." "Shades of Black," from *Mary* by Mary Mebane. Copyright © 1981 by Mary Elizabeth Mebane. Used by permission of Viking Penguin, a division of Penguin Books USA, Inc.

Momaday, N. Scott, "The Way to Rainy Mountain." First published in *The Reporter,* 26 January 1967. Reprinted from *The Way to Rainy Mountain,* copyright © 1969, The University of New Mexico Press.

Mourning Dove (Christine Quintasket), "Marriage Customs among the Salishan." Reprinted from *Mourning Dove: A Salishan Autobiography,* edited by Jay Miller, by permission of the University of Nebraska Press. Copyright © 1990 by the University of Nebraska Press.

Mura, David, "Bashed in the U.S.A." Copyright © 1992 by The New York Times Company. Reprinted by permission.

Nava, Michael, "Gardenland, Sacramento, California." Copyright by Michael Nava. Copyright © 1990.

Naylor, Gloria, "Mommy, What Does 'Nigger' Mean?" Reprinted by permission of Sterling Lord Literistic, Inc. Copyright © 1986 by Gloria Naylor.

Noda, Kesaya E., "Asian in America." From *Making Waves,* by Asian Women United. Copyright © 1989 by Asian Women United. Reprinted by permission of Beacon Press.

Ode, Kim, "A Farmer's Daughter." First appeared in *Minnesota Monthly,* January 1990. Copyright © 1990 by Kim Ode.

Oishi, Gene, "In Search of Hiroshi." Reprinted by permission of the author.

Otto, Whitney, "How to Make an American Quilt." From *How to Make an American Quilt* by Whitney Otto. Copyright © 1991, reprinted by permission of Villard Books, a division of Random House, Inc.

Pérez, Ramón, "The Day of the Dead." "The Day of the Dead," an excerpt from *Diary of an Undocumented Immigrant* by Ramón Pérez, is reprinted with the permission of the publisher (Houston: Arte Publico Press, University of Houston, 1991).

Reed, Ishmael, "America's Multinational Heritage." Reprinted with permission of Atheneum Publishers, an imprint of Macmillan Publishing Company from *Writin' Is Fightin': Thirty-Seven Years of Boxing on Paper* by Ishmael Reed. Copyright © 1988 by Ishmael Reed.

Reed, Ishmael, "My Neighborhood." "My Neighborhood" (originally titled "My Oakland, There Is a There There," Part I) is reprinted with the permission of Atheneum Publishers, an imprint of Macmillan Publishing Company from *Writin' Is Fightin': Thirty-Seven Years of Boxing on Paper* by Ishmael Reed. Copyright © 1988 by Ishmael Reed.

Rodriguez, Richard, "The Fear of Losing a Culture." From *Hunger of Memory* by Richard Rodriguez. Copyright © 1982 by Richard Rodriguez. Reprinted by permission of David R. Godine, Publisher.

Rosenthal, A. M., "A Haitian Father." Copyright © 1992 by The New York Times Company. Reprinted by permission.

Sanders, Scott Russell, "The Men We Carry in Our Minds." Copyright © 1984 by Scott Russell Sanders; this version reprinted from the *Utne Reader,* originally appeared in *Milkweed Chronicle* and reprinted in *The Paradise of Bombs* (in full) (University of Georgia Press, 1987); excerpted here by permission of the author and the author's agent, Virginia Kidd.

Santiago, Roberto, "Black *and* Latino." Copyright © 1989 by Roberto Santiago. Reprinted by permission of the author.

Scheller, Melanie, "On the Meaning of Plumbing and Poverty." Copyright © 1990 by Melanie Scheller. Reprinted with permission by the *Independent Weekly* of Durham, North Carolina.

Schlesinger, Arthur, Jr., "The Cult of Ethnicity, Good and Bad." Copyright © 1991 Time Inc. Reprinted by permission.

Shaheen, Jack G., "The Media's Image of Arabs." Copyright © 1988 by Jack G. Shaheen. Reprinted with permission of the author.

Soto, Gary, "The Savings Book." From *Living Up the Street,* Strawberry Hill Press. Copyright © 1985 by Gary Soto. Reprinted by permission of the author.

Staples, Brent, "A Brother's Murder." Reprinted by permission of the author. Brent Staples, who holds a Ph.D. in psychology from the University of Chicago, is a member of the editorial board of the *New York Times.*

Staples, Brent, "Just Walk on By." Reprinted by permission of the author.

Tan, Amy, "Mother Tongue." Copyright © 1990 by Amy Tan. First published in the *Threepenny Review*. Reprinted by permission of the author.

Torgovnick, Marianna De Marco, "On Being White, Female, and Born in Bensonhurst." First appeared in Partisan Review, Vol. 57, No. 3, 1990. Copyright © 1990, by Marianna De Marco Torgovnick. Reprinted by permission of the author.

Wong, Elizabeth, "The Struggle to Be an All-American Girl." Copyright © 1980. Reprinted by permission of the author.

Wong, Jade Snow, "Puritans from the Orient: A Chinese Evolution," by Jade Snow Wong, from *The Immigrant Experience* by Thomas C. Wheeler. Copyright © 1971 by Doubleday, a division of Bantam Doubleday Dell Publishing Group, Inc. Used by permission of Doubleday.

Wu, Shanlon, "In Search of Bruce Lee's Grave." Copyright © 1990 by Shanlon Wu. All rights reserved.

X, Malcolm, "My First Conk." From *The Autobiography of Malcolm X* by Malcolm X, with Alex Haley. Copyright © 1964 by Alex Haley and Malcolm X. Copyright © 1965 by Alex Haley and Betty Shabazz. Reprinted by permission of Random House, Inc.

Yuhfill, Ji-Yeon Mary, "Let's Tell the Story of All America's Cultures." First appeared in the *Philadelphia Inquirer*. Reprint permission granted by the author and the *Philadelphia Inquirer*. Copyright © 1991 by Ji-Yeon Mary Yuhfill.

Art Credits

p. 190 Alston, Charles, "Walking" (1958). Reprinted with permission of the Sydney Smith Gordon Collection.

p. 370 Bearden, Romare, "The Prevalance of Ritual: Baptism" (1964). Reprinted with permission of Scala/Art Resource, NY.

p. 88 Chapter Three Illustration is provided courtesy of the Third Street Music School Settlement, New York City. Painted by the children of the Charas Youth Summer Project, 1985; the After School Arts Project at P.S. 15, 1986; and the After School Arts Project at P.S. 142, 1987, all under the direction of Pablo Delano. Reprinted with permission.

p. 154 Garza, Carmen Lomas, "Cascarones" (1989). Reprinted with permission of the artist.

p. 228 Gee, Yun, "Where Is My Mother" (1926–27). Reprinted with permission of the Li-lan Collection.

p. 26 Gutiérrez, Marina, "Biography" (1988). Reprinted with permission of the artist.

p. 412 Kelley, Garrett, "Sounds of the Subway" (1992). Reprinted with permission of the artist.

p. 1 Lawrence, Jacob, "Bumbershoot" (1976). Reprinted with permission of the artist and the Seattle Arts Commission.

p. 275 Torres, Leyla, "Morning Women" © 1991 by Leyla Torres. Reprinted with permission of the artist.

p. 332 Wood, Grant, "Tree Planting Group" (1937). Reprinted with permission of Scala/Art Resource, NY.

INDEX